THE BOOK OF ANTIQUE

FURNITURE

An International Style Guide from the 16th to the 20th century

This edition published in North America in 2000
by Chartwell Books, Inc
a Division of Book Sales, Inc.
118 Northfield Avenue
Edison, NJ 08837

Originally created by Copyright Studio, as *Le Grand Livre des Meubles*

Translation: Lisa Davidson
Copyediting: Elizabeth Ayre
Graphic design: Ute-Charlotte Hettler
Typsetting: Jacqueline Leymarie
Editorial assistant: Isabelle Raimond

Printed in Spain

THE BOOK OF ANTIQUE FURNITURE

An International Style Guide from the 16th to the 20th century

by Francis Rousseau

CONTENTS

FROM ANTIQUITY

Styles have always traveled freely between France, Great Britain, Germany, Italy, Spain, the Netherlands, Scandinavia and Russia. Since the seventeenth century, however, France and Great Britain have stood out as the undisputed leaders in both determining and defining style. For three centuries, these two countries have launched and developed the largest number of styles.

The creation of a new style requires several stages, the first being a definition of the ornaments or ornamental vocabulary which form the building blocks of a style. These are dictated by fashion, by changing lifestyles and by a society's aesthetic tendencies. Most important of all, however, is the reigning architectural style of the time, which provides the principles of ornamentation.

In the past, once the ornamental elements achieved a sufficiently defined form, the ornamentalists and designers recorded them in sketchbooks and in printed collections of engravings, known as pattern books, to be used by decision-makers and other designers. At this point, a style had reached a definitive stage. All that remained was to obtain the approval of the political authorities—which was often a formality, as they generally monitored these developments and occasionally offered discreet suggestions concerning the choice of decorative elements. Political influence was not a decisive factor in the definition of style, as the process was too subtle to

▽ *Duck head from an Egyptian piece of furniture. Wood and ivory. Musée du Louvre, Paris.*

TO THE RENAISSANCE

succumb to any authoritative directive. Indeed, there are only two styles whose elements were imposed by a ruler: the Louis XIV style, which was the Sun King's way of consolidating and demonstrating his power; and the Empire style, developed by Napoleon I as a propaganda tool in support of his policies.

A final step remains before a style truly has truly been defined: its realization. This is where the carpenters, cabinetmakers, bronzesmiths, tapestry-makers, ceramicists and goldsmiths come in—without whom any style remains a mere concept, nothing more than drawings in a designer's pattern book. Artists and craftsmen drew their inspiration from these drawing collections, adding their own imagination, creative touch and skill to give form and character to a style through the ancient medium of furniture.

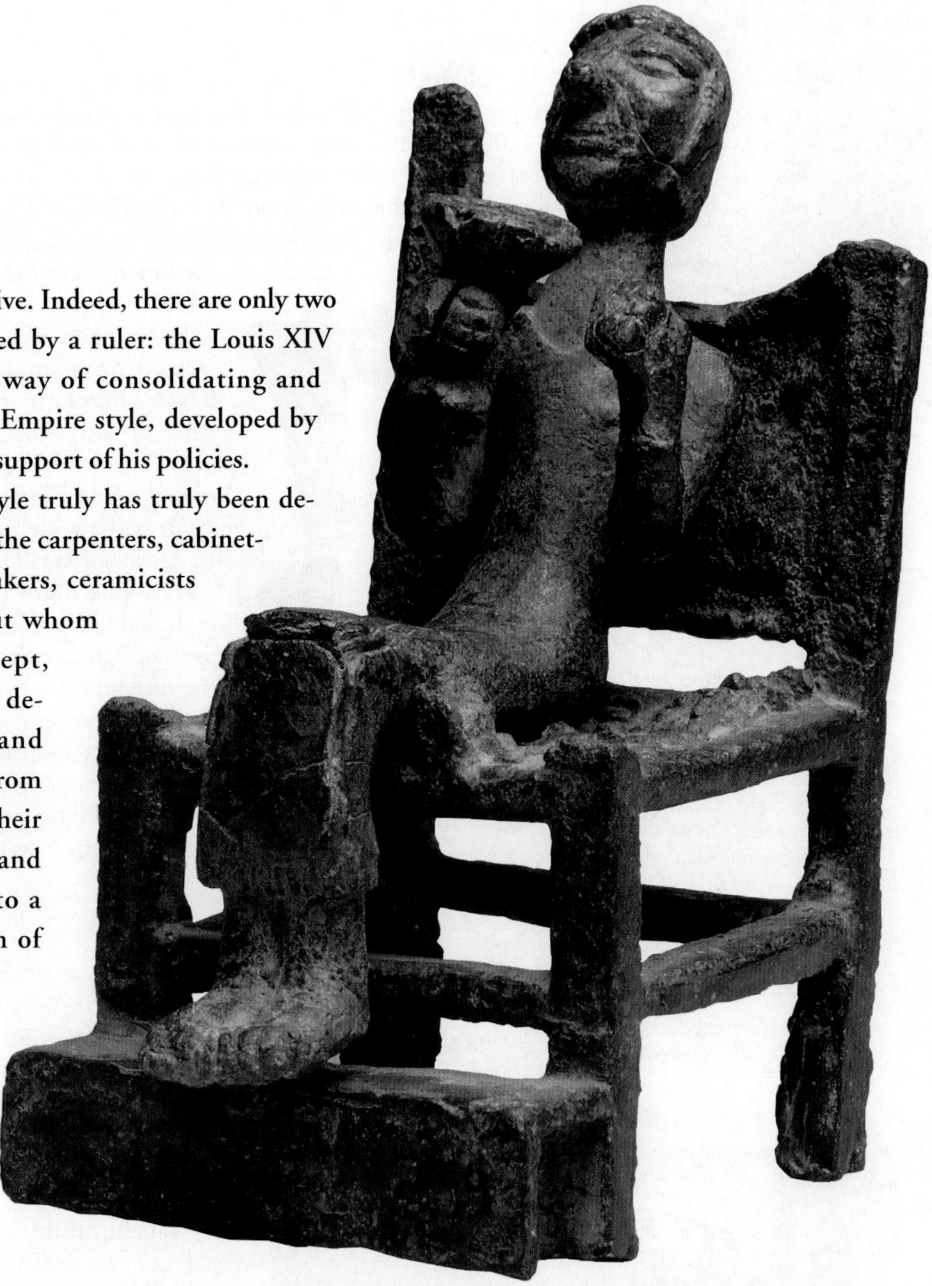

△ *Seated god drinking from a cup. Bronze. Cyprus. Musée du Louvre, Paris.*

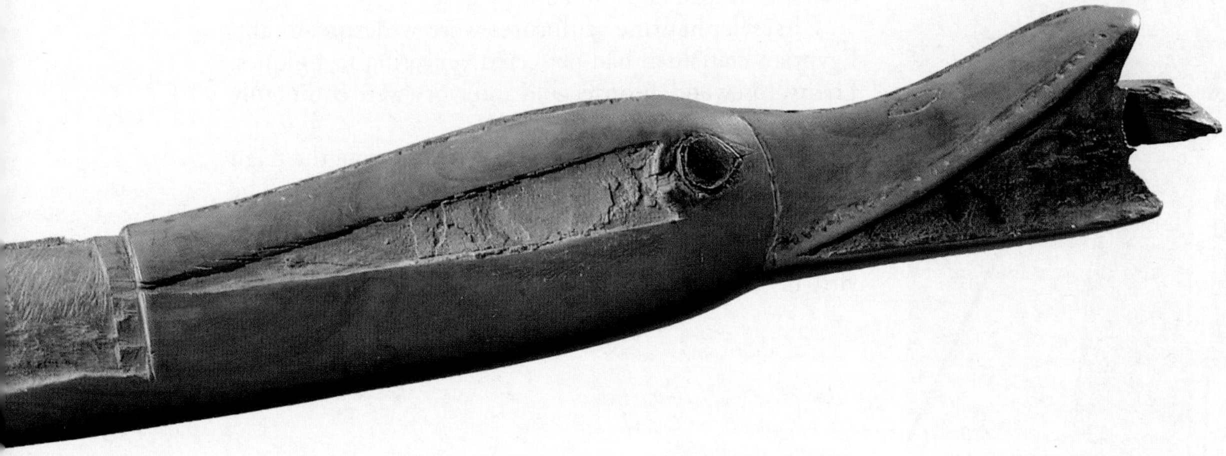

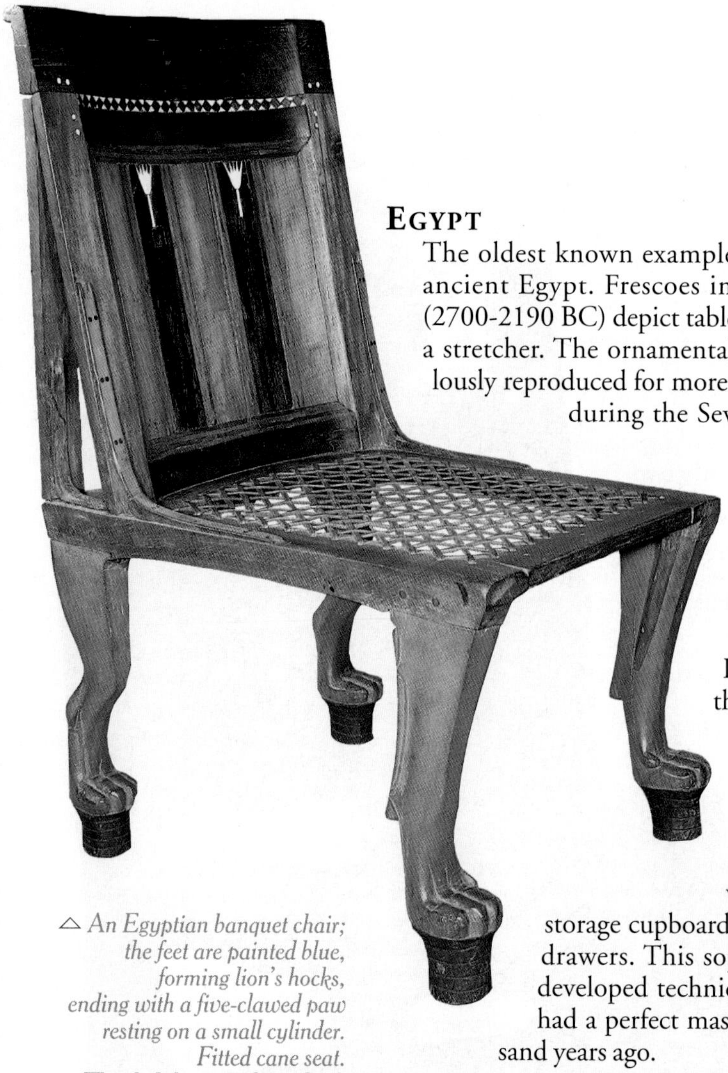

▷ *Egyptian toiletry chest made from carob with ebony lid. The design depicts a woman offering a cup to a couple seated on lion's-paw chairs. Musée du Louvre, Paris.*

Egypt

The oldest known examples of furniture were produced in ancient Egypt. Frescoes in tombs from the Old Kingdom (2700-2190 BC) depict tables with four legs interconnected by a stretcher. The ornamental elements that would be scrupulously reproduced for more than one thousand years appeared during the Seventh Dynasty (2300 BC). These included the famous lion's-paw feet supporting beds and chairs; each five-clawed paw rested on a small cylindrical base. The chair was the most common and most comfortable piece of furniture in ancient Egypt. During the New Kingdom dynasties (1580-1085 BC), the chair had a wide, comfortable seat made of woven straw or a lattice of small cords—the same caning method used today. The main patterns used to decorate furniture included stylized lotus flowers, gazelle and goat heads, the paws of lions, and the hooves of gazelles and bulls.

The different pieces of Egyptian furniture included tables with rectilinear legs, three-legged tables or pedestal tables, storage cupboards, small chests and cabinets, beds and superimposed sets of drawers. This sophisticated range of furniture was produced with highly developed techniques (such as ivory inlays), proof that Egyptian craftsmen had a perfect mastery of the furniture-making process more than four thousand years ago.

△ *An Egyptian banquet chair; the feet are painted blue, forming lion's hocks, ending with a five-clawed paw resting on a small cylinder. Fitted cane seat. The slightly curved seat back is made of wood with ivory inlays. Musée du Louvre, Paris.*

Assyria and Persia

During the ninth to the fourth centuries BC, the Assyrian civilization, followed by the Persians—particularly under the reigns of kings Darius and Xerxes—inherited and kept alive the skills of Egyptian craftsmen from the Pharaonic era. Babylon, with its hanging gardens and legendary palaces, represented the epitome of refinement in this ancient era.

The furniture, which was found "in abundance in the palaces" according to historians, is often described as being the most sophisticated and sumptuous of its era. Favorite motifs included lion's-paw and animal-hock feet, as well as winged lions' and horses' heads.

Chryselephantine sculptures were widespread, and Egyptian craftsmen had perfected veneering techniques. Ebony, rosewood, bronze, gold and ivory were commonly used.

These civilizations would be overrun during the reign of Alexander the Great in the fourth century BC. The fabulous skills, which had been developed over two thousand years by Egyptian craftsmen, would be transmitted virtually intact to ancient Greece.

◁ *Detail of an Assyrian fresco representing King Tiglath-pileser III holding an audience. Musée du Louvre, Paris.*

Greece

As in Egypt, Greek furniture design was inspired by the predominant architectural styles. Craftsmen adapted and miniaturized the patterns that were used on buildings—lotus leaves, palmettes, beads, grooves, denticulation, foliage and, of course, acanthus leaves—and placed them on furniture. The acanthus leaf, used for the first time in the fifth century BC by the goldsmith and sculptor Callimachus, became a permanent part of the ornamental vocabulary of European furniture up through the early twentieth century. Quite a success story for what is really a humble Mediterranean weed! Another famous ornamental device was the Greek key or meander pattern, which is a broken line with right angles forming hook shapes of squares and rectangles.

No examples of Greek furniture survive, as opposed to Egyptian or Roman furniture, but the many images on ceramics and bas-reliefs provide detailed descriptions of the various forms. The furniture—stools, chairs, chests and tables—was generally Egyptian in design. Yet Greek furniture makers were innovative in their chairs. The most famous is a wooden chair that appeared in the fifth century BC. Known as a *klismos,* it would be copied by the Directoire and Empire styles in France, by the Regency style in Great Britain and by Sweden and Russia. An extremely elegant and well-proportioned chair, the *klismos* had four saber legs which supported a seat made of plaited ropes or strips of leather, and a double curved back: vertically toward the back and horizontally toward the interior. The apron and the seat back were inlaid with geometric ivory patterns, creating a harmony never achieved before—and rarely since.

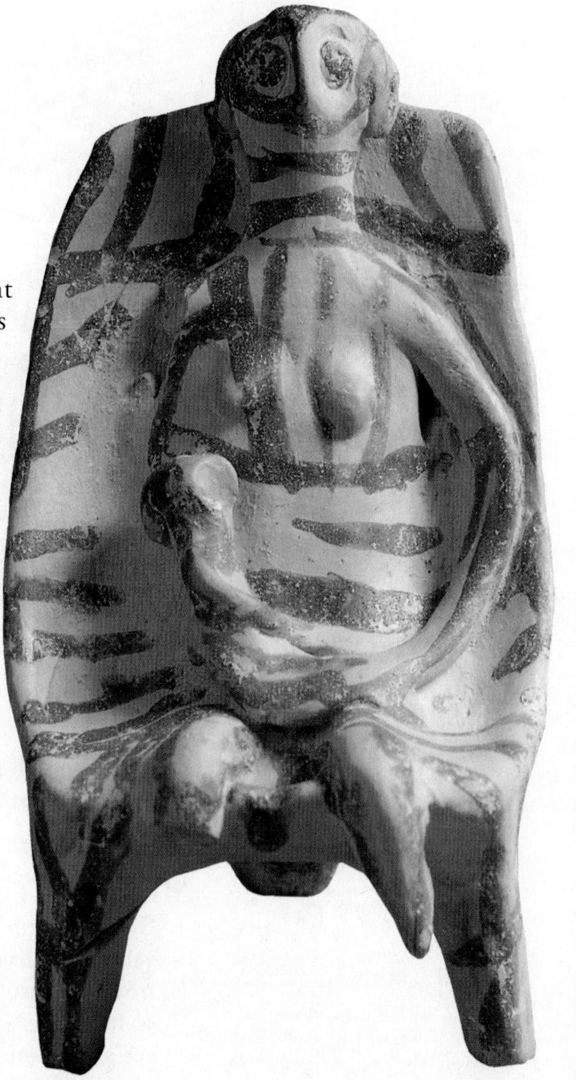

△ *Figurine seated on a throne. Painted terracotta statuette. Mycenaean era. Musée du Louvre, Paris.*

Rome

Roman furniture was modeled from Greek furniture, from which it borrowed the patterns and fashion for concave shapes. The Romans were highly skilled woodworkers and had perfected the technique of finely chased bronze ornaments and silver veneer. The furniture, at least toward the end of the Empire, was extraordinarily luxurious . Recent reconstructions of these pieces, made from architectural texts or excavations, reveal the sophistication and splendor of the work—something historians had imagined, but had never been able to fully assess.

Most of the wooden furniture was decorated systematically with chased bronze: lion's paw feet, chased acanthus leaf ornaments and rosettes. Geometric inlaid patterns made of ivory and ebony were also common. Some pieces of furniture were made entirely of bronze or of chased silver veneer (especially beds and couches). Seats were covered with stretched leather. Folding X-frame seats were also widespread, and used as stools or tables. The X-frames were later used by cabinetmakers working in the Louis XIV, Directoire, Empire and Regency styles.

The major innovation in furniture under Roman rule—which was, after all, a military civilization—was the chest for storing arms. This chest naturally acquired the name *armorium,* from which the word armoire is obviously derived. Many examples were unearthed in the eighteenth century during excavation work at Pompeii and Herculaneum; these pieces and others from these ancient sites sparked the neoclassical fashion that flourished in Europe, leading to the Transition, Louis XVI, Directoire (France), Regency (Great Britain) and Gustavian (Sweden) styles.

△ *Painting from Herculaneum. Musée du Louvre, Paris.*

△ *Ivory box, decorated with rectangular sculpted panels surrounded by rosettes. Byzantine Empire. Twelfth century. Musée national de la Préhistoire, Les Eyzies.*

Byzantine empire

The grandeur of the Roman Empire gradually crumbled during a long period of decadence marked by barbarian invasions. The final hour coincided with the Sack of Rome; at this point—the dawn of the fourth century—those craftsmen maintaining the heritage of the Egyptians, Assyrians and Greeks moved to the new capital of the empire created by Constantine: Constantinople. The craftsmen were especially gifted in ivory work. Depictions of religious subjects at that time (the predecessors of icons) adorned marvelous ivory seats, sculpted with flowers, foliage, animals and people. The chair, chest and lectern were the three most common pieces of furniture.

Medieval furniture

By the late fifth century, Clovis had founded the Frankish kingdom. Up through the eleventh century, furniture remained extremely simple. Folding X-frame chairs, inspired from the curule chair of the Roman Empire, seem to have been the most common item of furniture. Large bronze chairs sculpted with animal designs, which are depicted on certain illuminated manuscripts, were generally reserved for important figures, such as ecclesiastics or kings.

Chests, which were also used as tables and beds and for storage, were extremely rustic and simple, with little or no ornamentation. The only remarkable elements were produced by the blacksmiths who created iron straps and hinges to join the wooden pieces. Bench-chests and church benches had slightly more decoration (occasionally a plant motif). Oak was the only wood used during the Renaissance, as it is an extremely sturdy wood. Joints, made by *huchiers* (hutchmakers) were rough. It appeared as though the skills accumulated over the centuries by Egyptian, Assyrian, Greek and Roman craftsmen had been forgotten sometime between the third and tenth centuries.

▽ *Large chest, ca 1300. Musée de Cluny, Paris.*

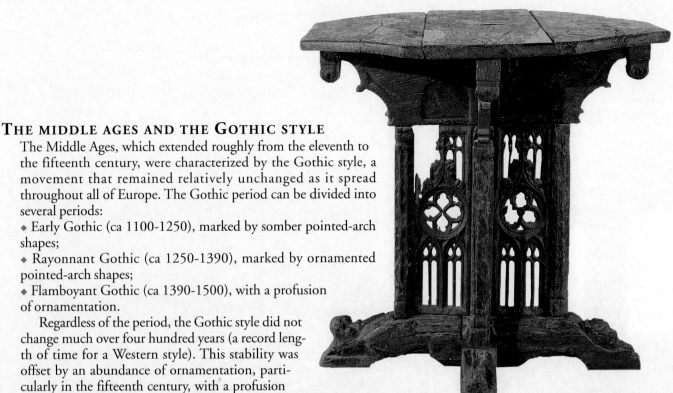

The Middle Ages and the Gothic style

The Middle Ages, which extended roughly from the eleventh to the fifteenth century, were characterized by the Gothic style, a movement that remained relatively unchanged as it spread throughout all of Europe. The Gothic period can be divided into several periods:

- Early Gothic (ca 1100-1250), marked by somber pointed-arch shapes;
- Rayonnant Gothic (ca 1250-1390), marked by ornamented pointed-arch shapes;
- Flamboyant Gothic (ca 1390-1500), with a profusion of ornamentation.

△ *Wooden table that could be taken apart. France, 1500. Musée de Cluny, Paris.*

Regardless of the period, the Gothic style did not change much over four hundred years (a record length of time for a Western style). This stability was offset by an abundance of ornamentation, particularly in the fifteenth century, with a profusion of tracery, foliage motifs and statues of apostles of all stripes. These decorative motifs were, for the most part, inspired from religion and reproduced the architectural themes used in the churches: ribbed vaults, semicircular arches, crockets and biblical scenes. Designs not drawn from the ecclesiastic world were usually taken from nature (rosettes, foliage, flower buds, fleur de lys, flowers and palmettes), from the geometric Romanesque vocabulary (tracery, checkerboards and chevrons) and sometimes from Celtic sources.

Oak was still the most commonly used wood and remained so through the late fifteenth century.

Wrought iron was the only other material used by furniture makers. It was shaped into hinges, straps, locks, handles and nails to attach leather. It was often shaped into elaborate forms, as the blacksmith was often more highly skilled than the hutchmaker.

The skills of marquetry and inlaid materials had been lost, except in southern Spain and Italy.

Furniture was usually brightly painted, as were the cathedrals (and, indeend, many the monuments in ancient Rome, Athens and Egypt). Most of the sculpted ornamentation was painted in vivid colors so that it stood out from the background, itself also highly colored.

The only real innovation introduced by the Gothic style was the dresser, a table-like base topped with a series of shelves. This furniture of state, called a buffet and designed to display plates and silver, prefigured the Italian Renaissance cabinets.

By the end of the Middle Ages, most of the woodworking and joining techniques, developed in ancient Egypt and lost over time, had been more or less rediscovered. From this point on, this knowledge would be carefully passed on from generation to generation, usually through the various guilds. Beginning in the thirteenth century, these guilds established strict guidelines for the transmission of these skills and access to the occupations of carpenter, woodworker and later cabinetmaker.

▽ *Chest with Venetian marquetry. Italy, 15th century. Musée de Cluny, Paris.*

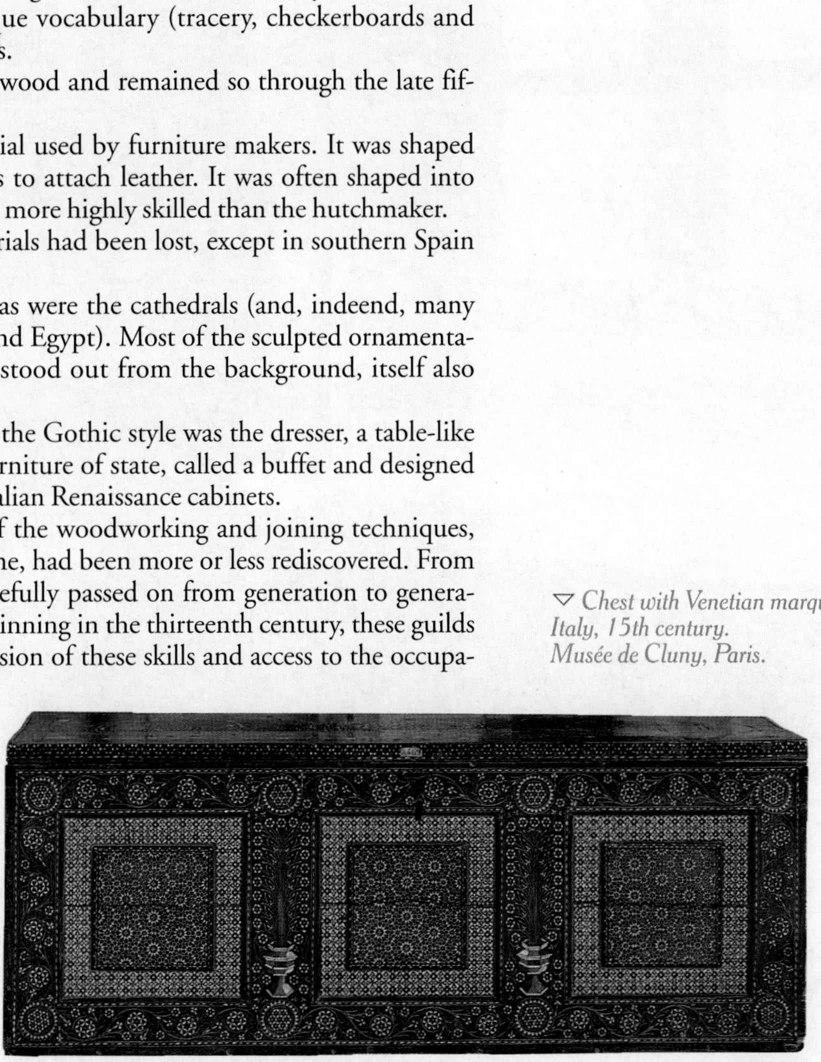

THE *16TH* CENTURY

THE RENAISSANCE CORRESPONDED TO A SPECTACULAR EXCHANGE OF IDEAS BETWEEN THE VARIOUS KINGDOMS, PRINCIPALITIES, DUCHIES, EMPIRES AND REPUBLICS THAT FORMED POST-MEDIEVAL EUROPE.

Many new ideas originated in the fourteenth century in Venice, during the period of the international Gothic style and after this fabulously wealthy trading town had discovered the Far East. This trend continued in the following century, particularly in Florence in Tuscany, home to the all-powerful Medici family.

In Florence from the early fifteenth century through the late sixteenth century—as well as in Siena, Milan and Rome (where Raphael's decorative frescoes in the papal apartments of the Vatican had a profound influence)—the Italian Renaissance offered a new style based primarily on two concepts: the revival of the ornamental vocabulary of Antiquity and the discovery of perspective. The latter would become the foundation of an innovative architectural and decorative style free from of any trace of Gothic rigidity.

By the early sixteenth century, the new movement had spread throughout Europe, under the influence of the artists who traveled between the royal courts of Europe and the political links of the countries under the rule of the Habsburg emperors. This phenomenon was further encouraged by the availability of Mannerist engravings produced in the 1560s. Exchanges between Venice and Castile, Flanders and Italy, Venice and London, and Augsburg and Nuremberg proved to be a constant source of new information. Each country adopted the Renaissance style, but adapted it to its individual aesthetic heritage.

In France, this adaptation occurred in several stages. The early Renaissance corresponds to the reign of François I (1515-1547) and the creation of the School of Fontainebleau, led by the Italian artists working on the chateau's construction site. The second phase of the Renaissance extended from the start of Henri II's reign in 1536 to the end of the century, and made abundant use of ancient Roman decors; the sculptor Jean Goujon was a leader in the Henri II style.

This same transition to the Renaissance style took place in England, starting with the reign of Henry VIII (this movement was placed under the generic title of Tudor style), and a fully defined style during Queen Elizabeth's reign. This pattern of successive stages also occurred in Spain with the Charles V and Philip II styles.

The Renaissance period also corresponded to the conquests of new worlds. Spain, liberated from the Mozarab occupation, discovered the Americas. Sources of inspiration seemed limitless. Each country outdid itself in displays of power and wealth. This translated into furniture designs in different ways. In Italy, for example, cabinetmakers invented marquetry (*intarsia*), incorporating precious materials and new techniques: *comesso,* a type of marquetry using *pietre dure* (hard stone), invented at the Florentine court of the Medici, is one such example.

◁ *The Renaissance beamed ceiling at the Château d'Amboise on the banks of the Loire River, France.*

ITALY

1450 1600

The Renaissance Styles

△ The Four Doctors of the Church with Symbols of the Four Evangelists.
Pier Francesco Sacchi. Musée du Louvre, Paris.

The movement that would release the decorative and fine arts from the Gothic style that reigned throughout Europe first appeared in Tuscany in the early fifteenth century. The Renaissance was born, paradoxically, from a desire to put the recent past behind, by drawing its inspiration from a more distant past. Indeed, the Renaissance invented its new stylistic vocabulary by borrowing a series of ornamental motifs from ancient Rome. The Tuscany Renaissance was characterized by an series of new technical processes that would travel throughout the world. The first of these was *intarsia,* which can be translated simply as "inlay."

Intarsia was first created in the Medici studios in Siena and Florence. The process consists in chiseling out geometric or serpentine designs in a wooden panel; these grooves and hollows were then filled with strips of different kinds of wood. At first, the designs were influenced by the Hispano-Mauresque style and consisted of arabesques with an ivory paste that stood out against the dark wood. This was the white Moorish style. Another technique, *certosina,* which may have been imported from the East, used very small pieces of colored wood in the hollowed-out areas. Another technique is pure marquetry, which differs from inlay in that strips of veneer from various different woods are glued side by side to create designs.

In 1588, Ferdinando I de' Medici created the Uffizi de Pietre Dure, a studio of stoneworkers, to create "stone paintings" from beautiful stones from all over the world. This technique produced extraordinary masterpieces. The favorite motifs of the Tuscany Renaissance were foliated scrolls, figures in low relief, putti, lion heads and caryatids. The Venetian Renaissance added an Oriental flavor to the Tuscan vocabulary—to such an extent that the style veered toward Baroque. *Sgraffito,* a technique of scraping off a paint layer to reveal a gold undercoat, was a favorite technique for wood furniture.

The masters

Mosaicists:
Alesso Baldovinetti, Domenico Ghirlandaio

Cabinetmakers, sculptors:
Aglomo Baglioni, Giovani De Baiso, Domenico Del Tasso

Wood and materials

Walnut

Ebony veneer

Rosewood

Pine

Ivory veneer

Pewter

Gold, ivory and mother-of-pearl inlay

Tortoise-shell inlay

Pietre dure *and painted stone inlay*

Tinted wood marquetry.

THE CABINET

The first stipi, or cabinets, appeared in Venice during the Italian Renaissance. In the seventeenth century, these elements became masterpieces of cabinetmaking.

Legs

The imposing table and chair legs were covered with sculpted foliate scroll designs. The table top was supported on each end by two triple-legs with a spiral and honeycomb decoration. Each leg ends with a pawed-foot base.

THE
TABLE À L'ITALIENNE

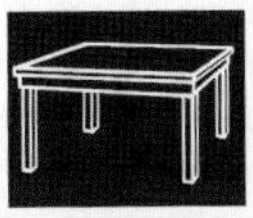

The design of the so-called* table à l'Italienne, *generally made of light walnut, was inspired from the ancient Roman marble table known as the carti*bulum. *The tabletop was supported on either end by massive slabs of wood sculpted to represent foliated scrolls or animal heads. In the Medici workshops in Florence, the end slabs were joined by a broad stretcher; columns or a lyre motif in the center of the stretcher supported the middle of the tabletop.

Stretcher

Ornately sculpted, this element joined the three-legged slabs supporting the heavy tabletop, contributing to the impression of stability, solidity and heaviness of the overall piece.

Apron

This element was often sculpted with foliated scrolls and geometric motifs or, as on this piece, a "convex mirror" design.

△ *Table with three-legged supports. 1580. Museo degli Argenti, Florence.*

Motifs and decorative elements

Acanthus leaves
Ionic columns
Foliated scrolls
Grooves
Molded rings
Concave-mirror motif
Figures sculpted in bas relief
Floral patterns
Animal heads
Cupids
Clawed paws
Islamic-style arabesques
Intertwined branches

SAVONAROLA CHAIR

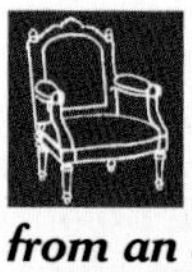

A large number of chairs were designed during this period. The early Italian Renaissance created the sedia dantesca, inspired from an ancient Roman design: it had a strip of leather stretched over an X-frame chair. The crest rail was decorated with gold, mother-of-pearl or ivory inlay. The first wooden chair, the Savonarola chair, appeared in the fifteenth century; it was an X-frame chair with six or more curved frames arranged from front to back. The back was a simple cross-piece with inlays of precious materials.

Crest rail

This consisted of a cross piece carved with the coat of arms of the owner, whose blazon was set in a tracery of floral designs and acanthus leaves. Precious materials were sometimes added to the carved designs on the seat back.

Legs

The legs were generally branch-like, curving frames that crossed underneath the chair seat.

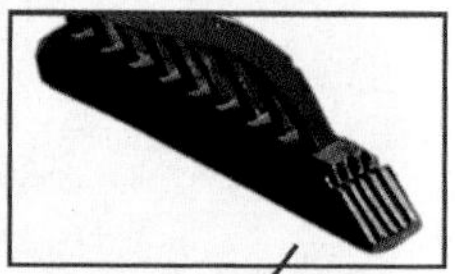

△ *Savonarola chair. Château du Plessis-Bourré, France.*

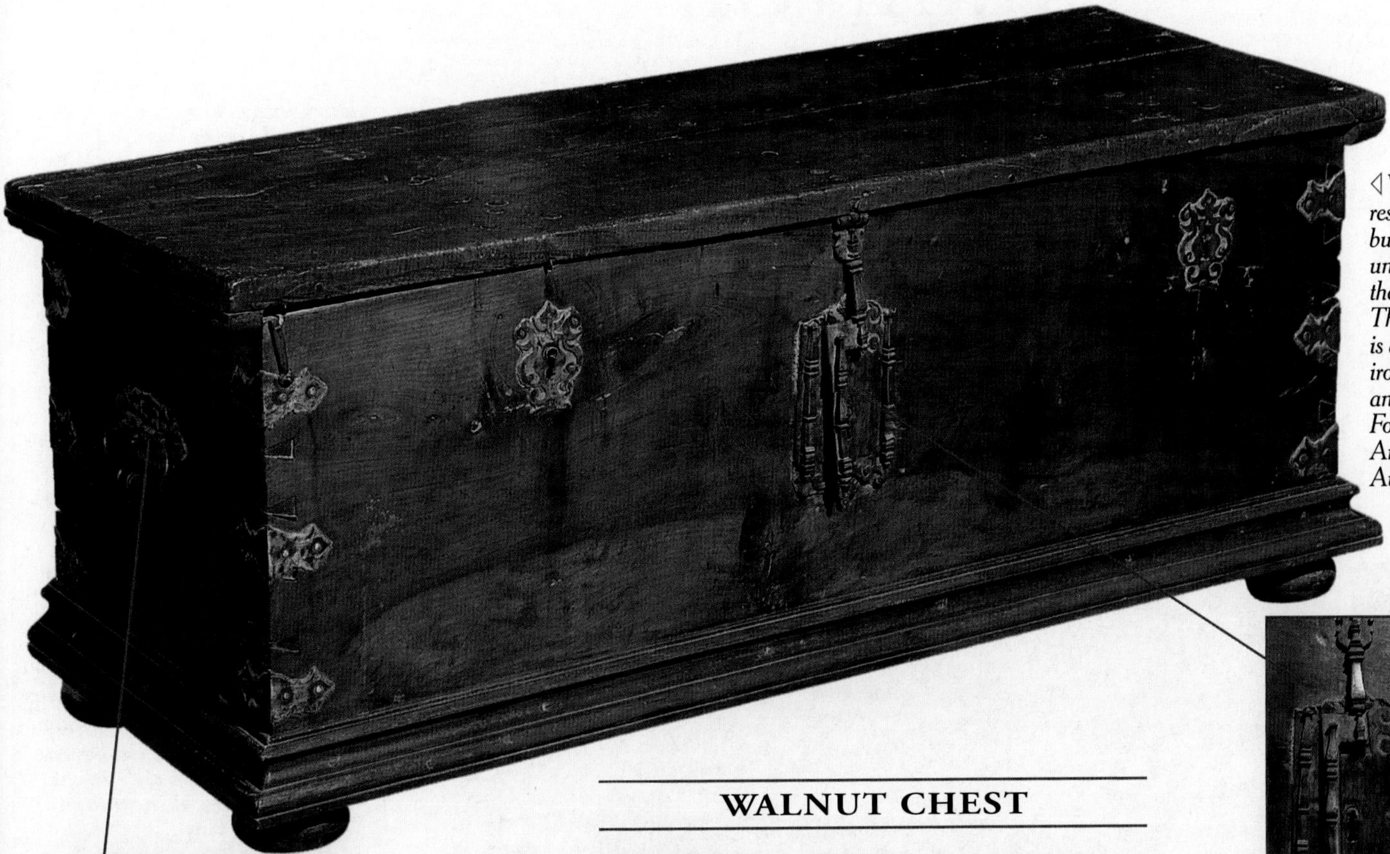

◁ *Walnut chest resting on bun feet underneath the apron. The chest is decorated with iron straps and handles. Fondation Angladon, Avignon.*

WALNUT CHEST

For many years, large chests, the one essential piece of furniture, were used as benches, tables and for storage. The Gothic tracery on these richly sculpted chests gradually was replaced by decorative floral elements.

Central lock

This lock and the side iron straps were the only decorative elements on this extremely austere chest, an unusually elegant and restrained design for this period. The lock resembles a blazon.

Handles

Fitted to the sides, the handles made it easy to transport the furniture during voyages. They were often sophisticated pieces of ironwork.

▽ *Walnut bench with a fan-leg support, interconnected by a twisted iron spacer. Italy, sixteenth century. Fondation Angladon, Avignon.*

Legs

The ornately sculpted front and rear legs of the bench, interconnected by a stretcher decorated with floral motifs, contrast with the simplicity of the rest of the bench and the rather austere ironwork.

BENCHES

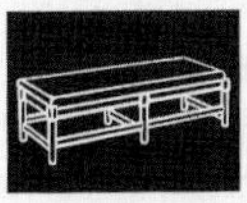

As in the Middle Ages, benches in the Renaissance were generally little more than simple planks of oak or walnut. A low back was often added, formed from a piece of walnut with beveled edges. The trestle, which was the usual support, was replaced by legs, decorated and sculpted in relief with acanthus leaves, elongated palmettes or various types of fruits.

FRANCE

1494 — 1610

Two Renaissance Styles

△ *Henri II's bedroom. Château d'Amboise, France.*

A distinction is generally made between the first Renaissance style or François I style (1494-1548) and the second Renaissance (1547-1610). The first Renaissance style was introduced to France by Charles VIII when he returned from his first Italian expedition (1483-1498). The second Renaissance is also known as the Henri II style, whose queen was Catherine de Médicis. This style covers the reign of this king, as well as the reigns of his three successors—François II, Henri III and Henri IV—and lasted until 1610.

The French Renaissance styles differed from the Italian styles in that they had a distinct preference for relief sculpture, figures sculpted in the round and ornamental sculpture, like the work produced by Jean Goujon—rather than for inlay, marquetry or painting on wood. Caryatid supports, recesses, mirrors, helmeted warriors, battle scenes, candelabras, grotesque ornaments, pilasters, grooved Ionic columns and ball feet are characteristic elements of the style. The principal pieces of furniture, which were always ornately decorated, were chests, cabinets, beds and—for the first time in France—cupboards designed to display silver, plates, enamels and faience. The most common decorative motif in the French Renaissance styles was the elongated acanthus leaf, which was sculpted onto most Henri II furniture.

The masters

Hugues Sambin

Jean Goujon

Jacques Androuet du Cerceau

Denis Bredin

Pierre Chenevières

Wood and materials

Oak

Mother-of-pearl, ebony and ivory inlays

Motifs and decorative elements

Elongated acanthus leaves

Foliated scrolls,

THE *TABLE À L'ITALIENNE*

Inspired from an ancient Roman piece of furniture, this table consisted of a rectangular tabletop surrounded by bas-relief sculptures of designs, gadroons, palmettes or ovolos. It was supported by a monumental fan-shaped base made of elaborately carved columns and arcading, joined by a broad stretcher. The tabletop was divided into two flaps, one of which folded over the other. The most beautiful examples were made in the style of the Burgundian cabinetmaker Hugues Sambin.

Winged chimera

Winged chimera and caryatids were the two favorite mythological motifs in the Henri II style. Chimeras, caryatids and female sphinxes were sometimes replaced by simple grooved columns or colonnettes.

THE HENRI II CUPBOARD

The display cupboard and the two-tiered Henri II cupboard are specific to the early French Renaissance style. This latter piece of furniture consisted of two sections topped by a broken pediment. It often included one or two drawers in the apron and four doors: two in the upper section, two in the lower. The cupboard formed a doubly symmetrical unit, as the various elements were repeated two by two. The legs were short and squat; sometimes they were replaced by a small base or a type of platform. The decorative elements were often drawn from mythological sources: Diana the Huntress, Mercury, Leda and Jupiter. Display buffets had a lower open section, forming a caryatid console that supported the upper section.

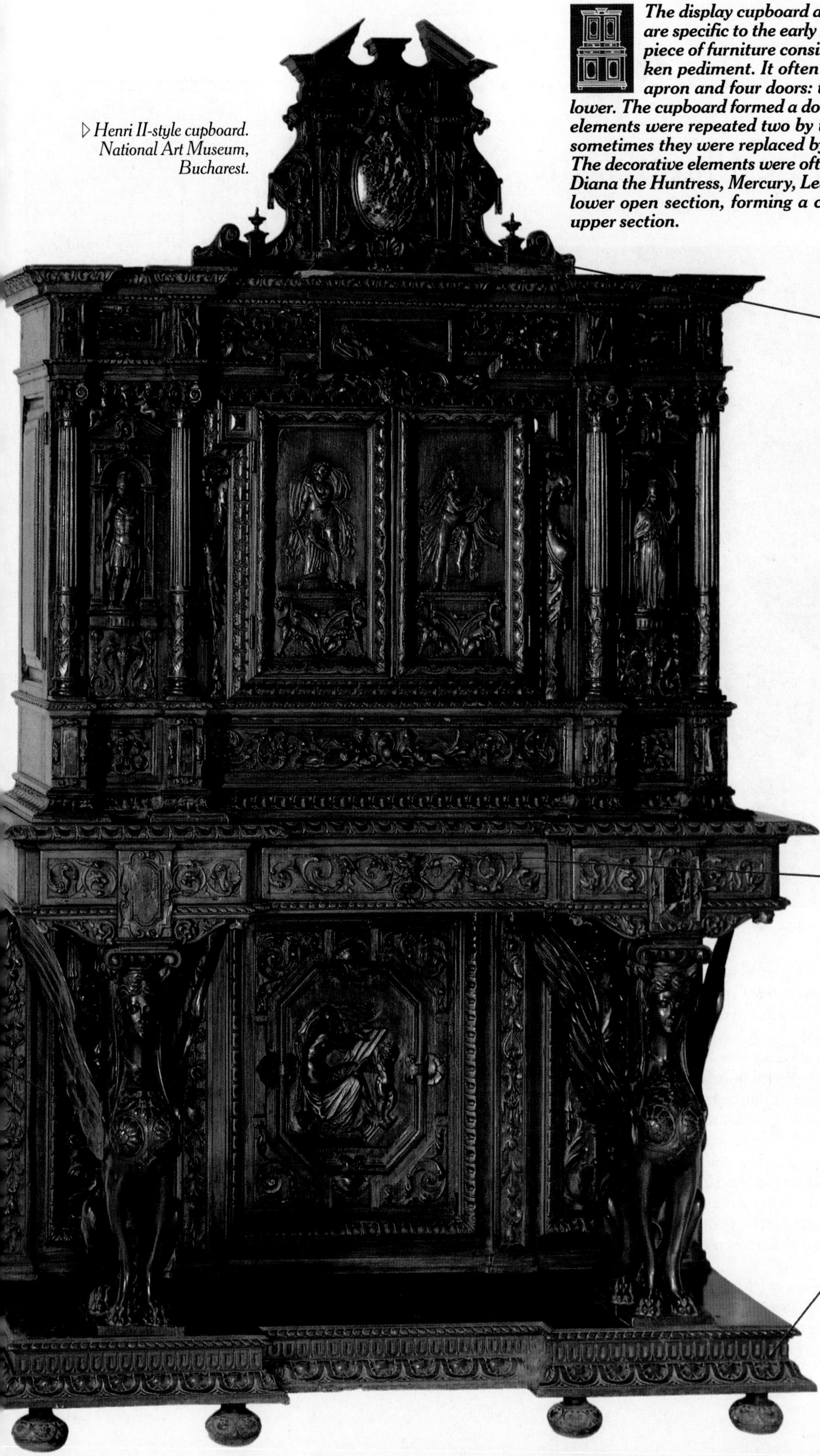

▷ *Henri II-style cupboard. National Art Museum, Bucharest.*

Sculpted pediment

These were broken pediments; the gap was sometimes used to display a statuette, an urn or a vase. It was always elaborately carved with acanthus leaves, winged chimera, molding and scrolls.

Drawers on the apron

These drawers separated the two sections of the cupboard; the decorative elements on either side were symmetrical.

Base

The columns or caryatids supporting the upper section of the cupboard rested on the base. It was supported by four bun feet on the front side.

SPAIN

1500 1598

The Plateresque Style

Wood and materials

Walnut
Ebony
Ivory
Bone
Painted wood
Gilded bronze

Motifs and decorative elements

Painted architectural elements
Arcatures
Colonnettes
Inlay with Mudéjar-style motifs and Islamic designs
Grotesque ornaments

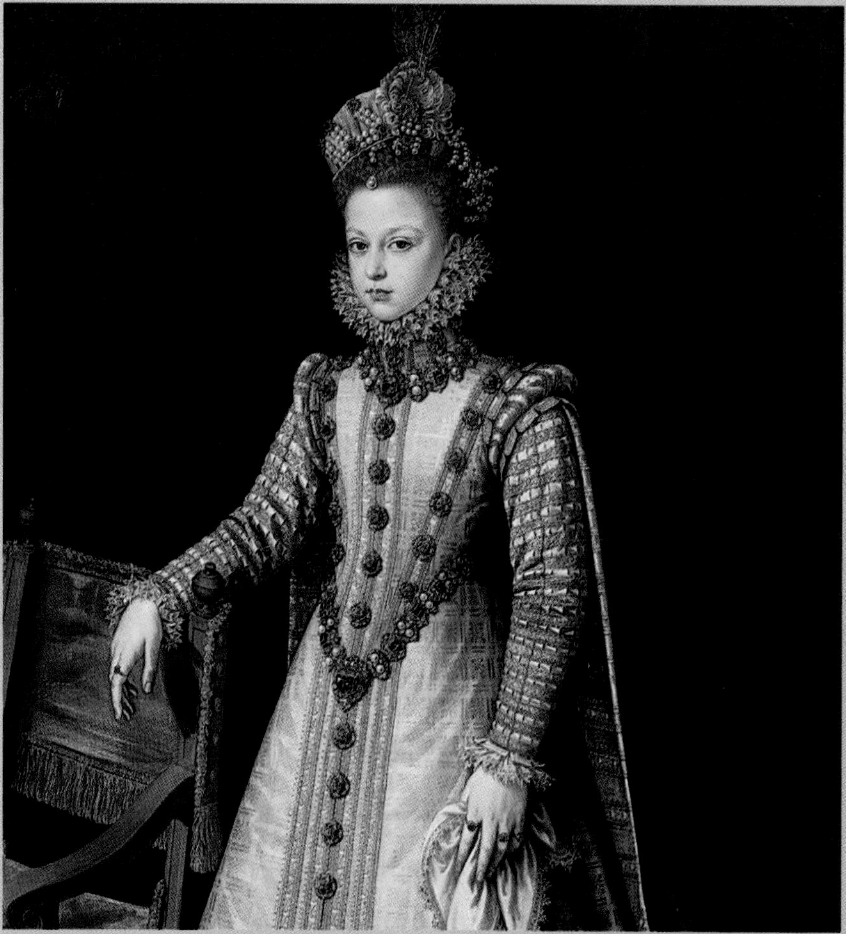

△ The Infante Isabel Clara Eugenia de Habsburg. *Alonso Sánchez Coello. Prado Museum, Madrid.*

When Charles V became king of Spain in 1516, the Moors had just been vanquished at Grenada. When he acceded to the throne, he also inherited the Habsburg dynasty, which included Castile, Aragon and the kingdoms of Naples and Sicily. From the moment he became king, he introduced an entirely new set of values into Spanish society. During this century, Spain set out to conquer the New World in search of its fabulous wealth. But the Spanish style acquired its real identity during the reign of Charles V's son, Philip II (1556-1598).

Under Charles V, furniture design began to borrow a number of decorative elements from the Italian Renaissance: urns, putti, masks, birds, laurel wreaths, grotesque ornaments, trophies, vases and shells. These elements, applied to the traditional structure of furniture that was still highly imbued with the Mudéjar culture—Muslims who remained on the reconquered land—formed striking contrasts. At the same time, the Plateresque style (from *plata,* which means "money,") took its inspiration from the bas-relief sculptures used on gold and silver pieces, which were then applied to furniture.

Under the reign of Philip II, the Mudéjar influence persisted, but was gradually replaced by more austere motifs inspired from the architectural ornamentation created by Juan Bautista de Herrera. Toward the end of the century, furniture was painted, and gilt bronze appeared on many pieces.

ARCAS

Arcas (chests) were extremely simple structures used as seats or beds (in the Moorish fashion with pillows covering the top) or used to transport objects. Toward the end of the century, they became more Italianate in style, with caryatids adorning the corners and a profusion of sculpted elements.

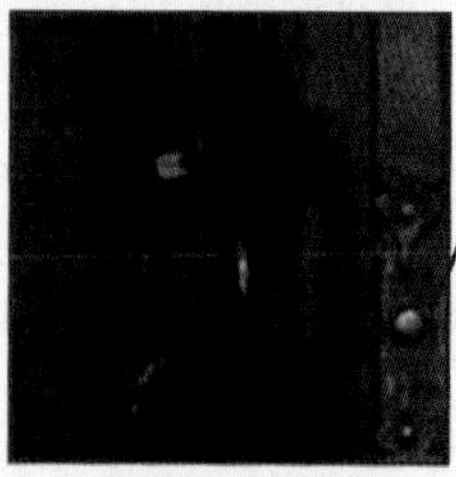

Side handles

These handles were used to carry the desk, as was done with the Hispano-Moresque-style fall-front chests.

Shell motif

The symbol of the Santiago de Compostela pilgrimage, the shell indicates that this *vargueño* belonged to a pilgrim.

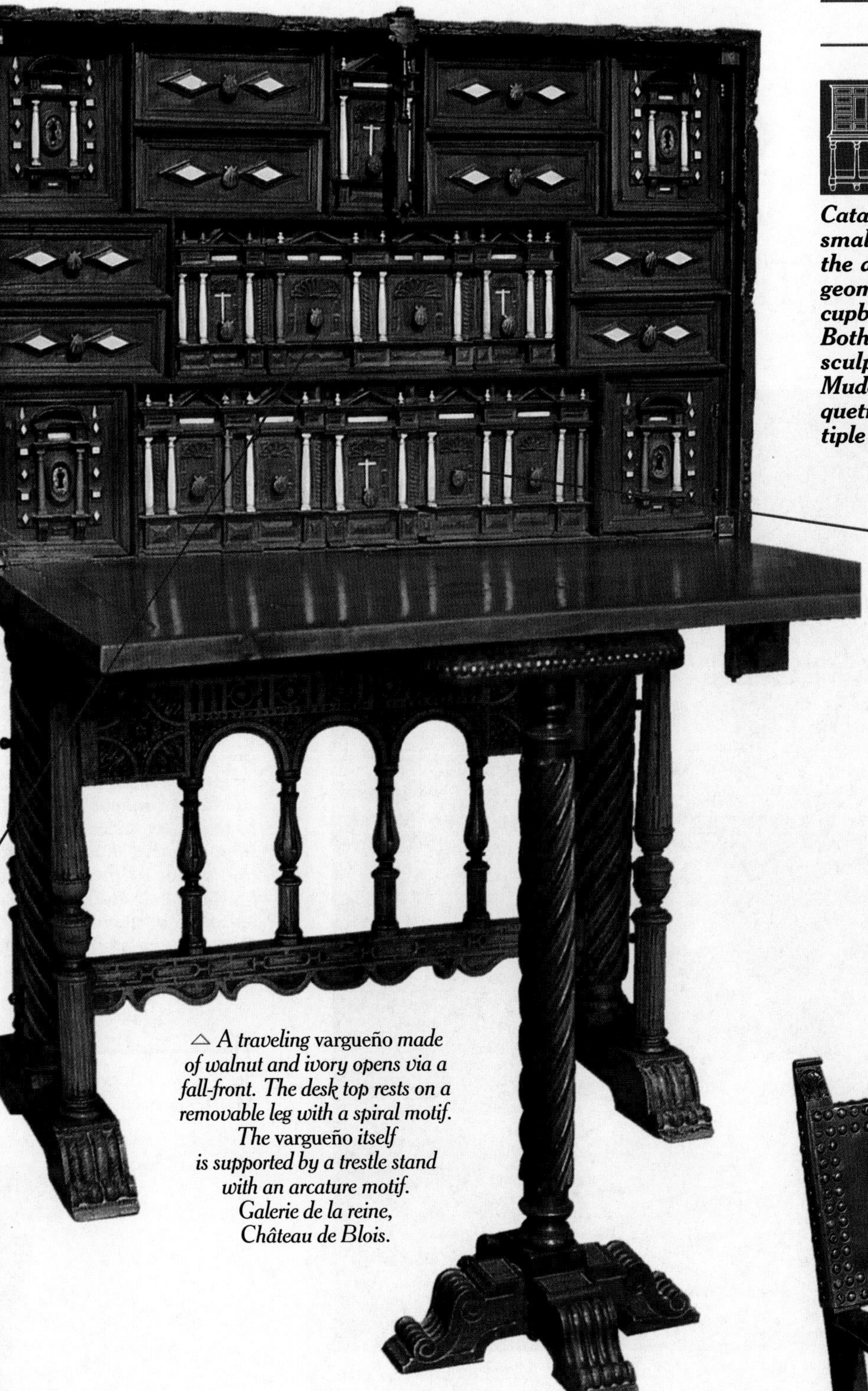

△ *A traveling* vargueño *made of walnut and ivory opens via a fall-front. The desk top rests on a removable leg with a spiral motif. The* vargueño *itself is supported by a trestle stand with an arcature motif. Galerie de la reine, Château de Blois.*

PHILIP II *VARGUEÑO*

Under Philip II's reign, a piece of furniture was created which would become the Spanish desk* par excellence*: the* vargueño*. It was a clever combination of the front-fall Moorish chest and the Catalan chest. It opened to reveal several rows of small drawers and compartments. When closed, the desk was perfectly symmetrical and austerely geometric. The* vargueño *rested on a four-legged cupboard or a trestle stand with a spiral-leg design. Both the inside and outside were decorated with sculpted colonnettes, arcatures, pediments and Mudéjar-style arabesques created with ivory marquetry. Some of these desks were painted in multiple colors or with a trompe-l'œil design.

Architectural sculptures

Miniature ivory colonnettes, arcatures and pediments reproducing the facades of palaces or church doors framed the compartments and drawers.

▷ *High-backed walnut armchair with acanthus leaves. Baluster armrests. Column legs in the front linked by an openwork stretcher. Upholstered with nailed leather. Fondation Angladon, Avignon.*

ARMCHAIRS

The* sillón de fraileros*, or "monk's chair," is a simple rectilinear wooden armchair upholstered with* guadamecil *(tooled and colored) leather attached with copper nails. The legs support wide arms and are linked by a box stretcher with an openwork design.
The simpler chair inspired the so-called Spanish chair, with a woven straw or leather and back with two or three sculpted wooden rods.

England

1509 — *1603*

The Tudor Style

Motifs and decorative elements

Man dominated by animals

Lions reclining or standing on their hind legs

Blazons held by monstrous animals

Winged dragons

Monumental vases

Ionic columns with women's heads

Religious figures and Evangelists

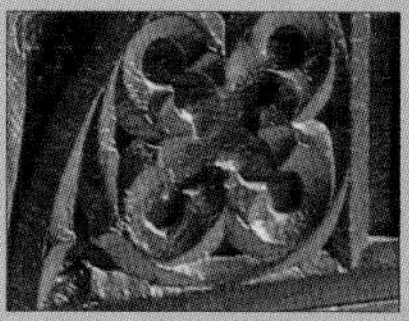

Wood and materials

Oak

Inlaid boxwood

Hard stone or precious stone marquetry

△ Death of Queen Elizabeth of England, in 1603. *Paul Delaroche. Musée du Louvre, Paris.*

The Tudor style continued throughout the entire sixteenth century and the reigns of King Henry VIII and Queen Elizabeth I. It was highly influenced (particularly in the second half of the century) by elements of the Italian Renaissance, especially the Venetian version. The linenfold motif that was sculpted on nearly all furniture through the end of Henry VIII's reign was replaced by tracery and shell motifs from Italy during Queen Elizabeth's rule. The four Evangelists were also a common motif on chests and bed corners. Other sculpted elements included stretchers, rings, rosettes, spiral motifs and chimera. This style was a clever mix of styles from the Italian Renaissance and the Celtic Renaissance, which had been a major influence on English furniture-makers during the Gothic period.

Furniture developed first in the monasteries and soon became a sign of prestige and wealth in aristocratic homes. These included chests, tables and beds, particularly the canopy or tester bed covered with fabric. An entirely new series of furniture pieces were invented for the hall, the large central room in English homes that was also used for banquets and entertainment.

OTHER FURNITURE

The sideboard, with two superimposed tables, rested on heavy supports.
The cupboard was made according to the same basic design as the sideboard, but with a solid upper section with a door that was used to store food. Bulb-turned columns decorated the corners.
The high table was a decorative table covered with opulent fabric on which silver and plates were displayed.
The refectory table sat on a stout support interconnected by stretchers just above the ground; it replaced the long trestle table and was surrounded by stools. By the end of the century, sculpted shells decorated the apron. At the same time, high-backed chairs were replaced by armchairs decorated with boxwood inlay on the seat back.

◁ *Oak chest with Gothic-inspired decoration elements, resting on short feet. Fifteenth-sixteenth centuries. Christie's, London.*

Legs

The chest no longer rested on a base set directly on the ground, as in earlier styles, but is supported on feet; with these elements, the chest started to resemble a low commode.

CHESTS

Chests made during the Elizabethan era, often with ornamentation still inspired from the Gothic style, were supported by short feet that raised it off the floor. At the same time as the feet were added, the furniture was also made higher, which transformed the chest into a commode. Indeed, the words commode and chest are virtually interchangeable.

DRAW-LEAF TABLES

This was a table with one or two leaves that rested beneath the tabletop. This tabletop, with intarsia-style inlay, rested on legs ornately sculpted with fantastic animals and vase motifs. The apron was decorated with acanthus leaves and godroons.

◁ *Table with two leaves concealed under the tabletop. The apron is decorated with acanthus leaves and the table top is supported by six legs, including four sculpted as fantastic animals on each corner bearing the owner's coat of arms, and two sculpted with religious figures in the center. Christie's, London.*

Germany

1500 1680

The masters

Peter Flötner, architect, engraver and designer of sculpted furniture

Lienhart Strohmeier, famous for the desk he designed for Charles V

Thomas Rucker, creator of a steel armchair for Emperor Rudolf II

Wood and materials

Walnut

Oak

Walnut bur

Ebony

Ivory

Steel

Shell

Hard stones

Precious metals

Augsburg and Nuremberg

△ *View of the Nuremberg goldsmith workshop, 1565. Musée de la Renaissance, Écouen.*

In the early fifteenth century, craftsmen in the various German principalities began to move away from Gothic ornamentation in favor of the vocabulary of the Italian Renaissance and for decorative motifs inspired from ancient Rome. Furniture production from this period was marked by masterpieces created by the trade-guilds, an extremely regimented hierarchical system. Cabinetmakers were highly skilled in Germany during the Renaissance. By the mid-sixteenth century, the architectural craftsmen—so-named for the architectural aspect of the furniture, which was inspired by the structure of monuments—specialized in massive furniture. The style in the southern principalities was a simple reproduction of the Italian style. In the north, however, particularly in Augsburg and Nuremberg, a specific Germanic style developed; it was characterized by ornate decoration, massive structures and an extremely high, nearly perfect, level of craftsmanship.

Other furniture

The double-door cabinet rested on a table-like support with rectilinear legs or straight columns. This aristocratic piece of furniture, often made of walnut bur, opened to reveal a series of drawers bordered with ebony, with inlaid scenes and landscapes in ivory, stone, tortoiseshell and precious metals. The center section had a secret compartment. A cornice molding inlaid with ebony often ran along the top of the cabinet. During this period, most chairs and armchairs were still Gothic in style, although cushions were added for greater comfort. Folding X-frame chairs in the Italian style were also made.

Lock mechanisms appear

The complex mechanism of this 13-bolt lock is visible once the chest is opened; this pile of arrows forms a fascinating motif for this particularly austere military chest.

WARDROBES AND CUPBOARDS

The wardrobe or cupboard was a very large piece of furniture: between 9 to 9 1/2 feet high, depending on the region. Sometimes formed of two separate sections, the wardrobe was constructed to resemble the facade of a Renaissance palace or monument. The structure was divided vertically into symmetrical sections. These contained compartments arranged on either side of a central column. Another type of wardrobe with two sections and double doors appeared in the second half of the century.

◁ *Two-tiered cupboard with architectural-style facade. Made in Augsburg by Clement Petel. The front panels of this cupboard reproduce the architectural elements of a Renaissance-style building. Stadtmuseum, Weilheim.*

Architectural ornamentation

The door reproduces the windows of an imaginary palace. It is framed by columns, which are the uprights. Each door is sculpted with a different motif: sculptures on the upper doors and marquetry on the lower ones.

◁ *A so-called Nuremberg chest, with an interwoven design. It is a remarkable example of high-quality workmanship and solidity. Musée du Vieux Marseille, Marseille.*

Recessed base

Each corner of the base is flanked by a double upright framing a recess. This recess is decorated with a statuette; this massive base was a common stylistic element during the Renaissance.

CHESTS

As was the case throughout all of Europe, chests were the single most important element of furniture. They were often ornately sculpted in bas-relief and sometimes painted. The outside ornamentation consisted of pilasters that framed medallions of people or landscapes with capitals or arcading along the top.

THE *17TH* CENTURY

THE BAROQUE STYLE, WHICH DEVELOPED IN ITALY IN THE LATE SIXTEENTH CENTURY, WAS BOTH AN AESTHETIC AND RELIGIOUS MOVEMENT. THE STYLE—ITS EXUBERANCE, APPEARANCE, LUXURY, EXAGGERATION, MONUMENTALITY AND PATHOS—OWES MUCH TO THE COUNCIL OF TRENT AND THE COUNTER-REFORMATION, AND NOTHING, IN FACT, TO CHANCE.

The expansion of the Baroque style was linked to the Catholic Church and its policy of using art as a vehicle for religion and as an expression of the sublimation of the Catholic faith. Worshipers were drawn to the spectacular nature of the Baroque style, which impressed them and reassured their religious beliefs with its vision of a joyous, radiant world. This was a contrast to the rationalist, austere and skeptical world view of the Protestants.

Extravagance, the essential characteristic of the Baroque style, was the reason this style was so quickly adopted by the European courts, as well as by their recently acquired American colonies and the Calvinist courts of the Netherlands and Germany—the ultimate aim of the operation.

France, which enjoyed unprecedented power and a flourishing economy in the early year of Louis XIV's reign, viewed the foreign movement with suspicion and maintained an independent course. At the same time, it wanted to flaunt its power and immense wealth. Louis XIV excelled at this game—so well, in fact, that he created an almost separate style, with the assistance of Charles Le Brun, who oversaw the furnishings and decoration of Versailles. He was also assisted by brilliant and imaginative designers and ornamentalists, one of whom even designed solid silver furniture for the Grande Galerie. This furniture, which became famous throughout the world, would later be melted down for economic reasons during Louis XIV's lifetime. Yet by that time, it had already impressed and influenced courts throughout Europe and the Middle East.

The volumes of pattern books, published by French and Dutch ornamentalists, were extremely important to furniture styles; they were a source of decors and motifs that cabinetmakers consulted frequently. The greatest cabinetmaker among them, Jean-André Boulle, often used these books to create elaborate, luxurious court furniture.

This was a period during which styles from the East began to influence artistic milieux. Rare porcelains, Chinese screens and extraordinary lacquerwork had a place on honor in the literary salon of Madame de Rambouillet. The impact was immediate. Fascination for this work spread throughout all of Europe; it remained fashionable up until the mid-twentieth century.

◁ View of Louis XIV's bedroom.
Victor Navlet.
Château de Versailles.

FRANCE

1589 1661

The Louis XIII Style

The masters

Jean Macé (1602-1672): King's furniture-maker.

Wood and materials

Walnut

Oak and poplar for frames and armoires

Ebonized pearwood and other fruit trees

Amaranth veneer

Inlays of ebony, ivory, mother-of-pearl, amber, bone, tortoiseshell, pewter

Stone and gilt bronze, mirrors, fake rocks, shells, coral for cabinet cases

Wood veneer, modeled after the Italian intarsia technique

△ *Louis XIII dining room. Fondation Angladon, Avignon.*

Although known as the Louis XIII style, this fashion actually began during Henri IV's reign (late sixteenth century), continued through Louis XIII's reign (1610 to 1643), and persisted through the end of the regencies of Anne d'Autriche and Cardinal Mazarin (1661). Henri IV was the first French ruler to seek out the best craftsmen from all over Europe—Italy, Spanish Netherlands, Germany and Spain—and bring them to his court. He wanted them to train apprentices who could revive the national industry that was still producing Renaissance pieces, which required imports of precious and extraordinarily expensive materials. Henri IV offered these famous artists twenty-seven apartments and five workshops on the ground floor of the Louvre, under the Galerie du Louvre, where they could work comfortably. Yet the decisive social phenomenon of the early years of this century was the appearance of a wealthy French merchant class. The bourgeoisie wanted to live in elegant, stylishly furnished apartments with—and this was a novel idea—a certain level of comfort. Chairs, for example, became more comfortable with leather and fabric upholstering attached by large copper-headed nails, along with decorative galoons and fringe.

The Louis XIII style produced the first bourgeois-style furniture and the first intended specifically for apartment and city-dwellers, different from the aristocratic furniture in châteaux and private mansions in Paris's Marais district.

This type of furniture reappeared during the French Revolution and the Directoire; it was diametrically opposed to the furniture of state reserved for the king and other lofty figures in the realm.

The Louis XIII style, initiated by the bourgeoisie, was highly influential for a long time, particularly in regional French furniture styles, which were by nature bourgeois.

THE FAUTEUIL

The fauteuil, or armchair, first appeared around 1650. Initially, it was little more than a chair with arms. Soon, however, the seat back, which had been low and square, became higher, rectangular and slightly curved in shape—and therefore more comfortable. The curved armrests ended in carved scrolls. The front crosspiece and H-stretcher were turned with the same pattern as the legs. The fabric covering the seat back and armrests became increasingly luxurious.

Curtains

These curtains concealed the four bedposts, which were simple, unadorned walnut posts. When the bed was open, the curtains were attached on either side of the posts to reveal the interior trimmings of the bed and the bedspread, both made from the same fabric as the curtains and canopy.

Bed valance

The bed valance consisted of a strip of fabric, positioned symmetrically to the upper valances, which concealed the bedframe underneath.

THE CANOPY BED

The canopy bed was an expensive and monumental piece of furniture, which was always placed in a corner of a room. The bedroom was the room in which people spent much of their time, and it served as a backdrop for much of the social life of the period: people received guests in their bedrooms, ate meals, played games and slept. Conversations were held in the narrow space between the bed and the wall, called a "ruelle" in French.
The bed consisted of four turned wooden posts supporting a canopy. Large finials rose above each corner; these were often decorated with carved wooden plumes or flames, or fabric and trim. The bed was covered with the same fabric used for the canopy, which also upholstered the chairs. The quality of these beds was judged by the richness of the fabric, which generally consisted of strips of Genoa velvets alternating with appliqués of silk embroidered with silver and gold thread; dark damask (purple and carmine) with wide gold strips of additional embroidery; or even velvet trimmed with silver and gold lace. Although luxurious, it was fairly practical—by necessity, as it was commonplace to transport the household bed during travels. As sumptuous as it was, the bed could always be dismantled and stored in large leather trunks during the frequent trips to and from city homes and country estates.
These Louis XIII beds were certainly imposing, but were rather short in length. This is not due to any difference in size between seventeenth-century people and people today; it is, rather, because the habit was to sleep in half-sitting positions, never reclining.

▷ *Bed from the Château d'Effiat, made of walnut and silk velvet. Musée du Louvre, Paris.*

Finials

Finials were most often sculpted in the same shapes as those used in the silk trim on the fabric or the gold and silver embroidery. Bouquets of plumes sometimes adorned the top of these finials, and the vase form was occasionally replaced by sculpted wooden flame shapes.

Valances

The valances surrounding the canopy (formed by the tester or framework itself) were often made of scalloped Genoa velvet; the fabric pattern was symmetrical to that of the bed valance.

Motifs and decorative elements

Spiral, baluster, twisted and ball turned legs

Square doweled joints

Festooned garlands of fabric, held by ribbons

Chimera ending in foliated scrolls

Eagle's claws

Winged cupids

Elongated (vertical and horizontal) cartouches

Feathers, cornucopia

Various motifs: diamond point, Maltese cross, mascarons, palmettes, coats of arms, lion heads, women's busts

First fine cabinetmakers and appearance of ebony furniture

TABLES

Several types of table were common during the Louis XIII period. They were always covered with a piece of fabric, a tablecloth or a valuable rug, a practice that continued throughout the entire seventeenth century.
The large table used for meals was generally rudimentary in design: the tabletop was supported by trestles on four legs interconnected by a thick stretcher; the legs often ended in bun-shaped feet.
Pedestal tables had thick heavy bases to increase stability. The tabletop was used as a candle-stand.
Walnut writing tables had a beveled tabletop supported by four turned legs; each of the legs stood on bun-shaped feet joined by a stretcher.
By the middle of the century, these small tables become more sophisticated with the addition of a large drawer in the apron; the tabletop rested on four baluster legs interconnected by a decorated H-stretcher or an X-stretcher with molded elements.

Stretcher

Also known as a crossbar, the stretcher for these tables was always H-shaped, formed of a large crosspiece and two side pieces, each connected to two legs. The mid-point of the central crosspiece was sometimes decorated with carved elements.

Tabletop

The tabletop was often bordered by a typical, quarter-round molding known as ovolo molding or a half-rosette sculpted ornament.

Legs

The legs were generally spiral-turned in a single piece. The joint where the stretcher joined the legs was generally left unsculpted, or was square in shape. The corners of the square-shaped parts were beveled. The entire support rested on flattened bun-shaped feet. The legs were turned in baluster or beaded shapes.

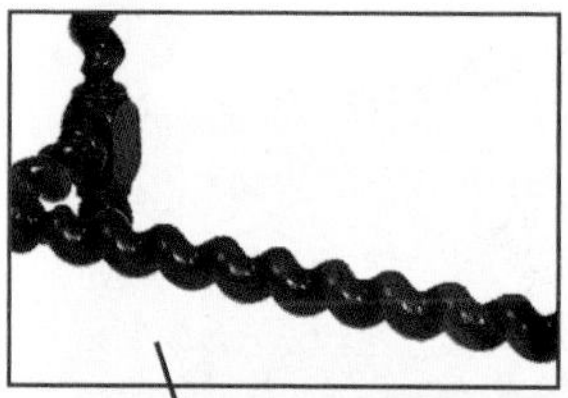

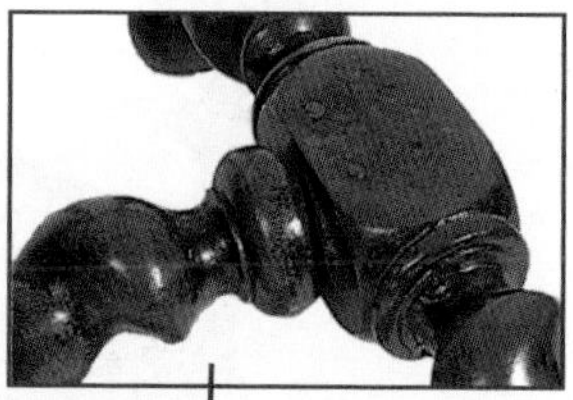

△*Walnut table on twist-turned legs and stretcher. Fondation Angladon, Avignon.*

▽ *The walnut two-tiered cupboard, or* armoire à deux corps, *has paneled doors sculpted with diamond-point designs, stylized foliage and cherub heads, and a base with bun-shaped feet. Fondation Angladon, Avignon.*

Cornice

Often richly molded, the cornice was symmetrical to the base. Another feature, also typical of the style, was a central broken pediment. Over the centuries, this element often disappeared from the furniture pieces.

Drawers

The drawers were placed between the two sections of the cupboard. In other designs, the drawers were placed just above the base.

Panel decoration

The panels were most often highly decorated with a diamond-point motif or sandpile design. The first consisted of square geometric subdivisions, while sandpile designs were rectangular geometric subdivisions. The two designs could be used on a single piece.

Base

The base was richly molded to confer a solid, massive appearance to the furniture. It rested on flattened bun-shaped feet. The rear feet were either rectilinear or the same as those in the front.

TWO-TIERED CUPBOARD

Also known as the armoire à deux corps, *the two-tiered cupboard was the most popular piece of furniture made in this style. They became popular among the bourgeoisie, who needed efficient, solid and handsome storage elements for the city apartments. The characteristics of these wardrobes remained unchanged for years in many regional French styles, particularly in the Périgord region.*

The monumental cupboard rested on flattened bun-shaped feet. Each of the doors was sculpted with a diamond-point or circular molded motif. Two drawers were sometimes fitted into the mid-section. Each element bore a heavy, molded cornice.

The two-tiered cupboard became highly fashionable in the middle of the seventeenth century. It was often decorated to excess.

The upper section was always smaller than the lower section. Each of the two sections had two panel doors, and the facade and pediment were richly adorned with molding and symmetrical sculpted motifs. The pediment was occasionally carved as a broken pediment, which had a central gap holding a statuette.

Fabrics

Described in inventories under the name of the furniture, fabric was the same for all the objects in a room: chairs, beds, wall hangings, drapes and door curtains.

Fabric could be removed from chairs and changed twice a year: Genoa velvet or silk velvet with embroidery for the winter, silks in the summer.

Silver and gold lace embroidery for beds of state.

Silks, silk velvet, damask, satin, tapestries and brocade.

Broadcloth or homespun cloth on writing tables.

Trimmings made of silk embroidered with silver and gold thread, fringed fabric, gold and silver, long fringes.

Colors: red, olive green, purple, beige, white.

CABINETS

△ *Cabinet with two panels, made of ebony, pearwood and rosewood, resting on baluster legs joined by a slab stretcher. Galerie de la Reine, Château de Blois.*

Central niche

The niche, framed by a series of drawers, could reproduce a complex decor designed as a theater set or containing a simple row of secret drawers. Cabinetmakers developed numerous designs.

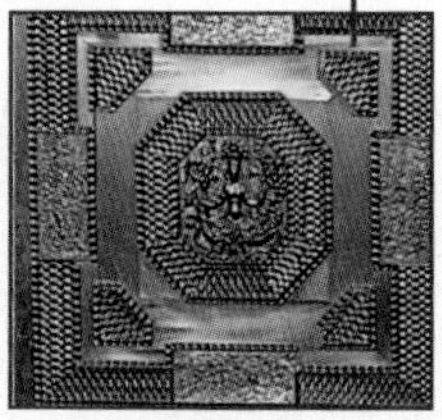

Panels

When closed, the panels hid the desk drawers. They opened to reveal the cabinet interior and its niche. The sculptures decorating the inside of the panels differed from those on the outside.

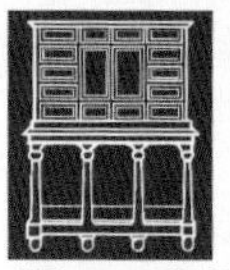

France was the last country in Europe to make cabinets; before the seventeenth century, they had been imported from Augsburg, Nuremberg, Antwerp, Amsterdam and, of course, Italy.
Henri IV, tired of paying such high prices for these luxury imports, sent furnituremaker Jean Macé to Holland to learn the art of cabinetmaking. After learning the trade, Macé returned to France, where he started his own workshop specializing in ebony cabinets and began to train apprentices. This was the beginning of the French-style cabinet developed by Macé.
The overall design basically remained the same throughout Europe (a piece of case furniture consisting of a number of drawers and set on legs), but the French version differed from the others in its size: it tended to be larger and the legs were more substantial and often turned. These legs were interconnected by a richly sculpted low, broad slab.
The cabinet itself, generally made of ebony, sat on the support and had two panels sculpted with bas-reliefs inspired from ancient history. These panels were framed by molding. Statuettes sometimes were sculpted on the sides of each panel.
The panels opened to reveal a row of drawers framing a central niche. In Italian cabinets, this section was designed to look like a palace facade; the French versions, however, resembled an elaborate theater stage, complete with foreground, backstage, wings, sets and tiers.
The decor of the "backstage" section was generally painted with a trompe-l'œil landscape framed by a row of small columns made of stone, bronze or coral. The "floor" had a checkerboard pattern made of ivory and ebony or rosewood.
The trompe-l'œil "ceiling" often depicted a mythological figure. The tiers consisted of a bronze baluster. Mirrors and fake rock grottoes made of shells, stones and corals add to the effect of depth. This piece of furniture was so luxurious that only the richest aristocrats could afford it, yet its sole purpose was to hold small, valuable collector's items.

▷ *Simple walnut chair supported by rectilinear legs in the back and beaded baluster legs in the front. The chair is upholstered with nailed Cordova leather. Fondation Angladon, Avignon.*

STRAIGHT-BACKED CHAIRS

Straight-backed chairs are exactly the same size as armchairs and designed the same way. The only difference between the two is that straight-backed chairs do not have armrests.

Like armchairs, they were lined up against the wall and could be moved to the center of the room for various purposes. Footstools and folding X-frame stools were used in the same way as these chairs were.

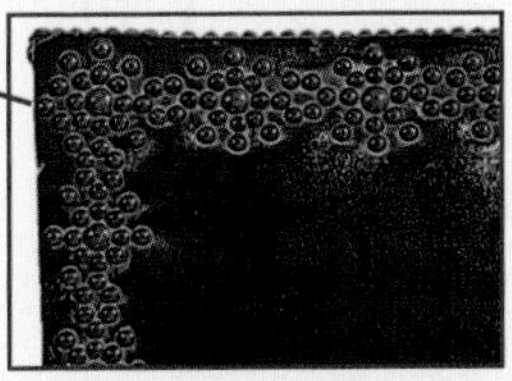

Daisy patterns

Round-headed nails were arranged in patterns to forms a stylized daisy or sun pattern. A less sophisticated nailing technique consisted of spacing the nails regularly along a galoon.

ARMCHAIRS

The armchair is a perfect example of the type of furniture used by apartment-dwellers. It did not take up much space and was easy to move.
These chairs had low backs, which were always wider than they were high.
The seat, considered to be extremely comfortable according to the standards of the period, were padded with horsehair and then upholstered with fabric or leather attached by nails or trim. For the first time, the seat and back were not made of cushions that could be removed, but were part of the chair structure and seat itself.
The four legs, or sometimes just the rear two legs, were turned in twist, beaded or baluster patterns. They were joined by an H-stretcher, rather than by the box stretcher that had been common during the Renaissance.
The joints were reinforced by square or rectangular sections of wood. The armrests and arm stumps were turned in spiral patterns and sometimes decorated with a lion's head or doll motif.

◁ *An armchair. Walnut. The stretcher, armrests and four legs are spiral turned. The arm stumps are decorated with a foliage motif. Ca 1630. Château d'Amboise.*

The masters

Jean Lepautre (1618-1682):* *Designer, trophy and divinity motifs

Jean Berain (1639-1711):* *The most famous designer, he created silver furniture pieces, scenery for royal festivities and pattern books that inspired cabinetmakers

Claude III Audran (1657-1734):* *Designer

André Charles Boulle (1642-1732):* *Louis XIV's favorite cabinetmaker, he invented a decorative system of marquetry using red tortoiseshell and brass veneer

Pierre Gole, died 1684:* *Cabinetmaker, chairs and furniture of state

Pierre Hache (1703-1776):* *Cabinetmaker, inlaid commodes

FRANCE

1661  1700

The Louis XIV Style

△ *The King's Bedroom, with alcove and fireplace. Château de Versailles.*

When Cardinal Mazarin died in 1661, King Lous XIV, just twenty-three years old at the time, was eager to prove his mettle. His aim was nothing less than to astonish and overwhelm his entourage with his glory. In 1682, Louis XIV moved to Versailles with his court, which was more brilliant than anything France had ever known. The influence of this fabulous era on royal courts around the world lasted nearly two centuries, as Versailles was considered the unattainable model of aristocratic life.

The Sun King was satisfied only with the most sumptuous, refined objects—indeed, he was well-versed in the fine arts and demonstrated impeccable good taste in everything he did. Early on, he brought to his court the most talented craftsmen of his time. His minister Colbert gave him valuable advice, and together they institutionalized architecture and the art of furniture, porcelain and decoration by creating or renovating national workshops: Gobelins, Saint-Gobain, Beauvais and Aubusson. Louis XIV wanted to differentiate his style from foreign influences—particularly the Italian Baroque style—to create a strong, distinctive personal style. He encouraged designers to seek out motifs, publish pattern books and create innovative designs. One of these designers, Jean Berain, created the solid silver state furniture that was later melted down for financial reasons. Yet every piece of royal furniture we know today was directly inspired from Berain's work. Louis XIV created a movement, more than a style, due primarily to his excessive desire for luxury. This movement, called French Classicism, was part of a larger movement that swept all of Europe and was known as Baroque.

BEDS

The French lit à la duchesse *was one of many beds that filled bedrooms, as these rooms were always used to receive guests and for ceremonies. It was different from the others in that it did not have corner posts. The canopy was suspended from the ceiling and stretched all around the bed.*
The angel bed, similar to the lit à la duchesse, *had a canopy suspended from a tester and covered only half the bed.*
The imperial bed had a dome-like canopy.
Column beds had four corner posts.
Daybeds, a new type of furniture, appeared around 1660. They were used by women of the court to recline as they received guests. It was a long, narrow bed; the frame was made of sculpted, gilt or Chinese lacquered wood, with lion's paw feet. No examples of these canopy beds or daybeds have survived from this period.

Legs

First a baluster in the early years of the reign, the legs evolved into scrolls, then pedestals, as in this photograph, by the end of the reign. All the bureaus sat on feet made of fluted gilt wood or covered with acanthus-leaf motifs.

THE MAZARIN DESK

The word "bureau" is derived from the French term "bure," or burlap, that covered writing tables in the seventeenth century. This bureau first appeared around 1670, however, several years after Cardinal Mazarin's death. For reasons unknown, nineteenth-century antique dealers started calling this desk the "Mazarin." It had four short legs at each end; each set of legs was joined by an X-stretcher and supported a pedestal housing three drawers. The shallow kneehole space also had a small drawer. The upper sections of the two sets of legs were often elaborately decorated with gilt bronze motifs. The tabletop might have been framed by a gilt bronze molding or divided into two sections, one of which could be raised up.

Certain designs included a small case consisting of one or two rows of drawers or pigeonholes. This element sat along one side of the top and was used for storage. The four sides of the bureau, which was usually placed near a window or in the center of the room, were decorated with the same marquetry designs used on the tabletop. The technique used was generally Boulle marquetry, consisting of thin sheets of brass, pewter and tortoiseshell. The designs came from the pattern books created by the designers, particularly the one by Jean Berain.

These desks were luxurious but notably uncomfortable, as it was difficult to fit both knees between the pedestal drawers. This bureau was soon replaced by a large rectangular writing table known as the **bureau plat.**

Central drawer

This drawer was slightly recessed behind the shallow kneehole space; this is an early form of the English-style "kneehole desk."

Tortoiseshell and copper inlay

The four sides of the bureau and the tabletop were covered in marquetry, as it often sat in the middle of a room and was designed to be seen from all sides.

△ Mazarin desk with tortoiseshell and copper inlay and gilt wood supported by eight console legs; each set of two legs are joined by an X-stretcher. Château du Plessis-Bourré.

Fabrics

Tapestries embroidered with foliated scrolls and flower motifs.

Linen damask, brocade, silk with gold embroidery, satin, Genoa velvets.

Silk ribbons to tie back bed canopies.

Gathered flounces framing seat backs, armrests and seat bottoms.

Velvet embroidered with gold thread for daybeds. No longer exists today.

Continuation of a custom, begun under Louis XIII, of changing fabrics twice a year: thick velvets, damask and brocade for the winter; light and flowery silks for the summer.

Serge, wool fabrics for bourgeois furniture.

Colors: red, blue, green and white.

THE *CHAISE À USAGE*

The use of chairs at the court of Versailles was strictly regulated by protocol. When the king was in a room, etiquette required that everyone remain standing; during conversations and games, however, courtiers were allowed to use stools, while chairs (meaning seats with backs) were reserved for lords and royal princes only. This type of chair was known as a chaise à usage.

Stools were used a great deal as they could be moved easily from one room to another. There were several different types of footstools: some had four baluster legs, interconnected by an H-stretcher, others were folding X-stretcher stools. They were generally made of sculpted and gilt beech and upholstered with red brocade or velvet and decorated with long fringe or tassels.

In accordance with a custom introduced to the French court by queens of Spanish origin, large embroidered and trimmed pillows known as carreaux were placed on the floor and reserved for untitled women at the court, who were then allowed to sit.

Several popular French expressions still in use come from this custom: "être sur le carreau," for example, means "to be as low as you can get."

Design of seat back

The tops of seat backs began to curve in approximately 1700, echoing the shapes of the shank legs and Dutch feet.

Apron

The apron consisted of two pieces of wood carved in a shank shape and joined together in the middle. It was often a simple straight piece of wood.

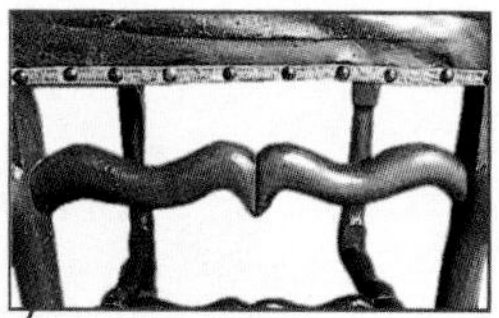

Shank leg

This was a waxed, carved wooden leg; it usually ended with a Dutch foot, also known as a pad or hoof foot. This shape first appeared in the 1700s.

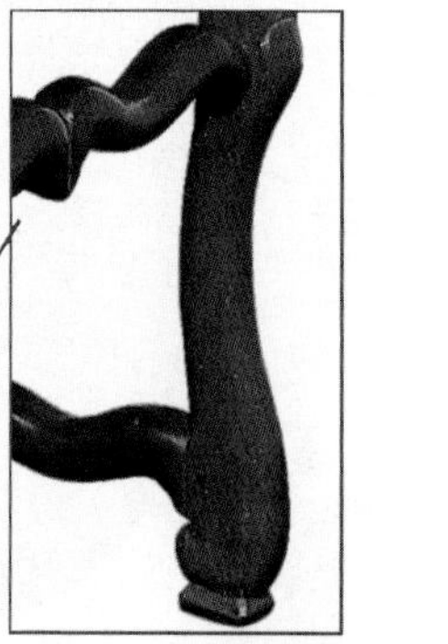

◁ *A so-called* chaise à usage *with a high walnut seat back, supported by shank legs. Upholstered with leather nailed along a binding. Musée Vouland, Avignon.*

Sloping, rounded seat back

Before this period, seat backs were vertical and rectilinear, then the back started to slope backward and curve toward the top. The seat back was completely padded and upholstered; none of the wood frame was visible. It was always separated from the seat itself.

Scroll armrest

The curving scroll shape echoed the shape of the leg, and often ended in a knob sculpted with an acanthus leaf. The armrest was supported by an arm shank situated directly above the legs.

▷ *Fauteuil with a curved back, made of carved, gilt beech. Late seventeenth century. The scroll legs resting on fluted balls are joined by a curving H-stretcher. Musée du Louvre, Paris.*

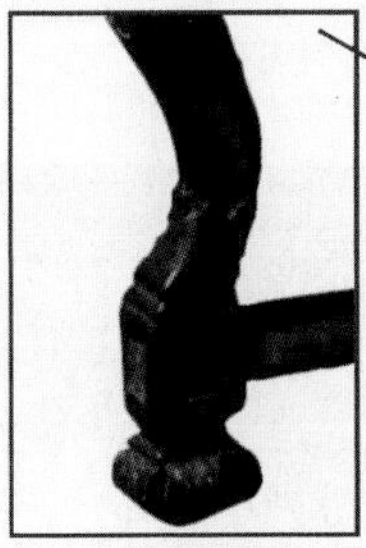

Scroll leg

The front legs were often carved in scroll shapes; this name refers to any form that is more or less in an "S" shape. The legs stood on lion's paw, fluted ball or bun feet, and sometimes on small decorated cube feet.

FAUTEUIL WITH A CURVED BACK

The design of fauteuils changed considerably during Louis XIV's reign. The seat became larger, and the back was sloped and became higher than it was wide. The shank legs curved inward; in later styles, they were rectilinear, becoming thinner toward the bottom.

The feet were joined together by an H-stretcher or an X-stretcher. The legs and stretchers were often decorated with gilt sculptures, while the legs ended in lion's paw or acanthus-leaf feet. The curved armrests often were fashioned into scrolls sculpted with acanthus leaves. The center section of the armrest sometimes was padded and upholstered.

Rounded backs started to appear after 1700, and the legs more often ended in scroll legs or bracket legs.

A new design appeared during this period: this was the confessional fauteuil, so-called because its back had two flat wooden panels, or "wings," protecting the sitter from drafts. This type of fauteuil was later adapted and reproduced many times by nineteenth-century English and American furniture-makers.

All the court chairs were upholstered in Genoa velvet, brocade, satin or damask cloth. Bourgeois chairs most often were upholstered in fabric with floral or foliated scroll patterns or a herringbone motif.

Wood and materials

Oak sawed into planks, which were then dried several years before being used. Treated in this way, the wood would not warp when marquetry was added.

Walnut and beech for chairs and armchairs.

Marquetry using exotic wood and contrasting colors, ebony, copper, brass, tortoiseshell, tinted horn, mother-of-pearl, ivory.

Gilt bronze sections to reinforce edges of furniture pieces.

Marble from the Languedoc and Pyrenee regions carved by the Gobelins workshops into tabletops.

Solid silver and silver veneer.

COMMODES

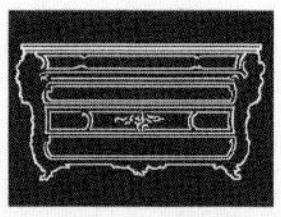

In the early years of Louis XIV's reign, the commode was the French version of a simple chest of drawers. Short legs were added to raise it up off the floor. This piece of case furniture had two or three drawers and was called, successively, **table en bureau,** ***then*** **bureau en commode,** ***then finally,*** **commode.** ***This basic design changed considerably through the Sun King's reign, resulting in two principal models: the so-called classical commode, an essential piece of furniture in bourgeois homes as well as in aristocratic dwellings; and the Boulle commode, which was a sumptuous, highly decorated piece reserved for state and court use. The classical commode was rectangular and was supported by short legs. The front was flat; the corners, beveled; the sides, straight. Three or four drawers with bronze handles slid open on shelves.***

The case was finished in polished wood, marquetry using fine hardwood or Chinese lacquer. The top, which was first made of marquetry veneer, would be replaced around 1700 by a more solid slab of marble.
The Boulle commode, named after the famous French cabinetmaker, was characterized by its highly ornate decoration on an ebony background or tortoiseshell and copper marquetry with gilt bronze masks or mascarons. The design could be austere or highly complex, if, for example, the piece of furniture was intended for the king himself. These commodes were not the only pieces of furniture at which Boulle excelled. He also created ornate marquetry patterns on cabinets and armoires, the monumental two-paneled elements that were covered with such motifs as bouquets of flowers and trophies, and decorated with spectacular gilt bronze work around the hinges and lock mechanisms.

Corners

The corners were decorated with ornate bronze elements: women's heads framed by wings, foliated scrolls and elongated acanthus supporting the griotte marble top.

Eight-leg support

This is an exceptional example that indicates the dual originals of the commode: both a table and a cabinet. The spiral legs support the lower tier of drawers; the lion's paw feet support the top.

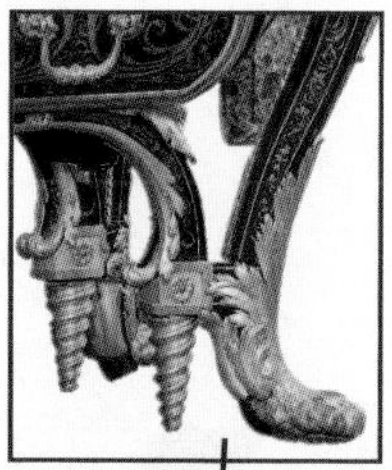

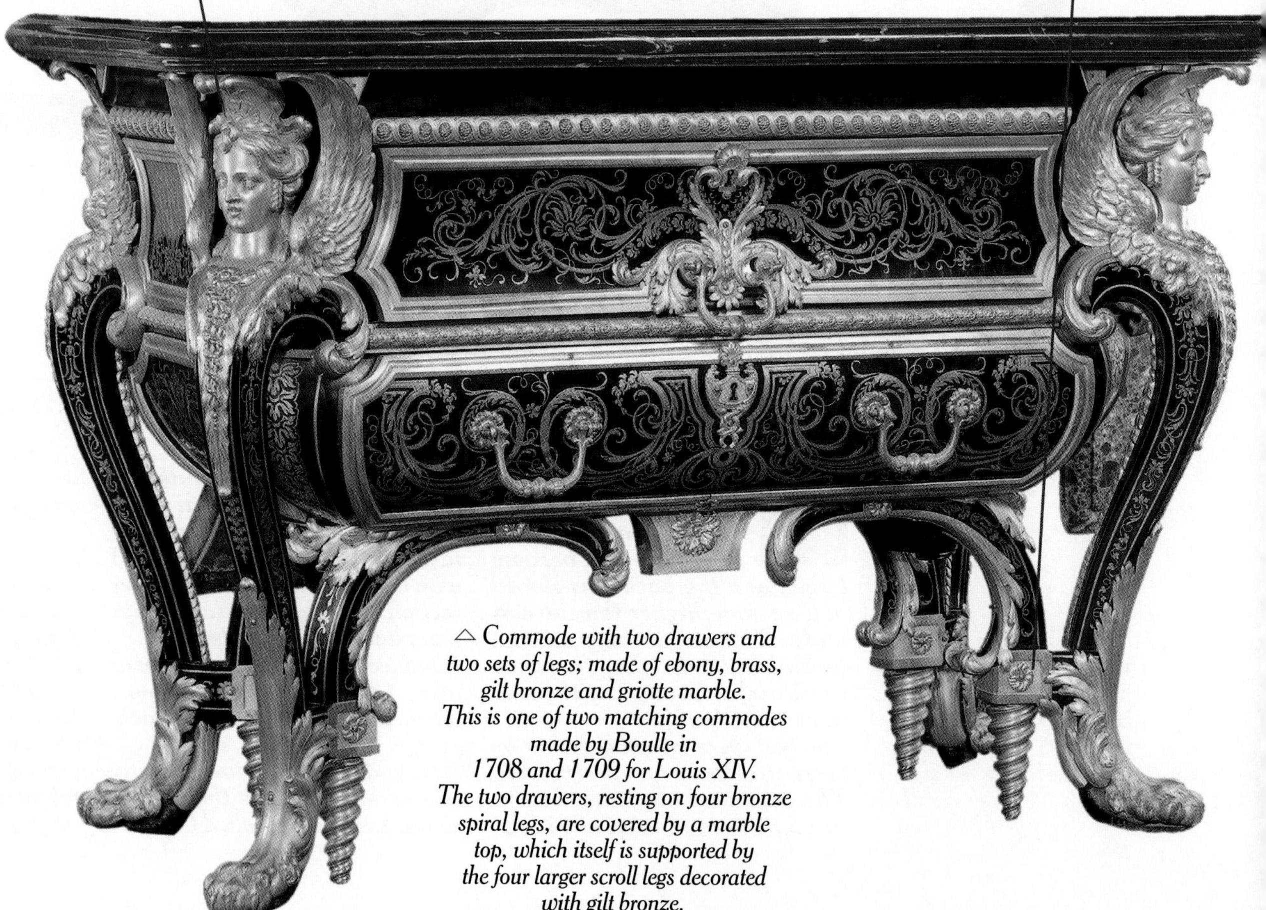

△ Commode with two drawers and two sets of legs; made of ebony, brass, gilt bronze and griotte marble. This is one of two matching commodes made by Boulle in 1708 and 1709 for Louis XIV. The two drawers, resting on four bronze spiral legs, are covered by a marble top, which itself is supported by the four larger scroll legs decorated with gilt bronze. Château de Versailles.

Scroll or console leg

The leg is named for its S-shape. The table leg here is covered with elongated acanthus leaf motifs.

Mascaron

The mascaron, which could be the head of an animal, man or woman, was a characteristic feature of the Louis XIV style. These elements were placed on the corners of the apron or slightly below the table apron.

Motif

Set in the middle of the apron, the motif was a carved ornament that reproduced a symbol or insignia of the owner. In this case, a cardinal's hat indicates that the table belonged to an imporant religious figure.

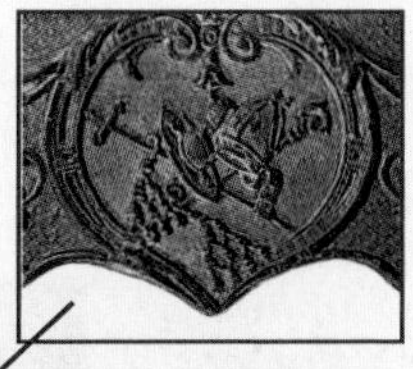

△ Console de milieu or table de milieu, *made of giltwood carved with acanthus leaf and foliated scroll motifs against a lozenge with grotesque ornaments and a cardinal's attributes in a central medallion. Musée Vouland, Avignon.*

THE *CONSOLE DE MILIEU*

The console table, sideboard, and table with console-shaped legs were the terms used to describe a wide array of furniture on which meals were served.

Under Louis XIV's reign, the dining table was much as it had been during medieval times: a simple tabletop set on trestles and covered with a cloth. "Real" tables were far more decorative. They were placed either in the middle of the room (*console de milieu*) or against a wall (*console d'applique*) and used to display precious objects such as marble and bronze statues. Two types of tables existed. The first was made of polished walnut with a rectangular tabletop and a drawer placed in the apron; these were generally made for bourgeois homes. The second kind, made of beech or oak, had an assortment of sculpted motifs inspired from Berain's silver furniture; these were designed for aristocratic residences. The carved and gilded scroll or bracket legs supported a marble top or stone marquetry tabletop.

A new piece of furniture appeared: the small portable table, different from the existing pedestal table. This small table could be moved easily; it was usually made of beech, or beech and mahogany, with a knob in the center of the stretcher. This type of table was inspired from the English gaming table developed under the reign of Queen Anne.

Another type of marquetry table also appeared around this time, called* tables à l'anglaise *or* tables de changeurs*. These were nothing more than French adaptations of the English gate-leg table.

ENGLAND

1603 1660

The Jacobean Style

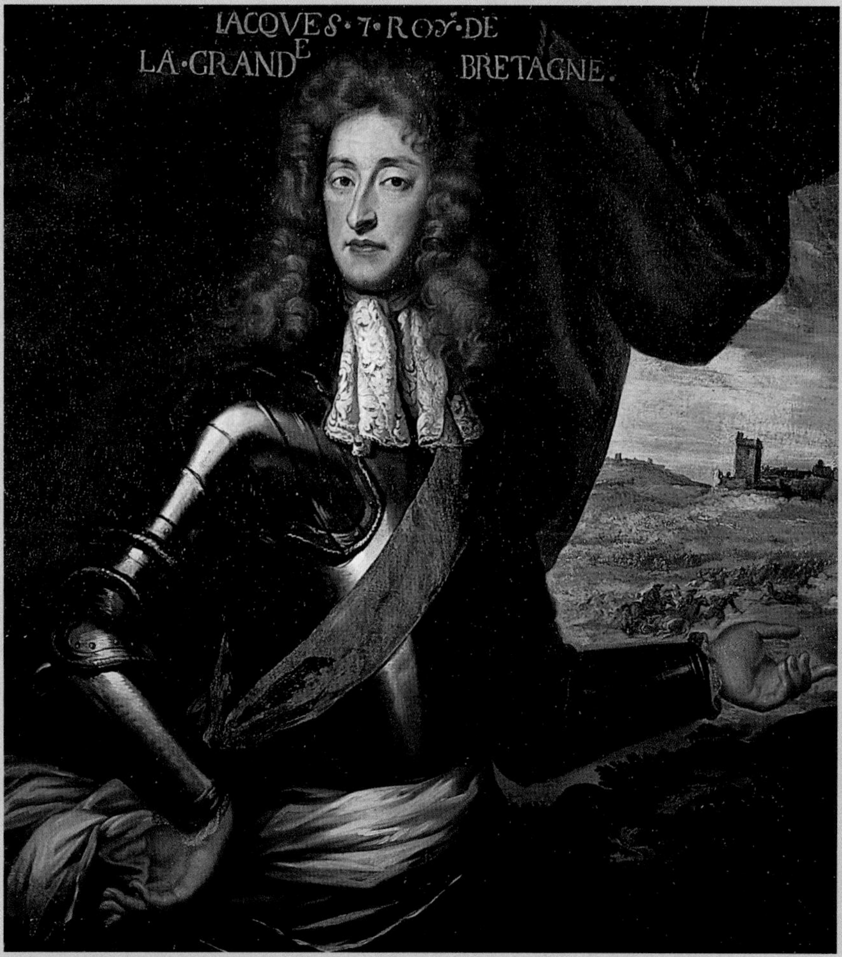

△ Portrait of James II, king of England. *Dutch School. Château de Versailles.*

This style covers the period from the beginning of the reign of King James I, who succeeded Elizabeth I (the last in the Tudor line), through the reigns of Charles I, decapitated at Whitehall in 1649, and Cromwell. During this last era, no new pieces of furniture were produced. The Jacobean style is roughly equivalent to the Louis XIII style in France. It was still highly influenced by Italy and the Renaissance, but it also borrowed elements from the Flemish and Spanish styles.

The elegant architectural style of the Palladian movement, brought to the kingdom by the architect Inigo Jones at the beginning of the seventeenth century, had a long-lasting influence on English aesthetics and, by extension, on furniture design.

The Flemish-style turnery and carved feet were considered so fashionable that they soon became the defining characteristics of the Jacobean style. Motifs featuring pearls, vases, balusters, St. Andrew's cross and star motifs covered doors and uprights.

Inlays of natural materials, as in Spanish furniture, were almost obligatory; tortoiseshell, mother-of-pearl and bone were all favorites.

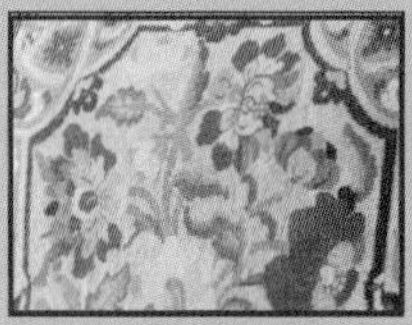

Fabrics

Turkeywork: tightly woven embroidered upholstery with flower and foliage motifs.

Leather-upholstered seats.

Damask and brocade for bed canopies and covers.

Wood and materials

Oak

Solid wood

Carved wood

Inlaid bone and mother-of-pearl

Tortoiseshell

OTHER FURNITURE

A certain number of subtle changes were made to existing pieces of furniture: two drawers appeared in the top section of cupboards. Sliding drawers were also built into the wider apron of sideboards.
Beds were decorated with rich fabrics and brocades. Armchairs of all kinds became common items of furniture in most homes: chairs with square backs and feet; stretchers and armrests carved in a style similar to the Louis XIII style; and seat and back upholstered in leather or turkeywork, a tightly embroidered, very thick fabric.

△ *Open gate-leg table made of oak.*

GATE-LEG TABLES

The gate-leg table was a major innovation: this design would be repeated and adapted in every future English style; indeed, it became one of the most characteristic elements of English furniture design in general.
These were oak tables made in round, oval or rectangular shapes. The tables could be made larger or smaller through a system of drop leafs and hinged legs. The tabletop was supported by a frame system from which the legs could swing out. The legs could be extended or retracted depending on the size of the table to be supported.
This was the first table in furniture history that could offer a variable surface size. And indeed, no one has yet to come up with a better concept.

◁ *Gate-leg table, oak, resting on eight hinged legs that could swing under or out from the tabletop. Fondation Angladon, Avignon.*

Tabletop hinges

The two sides of a round table could be dropped, so that the overall table formed a small rectangle that could be stored easily against a wall.

Gate-leg frame

This frame linked the eight legs of the table support. They could swing under the folded rectangular tabletop or swing out, depending on the surface area of the table to be supported.

Ball and ring turning

This motif was the only decorative element on this primarily functional table.

ENGLAND

1670  1695

The William and Mary Style

Fabrics

Petit-point embroidered fabrics with floral motifs

Trimming and galloons to conceal studs

Wood and materials

Walnut replaced oak

Development of veneer technique

Veneers using precious wood: violet wood, ash

Olive wood

Inlaid wood of contrasting colors

Wood burls, particularly walnut burl

Appearance of first Chinese lacquers and works reproduced in the Chinese style

Leather

Caning

△ King James II of England and his Family. *Pierre Mignard. Musée du Louvre, Paris.*

In 1660, the monarchy, which had been abolished by Cromwell during the Commonwealth, was restored by the King Charles II. The Restoration, or Charles II, style ushered in a new aesthetic that continued with the William and Mary style—named for William of Orange, who succeeded Charles II, and for his wife—through the end of the century.

Close in spirit to the French Louis XIV style, the William and Mary style represented an era of political transition. This was a highly prolific time for furniture designers, much as the Régence style would be in France several years later—although the historical context would be far less painful.

This new style proposed a completely new aesthetic. The idea was to leave behind the furniture of the past, linked to too many painful memories. A large number of old pieces of furniture simply disappeared: this was true of the sideboards, cupboards and refectory tables. New pieces of furniture surfaced, usually made of walnut or with hardwood veneer surfaces. This was an entirely new technique for Great Britain, and woodworkers explored the possibilities of wood grains and burls, and began to produce high-quality marquetry.

Legs were mostly inspired from the baluster legs of the French Louis XIV style. Chests of drawers and cabinets were decorated with foliated scrolls and lacquered panels imported directly from China or made in England in the style of Chinese lacquerware.

OTHER FURNITURE

The round pedestal table appeared for the first time in sitting rooms; the tabletop was supported by a central column rising from a tripod base with short legs.
Chairs were generally covered with a panel of caning, framed by turned columns supporting an open pediment.

Handles

Teardrop handles, although typical of English furniture in the early seventeenth century, were less important than the inlay work using light wood in quatrefoil motifs and foliated scrolls which constituted the major part of the furniture's ornamentation.

Bun foot

This style of foot was common throughout the seventeenth century. In English furniture, particularly chests of drawers, the bun foot was separate from the base it supported. In French furniture, this same bun foot was usually attached directly under the base.

▽ *A chest of drawers with three large drawers and two small ones. Walnut and marquetry with quatrefoil and decorative foliage motifs. The top is decorated with marquetry depicting crowns of English sovereigns. Bun feet. Teardrop handles. Sotheby's, London.*

CHEST OF DRAWERS

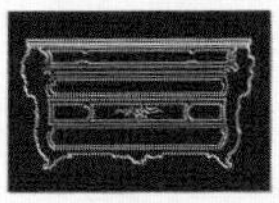

The chest of drawers became one of the most important pieces of furniture during this period. This case piece was usually a rectangular chest with four rows of drawers; the topmost row was often divided into two smaller drawers. The chest rested on bun, or onion, feet. In certain chests of drawers, the case was supported by a console table.

ARMCHAIRS

Armchairs from this period had high backs, scrolled armrests and carved legs. The seat back was sometimes made of wood sculpted in relief with geometric motifs. The seat was of wood or was fully upholstered to conceal the frame of the seat back.

Scroll arm

The scroll arm rested on an arm stump that repeated the same curve as the cabriole legs, but in reverse. It was often decorated with a thin strip of light wood inlaid along the entire edge of the pieces.

▷ *Walnut burl armchair with inlays of light wood. Covered with a petit-point fabric. The nails are concealed by an upholstery binding. Cabriole legs. H-stretcher. Christie's, London.*

NETHERLANDS

1550 1690

The Baroque Style

The masters

The designer Hans Vredeman de Vries (1527-1604): He published a pattern book which inspired furniture-makers throughout Europe.

Wood and materials

Walnut veneer, rosewood, fruit trees, including citron wood

Inlaid ivory, ebony, tortoiseshell, brass and silver

Walnut, olive wood (in marquetry), linden, pear, cherry, chestnut, sorb tree, almond, orange, lemon and mulberry trees

△ A Scholar in his Office. *Jacob van Spreeuwen. Musée du Louvre, Paris.*

The seventeenth and eighteenth centuries were particularly prosperous eras for the Netherlands, despite the division of the country into the Northern Netherlands and the Southern Netherlands. Toward 1620, the auricular style appeared, echoing the forms discovered by the budding science of anatomy. Woodworking and cabinetmaking guilds, much like those in Germany, flourished in the seventeenth century; these craftsmen imposed strict requirements on furniture quality. Marquetry workshops were so highly reputed that Henri IV, king of France and of Navarre, sent his favorite furniture-maker, Jean Macé, to the Netherlands to improve his talents. Marquetry was therefore the chief feature during the Dutch Golden Age. It inspired designs throughout the rest of Europe as well and remained important for over two centuries. Dutch marquetry was characterized by inlays of light wood over darker wood. These inlaid patterns covered every inch of the furniture pieces, including the legs. The primary motifs used for these inlays were flowers, shells, Moorish designs inspired from the Spanish, and trompe-l'œil architectural views. The sculpted decorative elements—decorative foliage, lions' heads, grotesque masks and caryatids—often were taken from the pattern books published by Hans Vredeman de Vries and his son, Paul Vredeman de Vries from the second half of the sixteenth century to the late seventeenth century.

CABINETS

Dutch cabinets differed from all other European cabinets in the large number of drawers they contained. Each drawer front was used to create a new decor. Cane chairs appeared as a new type of furniture; many nineteenth-century French chair-makers copied these designs.

BASIC FURNITURE PIECES

△ *Baroque table made of sculpted gilt wood and painted green in the kwabstijl or Dutch auricular style. The top and bottom of each leg are sculpted to resemble bird's beaks or dragons. The tabletop is made of veined marble. Second half of the eighteenth century. Christie's, Amsterdam.*

◁ *Walnut armchair. Fitted cane seat and seat back. The spiral-turned uprights frame a medallion decorated with acanthus leaves. Rectangular seat. Spiral H-stretcher with an additional crosspiece, made of two joined S-shapes. Late seventeenth century. Sotheby's, London.*

Dark caned seat back

The idea of using caned seats and seat backs originated in the Netherlands. This technique spread throughout Europe for outdoor furniture and later for dining room furniture.

Bird motif

The flat apron is decorated with a bird of prey with outspread wings, clutching a daisy in a wreath of flowers. This decorative motif is characteristic of the style adopted by the famous Dutch silversmith Johannes Lutma (1587-1669).

The design of Dutch armchairs was largely inspired by Spanish furniture. Common elements included repoussé leather seats held in place by sculpted or round-headed copper nails. The top of the high seat backs was always decorated with a lion's head or cupid head. The armchairs rested on baluster legs.

Tabletops were usually covered in elaborate marquetry patterns. Cupboards were the most distinctive items of furniture produced in the Netherlands. These included the Gueldre cupboard with grooved uprights; the Utrecht cupboard, which had ebony inlays and an engraved motif between the columns; and the two-tiered beeldenkast with wide panel doors, caryatids and geometric inlaid patterns.

GERMANY

1610 1680

The Auricular Baroque Style

Wood and materials

Walnut veneer

Walnut burl

Ebony

Inlaid silver

Inlaid ivory

Inlaid mother-of-pearl

Brass and tortoiseshell marquetry, developed by Boulle

Sheets of stone painted with landscapes, inspired from the Italian petre *paesine style, framed by gilt bronze*

Semi-precious stones for the colonnettes

Chased bronze

△ The Prodigal Son Among Courtesans. *Stefan Kessler. Musée Crozatier, Le Puy-en-Velay.*

The German Auricular Baroque style developed from the Dutch Auricular style (*kawbstijl*), created by the silversmiths Adam and Paulus van Vienen and by Johannes Lutma. The name comes from the curving designs used to decorate furniture; these resembled the interior of the human ear. Carved elements were covered with coils of budding acanthus leaves, intertwined foliage, double-curved S-scrolls, human figures concealed among branches and highly elaborate marquetry. Cabinetmakers covered an entire piece of furnitures with these motifs.

Court furniture developed in the workshops of specific palaces, duchies and principalities. Each of the political entities had its own cabinetmakers and woodworkers who were allowed a large measure of creative freedom. The furniture they created was so sophisticated and skillfully made that it inspired cabinetmakers throughout the rest of Europe, including the great French cabinetmaker Boulle himself. Germany returned the compliment: in the late seventeenth century, the Elector of Bavaria, Maximilian II, founded a cabinetmaking workshop that would become famous for its production of bureaus, cabinets and tables decorated with Boulle-style marquetry.

Furniture for bourgeois households complied with the strict regulations set forth by the guilds; this guaranteed a consistently high level of quality.

The cabinetmakers and woodworkers who adopted this exuberant Baroque style were also taking a political stance: they were reacting against the rigidity and austerity of the dominant Protestant dictates. From this time on, Catholicism, in application of the recommendations from the Council of Trent, would be synonymous with generous lines and decorative profusion in furniture design. The Protestant religion, however, was associated with rigor, spare lines and restraint.

OTHER FURNITURE

Massive wardrobes were the most typical form of Baroque furniture in Germany. These were imposing pieces with one or two sliding drawers along the wide base. The main section above had two or four doors. The decoration changed with each region: in the north, for example, wardrobes were covered with auricular-style motifs. They were all opulently sculpted with turned or grooved columns. Some pieces had marquetry motifs on the doors.

Drawer decors

The drawers formed frames for inlaid patterns representing mythological scenes, much like miniature paintings on a wall. The images on the two doors and the central compartment were meant to be seen together, like great medieval altarpieces.

▷ Upper section of a small display cabinet designed to be placed on top of a desk. The drawers, central compartments and inner sides of the doors are decorated with mythological scenes and inlays. Residenzmuseum, Munich.

Chased bronzework

Ornately chased bronze ball feet supported the cabinet. The door locks and hinges were finely shaped with Auricular-style motifs.

◁ Ebony cabinet with inlaid ivory in a Moorish motif. It is displayed closed and supported on rectilinear ebony legs with thin strips of inlaid ivory. Christie's, London.

Inlaid medallions

Ivory, tortoiseshell, mother-of pearl and brass were the most common materials used for inlaid patterns. The medallion featuring a horseman is framed by an inlaid motif inspired from the curving, intertwined auricular style.

DISPLAY CABINETS

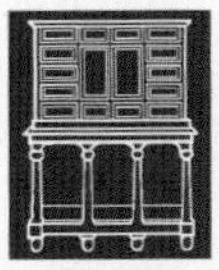

Display cabinets became the favorite piece of furniture in aristocratic houses. These were case pieces with drawers, designed to hold precious objects or unusual collections. Several different types were common, from a small cabinet placed on top of a desk, like a cartonnier or filing cabinet, to a more imposing form that stood atop a baluster or spiral support, decorated with intertwined foliage motifs or on a simple, rectilinear set of legs. The drawers were the main elements of an overall decorative pattern formed of small rectangles framing painted mythological scenes, marquetry with floral patterns or other motifs inspired from Boulle's designs, with inlaid silver, brass and tortoiseshell on an ebony background.

The masters

Buentalenti, known as Della Girandole (1536-1608): Cabinetmaker specializing in cabinets

Andrea Brustolini (1662-1732): Cabinetmaker who created unusual furniture with fantastic motifs

Wood and material

Ebony

Ivory veneer

Tin wires

Tortoiseshell marquetry

Gilt bronze

Compositions with hard stones

ITALY

1600  *1690*

The Baroque Style

△ Portrait of a Woman and Child. *Italian School. Musée du Louvre, Paris.*

After a period of two hundred years, the Renaissance period was waning. It had evolved into a transition style, Mannerism, which emphasized exaggerated human figures in contorted positions. Mannerism led to the Italian Baroque style, which was far less innovative than the Renaissance styles. Indeed, Italian designers had been resting on their laurels for nearly a century, as this new style known as Baroque was not really all that new. Its roots go back to the mid-sixteenth century, when the limits of the Renaissance style started to be felt, particularly among the eminent members of the clergy. The result was the Baroque style, which initially—and most notably in Italy—had its origins in religion. It began in Rome and quickly spread throughout all of Italy, where furniture-makers adapted it to regional styles. Bernini's design for the throne of St. Peter's Cathedral (1657) in Rome is the epitome of the Baroque style.

The actual purpose or design of the furniture had little importance; what mattered was the complexity, originality, beauty and opulence of the decorative elements. Straight angles were replaced by exuberant scroll shapes, and gilding covered every surface.

Furniture was characterized by an abundance of sculpted motifs, ranging from architectural forms to cupids, lion heads, chimera and eagle heads, as well as grotesque figures, busts of slaves, tree trunks and dragons. Furniture with extraordinarily sophisticated *pietre dure* or painted stone marquetry appeared. The pedestal tables with slave figures supporting the tabletop first appeared during this period. Cabinetmakers became extremely skilled at trompe-l'œil patterns that imitated all kinds of materials: wood, tortoiseshell, marble, ivory, bronze and even painting.

Balustrade pediment

This balustrade was inspired from the balustrade above Bernini's colonnade on St. Peter's Square in Rome. A bronze statue representing Atlas supporting the earth on his shoulders stands in the middle of the pediment.

TABLES

Tables were used as a means for cultivating decor for decor's sake. Most of the tabletops were so ornately decorated that they resembled real paintings. They were made of contrasting wood marquetry, or more often, black marble with inlays of colored stone forming compositions of flowers and birds intertwined with arabesque motifs. The legs were also covered with a wealth of ornamental motifs.

▷ *Rectangular ebony table with inlaid ivory and gilt wood. The tabletop is decorated with arabesques and floral motifs. It is supported by four turned, grooved legs interconnected by an X-stretcher decorated with inlaid floral designs. Ca 1664. Museo degli Argenti, Florence.*

STIPO

The stipo (cabinet), was first made in Venice around the early sixteenth century and reached a degree of absolute perfection in the seventeenth century. They were inspired by all the other known European cabinets (with the exception of the Spanish bargueños). The design was invariable: the upper section had many drawers and was supported by a series of atlas figures or caryatids. The composition of the top was characterized by a number of architectural elements meant to represent a palace: a window surrounded by columns, viewpoints and trompe-l'œil designs.

Central compartment

This part of the cabinet, in this case a decor of small columns of semi-precious stone and extremely theatrical miniature sculptures, was always ornately decorated.

▽ *Cabinet, or* stipo, *with a sculpted balustrade-shaped pediment along which stands a row of statuettes. The case is made of ebony with inlaid patterns of* pietra dura, *gilt bronze, ivory, tortoiseshell and small painted mythological scenes. The cabinet sits on a support consisting of atlas figures on the corners with caryatids in the center, each separated by draped scrolls of acanthus leaves. By Vittoria della Rovere, 1677. Palazzo Pitti, Florence.*

SPAIN

1605 1665

The Philip IV Style

Motifs and decorative elements

Mudéjar-style motifs continue to be used.

Capitals with two rows of leaves, topped with Ionic scrolls.

Wreathed columns with Ionic capitals.

Columns decorated with a climbing vine, ivy or leaf motif.

Sculpted blazons surrounded by scrolls of acanthus leaves.

Caryatids and cherubs decorating corners.

Wood and materials

Walnut

Chestnut

Ebonized pine

Ebony

Mahogany

Guaiacum (conifer from America)

Painted varnish

Marble designs

Bone veneer

Wrought iron

△ Interrogation During the Inquisition. *Matthias de Sallieth. Bibliothèque nationale de France, Paris.*

The Baroque style in Spain that took shape under Philip IV's reign was created by the German and Flemish artists who had been coming to court during the previous reigns of Charles V and Philip II. Under King Charles II, the styles of these foreign artists, combined with that of the architect Churriguera, created the specific decorative elements and motifs of the Philip II style. Indeed, this style was so distinctive that it was considered to be the most representative of all Spanish styles for many years. Furniture was covered with scrolls and curves, along with motifs of all kinds. The dominant elements were multicolored motifs highlighted with gilt and Moorish motifs, but designs incorporating the columns and towers of the Escurial Palace became increasingly common. The existing furniture designs began to evolve; new pieces appeared; and the Baroque designs inspired from local Spanish architects and Flemish and German designers added the remaining ingredients.

OTHER FURNITURE

The escritoria *was a small writing desk with a fall front that, when closed, concealed a painted design or a sculpted bone motif. The* contadores *were cabinets with broken pediments, columns and recesses housing bronze statues; these cabinets were similar to the French and Flemish cabinets. Like everywhere else in Europe, beds were covered with opulent fabrics and topped with decorative feathers. Tables leg were reinforced with wrought iron.*

Wide arm stumps

The arm stumps were always directly above the front leg. This chair offered a new level of comfort, as the armrest was slightly curved and wider than most chairs of the period.

FAN-BACK MONK'S CHAIR

Spanish furniture makers came up with a new chair design called the monk's chair (sillón de frailero). *It was either a sitting-room armchair or a folding chair designed for travelers. It was usually upholstered in Cordova leather and sometimes in brocade, held in place by enormous round- or diamond-headed gilded nails. The two solid rear legs continued upward to form a straight seat or inclined seat back. These stiles supported large, slightly curved armrests that ended in a downward scroll shape. The seat back was sometimes solid, sometimes completely open. In this case, it had a characteristic motif formed of three turned bars set in a fan-shape. The apron joining the front legs had an openwork design of geometric sculptures or was decorated with a coat of arms.*

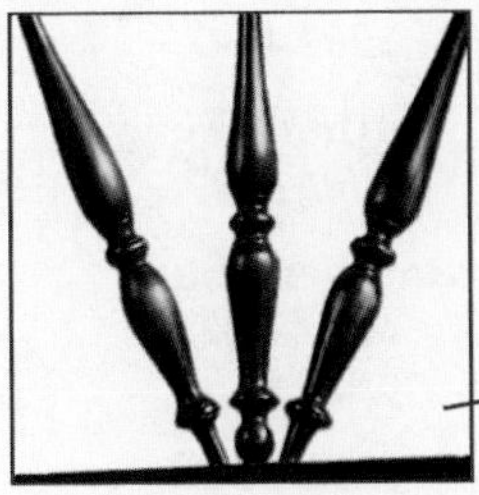

Three rods

This is a highly specific, classical design. The rods could be flat, carved or turned. They were always set in a fan shape, and the central rod was always slightly different from the other two.

Openwork crosspiece

This crosspiece joined the legs just above the H-stretcher. It was often sculpted with superimposed kidney-shaped openwork patterns or decorated with a coat of arms.

△ *Walnut armchair upholstered in nailed leather with a fan-back design. The rectilinear legs are joined by an openwork stretcher. Fondation Angladon, Avignon.*

CHINA

– 1200 1700

Functional Furniture

(1200 BC – AD 1700)

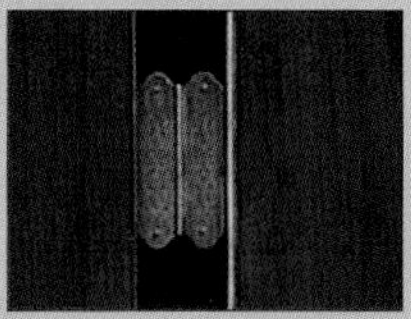

Wood

Veined red wood
Rosewood
Untreated teak
Palissander

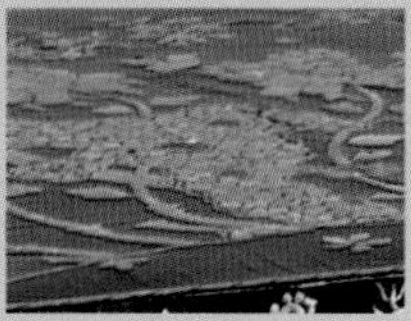

Laquers

Lacquer was used to protect furniture (tables, boxes, chests and trays) from weathering. Lacquer color varied with the different dynasties: deep purplish-red during the Ming dynasty, bright red during the Ch'ing dynasty. By the end of the Ming dynasty (throughout the latter sixteenth century and first half of the seventeenth), a type of lacquer known as yin ping tuo appeared; inlay jade, mother-of-pearl, beads, tortoiseshell and ivory were used to create landscapes on panels and screens. Many of these panels were imported to Europe—they inspired the Chinoiserie decorative style.

△ The Chinese Tapestry: "The Emperor's Audience." *Beauvais Tapestry. Guy-Louis de Vernansal. Château de Compiègne.*

The scale of time in China is always staggering. The history of lacquer in this country, for example, stretches over some thirty-two centuries. Historians estimate that the Chinese civilization, one of the oldest and most sophisticated in the world, invented the technique of lacquer about 1100 BC to cover funerary objects. This art grew considerably during the Han dynasty (206 BC-AD 220), became even more refined during the T'ang (618-907) and Sung (960-1279) dynasties, and reached a summit of perfection under the Ming dynasty (1368-1644).

During this period, a technique using thirty-six layers of lacquer was developed, and virtually all court furniture and pieces used for traveling were covered with lacquer. Brought to the West by the merchants and large guilds that traded with the Far East, India and China, lacquer furniture became fashionable in every European court starting in the early seventeenth century, and enjoyed an unprecedented popularity in European furniture design that would persist through the mid-nineteenth century.

The origin of Chinese furniture designs remains relatively unknown. Low tables and stools, designed with an opulent attention to detail, are visible in paintings dating from the early years of the T'ang dynasty (seventh-tenth centuries). The basic shape of these pieces of furniture has remained unchanged since that date.

No examples of this furniture have survived, as the pieces often accompanied a person after his death. The person's descendants made their own identical copies of the furniture; this is similar to the Muslim tradition, which does not allow people to live with someone else's furniture, even items that belonged to a family member.

THE GREAT CHINESE DYNASTIES

Han
206 B.C. to 220 A.D.

Ts'in
220-589

Sui
581-618

T'ang
618-907

Five Dynasties
907-960

Northern Sung
960-1127

Southern Sung
1127-1279

Yuan
1279-1368

Ming
1368-1644

Ch'ing
1644-1911

▷ Jiao yi *chair. Rosewood and light mahogany. Horseshoe-shaped back. Fitted cane seat. Ming dynasty (fourteenth-seventeenth centuries). Musée Guimet, Paris.*

STORAGE ELEMENTS

The first storage elements appeared in the eleventh century, during the Sung dynasty. Similar to the European chests and chests of drawers that Marco Polo discovered in the thirteenth century, they may have been the inspiration for the earliest cabinets made during the Italian Renaissance. The large, massive rosewood cupboards have two superimposed elements with bamboo doors and complex iron hinges. Most are from the Ch'ing dynasty (1644-1911) and were probably made between the early eighteenth and late nineteenth century.

▷ *Large redwood armoire from the Ch'ing dynasty. The case has two doors, each with two panels, and stands on bronze feet made in the West (late nineteenth century). The central locking mechanism was made in China. Fondation Angladon, Avignon.*

△ *Two-tiered cabinet with four doors. Rosewood. Ming dynasty. Wanli period. Musée Guimet, Paris.*

LOW TABLES AND STOOLS

Chinese furniture was basically designed to be functional. The first element, which appeared during the T'ang dynasty, included a large cushion made of precious silk and placed on the floor; a stool with a cushion; and a small, low table used for writing or playing games. A beautiful example of this type of stool can be seen in an eighth-century ink-on-silk work of art by painter Tcheou-Fang (Women Playing Backgammon). The cushion is attached to the stool, which stands on four sculpted legs which curve in slightly at the top, where they join the apron. The seat is very wide. Another popular piece of furniture can be seen in this same drawing: a cleverly designed and sculpted two-tiered shelf made for playing backgammon.

△ *Tall table. Wood covered with black lacquer with inlaid mother-of-pearl. Ming dynasty. Late fifteenth-early sixteenth century. Musée Guimet, Paris.*

THE 18TH CENTURY

FRANCE WAS EXTRAORDINARILY INFLUENTIAL IN EIGHTEENTH-CENTURY AESTHETICS AND IDEOLOGY. EVERY MAJOR INNOVATIVE MOVEMENT STARTED IN THIS COUNTRY AND SPREAD THROUGHOUT THE WORLD—AND EVERY OTHER COUNTRY KEPT A PERMANENT EYE ON WHAT WAS DEVELOPING IN FRANCE.

In the eighteenth century, French ornamentalists, architects, cabinetmakers, draftsmen and decorators, fueled by their desire to move away from the rigorous formality and grandeur of the Sun King, started to develop new styles. One movement, following the transitional Régence style, began to stand out from the others: this was the first phase of Rococo, which would lead to the Louis XV style. This style has been associated with the golden age of French furniture and an art de vivre distinguished by refinement, comfort and harmony.

The sacrosanct symmetry of the seventeenth century was quickly abandoned. Asymmetry, sinuous forms and S-shaped curves appeared everywhere, along with sumptuous marquetry pieces. During much of this century, cabinetmakers and furniture-makers were required by law to apply their signatures via a mark known as the *estampille* to their production.

Talented cabinetmakers in England began to seek their own original styles. In Italy, Spain and Germany, the elegant and refined Rococo style that reigned in France was transformed into a flashy, exaggerated, eye-catching and luxurious art: it was an excessive, overdone style. Yet all these variations on the Rococo style shared a common element: a fondness for Chinese and Japanese styles.

Furniture styles followed the ephemeral phenomenon of fashion. Everything served as a pretext for change. The discovery of the buried cities of Herculaneum and Pompeii, for example, immediately made everything concerning ancient Rome fashionable. This led to a complete redefinition of the stylistic vocabulary in France and England, followed by other countries around the world. This movement, known as neoclassicism, had several proponents: in France, the painter Joseph Marie Vien, the archeologist and engraver Caylus and the architect Germain Soufflot; and in England, the architect Robert Adam. This movement would lead to the Louis XVI style and the Directoire style in France, and to the George III style in England. Each country defined the new movement in its own way: it was characterized by unbridled luxury in Russia, a "bourgeoise" vision in the United States and an integration of popular traditions in Sweden.

The French Revolution was a barely perceptible pause in the Directoire movement that was evolving from the Louis XVI style. This movement continued through the Consulate style, a transitional mode named after Napoleon's first government, and developed into the Empire style.

This summary of eighteenth-century French styles is yet another example of how aesthetic movements accompany political and social movements.

◁ *Louis XVI game room. Château de Versailles.*

FRANCE

1715 1723

The Régence Style

△ Philippe, duc d'Orléans, Regent of France, in his office with his son, the Duc de Chartres. *French School. Château de Versailles and Trianon.*

King Louis XIV died in 1715. The crown passed to his great-grandson, Louis XV, who was just five years old. Until he reached his legal majority, the country was ruled by a regent, Philippe d'Orléans, son of Louis XIV's brother, who was known as "Monsieur." Philippe d'Orléans was regent for only eight years, but what is commonly known as the Régence style lasted slightly over twenty-five years. It first appeared in Paris, during Louis XIV's lifetime, among nobles who had fled the severity and stultifying hierarchy of the Château de Versailles. Although it retained certain elements of the Louis XIV style, by 1700 the Régence style reflected a desire for a better quality of life, which included more intimacy and comfort—factors that were unknown to attendants and followers of the all-powerful Sun King. Paris gradually replaced Versailles in importance. Apartments and small private mansions in the Marais or the Faubourg Saint-Germain were the fashionable places to live. A more frivolous climate of comfort and enjoyment replaced protocol and the staid sumptuous style of the earlier reign. The painter Antoine Watteau translated this lightheartedness onto canvas. No one wanted the pomp and circumstance or heavy styles, which were associated with boredom and constraints.

During this period, the most popular pieces of furniture were the commode, the *bureau plat* (a desk design that has an unsurpassed level of comfort, even today), and a multitude of different chairs with rounded seats designed to accommodate the record size of women's extravagant hoop skirts. In general, furniture was smaller and less solemn and had rounded and curved shapes. The proportions were well balanced, while symmetrical gilt-bronze motifs and whimsical designs were dominant features.

This was also the era when financial speculation first appeared, along with bankruptcies and the spectacular failure of Scottish financier John Law's reign as controller-general of France. Fortunes were acquired and lost with unprecedented speed; in furniture styles, this resulted in the creation of a series of objects designed to satisfy the whims of the rich.

The Régence was an incredible period of movement and belief in the inventive qualities of youth. It is no surprise, therefore, that it led straight to the most exaggerated of styles: Rococo.

The masters

Claude III Audran (1657-1734): ***Ornamentalist and Berain's successor, he attracted a clientele of princes and bankers in the early 17th century.***

Charles Cressent (1685-1768): ***Named* maître *in 1720, he worked for the Regent. He is rightly considered to be as talented a furniture-maker as was Boulle. Stamped works by Cressent are extremely rare. He developed all the characteristic features of the Régence style (powerful curves, impeccably cast bronze pieces used as symmetrical ornaments, adaptation of the espagnolette).***

André Charles Boulle (1642-1732): ***Great French cabinetmaker under Louis XIV; he continued to produce beautiful furniture throughout the early Regence period. He created the* bureau plat.**

CONSOLE TABLES

Sculptors often used console tables as a piece on which they could indulge their tastes for fantasy. In the early eighteenth century, this piece of furniture was still profusely decorated, as it was during Louis XIV's reign. There were small changes, however: the decor was less rigid and often included a multitude of shells, dragons, espagnolettes, masks, scrolls of foliage and diamond motifs against a lattice-like background. These ornamental devices prefigured the Rococo style.
Console tables were generally attached against a wall or along paneling, and were therefore supported by legs on the front side only (although a central back leg was sometimes used for stability).
The lower part of the S-shaped legs curved toward the wall; these were joined by an ornately carved X-stretcher, which had a large motif in the center or sometimes a circular base meant to hold a porcelain vase. The frieze was elaborately carved and also had a large motif in the central section.
The tabletop itself was made of marble with shaped edges. These console tables were purely decorative; they were designed to set off a vase, a rare piece of porcelain, a bust or a statuette.

THE *BUREAU PLAT*

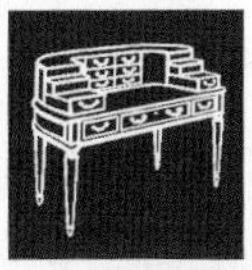

The invention of the bureau plat *is attributed to André Charles Boulle, Louis XIV's great cabinetmaker, who continued to design imaginative furniture during the Régence period. Early examples of this desk were supported on eight curved legs, separated into two groups of four legs; these were not joined together by a stretcher. The most common design had four legs with S-shaped legs curving at the top. In both these designs, the legs supported a large rectangular tabletop, often made of ebonized pearwood covered with leather. The edges were rounded and bordered by a quarter-round molding of bronze or copper. The frieze was slightly recessed and highly ornate; it often had three wide drawers. But Boulle's early, eight-legged models had five drawers (one drawer in the middle and two superimposed drawers on each side—perhaps a reference to the earlier kneehole desks from Louis XIV's era). The corners were decorated with ornamental mounts. Boulle's designs used gilt-bronze masks, while the bureaus attributed to Cressent are characterized by sumptuous bronzes and espagnolettes, and by highly ornate friezes.*
This type of bureau plat *remained popular throughout the eighteenth century and inspired designs for variations on this piece of furniture made in the Louis XV and Louis XVI styles. The* bureau plat *is a marvelous combination of functionality, luxury, imagination and harmony.*

Corners decorated with espagnolettes motifs

Espagnolettes, gilt-bronze busts of young women, were a typical motif in the furniture made by cabinetmaker Charles Cressent. The heads were turned slightly outward. The Spanish Infante, promised but never married to the future King Louis XV, inspired this design.

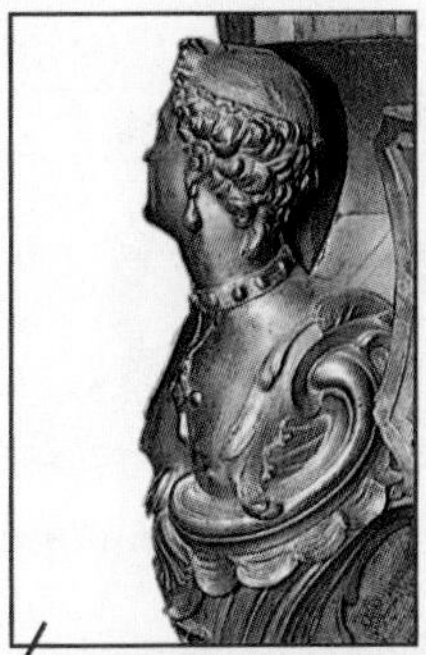

Tabletop

The top was always rectangular and rounded at the corners to avoid accidents. The edges were bordered by a strip of bronze molding for the same reasons.

Curve

The curve was situated high up on the leg, though it was not very prominent during the Régence. It started just below the espagnolette on the corner, so that the leg almost looks as if it is straight.

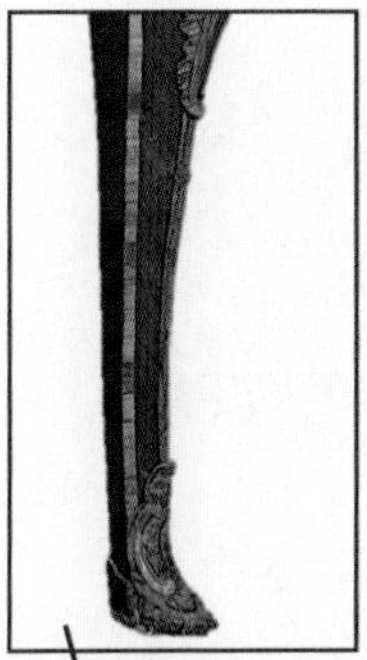

△ *Large* bureau plat *with three drawers, made of oak, walnut, pine, satinwood and violetwood veneer, and gilt bronze. Attributed to Charles Cressent. Musée du Louvre, Paris.*

Motifs and decorative elements

Shells with symmetrical ribs

Bat wings

Lambrequins on latticework (or diamond-shaped) background

Palmettes

Pomegranate motif

Costumed monkeys

Shepherds

Chimera, masks and mascarons

Chinese dragons and fantastic animals

Magots under parasols

Chinese motifs and pagodas from the East India Trading Company.

Espagnolettes

Musical instruments, fishing and hunting accoutrements

Warrior's attributes

Attributes inspired by courtly love: cupids, quivers, arrows, cherubs, crowns of roses, wreaths

FLAT-BACKED FAUTEUILS

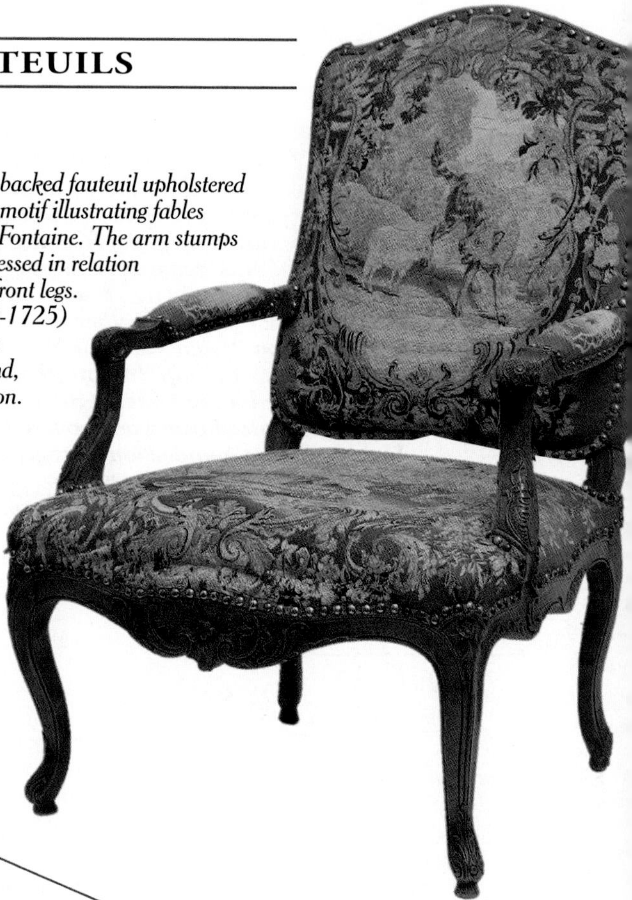

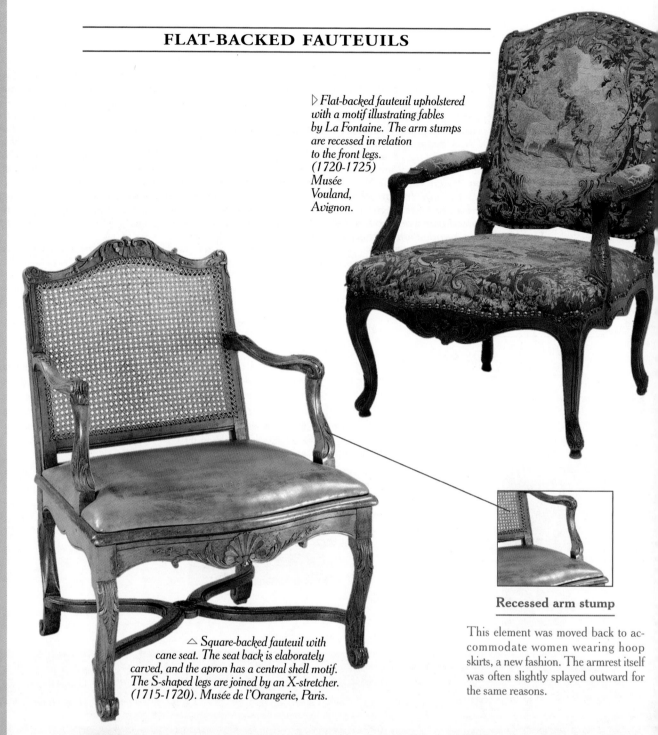

▷ *Flat-backed fauteuil upholstered with a motif illustrating fables by La Fontaine. The arm stumps are recessed in relation to the front legs. (1720-1725) Musée Vouland, Avignon.*

△ *Square-backed fauteuil with cane seat. The seat back is elaborately carved, and the apron has a central shell motif. The S-shaped legs are joined by an X-stretcher. (1715-1720). Musée de l'Orangerie, Paris.*

Recessed arm stump

This element was moved back to accommodate women wearing hoop skirts, a new fashion. The armrest itself was often slightly splayed outward for the same reasons.

Chairs are a good example of how Régence designers borrowed from the earlier Louis XIV style and how they prefigured what would follow. In hindsight, the chairs seemed to be a conglomeration of the Louis XIV and Louis XV styles, but in fact, there were several distinct periods. Between 1700 and 1715, chair designs remained similar to those common during Louis XIV's reign, and were characterized by the same stiff, imposing forms. The seat back was high and curved at the top, with straight sides. It was fully upholstered, with no visible wood. The arm stumps were straight and aligned with the chair legs. The so-called pied-de-biches, ***or slightly curved hoof feet, were joined by curved X- or H-stretchers.***

This design changed considerably between 1720 and 1725: wood appeared around the entire circumference of the seat back and the apron; the stretcher connecting the legs disappeared; and the arm stumps, which were still aligned over the legs, started to splay outward to accommodate the hoop skirts that were in fashion. The stiles along the seat backs were still rectilinear, and the curve of the legs was still very high.

Starting in 1725, the arm stumps moved toward the back, shortening the length of the armrest; this was also introduced to make chairs more comfortable for women wearing wide skirts. The armrests began to be upholstered. The wood, visible around the seat back, was curved. The legs became shorter and the S-shape was more prominent. Decors remained extremely luxurious: the wood may have been gilded, silvered or simply waxed. Cane-seat chairs appeared, influenced by a fashion that arrived from Britain and Holland.

Several new types of chairs were invented, each one offering increased comfort: the bergère, ***a chair with a removable cushion, upholstered between the arms and the seat; and the confessional, another upholstered chair with flat wooden panels, or "wings," projecting from the top stiles on which the sitter could rest her head.***

THE *LIT DE REPOS*

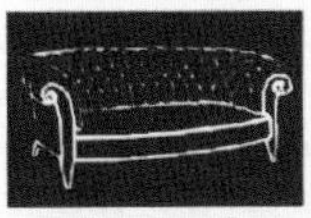

The* lit de repos, *also known as a* canapé *or* sultane, *developed from the* fauteuil*: this chair was expanded laterally to sit three people and rested on eight legs. This sofa was fitted with a mattress upholstered with the same fabric as on the sides, which were generally fairly low. This piece of furniture was placed against a wall or faced the fireplace. Square or cylindrical cushions were added for additional comfort. The fabric covering the cushions were changed twice a year: in the winter, either a petit-point fabric, silk velvet, or deep blue and red brocade or damask were used; for summer, pastel silks or printed fabrics.

Cabriole leg

Eight legs, identical in the front and back, supported the *lit de repos*, ensuring that the sofa remained perfectly stable.

Central shell motif

The shell, the favorite ornament of the budding Rococo style, was always placed in the center of the apron. It appears three times on this sofa, demonstrating that the design was based on the structure of three fauteuils.

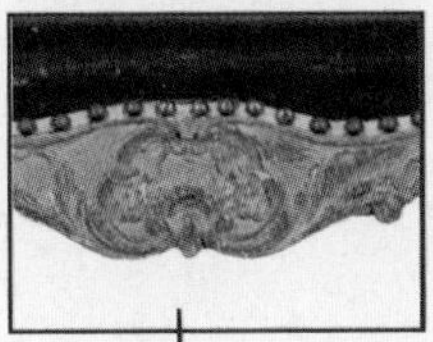

Cylindrical cushion

This long round cushion was placed at each end of the *lit de repos*. A tassel hangs from the center of each rounded end. A square cushion, decorated with similar trim, was often placed over this cylindrical one.

△ Lit de repos *with three low sides, resting on eight legs.*
Collection Jean Walter and Paul Guillaume. Musée de l'Orangerie, Paris.

Wood and materials

Oak for large furniture, armoires and buffets

Walnut and beech for chairs and armchairs

Linden-tree for all giltwood furniture

Pine for the frames of all furniture and base support for marquetry

Ebonized pearwood replaced ebony

Veneer: rosewood, satinwood, kingwood, citron wood, maple

Greater use of bronze elements designed to reinforce corners and protect locks and feet. Techniques included mercury or fire gilding, or the elements were simply covered with gold-colored varnish.

THE *COMMODE-TOMBEAU*

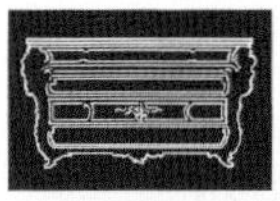

Along with the bureau, the commode, or chest of drawers, was the most characteristic piece of furniture during the Régence style, which aimed to increase domestic comfort. Indeed, it was so useful that it quickly replaced the armoire as a storage element. Two main types of commodes co-existed during the Régence.

The most famous design was the** commode-tombeau, **also known as the** commode à la Regence, **which was characterized by three rows of drawers. These drawers, separated by a cross piece, come in several variations: two wide drawers on top of each other at the bottom, with two drawers, side by side, at the top; or more simply, three wide superimposed drawers.

The element always curved outward in the middle. The uprights were covered with gilt-bronze decorative mounts representing acanthus leaves scrolls or caryatids. The handles, also made of gilt bronze, were hinged or attached by two bronze plates decorated with a rosette, oak leaf, acorn or female sphinx motif. The commode stood on short legs covered with gilt-bronze mountings. The marble tabletop was either rectangular or followed the curve of the drawers. The apron in the center of the lower cross piece was decorated with a large gilt-bronze motif.

The name "commode à la Régence" remained in use throughout the eighteenth century to describe this type of triple-drawered furniture on short legs—whether the piece dated from the Régence period or not.

The invention of the second type of commode is attributed either to Charles Cressent or to André-Charles Boulle. This piece of furniture had two drawers, separated by a crosspiece; it was characterized by the very long cabriole legs, which prefigured the Louis XV style. The corners were decorated with masks, caryatids or espagnolettes; the feet, with acanthus leaves, lion's paws or hands; and the apron, large gilt-bronze motifs.

▷ *A* commode-tombeau, *marquetry, bronze female sphinx motifs around the locks and caryatids on the corners, extending up from the legs. Red marble tabletop. Musée Vouland, Avignon.*

Base

The feet generally were covered with chased bronzed in the form of an acanthus scroll, in order to protect the wood.

Apron

The center of the apron was decorated with an ornament. Usually made of bronze, this motif was a foliated scroll, acanthus leaf-pattern or a shell against a a bat-wing design.

◁ *Oak occasional table with a palmette and diamond-star pattern; the frieze is carved on all four sides. Musée Vouland, Avignon.*

Diamond background

The diamond pattern appeared in the final years of Louis XIV's reign. It became the most common background pattern; others included gridded flowerette motifs or concave squares.

Leg with palmette motif

The palmette, or palm leaf motif, often associated with an eloganted acanthus leaf pattern, extended along the outer part of the leg from the frieze down, creating a relief that accentuated a fairly shallow curve at the top.

OCCASIONAL TABLE

Occasional tables, folding tables, portable tables and central tables decorated on all four sides were among the small, elegant tables in wide use at this time. The advantage to these tables is that they were far less imposing and far easier to move than those made in the Louis XIV style; they were thus perfectly suited to the urban lifestyle.

Central tables, which were ornately carved on all sides, were made of solid wood or giltwood and rested on four hoof feet. The legs were not connected by a stretcher. The tabletop was usually covered with a thick slab of marble.

Portable tables and occasional tables were used to compensate for a lack of servants (this occurred fairly frequently during the wild financial speculations of the Régence). These tables had multiple functions: they were used as serving tables for light meals, they supported candlesticks or candelabra or served as simple gaming tables (in this case, the frieze often had one or several drawers).

France

1723 1774

The Louis XV Style

△ *Tapestry Room. Château de Cheverny.*

The peaceful, prosperous and popular reign of Louis XV, known as the Bien-Aimé, or Well-Loved, encouraged the development of art and literature under the enlightened patronage of Madame de Pompadour, a royal favorite. She provided the impetus for the Rococo style in France, the result of a long stylistic quest (which began in the early eighteenth century) that aimed to free design and furniture from the solemn rigidity of the seventeenth century.

The process that led to the Rococo style did not, therefore, begin with the start of Louis XV's reign, but had already appeared during Louis XIV's lifetime; there was a collective awareness that a new style was beginning and that it had to be different from the preceding one. The Rococo style, like any new style, was associated with change and with youth, but stood out on its own as an elegant, imaginative style.

This new movement paralleled new lifestyles in which comfort was one of the primary goals. During this time, formal rooms were reserved for ceremonial events. The king ordered smaller rooms, lower ceilings, painted wood-paneling and efficient fireplaces for his apartments at the Château de Versailles. These apartments were cozier and offered an elegant intimacy, even in winter.

First the aristocracy, then the bourgeoisie, adopted this lifestyle that was popular at court. From this point on, when ordering a new piece of furniture, people went to specialized shops where they could view an array of new items, which could be adapted to the needs of each customer. The merchant then ordered the furniture from his usual cabinetmaker or furniture-maker and delivered the finished piece to his customer. The Comtesse de Barry, another of the king's favorites (starting in 1768), ordered furniture in this way; many of the existing pieces are considered masterpieces today.

Starting in 1751, as a guarantee of exceptional quality, cabinetmakers and furniture-makers had to stamp every piece of furniture leaving their shops with their name or initials; this was the beginning of the official *estampille*, or stamp, proving the provenance of a piece. On chairs, the stamp was usually placed under the rear crosspiece; on commodes and desks, under the marble tabletop; and on tables, concealed under the frieze. Other European countries soon adopted this procedure.

The masters

There were many cabinetmakers and furniture-makers in the 18th century. This list includes the most famous, with the date each one was named maître (master) by his guild. A book entitled the Salvert identifies each maître, along with his stamp.

Juste-Aurèle Meissonnier (1693-1750): Architect and designer for the Chambre du Roi.

Nicolas Pineau (1684-1754): Ornamentalist and creator of the Rococo style in the 1730s.

Bernard Van Riesenburgh, known as Bernard II: He became a maître in 1735. A cabinetmaker, he specialized in royal commissions.

Jacques Dubois, named maître in 1742. A cabinetmaker known for the sumptuous bronzework on his furniture.

Jean-François Œben, named maître ca. 1750. A German-born cabinetmaker, he specialized in

◆◆◆

The Poetry of Chairs

There were so many different designs that a chair existed for practically every specific event in the day and for each room of a house.

The voyeuse, or conversation chair, was an innovation inspired from a new, popular activity: games and an interest for watching them. Men would straddle these chairs, while women kneeled on them. Both would lean on the seat back, which became something like an armrest.

Certain Louis XV-style chairs had charming names in French. The sultane, for example, was an upholstered settee with matching scroll arms and eight legs. It could stand alone, such as a canapé, or be placed in an alcove framed with curtains and lined with fabric matching that of the sultane.

The piece of furniture known as the ottoman was a low, heavily upholstered seat or bench.

The paphos was a precursor to the convertible sofa-bed. The back of the canapé tilted to form a bed.

The turquoise was a sofa in which the seat between the symmetrical armrests could be removed.

Veilleuses were generally made in pairs and placed facing each other, often on either side of a fireplace. These were armchairs with high backs and thick cushions.

COMMODES WITH SERPENTINE FRONTS

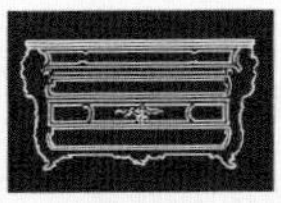

Louis XV commodes were among the most elegant and balanced pieces of furniture ever made. The **commode-tombeau,** ***also known as the*** **commode à la Régence** ***(or chest of drawers), was still popular, but the handles had evolved; they were no longer removable or symmetrical. New forms appeared, aided by the constantly increasing skill of the cabinetmakers. The legs became thinner and quite high, as, for example, with the*** **commode Cressent,** ***which generally had two or three drawers, a serpentine front and a shaped apron. In the early eighteenth century, the drawers were separated by a crosspiece, but starting in 1750, this element disappeared. When there was no lower crosspiece or lower drawer, a decorative apron often appeared, with a bronze mount placed in the center. The serpentine fronts and curved shapes were the most prominent feature of these pieces of furniture, which epitomized the Rococo style. These new shapes were accompanied by a new style of decor, best illustrated by the marquetry patterns. Framed with the serpentine structures, the marquetry presented an unusually sumptuous and exuberant inventory of every possible floral motif. Pieces of furniture were the backdrops for small, highly complex marquetry scenes made with sophisticated techniques and wood of different colors. The gilt bronze mounts also added to the ornamentation, notably on the corners, feet, handles, keyholes and central motifs on the apron. Chinese lacquer, also known as japanning, or hand-varnished decors were common. The*** **commode à vantaux** ***appeared toward the mid-eighteenth century; in this piece, the two or three drawers were concealed behind two doors decorated with marquetry or lacquered panels.***

◁ *Half commode-tombeau with a marquetry decor and two drawers (with no crosspiece). The handles, corners and keyholes are decorated with bronze foliage mounts. Marble tabletop. Stamped by Garnier, named* maître *in 1742. Fondation Angladon, Avignon.*

Asymmetrical, fixed handles

The handles were no longer removable, as on Louis XIV and Régence furniture, but were affixed to the front. They formed a remarkable gilt-bronze motif of leaf-covered branches or twigs. A darker marquetry pattern creates an extremely elegant frame for the attachment point on the front.

▷ *Commode with ornate marquetry, serpentine front, two drawers with a crosspiece, bronze foliage mounts, sculpted griotte marble tabletop. Stamped by Pierre III Migeon. Musée Vouland, Avignon.*

♦♦♦

marquetry. He also invented the roll-top desk.

***Nicolas Heurtault**, named* maître *in 1753. A furniture-maker, he was famous for his richly carved chairs.*

***Roger Vandercruse**, known as Lacroix (1728-1799), named* maître *in 1755. A cabinetmaker of Flemish origin, he is known for beautiful furniture with inlays of porcelain plaques, chairs and convertible furniture.*

***Louis Delanois** (1731-1792), named* maître *in 1761. A furniture-maker famous for his chairs, most often designed for the French bourgeoisie.*

***Charles Topino** (1725-1789), named* maître *in 1773. A cabinetmaker famous for his heart-shaped dressing-tables.*

***Pierre II** (1701-1734) and **Pierre III Migeon** (1733-1775): Cabinetmakers and furniture dealers specializing in commodes.*

CABRIOLE CHAIR AND *CHAISE À LA REINE*

Chair-makers (known as** chaisiers **in French), not furniture-makers, produced the many different kinds of chairs; these were custom chairs, made according to the specific instructions provided by the tapestry-haberdashers, architects-designers or ornamentalists who had produced pattern books.

French chairs generally fell into one of two main categories: the** chaise à la reine**, or straight-backed armchair, and the cabriole chair, with a curved back. Both categories had strict specifications—the sizes were defined to within half an inch.

In both these designs, the stretchers had disappeared. The curve of the S-shaped legs was more pronounced, and the legs usually ended in hoof feet.

The same curve was reproduced on the arm stumps (which also curved outward) and the seat back. The back sloped slightly backward, the edges were beveled and the crest rail had a central carved element.

Much of the chair frame itself was carved with motifs ranging from asymmetrical ribbed shells to budding flowers, fan-shaped palmettes and pomegranates.

The straight-backed** chaise à la reine **developed from the formal furniture of state and was similar to the** chaise meublante**, a heavy chair always placed against a wall. The seat back never exceeded the height of the wall paneling. The seat itself had to be from 14 to 16 inches from the floor.

The cabriole chair had a curved back and was therefore more comfortable. Lighter and more portable than the chaise à la reine, it was usually placed in the center of a room.

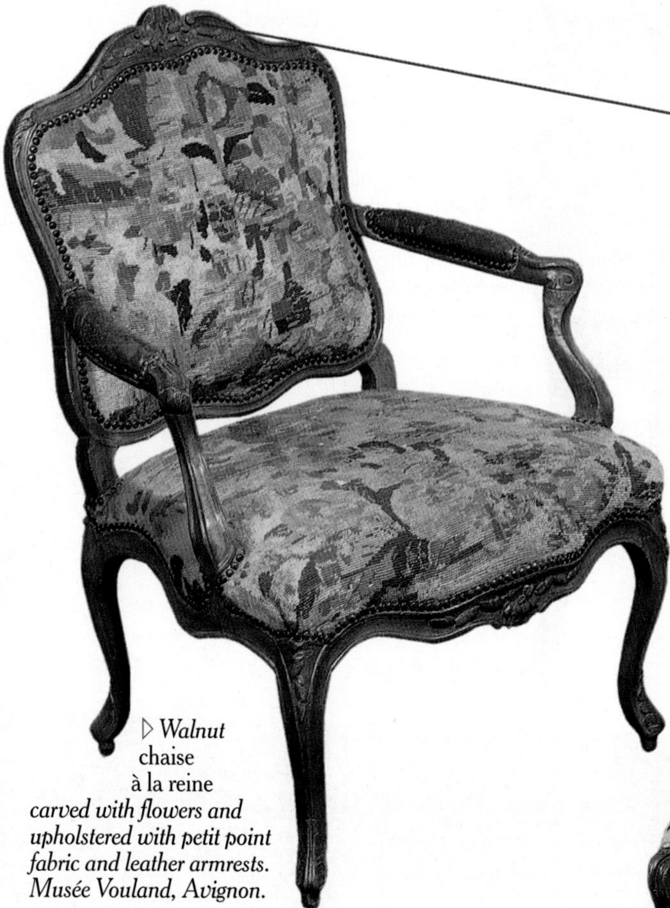

▷ *Walnut* chaise à la reine *carved with flowers and upholstered with petit point fabric and leather armrests. Musée Vouland, Avignon.*

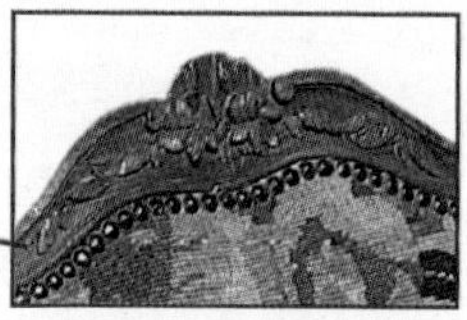

Sculpted crest rail

The center of the crest rail is decorated with a rose or other type of flower. The top of the seat back always ended at shoulder level, so that it would not interfere with hairstyles. Several forms were used: rounded, notched, undulating.

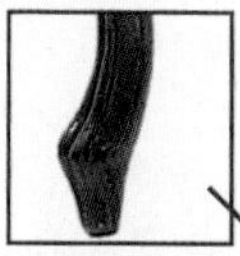

French scroll foot

This scroll foot, decorated with acanthus leaves, was also called the leaf scroll foot. This element is highly characteristic of the Louis XV style. It elegantly sets off the upward curve of the leg. Ths foor always rests on a small, barely visible cylinder.

△ *Walnut cabriole chair, carved with stylized flowers at the top of the seat back. Upholstered with petit point fabric decorated with small flowers. Musée Vouland, Avignon.*

◁ *Corner chair similar to the chair described by Roubo in his illustration no. 233. The rounded back curved into the arms, the legs are placed to the side and in the center. Fondation Angladon, Avignon.*

CORNER CHAIRS

The corner chair, or bureau chair, had an innovative shape; it was designed to be more comfortable for a person sitting and working at a desk. The deep round back curved into the arms. Gondola chairs, which appeared during the Directoire, repeated this exact design. The seat projected sharply in the front, so that the user's legs fitted more comfortably on the sides.

This singular shape meant that the furniture- or chair-maker arranged the legs in an unusual way so that the chair would remain stable: two legs were placed on the side, with one in the front and another in the back. Corner chairs were upholstered with leather, which was attached by gilt nails.

CANED CHAIRS AND *BERGÈRES*

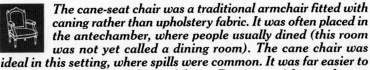

The cane-seat chair was a traditional armchair fitted with caning rather than upholstery fabric. It was often placed in the antechamber, where people usually dined (this room was not yet called a dining room). The cane chair was ideal in this setting, where spills were common. It was far easier to clean caning than upholstery fabrics. **Bergères** ***with caned seats also existed, but they were fairly rare and were generally placed in libraries.***

Bergères ***are different from armchairs in that they are upholstered between the arms and the seat. The*** **bergère** ***first appeared around 1730. It was an elegant version of the heavy winged chairs, or confessionals, from the final years of Louis XIV's reign, designed to protect the sitter from drafts. The wide seat usually had a large cushion, which made it an extremely comfortable chair. The*** **bergère** ***sometimes also had wings at the top of the seat back; in this case, it was called a*** **bergère confessional or fauteuil de commodité.**

△ *Cane* bergère *made of carved beech, decorated with leaf-work joints and cartouches on the front and rear of the seat back. Exhibited with its leather pillow. Fondation Angladon, Avignon.*

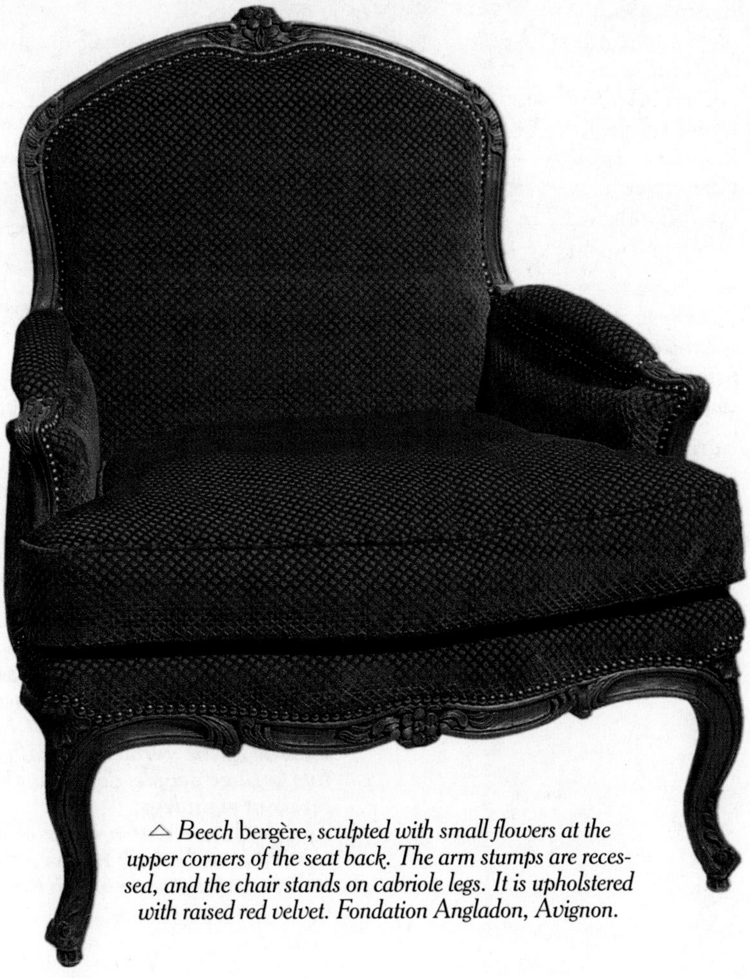

△ *Beech* bergère, *sculpted with small flowers at the upper corners of the seat back. The arm stumps are recessed, and the chair stands on cabriole legs. It is upholstered with raised red velvet. Fondation Angladon, Avignon.*

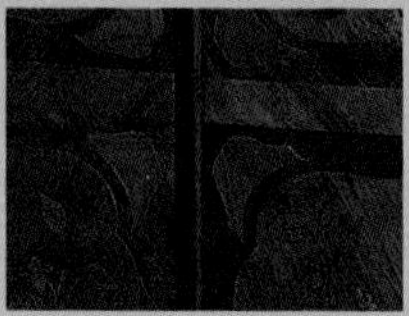

Wood and materials

Oak for large furniture pieces and for frames of high-quality items. Often used with linden and pine

Gilt or painted beech for chairs

Marquetries: holly, olivewood, boxwood, berberis, pear, plum, cherry, ebony, mahogany, rosewood, satinwood, sandalwood

Exotic wood, used especially for its diverse colors: violet wood (violet), rosewood (pink), citron tree (yellow) and kingwood (red)

Lacquered Japanese and Chinese panels, primarily black and gold in color

Coromandel lacquer (named for the trading ports along the Coromandel coast of India)

◆◆◆

△ *Three-seated painted wooden settee. The apron and armrests are decorated with stylized carved flowers. Curved legs. The settee is upholstered with yellow damask silk. Musée Vouland, Avignon.*

▷ *Beech* duchesse brisée, *or duchess, consisting of a round-backed armchair* (confessional) *decorated with stylized flowers, resting on S-shaped legs, and a matching footstool forming a small* bergère. *Upholstered with moiré silk with ribbon and flower pattern. Stamped by Jean-Baptiste Tilliard, named* maître *in 1752. Fondation Angladon, Avignon.*

THE SETTEE AND THE *DUCHESSE BRISÉE*

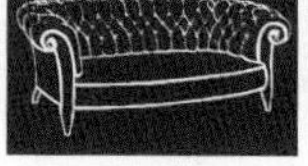

Settees, or sofas, developed from the simple armchair. The frame of this piece of furniture was extended laterally to accommodate two or three people; depending on its size, it rested on six or eight legs.
The duchesse ***was a chair midway between an armchair and a bed. It was a very deep upholstered chaise longue on which the sitter could extend his or her legs.***

When designed in two parts, it was called a duchesse brisé. ***This consisted of a*** bergère ***with a deep, round back (with or without wings on the seat back), and one or two stools of varying lengths. The front of the*** bergère ***and of the stool were designed to fit together to form a daybed.***
The duchesse en bateau ***was another version of the chaise longue; it was a single piece and the upholstered foot had a short back that matched the curve of the seat back.***

Marquetry design

The marquetry design was selected by the owner when the piece of furniture was ordered. Designs ranged from musical instruments to amorous attributes or, as in this piece, flowers set in a vase framing an ink pot and an envelope.

THE *BONHEUR-DU-JOUR*

The* bonheur-du-jour, *which appeared around 1760, was a delicate piece of furniture. A flat-topped desk, it had compartmentalized drawers in the upper section. The marble top was sometimes framed on three sides by a bronze railing. This small desk was almost always used as a pretext to showcase a masterpiece of marquetry work.

△ Bonheur-du-jour *with flower bouquet marquetry on the upper section and an ink-pot and envelope pattern on the lower section. The design was influenced by Topino's style of marquetry. Musée Vouland, Avignon.*

ARMOIRES

Armoires as we know them today were not popular during the reign of Louis XV. What we understand to be an armoire—an imposing piece of furniture designed for storage—did not even really exist during this period. Its large size was probably the reason it fell out of fashion. What contemporaries of Louis XV called armoires were small, rather shallow pieces of furniture, measuring 72 to 80 inches tall. The curved furniture was often covered with japanned marquetry patterns, framed by gilt-bronze mounts.

△ *Armoire with flower bouquet and bird marquetry on the doors. It is decorated with gilt-bronze mounts. Marble top. Stamped by Durand. Musée Vouland, Avignon.*

◆◆◆

Vernis Martin, a generic term for a French Japanning technique, named after Guillaume and Étienne Martin.

Porcelain plaques made by the Sèvres royal workshop.

Gilt bronze appliqués used to decorate and protect corners, feet, handles and keyholes of furniture pieces.

Marble moldings on chest of drawers and desks.

Fabrics and upholstery

Petit point embroidery with floral or small flower motifs.

Beauvais tapestries, brocaded fabrics, Genoese and Venetian velvets, lampas, damask, leather for office chairs.

Caning on seats used outdoors, in dining rooms and in the libraries.

OCCASIONAL TABLES

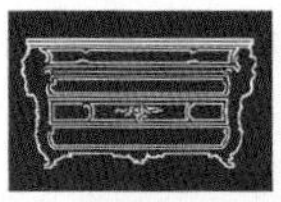

A large number of lightweight, easily transportable tables appeared during the eighteenth century. The most common were gaming tables, including backgammon tables with several superimposed tabletops and round card tables—all used as pretexts by cabinetmakers to showcase their skills.

At night, bedside tables were taken out of the wardrobes where they were stored during the day. Side tables had two glass-front or metal latticework doors, resembling small portable pantries with one or two drawers.

Cabaret tables with porcelain tabletops were designed for chocolate or coffee services, as well as for cups.

The table en chiffonière, *designed for sewing, was perched atop high S-shaped legs and had several drawers and a shelf between the legs.*

Dressing tables were the most important piece of furniture. They had side compartments with hinged covers. One side was used to store cosmetics, bottles, combs and brushes, while the other housed wigs. The surface of the table was often covered with fabric.

Reading tables had stands that could be tilted to any angle. Most also had a sliding panel for writing; tables designed specifically for writing, known as écritoires, *also had drawers for storing an ink pot and pen.*

△ Marquetry writing desk fitted with a pull-out panel and a drawers, supported by high curved legs and decorated with gilt-bronze elements. Fondation Angladon, Avignon.

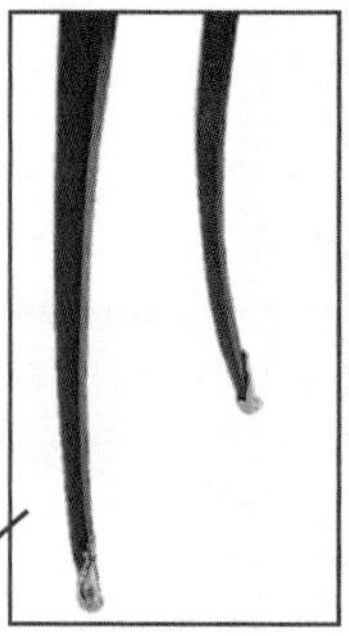

Cabriole leg

The elegant, graceful cabriole leg ended in a hoof foot, or pied-de-biche. It rested on a chased bronze base decorated with acanthus leaves, which protected the wood.

△ Backgammon table with checkerboard marquetry and gilt-bronze mounts, resting on cabriole legs. Stamped by Bourdin. Fondation Angladon, Avignon.

Removable tabletop

The tabletop was richly decorated with a checkerboard pattern; it could be lifted off, uncovering the ebony-and-ivory marquetry backgammon board in the frieze of the table.

△ *Slant-top desk decorated with foliated scroll marquetry patterns. The base of each curved leg is protected with a bronze mount. The slant-top is placed at a 45 degree angle. Musée Vouland, Avignon.*

SLANT-TOP DESK

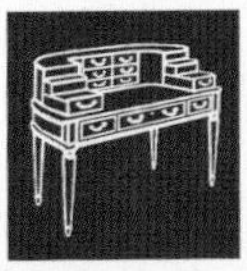

The slant-top desk, known in French as the **bureau en dos d'âne** ***or*** **secrétaire à dessus brisé,** ***was an innovation in furniture design. It was a curved piece of furniture, ornately decorated on all sides, which meant that it was designed to be placed in the middle of a room, not against a wall. These desks were both large and medium in size. The unique feature of these desks was the top, which, closed, slanted at a 45-degree angle and opened to reveal a series of drawers and a writing surface.***

Fall-front writing desk

When open, the fall front offers a writing surface usually covered with leather. Inside are a series of five drawers arranged in three rows, each decorated with marquetry patterns of foliated scrolls.

Chased bronze mounts

These mounts were placed at the top corners and extended all the way down the legs to the base, emphasizing the curved shape. The serpentine curve on the tabletop and the drawers in the frieze were also set off by luxurious gilt-bronze ornaments.

THE *BUREAU PLAT*

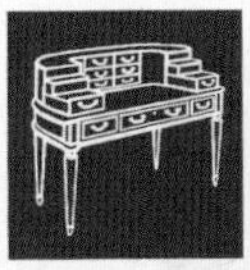

The bureau plat, invented by André-Charles Boulle and Charles Cressent during the Régence, did not change greatly during the Louis XV style. This piece of furniture was already quite luxurious and became even more so as chased bronze and gilt-bronze ornaments were added, emphasizing the curve of the legs and the serpentine lines of the apron. They also set off the geometric marquetry patterns.
Under Louis XV, a small serpentine shape piece of furniture was often placed under one of the sides; this was known as a cartonnier, a type of storage cabinet for papers. This small, free-standing elements was usually covered in leather and sometimes served as a base for a bronze desk clock.

△ Bureau plat *by Antoine-Robert Gaudreaux, ca 1740. Château de Versailles.*

FRANCE

1755 1770

The Transition Style

The masters

Jean-Charles Delafosse (1734-1789): Ornamentalist who supported a neoclassical style; influential for his designs published in 1768; these were "Greek-style models," which led to the creation of the Transition and Louis XVI styles.

Jean-François de Neufforge: Ornamentalist, author of **Recueil élémentaire d'architecture,** ***promoting the use of classical designs.***

Louis-Joseph Le Lorrain (1715-1759): Painter and furniture designer, he inspired neoclassicism.

Georges Jacob (1739-1814), named **maître** ***in 1765. Cabinetmaker and furniture-maker. He became well-known toward the end of the Empire. He was the first of a family of cabinetmakers, the Jacobs and Jacobs-Desmalter, who worked up to the beginning of the Restoration.***

△ Madame du Barry at her Toilette. *Jean-Baptiste-André Gautier-Dagoty. Château de Versailles.*

A new style began to appear in the middle of Louis XV's reign, first encouraged by Madame de Pompadour. This style was later actively promoted by the Comtesse du Barry after she became the king's favorite in 1768. The Rococo motifs and features of the Louis XV style were gradually replaced by neoclassical ornamentation and design. Two events contributed to Rococo's fall from grace. The first was the discovery in 1748 of Herculaneum and Pompeii, two ancient Roman cities buried during an eruption of Mount Vesuvius; this discovery had a major impact on the late eighteenth century and the first twenty-five years of the nineteenth century. The second event was a trip to Italy by a French mission that consisted of artists from the Académie de France (including the architect Germain Soufflot, invited by the Marquis de Marigny, Madame de Pompadour's brother). This group brought back a large number of antique ornaments, designs, bas-reliefs, columns and capitals. An interest in ancient Greece and Rome flourished soon after their return. Architecture was the first to reflect this revival, but the fashion soon spread to furniture, which was characterized by straighter lines and motifs that were decidedly—and sometimes ostentatiously—antique in inspiration. This marked the return to a classical and extremely dogmatic style. This was a typical reaction, and one that almost always occurs after a period of an exaggerated style, such as Rococo. It would lead to the Louis XVI style and an emphasis on straight lines and geometric shapes.

Antique corner plates

The corners were no longer decorated with caryatids, espagnolettes or other sculpted figures, but with corner plates influenced by the new fashion for ancient Greece and Rome. The various motifs decorating the plates included drapery, serpents and grooves.

Marquetry table

A specific feature of marquetry tables of this kind was the door, which was always decorated with marquetry reproducing a bucolic scene, a Chinese pattern or a sheepfold, inspired from the work of a fashionable painter, notably François Boucher.

GREEK-STYLE COMMODE

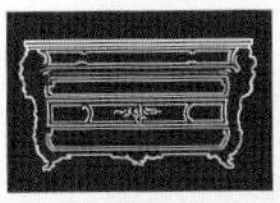

The facade is no longer curved and the uprights are straight. Only the short legs remain somewhat S-shaped. The two large drawers are separated from the three smaller drawers on the frieze. The marquetry has become more geometrical in design and includes ancient Greek motifs, such as amphorae, antique urns, rosettes and Vitruvian scrolls.

△ Greek-style commode made of beech with an oak frame, chased bronze and gilt-bronze mounts and clouded marble top. Marquetry with an antique-urn pattern. Stamped by Jean-Baptiste Henry. Musée Magnin, Dijon.

DRUM TABLE

The drum table was named for its particularly high apron and cylindrical shape. A curved door on the apron, which is supported by three S-shaped legs, is decorated with a marquetry scene; it opens to reveal three drawers or a large compartment. A marble top bordered by a bronze gallery sits on top of the chest.

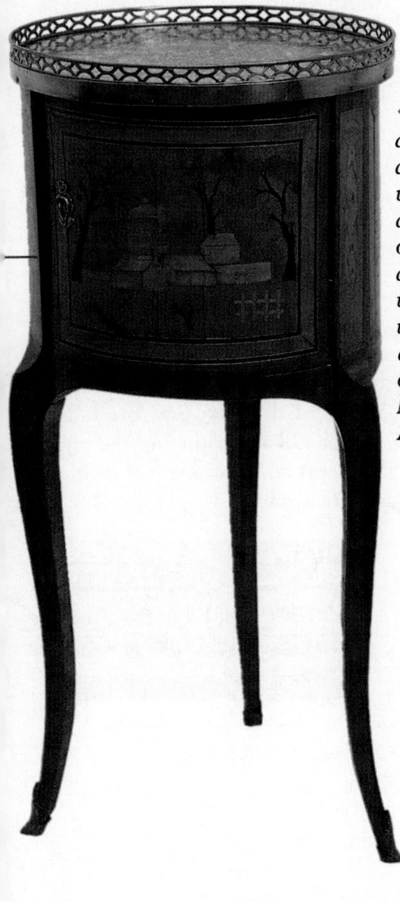

◁ Marquetry drum table decorated with wreaths and garlands on the edges above the legs, with a white marble top and an openwork gallery. Musée Vouland, Avignon.

BARREL CHAIR

This was a low chair with a deep, concave back, similar to the corner chair. The legs were either straight or curved, but were always short. A large cushion, typical of the Transition style, added to the chair's comfort; it could be removed, which changed the overall appearance of the chair.

Connecting block

A square or rectangular connecting block, decorated with a rosette pattern, became a common feature on chair aprons. First introduced by the cabinetmaker Georges Jacob, it persisted through the Louis XVI style and beyond.

△ Dressing table bergère, made of carved and painted beech, with an acanthus-leaf, bead and pilaster decor. The gondola-type back curved straight into the armrests. The legs are curved and involuted at the end. Stamped by Georges Jacob, named maître in 1765. Fondation Angladon, Avignon.

FRANCE

1774  1791

The Louis XVI Style

△ *The Grand Salon. Château de Valençay.*

When Louis XVI came to power at the age of twenty, the style named for him was already well-established in France. Indeed, under the influence Madame de Pompadour, who rejected the Rococo style out of hand, it first appeared during the late years of his grandfather's (Louis XV) reign. When Louis XVI was crowned in 1774, the antique style, known as the "Pompeian fashion," was the most popular style in architecture, the decorative arts and fashion. In other words, Louis XVI cannot really be credited with the style that bears his name, especially as he was utterly uninterested in the arts, literature and, in general, all aesthetic issues. Queen Marie-Antoinette, however, had extremely strong opinions and launched a large number of fashions (including a back-to-nature movement). She also commissioned a great deal of furniture from the most famous cabinetmakers of the era, and hired the best among them, including Riesener, Roëntgen and Jacob.

In comparison with the Transition style, the Louis XVI style seemed to be less dogmatic, less rigid, more generous and more feminine. This can certainly be seen as an example of the queen's strong influence. Flowers were everywhere: in bouquets, wreaths, baskets, ribbons, rosettes, draperies, swags and knots; they brightened up and tempered the rigid straight lines of the antique style.

The ornamentalists Gilles Paul Cauvet and Henri Salembier published pattern books containing floral arabesques; as usual, decorators, cabinetmakers and furniture-makers drew their inspiration from these motifs. Starting in 1780, the ornamentalist Richard de Lalonde began to publish *Cahiers d'ameublement* (Furnishing Notebooks), which provided a detailed inventory of the ornaments and the characteristic features of the style that would become known as Louis XVI. As for the Pompeian fashion, which triggered all these stylistic changes, it remained as popular as ever, although its name was changed to "Etruscan" by the ornamentalist Jean-Démosythène Dugourc.

The Louis XIV, Louis XV and Transition styles shared a common element, which was a fondness for exotic styles and the use of red and gold lacquered Chinese or black and gold Japanese panels. These remained popular with an extremely wealthy, demanding and extravagant clientele.

The masters

Georges Jacob (1739-1814), named maître in 1765. Cabinet-maker and furniture-maker. Known for his Louis XVI furniture. Invented the Directoire style.

Louis Delanois (1731-1792), named maître in 1761. Furniture-maker. He made chairs for many courts throughout Europe.

Jean-François Leleu (1729-1807), named maître in 1764. Cabinet-maker. His designs used marquetry and mahogany veneers.

Joseph Canabas (1712-1797), named maître in 1766. Cabinet-maker. He made small, extremely elegant mahogany furniture.

Martin Carlin (1730-1785), named maître in 1766. Cabinet-maker. Small furniture decorated with Sèvres porcelain plaques and lacquer.

Jean-Henri Riesener (1734-1806), named maître in 1768. Queen's cabinetmaker starting in 1776. Spectacular marquetry, perfect proportions, finely chased bronze.

Apron frieze

Exceptionally well-made, the bronze frieze decorated the entire length of the drawer in the apron. This was one of the most popular of the antique motifs, along with knots surrounding locks and laurel wreaths around the handles.

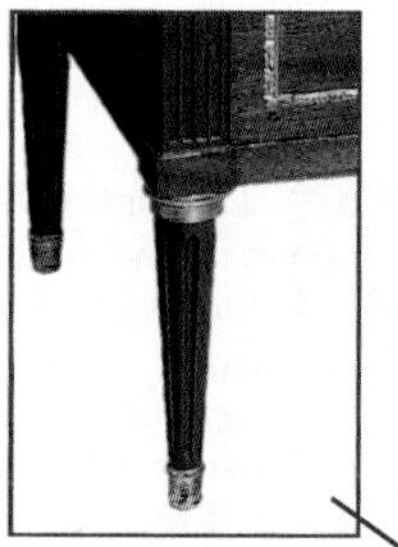

Short legs

The legs, encircled with bronze mounts at the top and at the base, were always short. They were either straight, as in this piece, or grooved, fluted or reeded, with a round or square profile.

Beaded molding

Also known as astragal molding, this bronze element clearly defined the shape of the drawers, the facade panels and the outline of the doors. This was an important feature in this style of furniture.

COMMODES

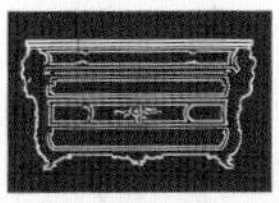

Commodes best represented the neoclassical style that had just come into fashion. The most common type was a rectangular commode with two or three large drawers (no crosspiece), supported by low fluted legs. To soften the rigidity of this rectangular shape, the corners were sometimes beveled or decorated with small fluted columns that extended up over the legs.

These large flat areas provided cabinetmakers with wide surfaces for beautiful mahogany veneers or ornate marquetry patterns. Bronze mounts were essential elements on these large mahogany surfaces, and they stood out more than ever before. These mounts were often exceptionally well-chased. Another type of commode, called a **demi-lune** ***or semicircular commode, also existed. The curving front appealed to a reigning fashion for oval shapes. These commodes had two central drawers and side doors (which were sometimes false). Extravagent bronze mounts were sometimes placed on the last drawer.***

The **commode à vantaux** ***was also popular. In this piece, the drawers were concealed behind doors.***

◁ *Mahogany commode with three drawers (no crosspiece), decorated with bronze mounts around the lock, bronze handles on the lower two drawers and a bronze frieze on the top drawer; white marble top. Stamped by Fidelis Schey, named* maître *in 1777. Fondation Angladon, Avignon.*

Side armoires

These small compartments were placed on either side of the *demi-lune* commode In some pieces, these were false doors and did not open. In such cases, the door had no keyhole, as opposed to the commode illustrated here.

△ *Mahogany* demi-lune, *or semicircular commode, decorated with bronze mounts on the locks and handles and bronze beaded molding; gray marble top. Musée Vouland, Avignon.*

CHAIRS

The main characteristic of the many different styles of chairs was the absolutely straight leg. Some legs were grooved or featured stopped fluting, in which the lower portion of each groove has a rounded convex strip resembling reeding. Some chairs had spiral-turned, square or cylindrical legs. Regardless of the shape of the leg, however, it was always straight. The rear legs, also straight, sloped slightly toward the back for better stability.
By the end of Louis XVI's reign, chair legs began to have an "Etruscan" shape, prefiguring the saber legs of the Directoire style.
Occasionally, all four legs of a chair had saber legs (especially voyeuses à genoux, or conversation chairs, designed for women to kneel on); this design was derived from chairs depicted on ancient vases. The legs were joined at the apron by a boss carved with a rosette motif framed within a rectangle or square, a characteristic feature of the Louis XVI style. The seat backs, whether straight (à la reine) or curved (cabriole) were highly diverse. The lower element of the seat back was always straight, except on medallion chairs, in which the seat backs were oval.
Chairs were named for the various shapes of the crest rail and the stiles: horseshoe, basket and so on. Generally, however, the seat backs were rectangular or square. Toward the end of Louis XVI's reign, the seat backs were pierced, like the chairs designed by the English cabinetmaker Thomas Chippendale. The splat was fashioned into various shapes, including lyres, hot-air balloons or wheat shucks.
The shape of armrests changed when wide hoop skirts fell out of fashion: slightly curved, they became straight, with column-type arm stumps or straight baluster arms.
A large number of different chairs co-existed: unfinished, waxed wood, painted or lacquered wood and giltwood.

△ Cabriole chair. Beech painted to imitate mahogany, horseshoe-shaped back, seat rounded in the front. The frame is carved with beads and ribbons, the legs are fluted. Upholstered with raised red velvet. Stamped by Georges Jacob, named maître in 1765. Fondation Angladon, Avignon.

▷ Voyeuse, or conversation chair, designed so that a man could straddle it and lean on the padded back to observe card players. Sculpted beech. The back splat is made to look like a stylized lyre. Upholstered in pastel silk fabric. Stamped by Jean-Baptiste III Lelarge, named maître in 1775. Fondation Angladon, Avignon.

◆◆◆

Jean-Baptiste Claude Sené (1747-1803), named maître in 1769. Furniture-maker. Made chairs for the king.

Jean-Baptiste III Lelarge (1743-1802), named maître in 1775. Furniture-maker. Made chairs with openwork backs, inspired by the Chippendale style.

David Röentgen (1743-1807), named maître in 1780. German. Cabinetmaker/mechanic for Louis XVI. Convertible furniture.

Guillaume Benneman (died 1803), named maître in 1785. German cabinet-maker. Prefigured the Empire style.

Motifs and decorative elements

Flowers, ovolo, pine cones, molding, pilasters, strings of beads, laurel leaves

Cubes, crowns, knots, ribbons, drapery, acorns

Palmette friezes, Carved plaques

◆◆◆

▷ Chaise à la reine *with a square back, made of gray lacquered beech. The frame is decorated with carved ribbons and flowers. The legs are slender, with stopped fluting. Upholstered with green velvet. Fondation Angladon, Avignon.*

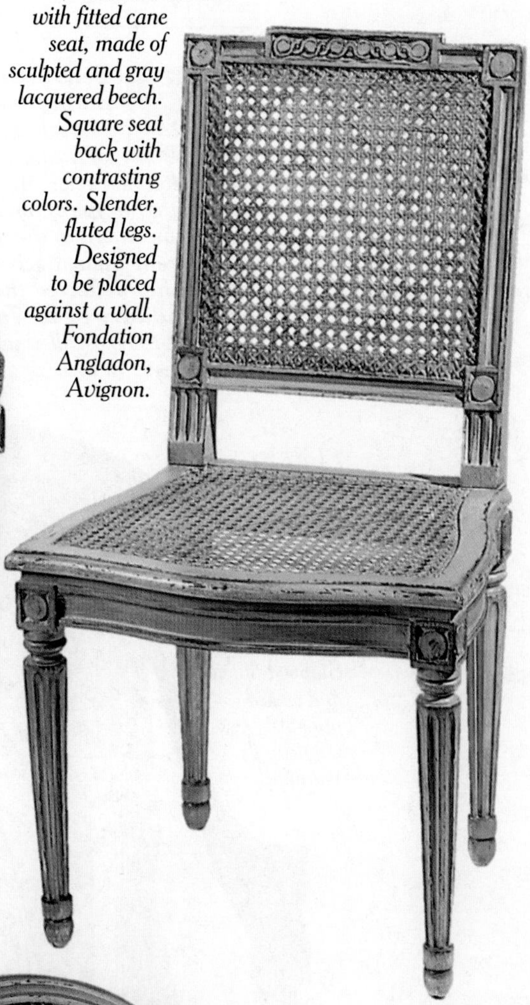

▷ Chaise à la reine *with fitted cane seat, made of sculpted and gray lacquered beech. Square seat back with contrasting colors. Slender, fluted legs. Designed to be placed against a wall. Fondation Angladon, Avignon.*

◁ *Medallion cabriole chair, decorated with carved knots around the apron and in the center of the seat back. Upholstered with red and beige striped cotton fabric. Stamped by Pierre Carpentier. Musée Vouland, Avignon.*

◁ *Medallion cabriole chair supported by tapered legs with stopped fluting. Upholstered with blue petit point embroidered fabric. Musée Vouland, Avignon.*

◆◆◆

Foliated scrolls

Bronze rings

Medallions surrounded by wreaths

Antique vases, lyres

Hot-air balloons, pens, ink pots

Sheets of paper

Books

Dance scenes

Bucolic scenes

Arabesques

Ruins

Wood and material

Mahogany, beech, walnut and chestnut

Chinese lacquer (red and gold) and Japanning (black and gold)

Marquetry using rosewood, violetwood, amaranthus, satinwood

Light-colored beveled marble

THE *LIT À LA POLONAISE*

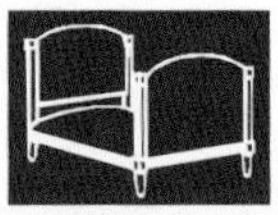

Beds became extremely ornate objects during this period. Tapestry-makers did not select a fabric, then use it for a piece of furniture; instead, they had it specially made after first selecting a pattern and colors in accordance with the type of furniture and its shape, and above all, its placement in the room. There were a multitude of different beds, each with its own specific name, which often reflected the type of decoration: Chinese beds, military beds, Turkish beds, Italian beds or English beds (so-called when it was on rollers). The **lit à la duchesse** ***(a type of canopy bed, also known as an angel bed), with the tester placed against a wall extending the entire length of the bed, was a popular design. Another canopy bed, the*** **lit à la polonaise**, ***remained extremely popular through the end of the eighteenth century. It was covered with a richly carved round or oval tester, which was supported by tall, fluted columns that rose from the edges of the footboard and headboard. The wood of the bed was generally painted the same color as the woodwork in the room in which it was placed. When covered with gold leaf, it was a bed of estate, reserved for high-ranking individuals and used exclusively for receiving official visitors.***

▷ Lit à la polonaise. *Sculpted wood and giltwood. Rounded canopy frame made of wood carved with lion heads. Stopped-fluted and reeded uprights. Château de Versailles.*

Sculpted canopy

Oval-, round- or dome-shaped, the canopy, sometimes crowned with giltwood or carved feather elements, was connected to the bedposts by a rounded metal or wooden frame that was concealed by a tester decorated with brocade and trim.

Frame

The frame was usually made of metal and concealed by the tester, but it could also be visible (as in this photograph) and elaborately carved in an outward curve ending in lion heads at the top of the bedposts.

Fluted bedposts

The bedposts were very high and framed the headboard and footboard. The crosspiece, sometimes decorated with flower baskets, always remained visible.

Bed curtains

These were always tied up at the corners and held by small cords and tassels from the highest point on the bedposts, so that the headboard, footboard and sides remained visible.

▷ *Tronchin-style table that belonged to Voltaire. Mahogany. Château de Serrant.*

TRONCHIN-STYLE TABLE

The Tronchin-style table was derived directly from the fashion for mechanical devices and modernism. It was an architect's table, in which the top can be raised and tilted to any angle, through the use of a rack and gear system.
Röentgen, a cabinetmaker and mechanic who worked for Queen Marie-Antoinette, excelled at this type of furniture, creating slant-top desks that concealed reading desks and even safes, or guéridons that could be transformed into music tables or with drawers that popped out simply by pressing a button.
This passion for mechanics was shared by other famous cabinetmakers, including Jean-Henri Riesener and Jean-François Œben, who, one after the other, began to make new furniture pieces designed to conceal secret documents; this became famous as the cylinder-top desk. A model designed for the king had a mechanical closing device (he loved locks; this was probably the only thing he could appreciate in a piece of furniture).

Mechanism

Moving parts were a defining element of the Louis XVI style, as, for example, in this architect's desk, which was even fitted with casters so that it could be moved easily.

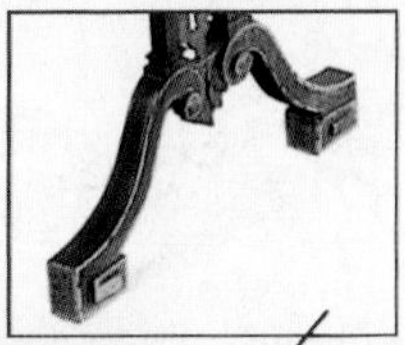

Blued-steel base

Inspired by a fashion popular in Russia at the time, some pieces of furniture, such as this one, used blued steel from Tula, which was magnificently chased and combined with geometric, diamond-pattern marquetry.

TABLES

Small tables remained extremely popular as they were portable and elegant. New designs began to appear, including the dining room table, a mahogany table modeled after an English design that was usually round or oval in shape. Instead of moving it around, as had been the custom, it was left in place in the center of the room for lunch and dinner. Around this time, the room began to be called a dining room. A demi-lune console table or sideboard with several trays was often made to accompany the table.

△ *Extremely rare example of a small sidetable with two trays, decorated with marquetry, supported by two side legs made of blued steel and gilt bronze. Fondation Angladon, Avignon.*

FRANCE

1795 1804

The Directoire Style

△ *Furniture by the Jacob Frères, placed in a dining room designed by Percier and Fontaine. Château de Malmaison.*

The French Revolution overturned everything, including design and style. The Directoire style that appeared afterward was viewed as the calm after the storm. A segment of the population was newly wealthly and was looking to spend its money on tasteful designs. The revival of the decorative art industries was one of the primary components of France's economic recovery plan.

A new ornamental vocabulary, new behaviors, new homes and new furniture were required for this new society. Yet the Directoire (which also encompassed the political period of Napoleon Bonaparte's Consulate) appeared to be a logical continuation of the overwhelming popularity for all things ancient. After the Transition style, with its Roman elements, came the Louis XVI style, and a fashion for Greek and Etruscan designs. Next was the Egyptian trend, which was intensified by Napoleon's military campaign to Egypt (1798-1801) and launched an Egyptian revival style. Although the Roman lictor motifs, with shucks of wheat and sickles, appeared to be revolutionary designs, they were actually first chosen by Queen Marie-Antoinette and the king's brothers for certain avant-garde projects submitted by the ornamentalist Dugourc, long before 1789.

Interiors continued to move toward a more austere style than before. In the first buildings constructed in Paris with all modern facilities, apartments were arranged by floors. The rooms were smaller than in private mansions, and the building fronts were rather unadorned, but well-proportioned. Certain rooms were reserved for specific purposes, a movement that had begun under Louis XVI. The dining room and the bathroom, for example, became separate rooms, with furniture specially designed for each room. A large extension table was placed in the middle of the dining room, with a matching set of chairs and sidetables. New furniture designs for the bathroom included a sink on a metal stand, an antique-style copper or marble bathtub, a mahogany dressing table with a mirror, a psyche, or cheval glass (a full-length mirror) with a mahogany and bronze frame, an *athénienne* (washstand) and a great number of other small pieces of furniture, including a few rare pieces made of precious metals, silver and vermeil.

The masters

When the guilds were eliminated in 1791, furniture-makers, cabinetmakers and sculptors worked with fewer regulations.

Furniture-makers could then make chests of drawers, not just chairs, and cabinetmakers could make chairs.

Furniture no longer had to be stamped by its maker. The best cabinetmakers, however, continued to sign their work.

Jacob Frères, rue Meslée (1796-1803): In 1796, Georges Jacob, whose designs led to the Directoire style, gave his business to his sons, Georges II Jacob and François-Honoré Jacob, who signed their work, "Jacob Frères, rue Meslée," until 1803.

◆◆◆

PRINTED FABRICS

Solid-color fabrics, silk velvet, Alsacian cotton fabrics, plate-printed cotton (toile de Jouy) and chintz. The novelty fabric of the day was printed with panther motifs; this was generally used to upholster chairs with feline feet, made by the cabinetmaker Bernard Molitor. Pastel colors, with a preference for yellow, alternated with bright shades, such as those discovered on the Pompeii frescoes—orange yellow, orange, Pompeii red and violet—as well as colors with such exotic names as "Spanish tobacco" and "Egyptian earth."

THE *MÉRIDIENNE*

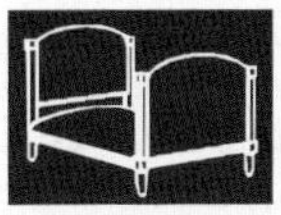

The méridienne, a type of short sofa or daybed launched by Madame Récamier, became extremely popular. Its success is most likely due to its similarity to ancient Roman beds. This piece generally had one high scroll arm, or else two scroll arms, one higher than the other.
The scroll arms were decorated with relief carvings of fantastic animals or knotted and woven laurel wreaths.

Méridiennes were supported on baluster-turned legs or animal hooves, which could be disturbingly realistic, especially in the pieces made by the cabinetmaker Bernard Molitor. Some daybeds were designed to be placed lengthwise against a wall. These had two scroll arms, each one decorated with a sculpted ball at the top. Others may have been placed on a small platform, with a Roman-style piece of fabric arranged around the foot end of the sofa.

Scroll arms

A characteristic Directoire element used for most of the daybeds and chairs. It was more or less offset to the outside, and was directly inspired by the Greek *klismos* chair.

Baluster-turned legs

This unusual leg, ordered by Madame Récamier, was considered to be a perfect symbol of the Orient.

Flange

This curved element widened out toward the bottom and joined the scroll arms to the support. The ends of these flanges were often decorated with a carved figure: the head of a dog, ram, lion, female sphinx or swan.

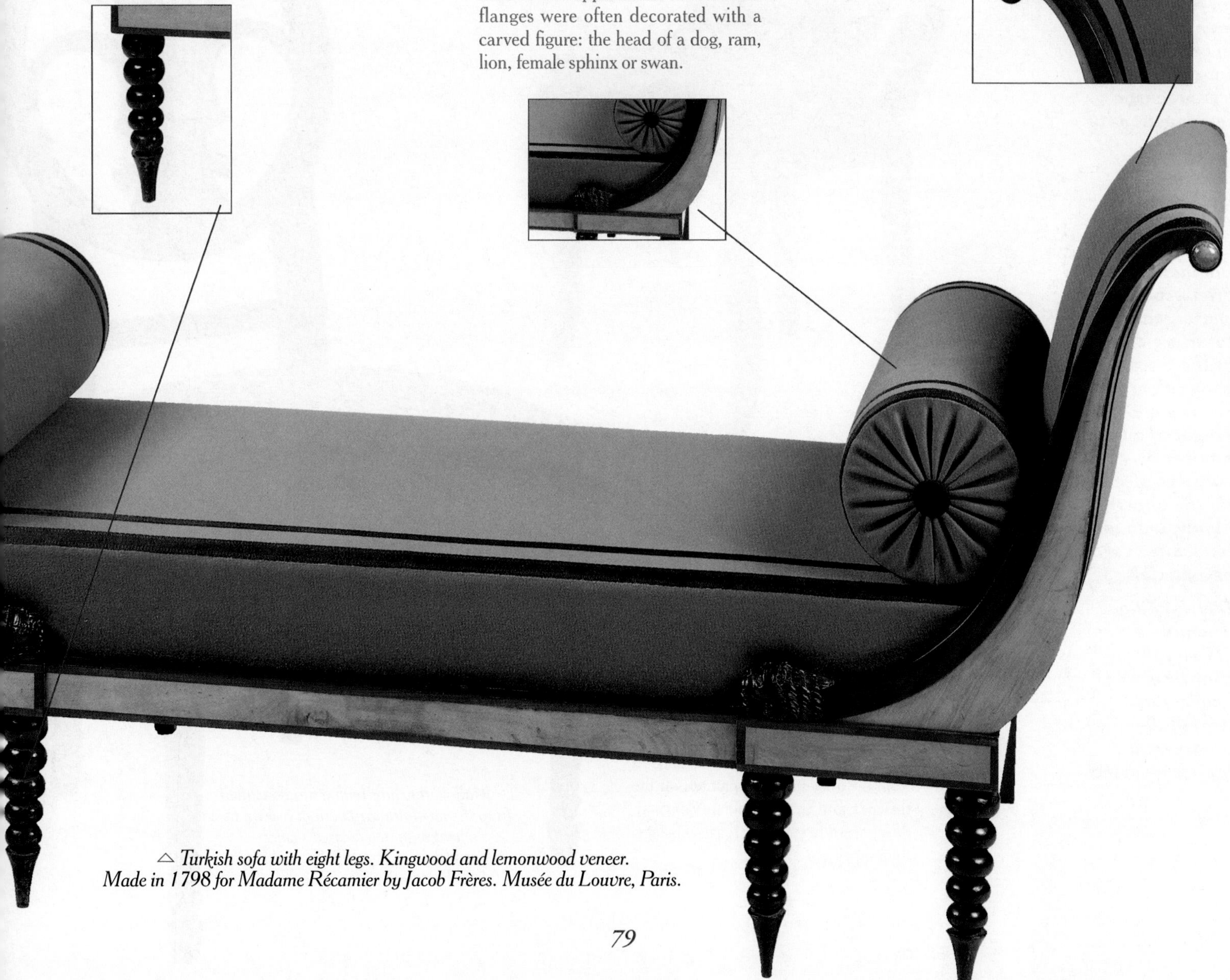

△ *Turkish sofa with eight legs. Kingwood and lemonwood veneer. Made in 1798 for Madame Récamier by Jacob Frères. Musée du Louvre, Paris.*

◆◆◆

***Georges Jacob** produced and signed a few masterpieces through 1795-1796, notably chests of drawers, which prefigured the Empire style several years before it actually developed.*

***Bernard Molitor**, named maître in 1787: Cabinetmaker, known for his inventive adaptations of antique models and his fondness for fantastic animals sculpted in relief and supports that were realistic reproductions of feline legs.*

***Martin-Guillaume Biennais** (1764-1843): Cabinetmaker, bronzesmith and chaser, and furniture-dealer at the Singe Violet shop on rue Honoré. He produced a large number of valuable pieces for the imperial family, with an innovative use of materials.*

***Pierre-Philippe Thomire** (1751-1843): Bronzesmith who created beautiful ornamental bronze elements.*

CHAIRS

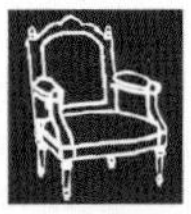

The first significant changes in furniture design appeared in chairs (bergères, stools, armchairs), with a few details prefiguring new shapes. Seat backs began to slope more toward the back and curved upward, in a break with the rigid, straight seat backs of the Louis XVI style.

Legs were no longer symmetrical in front and in back. In the front, they were tapered or turned and fluted, but always slender and high. The back legs were square and curved outward; these were known as saber legs. Aprons were not highly decorated. A new shape, a diamond pattern, appeared on the connecting boss. Arm stumps, in accordance with changing clothes designs (straight rather than hoop skirts), extended directly over the legs. These were generally baluster or column shapes, although occasionally, a winged female sphinx appeared, as in a chair by Georges Jacob, a copy of a Greek klismos. Some chair designs, such as Jacob's Etruscan chair, seemed to defy any semblance of stability. The legs were curved, forming arches that imitated elephant tusks resting on the tips. The narrow seat backs sloped backward and curved directly into the seat itself and were balanced on curved legs. Tassels, drapery and fringe were often included on these extraordinary chairs.

The favorite material in Paris was mahogany, natural beech or beech painted white or with light color. The French regions, however, demonstrated a preference for walnut left natural or painted white, and fruit wood, such as cherry.

◁ *Gondola chair, decorated with inlays. Made during the French Restauration (1814-1830) and signed by Jacob-Desmalter, from an original model by Percier. Château de Versailles.*

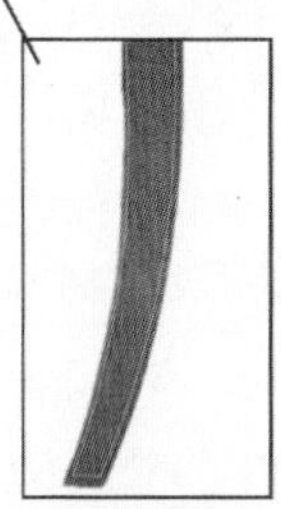

Saber leg

The rear legs were characterized by an outward curve; this design was derived from the ancient chairs painted on the frescoes and urns found in Pompeii. They were first called Etruscan legs, then saber legs.

△ *Mahogany chair with a motif inspired from the revolutionary period: a sheaf of wheat with two crossed sickles. Signed by Jean-Baptiste Séné. Musée de la Révolution française, Vizille.*

DINING ROOM TABLE

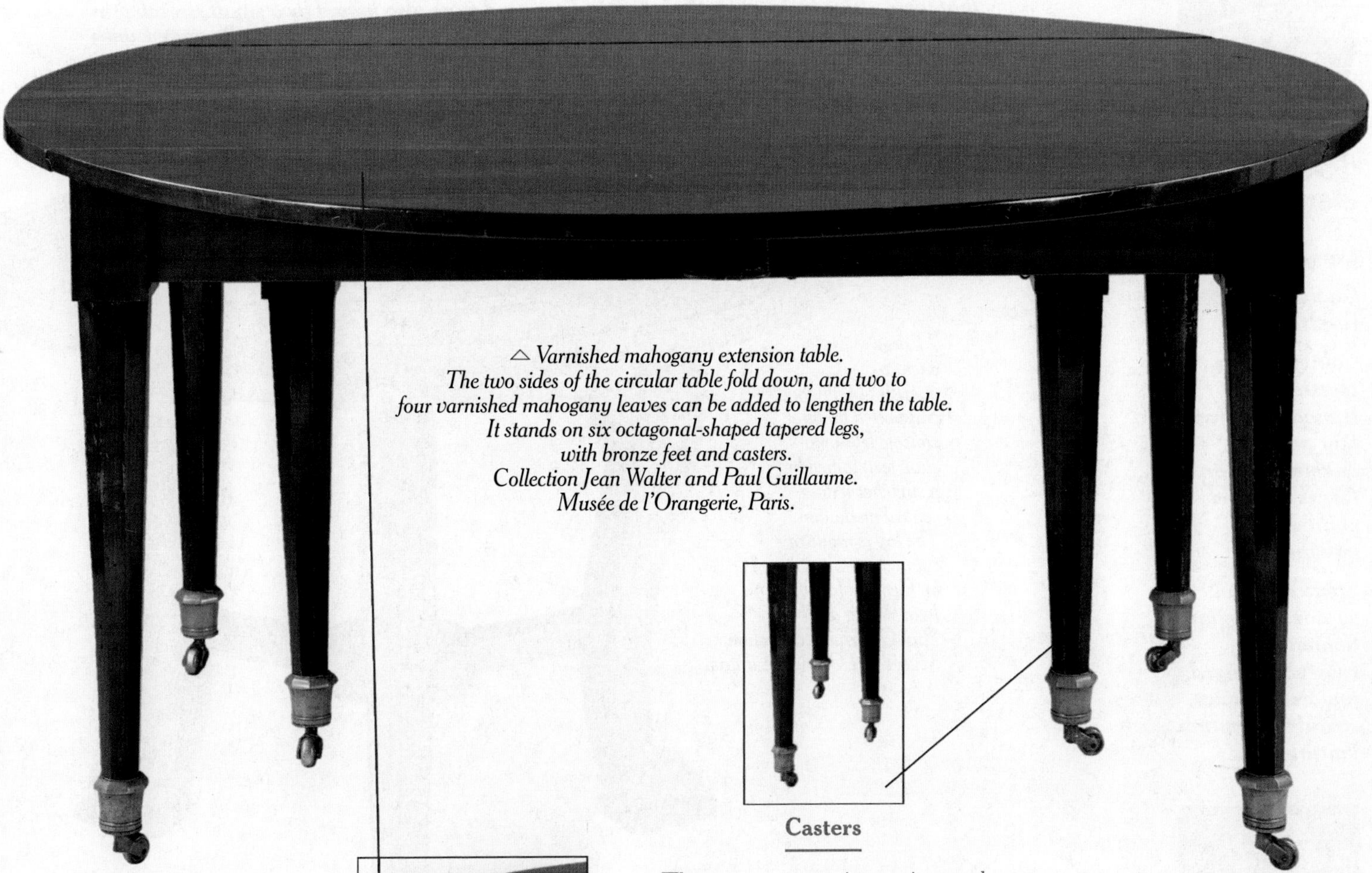

△ *Varnished mahogany extension table.*
The two sides of the circular table fold down, and two to four varnished mahogany leaves can be added to lengthen the table.
It stands on six octagonal-shaped tapered legs, with bronze feet and casters.
Collection Jean Walter and Paul Guillaume.
Musée de l'Orangerie, Paris.

Casters

These were a great innovation, and both France and Great Britain claimed to have invented them. The casters were attached to the bronze feet, making these large pieces of furniture easy to move.

Tabletop

The elegance of the table depended largely on the mahogany top, which was supposed to be thin. As in England, the thinner and straighter the tabletop, the greater its elegance.

The dining room became a specific room with permanent furniture. This new type of furniture included an oval or round mahogany table with leaves to accommodate a large number of guests. The varnished mahogany tabletop was divided into two halves that could be pulled apart, leaving room to insert extra table leaves, which were varnished like the tabletop. The table was supported by six tapered, fluted legs, ending with turned feet fitted with small bronze mounts that were sometimes fitted with casters.
A matching set of at least twelve chairs, which had sloping seat backs and were upholstered in leather or caned (for easier upkeep) surrounded the table. Other new pieces of furniture, essential to the dining room equipment, were sideboards, which were generally made in matching pairs. They were placed against the wall on either side of the entrance to the dining room. They were semicircular (called **demi-lune*****) or, more often, rectangular. These sideboards had two trays, protected by a marble slab.***
A large, deep drawer, designed for flatware, was fitted into the apron. The legs were straight, and either fluted or baluster-turned. These rested on the lower tray and ended in a characteristic ball-shaped foot.

Motifs and decorative elements

Diamond motifs

Gadrooned rosettes

Columns, urns, pilasters, truncated horns, lion paws, ancient Roman fasces, winged chimera, palemettes

Sphinxes, lion snouts, Phrygian bonnets, roosters, winged female sphinxes, scarabs, Egyptian vultures

Wood and materials

Various types of mahogany

Natural or painted beech

Walnut

Fruit trees

Elm burl, ash plane tree

Yew for expensive pieces of furniture

Gilt copper, silver, silver-gilt, blued steel

THE *GUÉRIDON*

Guéridons, or candlestands, were extremely popular. The design was inspired directly from ancient Roman tables that were often depicted on the recently discovered frescoes in Pompeii. They had a circular tabletop that rested on a tripod support. They were made of wood or marble or a combination of these different materials: for example, a table with a marble top and a giltwood stand, or a marble top with a metal stand.
The three curved legs joined up at the top and were also joined by a small stretcher in the middle. The legs generally ended with lion's paw feet. The top on smaller versions of these tables sometimes folded down, like the English sun tables.

▷ *Large circular guéridon. Giltwood. Supported by three console legs with claw feet, joined by a stretcher with a central medallion. The top is made of colored marble. Signed by Georges Jacob. Jean Walter and Paul Guillaume collection. Musée de l'Orangerie, Paris.*

◁ *Jardinière, or plant-holder, oak frame, mahogany, giltwood, gilt bronze and copper. Signed by Martin-Guillaume Biennais. 1800-1801. Musée du Louvre, Paris.*

THE *JARDINIÈRE*

A number of small, odd-shaped pieces of furniture, including work tables and vide-poches (small tables with rimmed tops to hold the contents of a man's pockets) appeared. Others, such as the jardinière (plantholder), perfume burner and athénienne (washstand), were often made, at least partly, of metal.

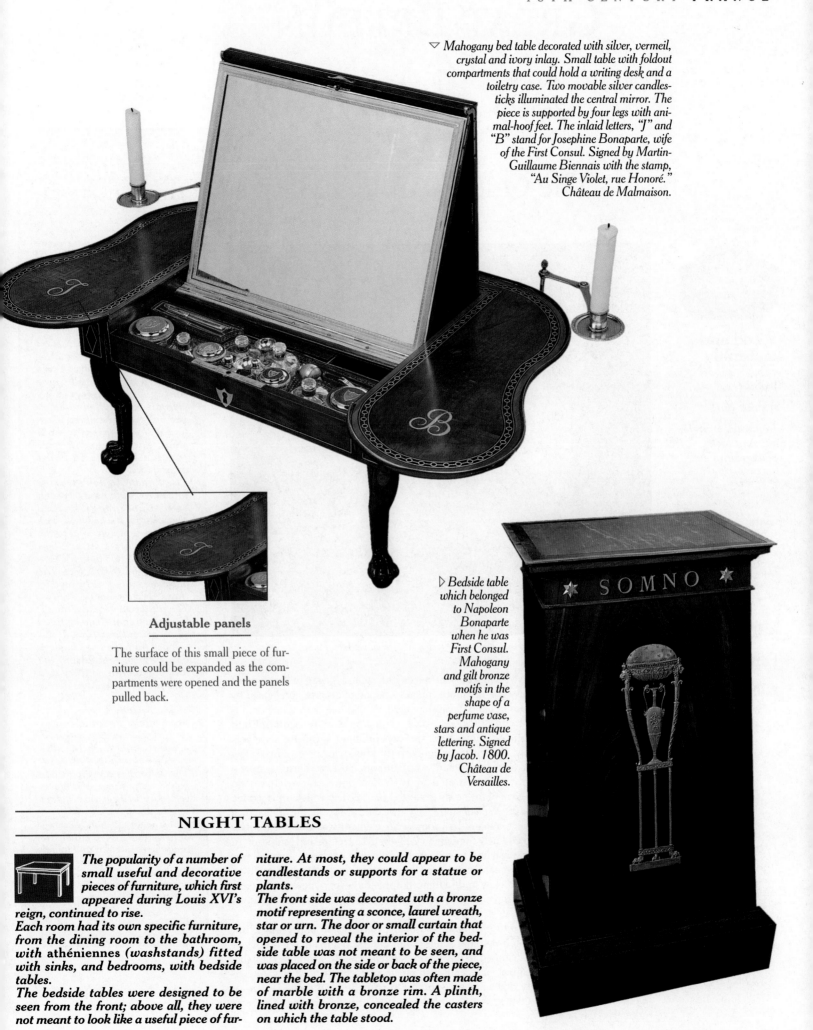

▽ *Mahogany bed table decorated with silver, vermeil, crystal and ivory inlay. Small table with foldout compartments that could hold a writing desk and a toiletry case. Two movable silver candlesticks illuminated the central mirror. The piece is supported by four legs with animal-hoof feet. The inlaid letters, "J" and "B" stand for Josephine Bonaparte, wife of the First Consul. Signed by Martin-Guillaume Biennais with the stamp, "Au Singe Violet, rue Honoré." Château de Malmaison.*

Adjustable panels

The surface of this small piece of furniture could be expanded as the compartments were opened and the panels pulled back.

▷ *Bedside table which belonged to Napoleon Bonaparte when he was First Consul. Mahogany and gilt bronze motifs in the shape of a perfume vase, stars and antique lettering. Signed by Jacob. 1800. Château de Versailles.*

NIGHT TABLES

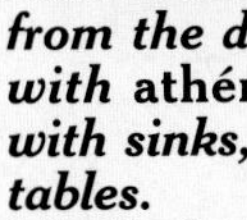

The popularity of a number of small useful and decorative pieces of furniture, which first appeared during Louis XVI's reign, continued to rise.
Each room had its own specific furniture, from the dining room to the bathroom, with athéniennes ***(washstands) fitted with sinks, and bedrooms, with bedside tables.***
The bedside tables were designed to be seen from the front; above all, they were not meant to look like a useful piece of furniture. At most, they could appear to be candlestands or supports for a statue or plants.
The front side was decorated wth a bronze motif representing a sconce, laurel wreath, star or urn. The door or small curtain that opened to reveal the interior of the bedside table was not meant to be seen, and was placed on the side or back of the piece, near the bed. The tabletop was often made of marble with a bronze rim. A plinth, lined with bronze, concealed the casters on which the table stood.

GREAT BRITAIN

1695 1714

The Queen Anne Style

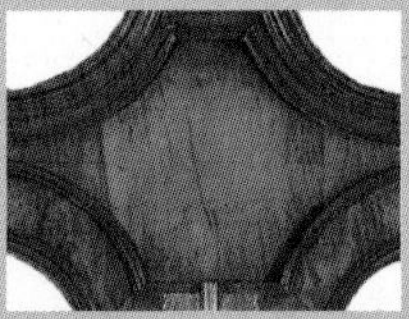

Wood and material

Walnut

Walnut burl

Japanned panels, gilt on black background

Bronze

Mirrors

Glass

Fabrics

Petit point embroidery

Leather

△ The Conjurer. *Philippe Mercier. Musée du Louvre, Paris.*

The Queen Anne style, named for the queen of England, began to develop just as the reign of Louis XIV in France entered a period of decline, accelerated by the king's illness, famines and the austere taste of Madame de Maintenon, his wife. During the reign of Queen Anne, who would unite Scotland and England and fiercely oppose Louis XIV, the predominant furniture style was characterized by simplicity, efficiency and modernity. This style borrowed very few elements from the Rococo fashion that had swept through most northern European countries. This modernity was illustrated by two major innovations: curves on furniture supports, in the form of the newly perfected cabriole leg, which replaced the turned legs popular during the William and Mary style, and above all, the appearance of the highly characteristic claw-and-ball foot. This element was derived directly from an element that was extremely common in Chinese architecture and sculpture. In China, this motif was generally a lion's paw, clutching a ball in its claws. This ball was of varying size: it could be much larger than the claws or tiny, offering numerous decorative possibilities. The claw-and-ball motif appeared everywhere on English furniture throughout the eighteenth and nineteenth centuries, becoming the most defining feature of the English style.

It also appeared in furniture made in Germany, Italy, Spain and Russia, but rarely in French furniture. The success of this motif, unprecedented in the history of ornamentation, must be attributed to power and strength clearly symbolized by this motif, a vitality that all the great eighteenth- and nineteenth-century powers wanted to secure. Furthermore, few other ancient Chinese ornamental motifs had such an impact on European aesthetics. On the other hand, no European ornament has ever influenced Chinese styles.

MAIN PIECES OF FURNITURE

The tallboy was a case piece that consisted of one chest of drawers on top of another. The bottom chest had two drawers and was wider than the top chest, which was slightly recessed and had three long drawers and a row of short drawers.
Card tables were either rectangular or semicircular; the latter was a folding table that could be placed against a wall. These tables were supported by cabriole legs ending in claw-and-ball feet. The apron often had dished corners to hold chips. They were sometimes covered with petit point embroidery.
The kneehole desk was as uncomfortable as its French equivalent, the bureau Mazarin, *but the kneehole desk was wide enough to actually accommodate a sitter's legs between the two uprights supported by fairly high feet. The kneehole space was framed by three deep drawers.*
The tilt-top table had a round, hinged top that could be tilted to a vertical position. It developed from the French guéridon, *or pedestal table, in the late eighteenth century and became fairly common during the reigns of Louis-Philippe and Napoleon III.*
Seat backs became lower, creating a chair that was well-proportioned with the ubiquitous claw-and-ball foot. The splat was an unadorned panel in the shape of a baluster. The arm stumps were scroll-shaped.
Stools were extremely simple in design and were either rectangular or circular and upholstered with petit point fabric. The legs ended in claw-and-ball feet.

THE *SCRIBAN*

The design of secretaries and scribans kept certain elements from the previous centuries: an upper section in the form of a chest of drawers, with compartments arranged asymmetrically in relation to the central niche. The three compartments generally framed three rows of drawers. The chest had two doors, which were solid, covered with mirrors or japanning or—an innovation—made of glass, revealing the chest inside. This piece was topped by a bonnet top pediment, which was sometimes decorated with a carved finial. The upper section rested on a chest of drawers of differing sizes; when the top one could be folded or pulled out to form a desk, the piece was called a scriban. The desk was sometimes a slant-top. The entire piece of furniture stood on bracket feet or on a molded plinth.

Elaborate pediment

The extremely serpentine pediment has a bonnet shape that caps two glass doors; these repeat the same curve as the pediment, forming an extremely elegant geometric design.

▷ *Secretary made of walnut burl with molded pediment. Double glass doors open to reveal a chest with drawers and compartments, resting on a chest of drawers with four rows of drawers of different sizes. Low bracket feet. Ca 1710. Sotheby's, London.*

▽ Walnut bachelor's chest. *Ca 1710. The top folds down. Two narrow drawers and three long drawers. Sotheby's, London.*

BACHELOR'S CHEST

The bachelor's chest was the most famous chest of drawers designed during the Queen Anne style. It consisted of four rows of drawers, three wide ones and two narrow. The top had a hinged leaf that could be folded out to form a desk. The writing surface was supported by two lopers, or sliding arms that extended on either side of the two small drawers. An unusual feature of this chest of drawers is that none of the drawers were the same size, as they became smaller toward the top of the chest. The piece of furniture rested on short legs known as bracket feet.

GREAT BRITAIN

1714  1760

The Early Georgian Style

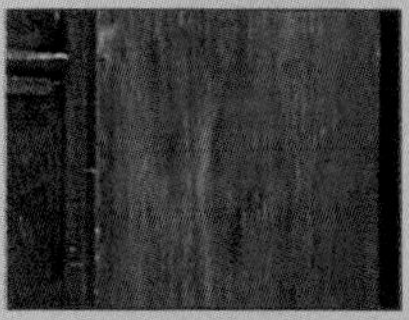

Wood and material

West Indian mahogany

△ Family reunion. *William Hogarth. Christie's, London.*

With the ascendancy of King George I (1660-1727), a German, to the throne in 1714, England changed dynasties from the house of Stuart to the house of Hanover. This German dynasty would rule the country throughout the eighteenth and nineteenth centuries and part of the twentieth century. When an embargo on walnut was imposed by the French government in 1720, English designers and furniture-makers turned to a wood that became widely used: mahogany, particularly West Indian mahogany. Throughout the eighteenth century and early nineteenth century, its red color, usually heightened by varnish, became the chief feature of English furniture. One of the advantages of mahogany is that the entire length of the tree trunk can be used; furniture-makers could create immense tables from a single piece. More resistant to rotting than other wood, mahogany became the favorite material, especially as it could be carved into spectacularly precise and delicate forms.

This period, known as Early Georgian, also includes the reign of George II (1727-1760). From a stylistic point of view, the start of George I's reign was distinguished by a revival of the Italian Renaissance and the Palladian style, but was soon after replaced by the French Rococo style, with its curves and serpentine forms. The most striking stylistic influence, however, came from China; English design was soon subjugated by this country (as evidenced by the claw-and-ball motif introduced during Queen Anne's reign). Under George I, the Chinese influence was most clearly marked by the use of lacquers, a technique adopted by almost every other European country as well. Entire lacquered panels and furniture pieces were imported from China and then adapted to European fashions.

The Georgian style in England was influenced not only by Chinese lacquer, but also by specific stylistic elements such as geometric patterns and tracery. These were combined, in a somewhat startling way, with figures derived from Gothic and Celtic art. By the end of George I's reign, mahogany had become the most widely used wood by far and was adorned with bronze or contrasting wood marquetry, similar to styles that were in practice elsewhere through Europe, notably in France under Louis XV and Louis XVI.

OTHER FURNITURE

The dressing table was a new furniture design. It consisted of a case piece resting on four legs interconnected by a stretcher. It may have been fitted with a kneehole. Another feature was an adjustable mirror attached to the rear crosspiece of the table frieze.

Kneehole

As its name suggests, this element allowed a person to sit at the desk without bumping his knees against the desk drawers. In this piece, the kneehole section has an elaborate cut-out design.

Adjustable writing surface

The sliding panel is pulled out by two small rings on either side of the panel.

CHAIRS

Almost all chairs had claw-and-ball feet, but the legs could be straight and square in shape and interconnected by a stretcher. The seat backs were decorated with arabesques and scrolls or openwork motifs derived from Chinese design, with a pagoda motif on the crest rail. The armrests were supported by S-shaped arm stumps. The chairs were upholstered with fabric or leather. The grandfather chair, or wing chair, differed from the French version, called a confessional chair, in that it was entirely covered with fabric.

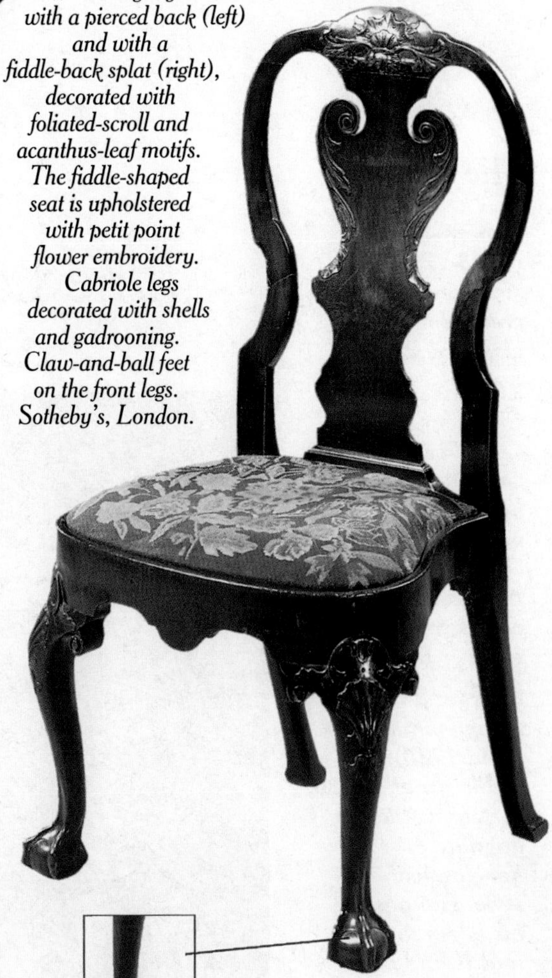

◁▷ *Mahogany chairs with a pierced back (left) and with a fiddle-back splat (right), decorated with foliated-scroll and acanthus-leaf motifs. The fiddle-shaped seat is upholstered with petit point flower embroidery. Cabriole legs decorated with shells and gadrooning. Claw-and-ball feet on the front legs. Sotheby's, London.*

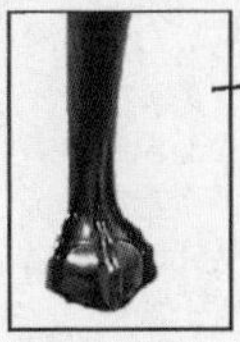

Claw-and-ball foot

The claw-and-ball motif (three claws holding a wall) was derived directly from an ornament common in Chinese furniture. It became one of the most characteristic features of English chair and table legs during the eighteenth and nineteenth centuries.

△ Walnut chest on stand. *It consists of a chest of drawers (four rows) topped by a straight cornice, which rests on a desk with a sliding writing surface, and two rows of drawers separated by a kneehole space. George II. Christie's, London.*

SECRETARIES AND DESKS

Several types of secretaries and desks coexisted: a chest on stand, a chest on a chest, a tallboy chest, a scriban (desk-bookcase) or a simple desk, a chest of drawers with a fall-front or slant-top writing surface. These various types of desks, which generally had two sections, gradually developed into a single piece with drawers under the tabletop. Desks generally consisted of a chest of drawers with two rows of wide drawers and a single row of smaller drawers, with a slanted top that could be used as a writing surface.
In more sophisticated designs, the desk had an upper section that formed a cabinet. In this case, the furniture had a pediment, scalloped cornices or openwork motifs.

The masters

***Robert Adam (1728-1792):** Architect; he created a neo-classical style.*

***Thomas Chippendale (1718-1779):** Cabinetmaker; he invented the pierced-back chair, a design repeated by cabinetmakers all over Europe.*

***George Hepplewhite (died 1786):** Cabinetmaker; softened Adam's angular neoclassical style. Famous for his geometric motifs and book of designs,* **The Cabinet Maker and Upholsterer's Guide,** *published in 1788.*

***Thomas Sheraton (1751-1806):** Cabinetmaker; his elegant style, drawn from the French Louis XVI and Directoire styles, spread throughout Europe and to the United States.*

Wood and materials

Mahogany, lemonwood, beech, maple, satinwood

GREAT BRITAIN

1760 — *1800*

The Late Georgian Style

△ Ralph Willett, bibliophile and collector. *George Romney. Musée du Louvre, Paris.*

This style refers to furniture made during the reign of George III and parallels the Transition, Louis XVI, Directoire and, to a certain extent, the Empire styles. This was a flourishing period in English art, so much so that when people speak of the Georgian style, they are really referring to the Late Georgian, or George III, style. It is characterized by a high degree of refinement, a quest for greater comfort, references to past centuries and foreign civilizations, and by innovations that ran counter to the aesthetic directives of the era. These stylistic innovations were developed primarily by three great cabinetmakers: Thomas Chippendale, George Hepplewhite and Thomas Sheraton. The first two are famous for the neoclassical elegance of their furniture designs, while Sheraton is known for his pattern works, especially his Drawing Book. The most common marquetry motif was the umbrella, placed within an oval or triangular shape. Thin lines of marquetry and light wood rosettes on mahogany were often included with this motif. For lighter-colored furniture, mahogany dominated, with inlays of wreaths, bouquets and cameos inspired from Wedgwood pottery. Wedgwood plaques featuring white cameos on a darker background (blue, beige, green, red or, more rarely, black) were fitted into furniture pieces. Japanning was used for diverse pieces of furniture, from chests of drawers to large secretaries.

SETTEE

The settee, made of mahogany and upholstered with fabric, was an elegant piece of furniture. It consisted of a carved open seat back that repeated the motif on the splat, or central panel, of matching armchairs. The upholstered seat was supported by cabriole legs, decorated with acanthus leaves or foliated scrolls, which ended in scroll or claw-and-ball feet.

▽ *Semicircular console with giltwood and marquetry. The tabletop is decorated with marquetry: foliage in the center, with radiating motifs of shells, fans and stylized flowers. Giltwood support, consisting of a fluted frieze and central shell motif surrounded by acanthus leaves, with four fluted giltwood legs. Attributed to Thomas Chippendale. 1770. Sotheby's, London.*

▽ Breakfront library bookcase made of mahogany. It consists of a large central case with diamond-pattern glass doors and a broken pediment framed by two side cases with star-pattern glass doors with bonnet pediments. These rest on a lower section with two sets of molded panel doors over a wide plinth. Thomas Chippendale. 1760. Sotheby's, London.

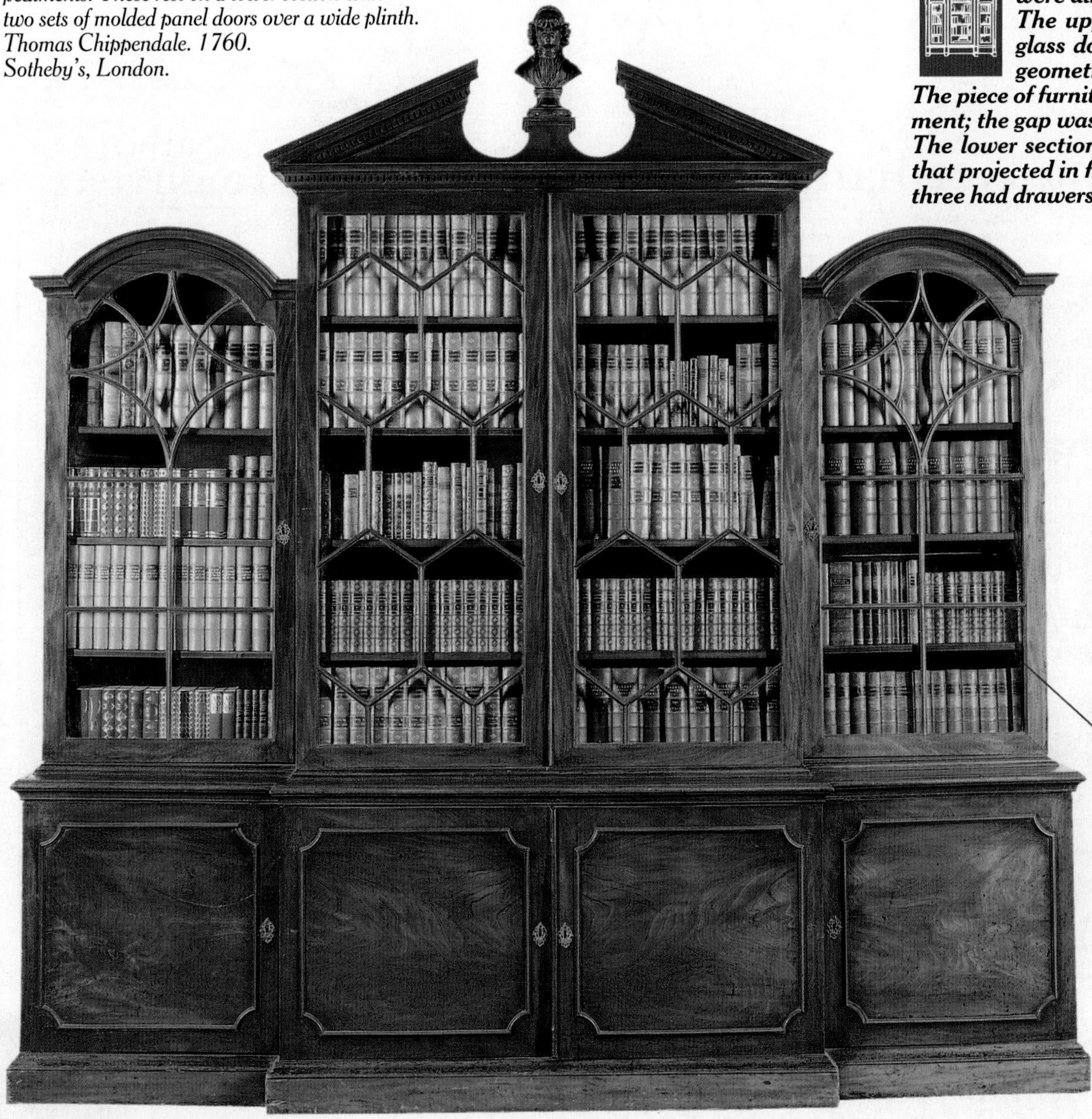

BOOKCASE

Bookcases, consisting of two sections, were almost always made of mahogany. The upper section had a series of four glass doors, decorated with fretwork in geometric patterns. The piece of furniture is topped with a broken pediment; the gap was used to display a bust or a vase. The lower section consisted of a central element that projected in front of the two side elements; all three had drawers or doors.

Partitioned glass doors

The glass doors were divided into sections by mahogany fretwork that formed stylized geometric patterns, such as diamonds, squares, rectangles, stars or half-circles, which recall motifs used in stained glass.

TABLES

The George III style inaugurated several innovations to table design. The dining room table, a well-proportioned piece usually made of mahogany, could be extended by means of extra leaves. The tabletop was rectangular, round, octagonal or sometimes even pentagonal. Depending on how long it was, it rested on one or two tripod supports, which were fitted with copper rollers to make it easier to move around. The side table and the sofa table began to appear in living rooms, placed next to chairs or behind canapés and sofas, as they are today. The writing table, still an extremely simple piece of furniture, was covered with leather and was roomy enough for two people to sit across from each other. A smaller version of this writing table existed; it had a drawer that opened on the side and a pull-out slide on the front. Even more surprising was the design of some fireplace screens, which sometimes had a built-in writing surface. The Pembroke table, a type of drop-leaf table, was the pièce de resistance among furniture design during George III's reign. It was a small table with two drop leaves and a rectangular, oval or serpentine-shape tabletop made of mahogany or maple and decorated with marquetry or arabesques. The legs were square, tapered or oval in shape. Every great English cabinetmaker designed a version of the Pembroke table. The most remarkable are the designs made by Thomas Chippendale, featuring drawers, and by Sheraton, in which the body of the table conceals a series of compartments that lifted up mechanically, somewhat like toolboxes today.

Germany

1725 — 1788

The German Rococo Style

△ *New Palace, 1763-1769. Potsdam.*

Eighteenth-century Germany, or Prussia as it was called at the time, was not a unified country. The principalities, duchies and earldoms of Germany formed a diverse group. There were two movements: the English influence, which was strong in the northern principalities, and Louis XV's Rococo style, introduced by the king of Prussia, Frederick the Great. These two influences, along with an Italian influence in the southern principalities, co-existed and even exchanged certain elements; in any case, these styles were always freely reinterpreted. Toward the middle of the century, the Rococo style finally became predominant, starting in Berlin. Rarely has there been such an exuberant official style, encouraged by the brilliant skills of the best German artists and craftsmen. The reputation of the German cabinetmakers spread far beyond the country's borders to all of Europe. In France, Queen Marie-Antoinette granted the highly coveted title, queen's cabinetmaker, to a German who lived and worked in Germany: David Röentgen. Catherine the Great, empress of Russia, invited this same Röentgen to settle in Saint Petersburg.

German Rococo was a style of exaggerated curves, exuberant decors and profuse ornamentation. Furniture, which had to fit with the decor of a room, became lighter in color. Curves and S-shapes proliferated. Everything was excessively denticulated, outlined, destructured and asymmetrical. The fashion was to accumulate motifs and use different materials: gigantic acanthus leaves, immense openwork shells, overwhelming drapery, chubby cupids, overstuffed quivers, wide palm leaves, full bouquets, cornucopias and jagged bat wings. Profusion was the word of the day. Bronze, gold, silver, mother-of-pearl, stone, ivory and porcelain were used in abundance for furniture designed specifically to dazzle. The only exceptions to this taste of the spectacular were chairs: most of them were designed simply and made of mahogany, with pierced splats (the central piece of the seat back).

The masters

***Joan Melchior Kambli (1718-1783):* Based in Potsdam, he was famous for his marquetry chairs with gilt-bronze mounts.**

***Johann and Heinrich Spindler:* They created spectacular furniture of state with sumptuously ornate mother-of-pearl, tortoiseshell, ivory and silver inlays (see the Frederick II commode in Potsdam's New Palace).**

***Abraham Röentgen (1711-1793):* Father of David Röentgen, the famous cabinetmaker and engineer; worked for Queen Marie-Antoinette of France and was the favorite cabinetmaker of Catherine the Great, empress of Russia.**

MAIN PIECES OF FURNITURE

Consoles and tables provided a backdrop for exaggerated displays of the Rococo style. Some of these are masterpieces of invention and skill, due to the complexity of the figures depicted on them.

Chairs and armchairs adopted and exaggerated the Rococo curves and counter-curves, but most were derived from the English caned chair with a pierced back.

Armoires were still extremely popular and remained so, despite the growing fashion for chests of drawers. Still decorated with strong curves, they were made in the Rococo style with curving shapes and protruding facades. These same characteristics appeared on ebony cabinets and buffets.

DESKS

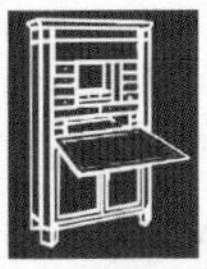

French-style slant-top desks were often decorated with masterpieces of marquetry. Toward the end of the century, roll-top desks with a tambour (narrow strips of wood glued side by side against a cloth backing) appeared, modeled after a famous French desk invented by two German cabinetmakers living in France and working for the crown: Jean-François Œben et Jean-Henri Riesener.

▷ *Secretary-cabinet with a marquetry pattern of foliated scrolls and flowers, and gilt metal. The upper section consists of a central glass case with curved legs, topped with an ebony pediment and framed by side shelves. It rests on a chest of drawers with a curved front and two doors. Christie's, London.*

Marquetry

German cabinetmakers were renowned for their marquetry skills, and the Rococo style gave them a free rein to demonstrate their imagination and talent in remarkably delicate works.

lant-top desk and drawers, made of walnut. entine front with three drawers a slant-top writing surface. Southern Germany. stie's, London.

DESKS WITH DRAWERS

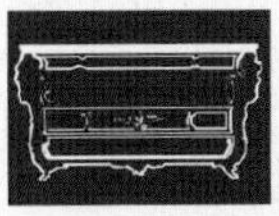

Chests of drawers first appeared in Germany in the early eighteenth century. They were generally made of walnut or a veneer of exotic woods. With the advent of the Rococo style, they became more rounded in shape, but still well-proportioned; they were ornately decorated or even painted in the Italian style in the southern principalities. Inspired directly from the English scriban, a chest-bookcase appeared in the north; it consisted of a lower section with two or three drawers, on which sat a glass-front armoire, which was relatively austere for the era.

ITALY

1700 — 1769

The Baroque Style

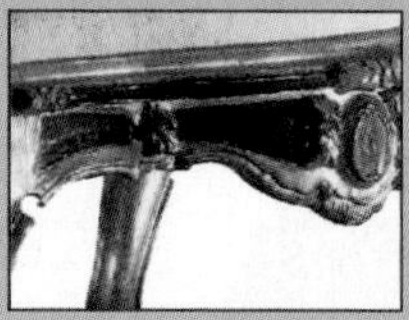

Wood and materials

Walnut for chests of drawers

Veneers of various woods and walnut but for marquetry

Gilt and silvered wood

Scagliola: *a material used to imitate marble, made from lime, gypsum, powdered marble and sand, bound together with water, glue and colors*

Mother-of-pearl, shells

Stone, marble and wood trompe-l'œil patterns

△ Benoît XIV. *Giuseppe Maria Crespi. Vatican, Rome.*

The Rococo style reached its peak in early eighteenth-century Italy. This style, also called the Petit Baroque, appeared as the final stage of Baroque aesthetics. The excesses in examples of this style have a certain charm. The guiding principle was decor for the sake of decor—a concept at which Venetian artists excelled. Furniture was designed to be seen rather than actually used, and indeed, most of it was unimaginably uncomfortable. Some pieces disappeared almost completely under the excessive sculptural elements. Chubby, winged cupids climbed up the sides of seat backs and the legs of armchairs, as they clutched coats of arms, quivers or hearts. Acanthus leaves were intertwined to excess, while jagged shells and bat wings filled up any remaining available space. These distorted sculptures and molding were often painted green, yellow or light blue with gold highlights. Imitation was encouraged: imitation marble, stone, multicolored stones, wood, draperies and Chinese lacquered panels. Every surface was an opportunity for a trompe-l'œil element, applied using such techniques as *alla povera*, *scagliola*, a mixture of plaster and powdered stone use to imitate marble, collage and varnishing of printed papers, and colored plaster made from a base of lime and glue. Stylized and natural shells became a major decorative motif.

MAIN PIECES OF FURNITURE

Venetian chests of drawers in the early eighteenth century somewhat resembled the French commode-tombeau, with the exception that the curve of the facade and sides was much more pronounced on the Venetian furniture, and that the tabletop was decorated with a trompe-l'oeil motif, rather than real marble.
The studiolo was a secretary that was a direct inspiration from the stipi cabinets.
The scriban was a type of slant-type desk or bureau on short, extremely curved feet.
Flat desks were characterized by an upper section and excessively curved legs, a tabletop and frieze covered with carved wreaths and often inlaid with mother-of-pearl and shells.

Sculpted decor

This defining feature of the Rococo style was generally placed at the bottom of consoles. On this piece, the decor represents a bucolic scene with several figures in a grotto formed by the asymmetrical pattern of the intertwined plants.

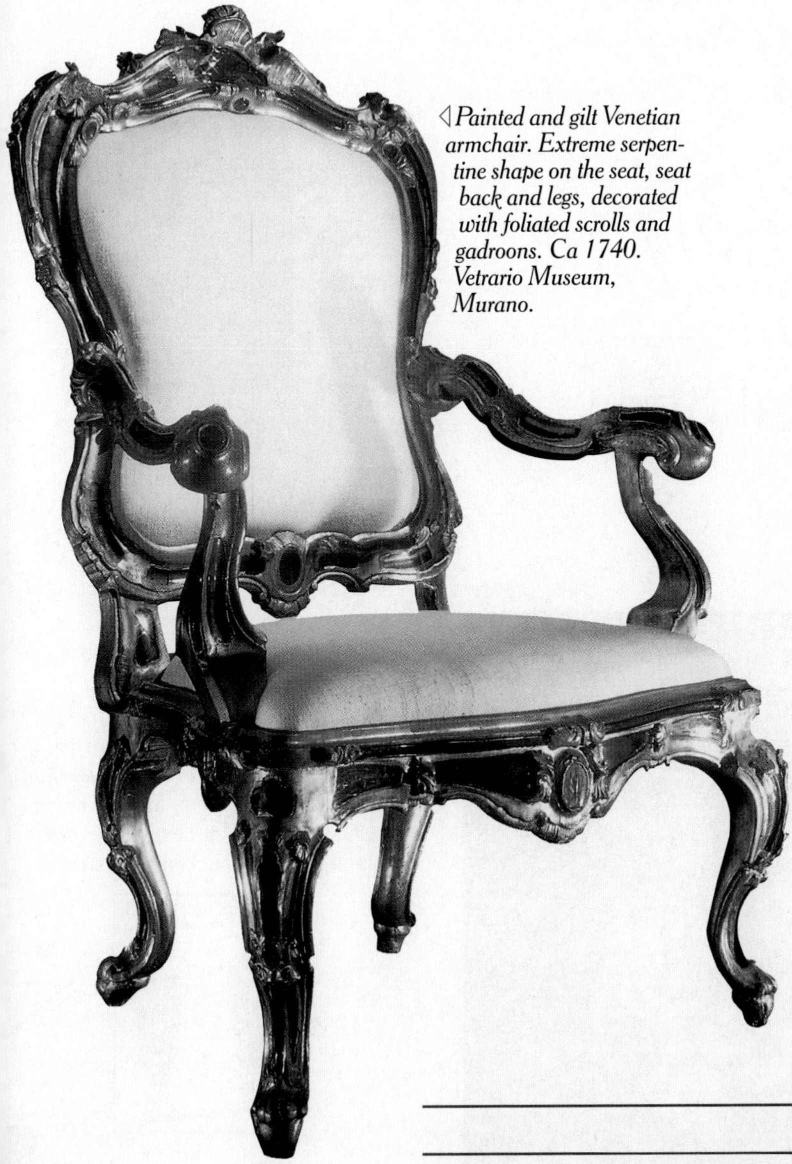

◁ Painted and gilt Venetian armchair. Extreme serpentine shape on the seat, seat back and legs, decorated with foliated scrolls and gadroons. Ca 1740. Vetrario Museum, Murano.

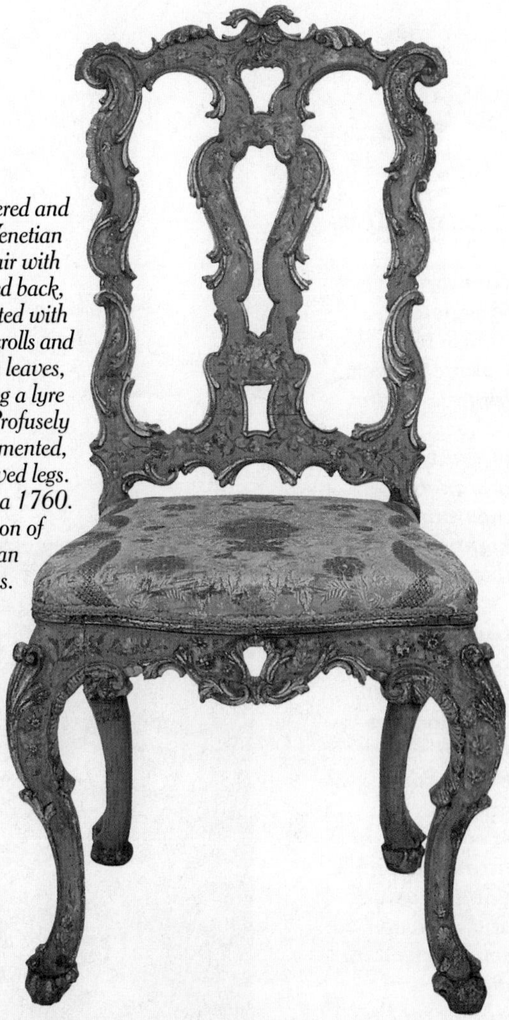

▷ Lacquered and gilt Venetian chair with pierced back, decorated with foliated scrolls and acanthus leaves, forming a lyre shape. Profusely ornamented, curved legs. Ca 1760. Collection of the Milan museums.

CHAIRS

Chairs were no exception to the rule of abundant ornamentation. These chairs of state were notoriously uncomfortable, designed to fill up reception rooms with additional sculptural pieces. The seat backs were so straight and so highly carved and shaped that it was difficult to remain seated for long. Yet they were unrivaled as symbols of luxury, splendor and wealth.

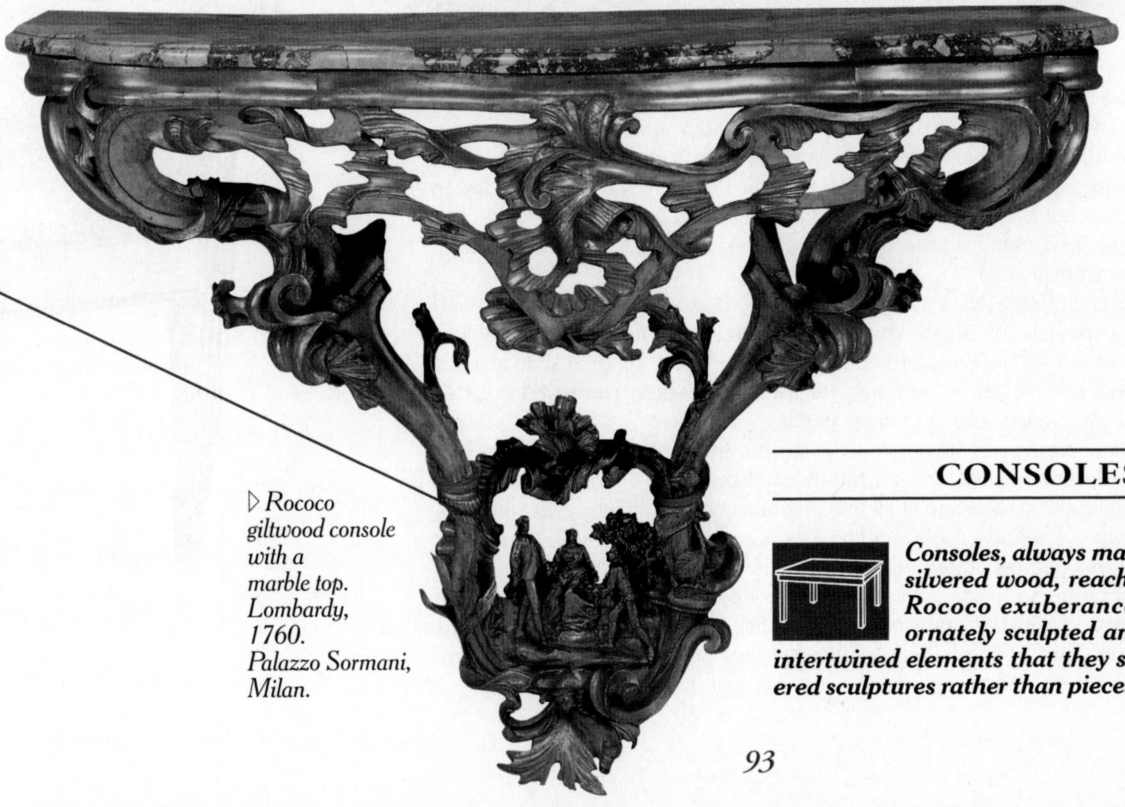

▷ Rococo giltwood console with a marble top. Lombardy, 1760. Palazzo Sormani, Milan.

CONSOLES

Consoles, always made of giltwood or silvered wood, reached an apogee of Rococo exuberance; they were so ornately sculpted and with so many intertwined elements that they should be considered sculptures rather than pieces of furniture.

The masters

Giuseppe Maggiolini (1738-1814): Cabinetmaker, famous for his remarkable chest of drawers with marquetry incorporating highly diverse woods.

Giuseppe Maria Bonzanigo (1745-1820): Sculptor and Italian neoclassical master specializing in furniture with painted wood and giltwood sculptures with wreath and ribbon motifs.

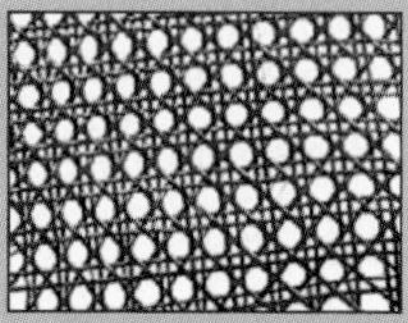

Wood and materials

Walnut

Walnut burl

Wood painted in colors of cream, gray, sea green

Giltwood

Caned seats with wide weave

Marble

Gilt bronze

ITALY

1769  *1804*

The Neoclassical Style

△ Family concert. *Pietro Longhi. Pinacoteca des palazzo di Brera, Milan.*

The discovery of Herculaneum and Pompeii did not produce the same results in Italy as in France. A return to neoclassical design and decoration did not occur until the early 1770s, when the architect Giovanni Piranesi published engravings depicting ancient Rome. It is ironic that Italy was one of the last to be inspired by neoclassical design, given that the inspiration for the movement—the ancient cultures—originated on the Italian penisula, and ruins of the civilization were part of everyday life.

Using the French Louis XVI style as an example, the neoclassical movement and imitations of ancient styles did finally come to Italy, and several master cabinetmakers adopted it to produce brilliant masterpieces. Nevertheless, the Rococo style was not completely abandoned and, as in Germany, Italian cabinetmakers continued to create floral decors, ornate tracery and gilt foliage motifs.

The curvilinear forms of furniture were gradually ironed out, straight lines reappeared, and curves, although not totally excluded from furniture, were less exaggerated, especially on table and chair legs. Motifs such as palmettes, wreaths, scallops, ovolos, rosettes, garlands, cable molding, beads and ribbons replaced the tracery. Chests of drawers were decorated with sumptuous geometric marquetry patterns, inspired from Pompeian frescoes, or marquetry depicting allegorical scenes and mythological figures. Venetian craftsmen adapted their skills in Rococo design to the neoclassical rules, but none of them totally gave up polychrome wood and gilt sculptures, which remained permanent characteristics of Italian furniture design.

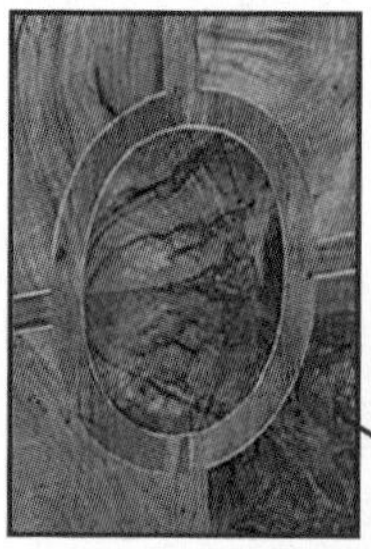

Marquetry

Oval or medallion marquetry motifs were derived from an ancient figure that was widespread on frescoes found in wealthy homes in Pompeii.

Antique urns

The Roman urn was copied from frescoes found in Pompeii. In this piece, the reference to ancient Rome is heightened by repeating the motif along the entire back of the settee.

MAIN PIECES OF FURNITURE

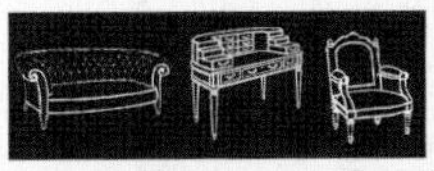

Generally speaking, these were the same as during the preceding period, with a distinct increase in the number of chests of drawers, which gradually replaced cabinets. Console tables were still in fashion and were often decorated with neoclassical attributes. Settees and sofas finally became more comfortable, and were designed to be used, rather than merely seen.

◁ *Writing cabinet made of walnut burl and geometric marquetry patterns. The top folds out over the top four drawers (two of which are false) to form a writing surface. It has two front doors and two side doors. Late eighteenth century. Christie's, London.*

▷ *Neoclassical Piedmontese armchair, inspired from the French style, with caned back and upholstered seat with a silk festoon pattern. Private collection. Avignon.*

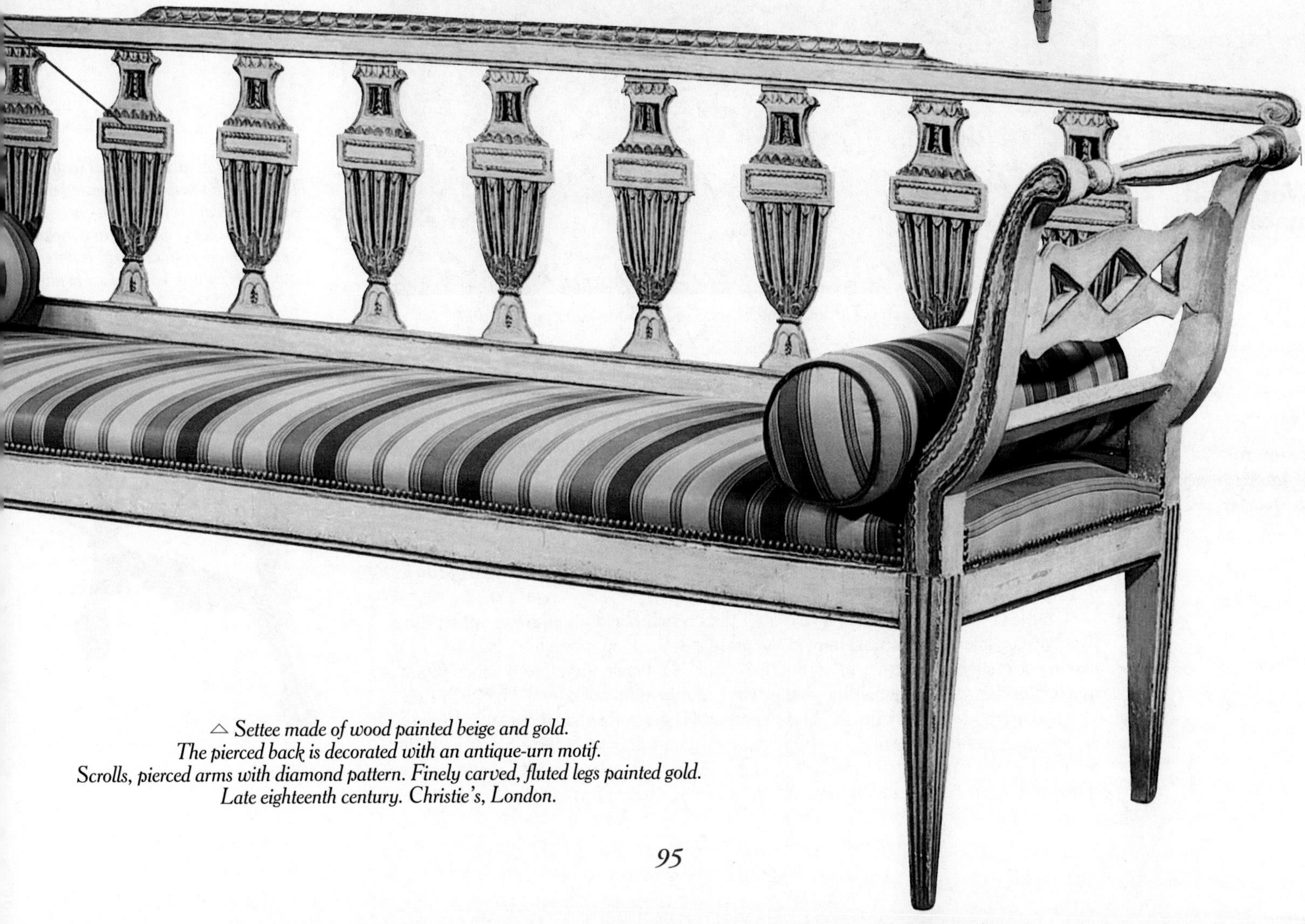

△ *Settee made of wood painted beige and gold. The pierced back is decorated with an antique-urn motif. Scrolls, pierced arms with diamond pattern. Finely carved, fluted legs painted gold. Late eighteenth century. Christie's, London.*

Spain

1715 1808

Rococo and Neoclassicism

△ General Antonio Ricardos. *Francisco de Goya. Prado Museum, Madrid.*

Spain could not escape the influence of France and England in furniture design, no more than any other European country could. The French influence on Spain was even greater in that the king crowned in 1700, Philip V, was none other than a grandson of Louis XIV. Because of this rather unique political context—a result of the Treaty of Utrecht ending the Spanish War of Secession—Spanish cabinetmakers and furniture-makers naturally adopted the Rococo style reigning in France. Philip V, however, then had two successive wives, both Italian princesses, which tempered the omnipresent French influence somewhat and added a slight touch of the Italian Rococo. This trend intensified with the appointment of the Neapolitan decorator Gasparini as director of the Manufactura Real (Royal Workshops).

Charles IV's reign began one year after the French Revolution broke out, ending twenty years later by his abdication, in the middle of the Bonaparte era. The aesthetic canons of French neoclassicism and of the Louis XVI style therefore reached Spain much later than elsewhere, although they were highly influenced by the English style, which arrived by way of Portugal. This period was characterized by a return to straighter lines in overall shapes and less highly curved chair and table legs, along with the adoption of the English claw-and-ball motif for chairs with pierced backs, developed by Thomas Chippendale. These were altered somewhat to conform to Spanish tastes.

The masters

***Ventura Rodriguez:* Architect, furniture designer and director of the royal workshops.**

***Pedro Palencia, Angel Maeos and Quintana* were the greatest eighteenth-century Spanish cabinetmakers.**

Wood and materials

Walnut

Ebony

Palisander veneer, ivory and tortoiseshell inlay

Beech for Neapolitan-style carved brackets

COURT FURNITURE

Furniture in Spain was designed exclusively for the king and the high aristocracy. It was not yet common in the homes of ordinary people, including the lesser aristocracy and the middle classes. These people continued to use furniture modeled after the Mudéjar, or Hispano-Moresque style, notable the vargueño (a desk with a fall-front).

Court furniture, especially under Philip V, was characterized by gilt sculptures, trompe l'oeil marquetry patterns, colored backgrounds and chinoiseries.

In royal palaces, gilt pier tables were extremely popular.

▽ Occasional table. *Carved walnut. The apron drawers are decorated with acanthus leaves. It rests on curved, trestle-style legs joined by two metal bars. Seventeenth century, restored eighteenth century. Christie's, London.*

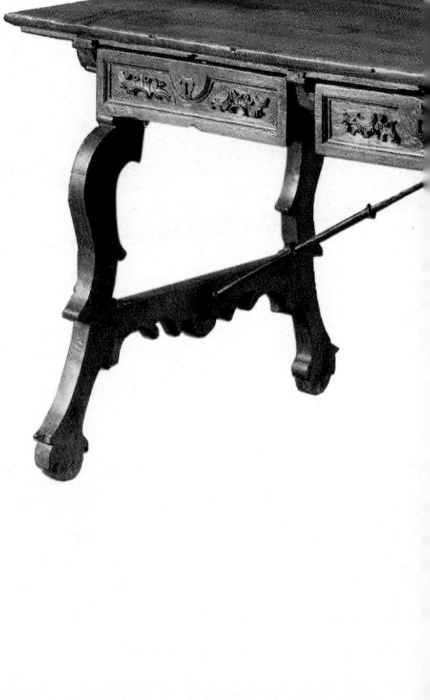

MAIN PIECES OF FURNITURE

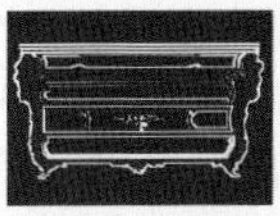

Chair designs generally followed those popular in France and England. The seat backs were always high and tilted slightly backward, or were curved, as in cabriole chairs, offering a level of comfort never before seen in Spain. Some chairs had pierced backs and claw-and-ball feet, derived from Thomas Chippendale's chairs.
All kinds of tables—occasional tables, sidetables, corner tables and flat desks—all highly decorated with marquetry and gilding, were as popular in Spain as they were in France.
The chest of drawers with three drawers, decorated with trompe l'œil or geometric marquetry patterns (modeled after the Louis XV style) and the English-style scriban gradually replaced the vargueño at court; late examples of this piece of furniture were covered with ivory, mother-of-pearl and tortoiseshell inlays.
Canopies disappeared from beds, which became longer as the century progressed.

△ Rococo chair with japanned black lacquer and gold. The richly decorated seat back is fitted with caning, with a chinoiserie decor on the central section. The crest rail has a carved mask framed by women's heads. Paw feet. Second half of the eighteenth century. Christie's, London.

△ Majolica chair made of walnut and pine. Pierced seat back with an urn-shaped splat. Padded seat upholstered with cotton fabric. Scalloped apron. English-style cabriole legs joined by a typically Spanish-style H-stretcher. Early eighteenth century. Christie's, London.

◁ Neoclassical table made of walnut and decorated with marquetry. Antique-style garlands on the frieze. Straight legs, fluted on the upper section only, ending in cylinder feet. Late eighteenth, early nineteenth century. Christie's, London.

Russia

1730 1801

The Nationalist Style

The masters

Charles Cameron (1740-1812): Scottish architect

David Röentgen (1741-1809): German cabinetmaker

Christian Meyer: German cabinetmaker

Heinrich Gambs (1765-1831): German cabinetmaker, the only one to live in Saint Petersburg.

Wood and materials

Mahogany, Karelian birch

Silver and gold leaf, Tula steel

Malachite and lazulite from the Urals. White and red jasper agate from Tulyakov, green agate from Revna, red from the Urals, black and white from Orsk and from Kuchkuldin.

Amazonite and turquoise from the Urals, gray porphyry from Korgon

Red aventurine from Siberia, white and orange from Korgon

Milky quartz, rhodonite, chalcedony and ivory

△ *Antechamber in Maria Fedorovna's apartment. Pavlovsk Palace, Saint Petersburg.*

When the French author Stendhal arrived in Moscow, in the wake of Napoleon's army, he wrote: "The beauty of Russian interiors surpasses anything one could see in Paris... the rooms are decorated with the most refined furniture, everything is in the most perfect taste." In 1750, however, some sixty years earlier, the Russian imperial court was so poorly furnished that elements had to be carried from one imperial residence to another.

How, in under 100 years, did styles change from such penury to the profusion and luxury noted by Stendhal? The answer lies in two major historical events:

◆ Russia's opening up to the west and modernization under Peter the Great's rule in the late seventeenth century. An enormous amount of furniture was then imported into Russia. Soon after, individuals began to send specific orders to the greatest cabinetmakers, furniture-makers, bronzesmiths and porcelain-makers in France, Italy, Germany and England.

◆ The second event was the coronation of Catherine the Great. Starting in 1762, the determined empress encouraged the development of Russian furniture production. She wanted grandiose, splendid furniture for her country, furniture that no longer imitated other styles, but innovated. In other words, she wanted a more Russian style. To achieve this goal, she turned to the European cabinetmakers with whom she already was working, but went one step further by encouraging them to move to Saint Petersburg. Russian craftsmen were also sought out to contribute their skills and techniques to a specifically Russian style of furniture. The Tula military steelworks, which had been specialized in the production of ornamented weapons, started manufacturing amazing blued-steel furniture with applications of faceted metal diamonds. The Peterhof gem-cutting workshop took advantage of the rich mineral resources in Russia and started to produce sumptuous stone furniture in various shapes of green, red and intense blue.

Fretwork

A fretwork, or gallery, placed around a desktop, was purely ornamental. Delicately chased, this bronze element compensated for the sumptuous and stately ornamentation by providing a touch of femininity and delicacy.

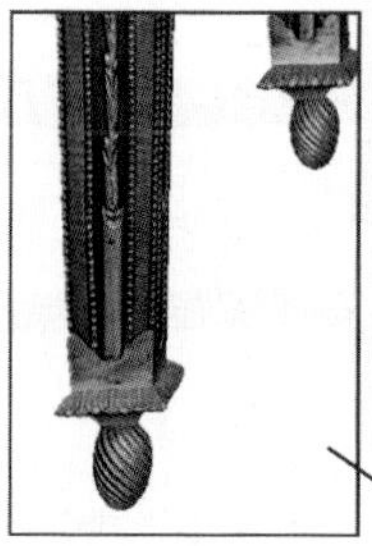

Egg-shaped spiral sabot

The rather hefty legs were decorated with marquetry of different colored woods bordered by a beaded bronze fillet framing a delicately chased central twig shape. The leg is fitted into a sumptuous egg-shaped spiral sabot made of gilt bronze.

△ *Roll-top desk. Marquetry incorporating various types of wood. Luxurious gilt bronze ornamentation. Made by David Röentgen specially for the Russian market. This desk belonged to Catherine II. Ca 1780. Musée du Louvre, Paris.*

Drapery

A French-style bronze drapery motif ran along the long, narrow central drawer, designed to hold military maps. Adapting to Russian tastes, the cabinetmaker covered each section of the desk with different bronze decorative motifs.

MAIN PIECES OF FURNITURE

European cabinetmakers working for Russia understood very quickly that their clients did not want new furniture designs, but instead, a specifically Russian style for luxury pieces that would surpass anything made elsewhere in Europe.

Typically, Russian pieces included the Tula steel furniture and the Peterhof stone furniture. In general, Russian furniture was excessively decorated, and each piece was seemingly more luxurious than the last. Decorative elements included inlays of eglomisé (gold glass), porcelain, painted glass, opaline and ivory, along with cameos and magnificently chiseled bronzes.

Marquetry motifs incorporated extremely rare woods of contrasting colors and depicted genre or topographical scenes.

Everything was extravagant. Even the proportions of the furniture pieces were unusually oversized. Although the main principles of the Louis XV, Louis XVI and Directoire styles were followed, it was sometimes hard to identify them, as they were almost submerged by the quest for luxury and grandeur.

NETHERLANDS

1700 1790

English and French Influences

△ The Family Meal. *Jan Josef Horemans. Château de Compiègne.*

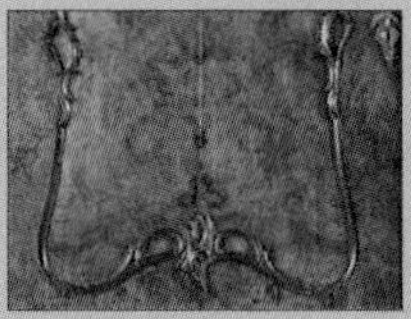

Wood and materials

Walnut

Walnut veneer

Marquetry with woods of contrasting colors and ivory

The Netherlands readily accepted styles and cultures, and in the eighteenth century, was exposed to the successive influences of France and England. Few countries in the early years of the eighteenth century could avoid being engulfed by the Rococo style of France. This phenomenon was even more striking in the Netherlands because of the massive influx of Protestant cabinetmakers from France, who left the country following the revocation of the Edict of Nantes in 1685. England's influence spread to the Netherlands as a result of the many commercial and political links between the two countries. Many pieces of furniture were imported. This did not, however, prevent Dutch workshops from producing a respectable amount of national pieces or from inventing their own Rococo style that was primarily illustrated in extremely sophisticated marquetry work. Most furniture was covered with walnut veneer or extremely complex marquetry patterns of flowers, ribbons and wreaths, made from ivory and woods of contrasting colors. With a great marquetry tradition that dated from the sixteenth and seventeenth centuries, the Netherlands reached an amazing level of beauty, delicacy and sophistication in its eighteenth-century marquetry. Furniture bodies became curved; this tendency was even more strongly exaggerated in table and chair legs, to the point that the sickle-shaped legs became a defining feature of the Dutch style. Bookcases, secretaries and chests of drawers were fashioned with bulging shapes that extended almost to the floor, creating a rather cozy aspect. Bronze mounts and ornaments were limited to keyholes and handles. Chinese lacquered panels and japanning were widely copied, as they were throughout the rest of Europe.

The Louis XVI style and neoclassicism had some influence in the Netherlands, but it arrived later than in other countries and was somewhat dampened by the prevalence of the English style toward the end of the century. The Napoleonic period, when Louis Bonaparte was placed on the throne of the Netherlands, imposed the Empire style which, because of the political context, was adopted by many European countries.

OTHER FURNITURE

Chests of drawers had three or four drawers. The sides bulged out at the base and the serpentine shape rested on bun or low curved feet.

Small desks were decorated with remarkably beautiful marquetry scenes. These pieces were sometimes so small that they could be placed on a table.

Mahogany chairs were derived largely from English chairs and rested on claw-and-ball feet. By the end of the century, seat backs had become rectangular and grooved, and the corners were ornamented.

△ *Gaming table. Ebonized wood and mahogany. A tabletop and shelf with a drawer on the frieze. Sickle-shaped legs. Fondation Angladon, Avignon.*

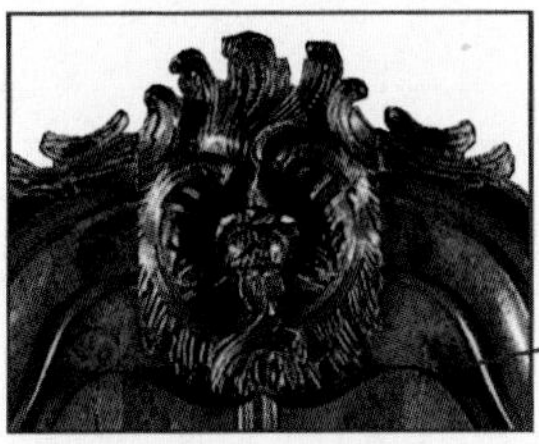

Arcaded cornice

This cornice appeared on all types of Dutch furniture during this period. In general, it was carved and decorated with shell, pine-cone, urn and even intertwined feather motifs.

▽ *Rococo cabinet-armoire with two doors. Walnut burl. The piece is topped by an arcaded cornice and rests on top of a lower chest with three rows of drawers. Mid-eighteenth century. Christie's, Amsterdam.*

Bulging chests or drawers

The serpentine shape rested on extremely curved feet, creating an impression of heaviness and solidity.

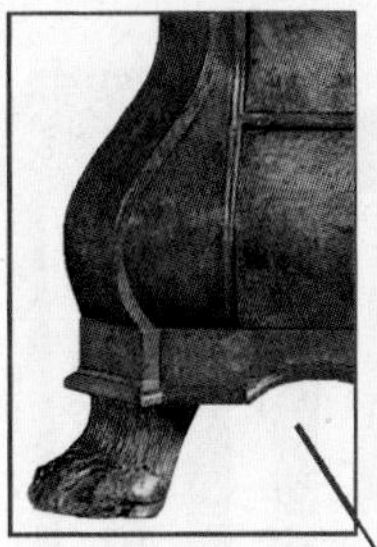

TABLES

Small tables were extremely popular, notably living room tables. These often had friezes covered with delicate marquetry patterns. The tables sometimes had surprisingly exaggerated curves.

CABINETS

Rococo cabinets were still in fashion, although the shape of these pieces increasingly resembled that of the bureau-bookcase. The lower section consisted of a wide chest with three or four drawers, with a fall-front that formed a writing surface. The chest of drawers bulged out at the base and rested on bun feet. The tall upper section, derived from the English writing cabinet, was a bookcase. Two doors, richly decorated with marquetry patterns of flowers, ribbons, urns and wreaths, were topped by an arcaded cornice.

SCANDINAVIA

1771 1792

The Gustavian Style

The masters

***Louis Masreliez:* French decorator who designed the Etruscan-style decors for the Hägä pavilion.**

***Louis Desprez:* Art director for the theater, he designed the Drottningholm theater.**

Wood and materials

Natural pine or pine with several coats of scumbled paint

Mahogany, walnut burl, beech

Scumbled paint: several transparent coats, sanded for a milky or lacquered effect

Colors: green-blue-gray and pearl gray

Fabrics and coverings

Striped silks, linen with large red-and-white, blue and white, or green and white squares, Vichy cotton. Reindeer leather.

△ An Intimate Lunch. *Nicolas Lafrensen. Musée du Louvre, Paris.*

Gustav III (1771-1792) was, like Emperor Frederick of Prussia and Catherine the Great of Russia, an enlightened despot; arts and literature flourished during his reign. His country remembers him as a cultivated king, who was extremely fond of French culture and encouraged the liberal ideas being developed by the French philosophers. A German neoclassical furniture and architectural style, highly inspired by the French Louis XVI style, is named for him. But, like French monarchs, his popularity decreased over the years, and he became decidedly unpopular during the last twenty years of his reign—a period that was also characterized by unbridled extravagance and luxury. In the early eighteenth century, Swedish furniture designers drew their inspiration from French furniture, which introduced a Rococo style to Sweden. Yet the Swedish Rococo was delicate and somewhat whimsical; it consisted of furniture with highly profiled sculptures, painted to look like marble. This aristocratic style co-existed with a provincial or peasant style, which produced solid, simple pine furniture covered with several layers of scumbled paint. Swedish furniture-makers had started using this technique in the Renaissance and it had remained steadily popular since then. The most common colors were green, yellow and deep red.

In the mid-eighteenth century, after the style had been adopted by the aristocracy and the new bourgeois class, this type of furniture became more common throughout the country. Furniture colors at this time tended toward a very pale, grayish blue-green, which would remain a characteristic color of Swedish furniture.

Under Gustav III, the success of painted and scumbled furniture grew with the influence of the neoclassical style, which the king brought back to Sweden from Italy. Common motifs included garlands, sculpted knots and sheaves of wheat, while the dominant color was pearl gray. In addition to the exceptionally beautiful royal pieces, the most charming examples of Swedish furniture were made in the provincial style. These had a simple elegance and were more modest, with extremely delicate scumbled colors. These painted pieces of furniture, arranged parsimoniously in the nearly empty large rooms of Scandinavian homes, matched the interior decoration and were extremely beautiful.

Festooned apron

This garland of cording, painted against a scumbled background (according to a Swedish tradition that dates to the eleventh century) reproduces a motif that was probably painted as a frieze on the walls of the room in which the chair was placed.

△ *Painted wood chair with foliage motifs on the stiles and with garlands on the apron. Pierced seat back with five rods. Rectilinear lines joined by an H-stretcher. Finnish Art and Design Company.*

CHEST OF DRAWERS

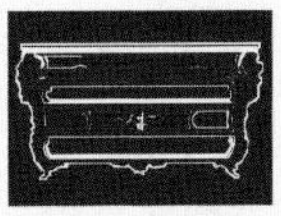

Chests with three drawers, curved fronts and straight uprights were made of waxed pine, painted to look like marble or covered with scumbled paint. Certain chests, designed for city-dwellers, were designed as slant-top desks over a chest of drawers. Flat-topped desks were placed perpendicularly to a wall and rested on rectilinear legs joined by a stretcher. They were made of walnut burl or birch and had a small superstructure fitted with drawers or compartments. They were made of wood decorated with scumbled paint and a thin gold fillet. Rustic desks had drop-leaves and heavy legs. They were covered with bright blue scumbled paint.

CHAIRS

Chairs with pierced splats, derived from English designs, were often painted in pale colors. The crest rail often had a sculpted or gilded motif, repeating a feature on the walls in which the chair was placed.
Round-backed klismos *chairs with saber legs front and back, made for King Gustav III's Hägä pavilion, were the inspiration for many Swedish chair designs.*

△ Danish scriban-desk, made of walnut and walnut burl, with a slant-top writing surface. A curved front with three drawers, resting on thick, short legs. Sotheby's, London.

△ Wood chair covered with scumbled paint. Pierced splat with stylized wheat-sheaf motif. Wooden seat. Rectilinear legs joined by an H-stretcher. Finnish Art and Design Company.

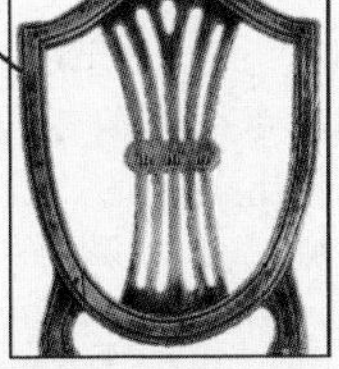

Sheaf-backed chair

A rough imitation of an English chair design, this sheaf design nevertheless gives this chair a naive elegance.

Lopers

These extremely simple slides are placed between the top drawer and the slant top. They pull out to support the opened writing surface, forming a desk.

UNITED STATES

1750 1810

Chippendale and Federal Styles

The masters

Stephan Goddard and John Townsend, cabinetmakers and furniture-makers. They became famous for their adaptations of the English Georgian style into what would be called the American Chippendale style; they originated a school of furniture.

△ The Open Window. *E. Nourse.*

The creation of the Federal style, as its name indicates, coincided with the writing of the constitution of the United States of America and with the nomination of the first president, George Washington, in 1789. Some time around 1750, furniture made in an American Chippendale style, inspired from the English Chippendale style, was made in North America by the cabinetmakers Stephen Goddard and John Townsend, working in their Newport, Rhode Island workshop. A beautiful example of the Quaker sensibility, this style was immediately successful and remained in fashion for about twenty years, when it was replaced by a neoclassical style that was very similar to the work of George Adam and to French Louis XVI furniture. Far from being a stylistic declaration of independence vis-à-vis the Old World, the Federal style was the first in a series of American adaptations of European styles—this process lasted throughout the entire nineteenth century with the Sheraton, Empire and Victorian styles.

American Chippendale furniture was a combination of straight lines and curves. Decors consisted of wreaths and shells: Goddard and Townsend's favorite motif was a highly stylized, perfectly symmetrical shell that resembled a fan. During this period, while Rococo reigned in Europe, American cabinetmakers adopted a methodic symmetry in their designs. Some pieces had extremely long, slender lines; they were generally much higher than European pieces. The legs were heavyset and curved. Bronze mounts were used only for keyholes and handles. Broken pediments were extremely popular and were used to introduce new types of curves, original ornaments and almost Rococo-like serpentines.

Federal style furniture followed the English neoclassical movement promoted by the architect Robert Adam, then began to adopt openly the French Directoire style.

Wood and materials

Mahogany

Curly-grained mahogany

Walnut

Walnut burl

Birch

Gilt bronze

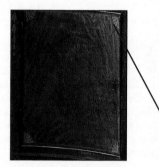

Concave side doors

The wood was specially worked and treated to obtain a concave shape for the doors to side compartments. They were a major factor in the elegance of this piece of furniture.

Fan motif

This is one of the most widely used motifs in American furniture, along with the concave or convex shell. In this piece, it is a quarter-fan placed at the corners or the doors and drawers.

ARMCHAIRS

A wing chair was a more comfortable version of the Queen Anne-style winged armchair (called a "confessional" in France). The wings were designed to protect the sitter from drafts.

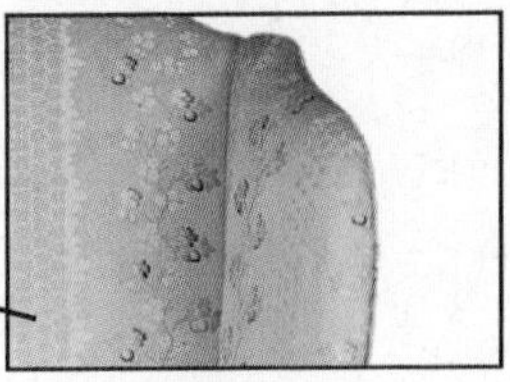

Wings

Entirely padded, the wings connected the seat back to the armrests. This element became the most popular characteristic of American armchairs.

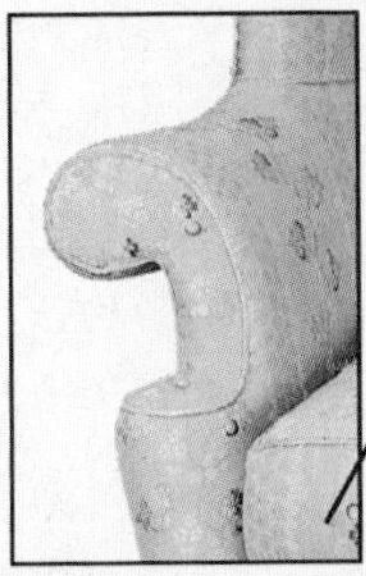

The compass seat

This seat was very round in front, as though it had been drawn by a compass. It projected slightly beyond the armrest. The small, padded space between the seat and the armrest was large enough for a child to sit on.

△ A confessional or winged chair, entirely padded and upholstered. The armrests have a crook in the front, the seat is called a compass seat. Cabriole legs made of mahogany carved with convex shell motifs. Claw-and-ball feet. Philadelphia. Ca 1760. Christie's, New York.

CHEST OF DRAWERS

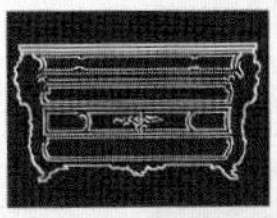

The most famous chest of drawers made in the Chippendale style was the blockfront, a specialty of cabinetmakers Goddard and Townsend. It was named for the blocks forming the front, which was divided in three sections of equal width and set off by an edge molding. Copper and brass openwork decorated the handles and keyholes. The legs were low and curved.

△ Federal sideboard made of mahogany. Serpentine front with two drawers of different sizes, decorated with bronze handles, and two side compartments with concave doors. Rhode Island 1790-1810. Christie's, New York.

THE *19th* CENTURY

AT THE BEGINNING OF THE CENTURY, NAPOLEON BONAPARTE WAS LEADING FRANCE TOWARD A NEW WORLD. ONCE PROCLAIMED EMPEROR, NAPOLEON OVERTURNED THE ANCIEN RÉGIME AND ESTABLISHED NEW REGIMES THROUGHOUT MOST OF THE COUNTRIES OF EUROPE.

In order to convey his new order, Napoleon needed a style that could also function as a powerful propaganda tool. He called on designers to create the Empire style, based on the ancient Greek and Roman stylistic vocabulary that first developed during the Ancien Régime—adding a typically Napoleonic element: a fondness for all things Egyptian. This was the beginning of the Empire style, which had a profound influence throughout several European countries for nearly fifty years. England, stronger than ever in furniture design and production, became the last refuge of good taste for those who considered the Empire as a regime of usurpers and upstarts. Yet nineteenth-century England deserves more than being relegated to this secondary role. One of the world's most brilliant cabinetmakers, Thomas Sheraton, lived in England at this time. Although he never crafted his own pieces of furniture, his designs during the Regency period were unrivaled models of elegance. England also produced the imaginative eclecticism characterizing the Victorian style, which was a far cry from the conformist reign for which it was named.

The most striking characteristic of the nineteenth century, however, was the triumph of a bourgeois style throughout all of Europe, with the Restauration and Louis-Philippe styles in France and the Biedermeier style in Germany and Austria.

As the century unfolded, the bourgeoisie, looking to legitimize its newfound role in society, turned to the past—all pasts—for stylistic elements. This resulted in an eclectic style characterized by pastiche, copies and a synthesis of all styles from all countries. The foremost example was the pastiche of Gothic and Renaissance styles, followed by a pastiche of Boulle and Louis XV styles—easily the most outrageous of all the stylistic expressions. The various styles were decorated with English, Spanish, Italian, Dutch, Celtic, Hebrew and early Christian touches, with, in addition, a strong dose of Japanese and medieval inspiration (Europe discovered Japanese culture with the advent of the Meiji dynasty in 1868). This unbelievable mixture of styles spread to the four corners of the world with the development of mass production of furniture.

The Universal Exhibitions, held regularly from 1851 on, stimulated exchanges between designers and diverse countries, and were influential in the appearance of the so-called eclectic or historicist fin-de-siècle style.

The succession of exaggerated forms, caricatures and stylistic extravagance that continued through 1900 led to the Secession movement in Austria. This movement provided the stimulus for the Art Nouveau style (known as Jugendstil in German‡), the first self-proclaimed pan-European movement, which was as innovative as were the Gothic, Renaissance and Rococo styles in their own times.

◁ *Empire Room. Château d'Amboise.*

FRANCE

1804 1815

The Empire Style

△ *The Emperor's office, with his folding baldachin bed. Château de Fontainebleau.*

The creation of the Empire in 1804 was the impetus for a new style based on simplicity, majesty and theatricality. The Empire style maintained a fondness for ancient styles, and promoted greater symmetry and a taste for "the true and the beautiful." Yet the most important function of these stylistic principles was to contribute to the propaganda of grandeur, based on historical similarities between the Napoleonic regime and that of Alexander the Great, Caesar and the Pharaohs. Napoleon consulted the architects Charles Percier and Pierre-François-Léonard Fontaine, and the painters Jacques David and Pierre Prud'hon to convey this new dream of French greatness. The exceptional quality of the furniture, the many commissions from imperial dignitaries and the export of furniture throughout Europe all contributed to the spectacular and universal success of the Empire style.

In the rest of Europe, where the emperor's brothers sat on most of the thrones, the Empire style was considered an "occupier's" style, which completely replaced the local styles through the mid-nineteenth century, particularly in Italy, Spain and, to a lesser extent, Scandinavia and the Netherlands.

Like all furniture of state, Empire furniture was designed to be viewed from the front. Marquetry disappeared completely (it actually began to disappear during the Directoire, for economic reasons), and bronze mounts became predominant ornamental elements. The quasi-military, geometric placement of these bronze mounts was quite spectacular.

The use of furniture at the imperial court, as at Louis XIV's court, was once again governed by a strict protocol: any piece of furniture covered with gold leaf, for example, was reserved for the emperor, the empress or sovereigns of the imperial family.

The masters

***Charles Percier and Pierre Fontaine:* Architects and founders of the Empire style.**

***Jacques Louis David (1748-1825):* Included ancient furniture in his paintings.**

***Pierre Paul Prud'hon (1758-1823):* A painter, he designed ancient Roman-style furniture for Empress Marie-Louise.**

***Pierre Philippe Thomire (1751-1843):* Bronzesmith and bronze-chaser.**

***Martin-Guillaume Biennais (1800-1832):* Bronzesmith, bronze-chaser, he created magnificent furniture in his shop, Le Singe Violet.**

***Jacob Frères, then Jacob-Desmalter:* Cabinetmakers, furniture-makers, successors of Georges Jacob.**

***Pierre-Benoît Marcion:* Cabinetmaker, he worked primarily for the emperor, ministers and officers to the crown.**

THE *MÉRIDIENNE*

The Empire-style* méridienne *differed slightly from the Directoire-style version. The later* méridienne *was a short* canapé *with two scroll arms; the head end was higher than the foot, and the back sloped from the top of one end to the other.

Padded armrests

The armrests were so thickly padded that the padding formed a distinct cylinder shape above the armrest itself. Tapestry-makers poured all their talents into this element, designing specific motifs for the damask upholstery.

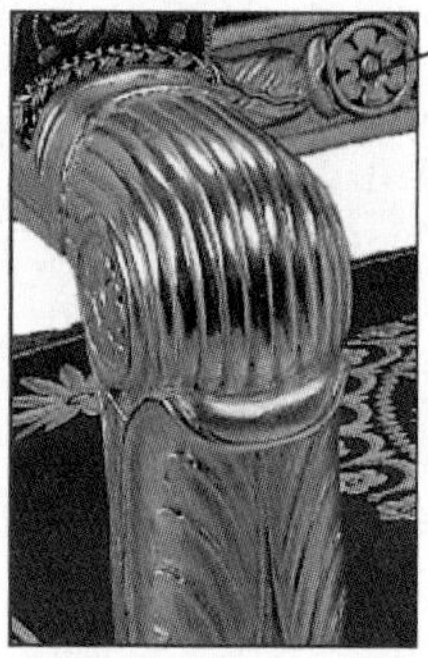

Egyptian inspiration

A characteristic feature of the Empire style, the right-angle joint between the arm stump and the armrest combined two Egyptian-style motifs: a scroll of striated foliage and a sheaf of gilt palmettes.

THE ARMCHAIR

All kinds of chairs (whose frames were more often ordered from the upholsterer) were used during the Empire. Folding stools, even though they didn't fold at all, kept the same name. These stools reappeared at the imperial court, their use governed by the same protocols and same decorative directives as during Louis XIV's reign.

In honor of this newly fashionable antique style, this stool, called a curule-stool, was supported by an X-frame sometimes decorated with swords. Dozens of these stools were used throughout the imperial apartments and, in private apartments, were arranged in pairs. Bathrooms, which appeared during the Directoire, were increasingly elaborate. Gondola chairs and gondola armchairs were first designed for bathrooms; they were so comfortable that they were soon used throughout the entire house. Gondola chairs were characterized by a padded, deep, concave back whose stiles curved down to join the top of the seat rail. Gondola chairs had elegant saber legs in front and in back, as opposed to all other types of chairs, which had rectilinear legs in the front and saber legs in the back. The most common type of chair for dining rooms was that with a straight or curved pierced back, decorated with lyre or palmette motifs and with a fitted cane seat. Armchairs had straight armrests, joined to the seat back by a palmette. Arm stumps extended straight up from the legs or were joined to the apron in the shape of winged lions, chimeras, sphinxes, swans or eagles with outspread wings. The front legs took the forms of monopod lions, caryatids, busts of women and Egyptian heads coiffed with Nemes.

The legs ended with a clawed foot, a bare foot or a reversed palmette.

Rounded seats

Chair fronts had a slight curve, the only rounded element aside from the saber legs in the rear. The curves and straight lines form a well-proportioned ensemble, creating an extraordinary impression of solidity.

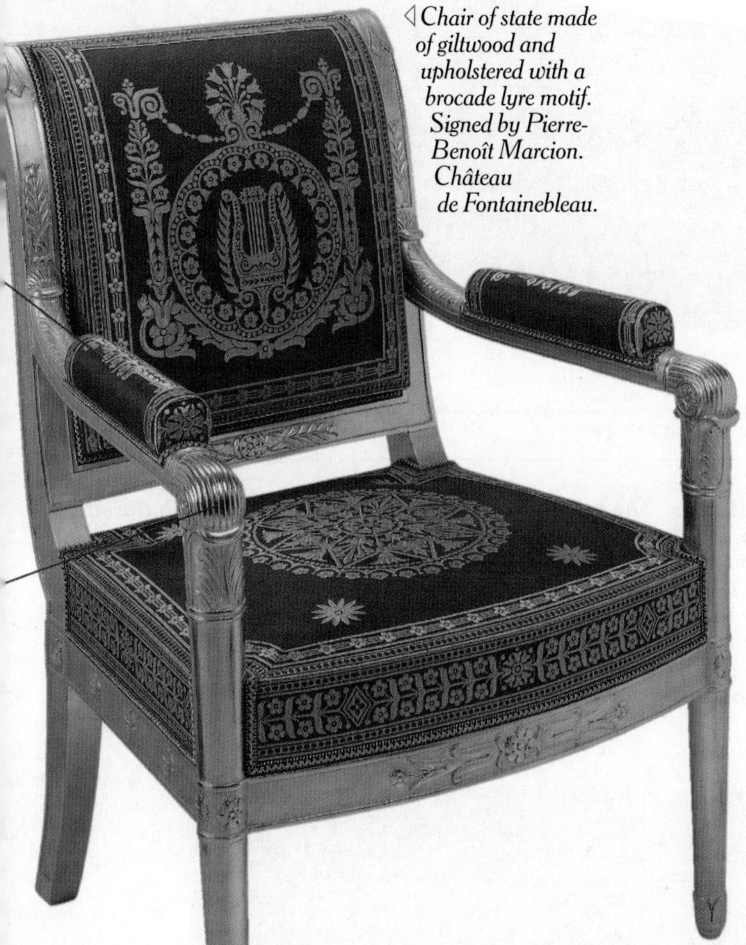

◁ *Chair of state made of giltwood and upholstered with a brocade lyre motif. Signed by Pierre-Benoît Marcion. Château de Fontainebleau.*

▷ *Mahogany and gilt bronze armchair. Rectilinear uprights and seat back, saber legs in the back. Signed by Pierre-Benoît Marcion. 1809. Château de Fontainebleau.*

CHAIRS OF STATE

Giltwood armchairs were designed as chairs of state, for the exclusive use of the emperor, members of the imperial family and princes. Bergères *had the same appearance and ornamentation as the rectilinear armchairs, differing only in that there was no gap between the armrests and the seat rail.*

Motifs and decorative elements

Imperial crowns (laurel wreaths), bees (Napoleon I's heraldic device), eagles, the letter "N" for Napoleon, "I" for* Imperator, *lion heads, caryatid mounts, obelisks, pyramids, winged solar disks, winged sphinxes, quadriga, winged victories, or victories wearing wreaths or bearing torches, draped tunics, swans, helmets, bucrania, amphorae, tridents, urns, swords, torches, trumpets, lyres, caducei, palmettes, rosettes, acanthus leaf scrolls, mythological scenes for bronze sconces, naiads for bathroom furniture.

THE *LIT EN BATEAU*

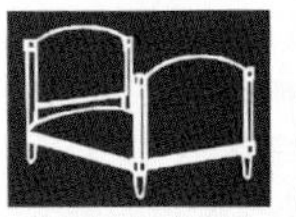

The most surprising furniture design, which remained popular through the entire nineteenth century, was the* lit en bateau, *(also known as the lit en corbeille, or "basket-bed") first commissioned by Madame Récamier, a great furniture-lover, during the Consulat.

The initial idea was to create a bed that had no sharp corners or edges. The sideboards curved like a boat ("bateau" in French) to join the headboard and footboard, which ended in an outward-turning scroll.

The* lits en bateaux *were decorated with bronze mounts on the theme of Diana the Huntress, crescent moons, torches, poppies and, in general, any motif relating to love and the night.

Saber-legged daybeds replaced chaise longues; the headboards and footboards were the same height in these pieces. These daybeds were usually extremely simple in design, though heavily ornamented with bronze mounts.

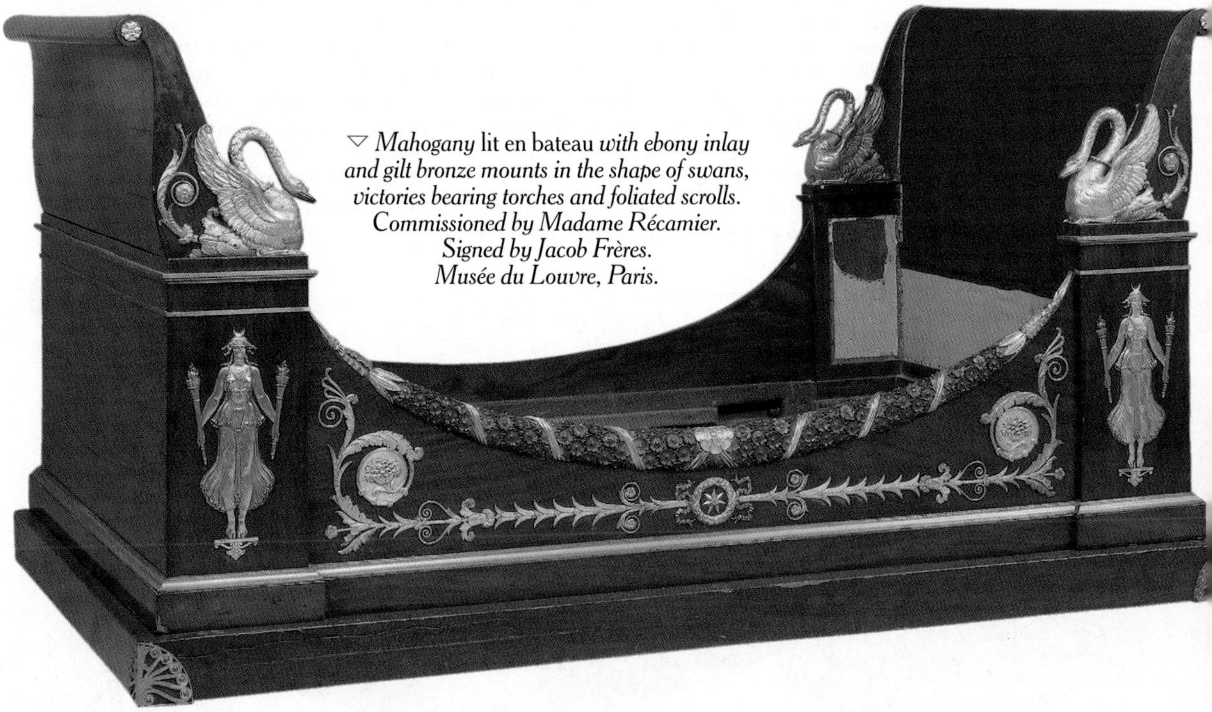

▽ *Mahogany* lit en bateau *with ebony inlay and gilt bronze mounts in the shape of swans, victories bearing torches and foliated scrolls. Commissioned by Madame Récamier. Signed by Jacob Frères. Musée du Louvre, Paris.*

THE SOFA

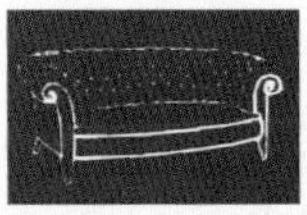

Sofas during this period became quite impressive in size (some six feet long) and resembled beds more than chairs.

The* tête-à-tête, *or* causeuse, *was somewhat shorter than the usual sofa designs. The back and ends were similar to those of armchairs. It was supported by six or eight legs that matched the armchair legs, by a thick base that rested on the floor or by lion's paws or cubes.

The* paumier *was a piece of furniture halfway between the sofa and the* méridienne. *It was intended to be placed near the fireplace. The ends were very low and turned outward, forming comfortable armrests. This type of sofa was entirely covered in upholstery.

◁ A tête-à-tête or causeuse *sofa, made of gilt wood sculpted with motifs of Roman fasces an laurel leaves. Upholstered in damask with a laurel-leaf pattern. This pie was part of the emperor's person furniture collectio Signed by Pierre-Benoît Marcion. Château de Fontainebleau.*

CHESTS OF DRAWERS

Three main types of chests of drawers existed during the Empire.

The chest with three drawers, with no exposed crosspiece, had straight, pilaster or sheath uprights with wood or bronze ornaments. The drawer in the apron projected and rested on caryatid supports. This massive chest rested directly on the floor and was sometimes decorated with lion's paw ornaments.

These chests were profusely decorated with bronze mounts on the three drawers and on the apron. Motifs used on the keyholes included lyres, cornucopias and palmettes, while drawer handles were decorated with crowns, knobs or rings in lions' snouts. Egyptian heads with Nemes headdresses or female busts decorated the top of the pilasters.

In some three-drawer chests, only the central drawer, the apron and the top of the pilasters were decorated. In this case, the central drawer was decorated with bronze mounts depicting mythological scenes. The top was covered with black or gray marble.

La commode à vantaux was a chest whose drawers were concealed by two solid wood doors. There was often a drawer under the marble top. The wide surface of the doors was often richly decorated.

The chiffonnière or semainier perpetuated the Louis XVI design; it was a tall chest with six or seven drawers.

Keyholes

The keyholes on this piece of furniture are sumptuously decorated with lyre-shaped bronze mounts surrounded by two opposing cornucopia. The strict symmetry of these bronze mounts is repeated on the handles, with rosettes, laurel leaves and palmettes.

△ *Chest with three drawers and exposed crosspiece.*
Mahogany, gilt bronze, veined white marble. The bronze mounts are arranged in a highly symmetrical pattern. Unusual gilt bronze feet. Signed by Pierre-Benoît Marcion, 1810. Château de Versailles.

Wood and materials

Swirl, curly-grained, solid or veneered mahogany

Elm burl, beech, walnut, cedar and ebony

Curled yew, boxwood, olivewood, maple and lemonwood for inlays

Symmetrically arranged bas-relief chased bronzes

Gilt copper

Sèvres porcelain

Gray, black and white marble sculpted with sharp edges

Fabric

Brocaded silk and brocaded, sheared silk velvet, rep with silk embroidery, Neuilly tapestry, Indian silk. Motifs included stripes on matching background, bees, laurel wreaths, rosettes, palmettes. Trim in contrasting colors.

▽ *Mahogany somno decorated with gilt bronze mounts: cameos, palmettes, stars and Roman fasces. Gilt bronze feet. Signed by Jacob-Desmalter. Château de Fontainebleau.*

NEW TABLES

A large number of new designs appeared during the Empire. Most of these were for tables or table-like objects, all revolving around the intimate spheres of dining, sleep or bathing rituals. They were meant to be placed in bedrooms, bathrooms and dining rooms.

The somno, *or bedside table, was not much different from the model developed during the Directoire; it had a marble top that projected slightly over the sides and rested on a cylindrical, square or, occasionally, truncated pyramid base. Bronze mounts decorated the visible surfaces. The door was always placed on the side facing the bed.*

The dressing table, *also known as a* coiffeuse *or* table de toilette, *was a rectangular table generally fitted with a gray or white marble top resting on a wooden apron, which included a drawer with bronze ornaments. The X-frame or lyre support, decorated with bronze, was never concealed by fabric, as it had been during the previous century. An adjustable oval, round or rectangular mirror, framed by torch- or quiver-shaped uprights, surmounted the dressing table.*

The psyche, *or cheval glass, was another piece of furniture designed for the bedroom. This was a large rectangular or oval mirror attached to two side uprights in such a way that it could be tilted. These uprights were made in various shapes, columns, pyramids or rectangles, and the top of the mirror was always decorated with a bronze emblem (usually an urn or a vase). Bronze candlesticks were placed halfway up the uprights. The base was always very heavy, for reasons of stability, and was formed of two X-frames or a solid base.*

The athénienne, *or washstand, consisted of a tripod support made of bronze, steel, iron and sometimes wood, modeled after ancient furniture forms and decorated with sphinxes, lions or naiads. It supported a large porcelain basin. Some of these tripods served several functions and could also support a perfume-burner, flowers or plants.*

The barbière, *or shaving table, was a tall, narrow piece of bathroom furniture. The lower section had a series of drawers, while the upper section had four columns supporting a marble shelf and a small drawer. A sliding mirror was placed between the two rear columns.*

◁ *Pedestal table, made of mahogany and ebonized wood, in imitation of bronze. Mahogany tabletop. Tripod base weighted with lead. Château de Fontainebleau.*

PEDESTAL TABLES

The pedestal table, also known as a guéridon *or a* tea table, *contributed to the overall comfort in the home. It was often used as a dining room table or for tea, hence its name. The round tabletop was made of wood, marble, mosaic,* pietre dure *and, more rarely, malachite or porphyry. The wide apron was sometimes decorated with bronze. There were several different types of supports:*

- *A large central column resting on a tripod base with concave sides;*
- *Three or four columns or caryatids, winged sphinxes or griffons resting on a round or triangular base with concave sides; this piece of furniture may have had a central urn;*
- *Three inward-curving legs ending in claw feet and surmounted by a lion's head or eagle's head, interconnected by a shelf or a ring.*

CONSOLE TABLE

The console table was an essential piece of furniture. It was used as a sideboard in dining rooms and elsewhere in the house as a support for the candlesticks illuminating the rooms.
This table was rectangular, with straight uprights. The tabletop was always made of marble and rested on legs attached to a thick, solid base that replaced the usual stretchers. A silvered mirror was often placed between the two rear columns under the tabletop.

▷ *Mahogany and veined marble.*
Uprights decorated with bronze mounts.
Silvered glass joining the rear legs.
Signed by Jacob-Desmalter, rue Chantereine.
Château de Malmaison.

Apron drawer

This drawer was sometimes visible, i.e., it had a keyhole, or it was concealed. In this case, it had no keyhole and opened by means of a bolt system. Another version was an entirely fake drawer with a fake keyhole.

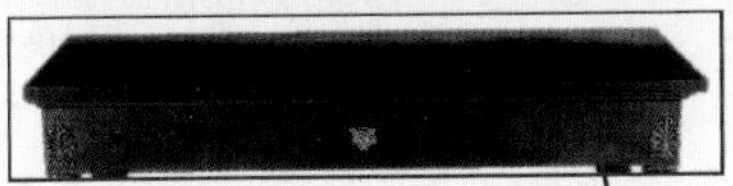

Silvered glass

This glass reflects the front uprights, creating an artificial effect of depth, which helps the overall proportions of this piece of furniture. The silvered glass is sometimes the extension of a mirror placed above the console table.

Uprights

The uprights were square, round, decorated with gilt bronze or sculptures, or free of any decoration whatsoever. The joint with the base is often encircled with bronze or highlighted with a bronze palmette motif.

◁ *Mahogany console.*
Gilt bronze and black marble.
Drawer visible in the apron.
Musée des Arts décoratifs, Paris.

FRANCE

1815  1830

The Restauration Style

△ King Louis XVIII Reflecting on the Charter, Seated at His Desk in the Palais des Tuileries. *Michel Marigny and François Gérard. Château de Versailles.*

The term "Restauration" designates the years 1815 to 1830 and corresponds to the Bourbons' return to the throne with Louis XVI's two brothers, the Comte de Provence and the Comte d'Artois. The former ruled from 1814 to 1824 as King Louis XVIII, the latter, from 1825 to 1830 as King Charles X.

The Restauration ushered in a radical change in the use, though not the materials, of furniture. Starting with this period, court commissions no longer governed stylistic trends, which were far more sensitive to the tastes of individuals and the bourgeois class. In any case, Louis XVIII, who became leader of an exhausted nation, could not afford to spend any money, and merely selected his furniture from the imperial palaces (and had the Napoleonic emblems removed). Similarly, Charles X did not order any large furniture projects. He left this task to his daughter-in-law, the Duchesse de Berry, who hired the greatest cabinetmakers of the period and was responsible for the newfound fashion for light-colored woods. The Duchesse de Berry was quick to introduce into the palace ideas or fashions she had discovered throughout the city. This modern approach was influenced by the increasing power of the business class and by the importance of the trade fairs and exhibitions, including an exhibition of French industrial products. This is how the Duchesse became one of the first to adhere to the neo-Gothic style, known in France as the Troubadour style, also called the Cathedral style, which so charmed the turbulent young writers and painters of the Romantic movement. It was during the Restauration that French society gradually began to accept the new ideas that had overwhelmed the rest of Europe.

The masters

Félix Remond (born 1779): *The Duchesse de Berry's favorite cabinetmaker.*

François Baudry: *Cabinetmaker, designer of the gondola bed for Charles X.*

Georges-Alphonse Desmalter (1799-1870): *The last in the Jacob dynasty of cabinetmakers.*

Jean-Christophe Fischer (1779-1854): *Cabinetmaker famous for his austere chests of drawers and secretaries.*

Jean-Jacques Werner (1791-1849): *Cabinetmaker famous for light-wood furniture with martial decors of gilt bronze mounts.*

Pierre-Antoine Bellangé (1760-1844): *He worked for Charles X and Louis-Philippe.*

L'Escalier de Cristal: *Name of the shop where reproductions of Louis XVI-style furniture and extremely extravagant pieces such as the Duchesse de Berry's crystal staircase were made.*

SOFAS AND *MÉRIDIENNES*

The Restauration méridienne *differed from the earlier designs in its use of light-colored wood and its ornamentation.*
The baigneuse *chair had a deeply curved back, which dropped down on one side to the level of the apron.*
The causeuse *and the* dormeuse *were sofas with scroll ends of different heights that curved forward.*
The canapé en chapeau de gendarme, *or camel-back sofa, was modeled after the English-style sofa. It had wooden scroll ends and an upward, serpentine curve in the back. It was decorated with inlaid work. The classic sofa had a straight back and curved armrests. Cushions appeared for the first time on sofas, which were also completely upholstered and decorated with all kinds of trim (tassels, fringe and piping).*

Removable porcelain plaques

This plaque, often decorated with flower bouquets and mythological scenes (as with this piece, which depicts the Muses), is also a door. This piece illustrates the use of bold, bright colors that were extremely popular during the Restauration.

THE BUREAU-SECRETARY

The bureau-secretary consisted of a closed cabinet, which was usually quite luxuriously decorated. Many of the earlier styles of bureaux were made during the Restauration: the large minister's desk, a descendant of the bureau Mazarin, *which rested on four or eight legs.*

The smaller and simpler writing table had turned legs and included a projecting tabletop that was supported by a strip of one or two drawers.

The roll-top desk was more unusual. It had straight, tapered legs and a single large motif inlaid on the cylinder top.

Different versions of the light-colored fall-front desk, highly architectural in design, were made. The upper compartment always opened to reveal a series of mahogany or amaranthus drawers (according to a design principle by which light-colored wood revealed a darker wood). The outer side of the fall-front may have had a mirror. It could open to reveal an ebony compartment modeled after the mid-seventeenth-century compartments. These desks became extremely elegant and, with the designs by cabinetmaker Jean-Christophe Fischer, were probably the most refined pieces made during the Restauration.

◁ Bureau-secretary. Wood, Sèvres porcelain and gilt bronze mounts. The cabinet is decorated with a bronze gallery, and bronze strips framing a porcelain plaque. The bureau is designed as a console with drawers in the apron, which is supported by two columns joined by a solid base. Signed by Leguay 1827. Musée de Céramique, Sèvres.

Motifs and decorative elements

Crowns of densely arranged roses, ivy wreaths and flowers clusters, oak and laurel branches, heraldic lilies.

Rosettes, palmettes, stars, swans, lyres, dolphins, griffons and seahorses.

Mythological scenes and figures, cameos.

Return of curved shapes and fewer ornamental devices.

Spiral backs and armrests, tulip-shaped friezes on chests of drawers and secretaries, saber legs, bases, gondola seat backs.

Use of extremely light-colored wood, except for Gothic-style pieces, inlays of dark wood on a light-wood background or inlays of matching tones.

Gothic motifs: dentelures, scallops, lattice structures, small turrets set off with inlaid fillets and rosettes.

◁ Lit en bateau *made of ash burl and gilt bronze mounts, displayed here with its canopy. This piece came from the Duchesse de Berry's room. 1820. Château de Compiègne.*

BEDS

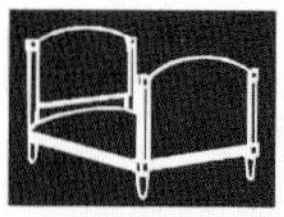

The* lit en bateau, *the most popular type of bed, was placed alongside a wall. Its most striking characteristic was the outward-scrolling ends. Here again, the differences between the Empire-style bed are primarily the use of a light-colored wood and a sophisticated decoration consisting of fine inlay along the uprights and lower crosspiece. The* lit à nacelle *(*lit en bateau *or* gondola bed*) was an imitation of a piece invented by the cabinetmaker Baudry for King Charles X, was so deeply curved and covered with outward-scrolling curves that it looked more like a bathtub than a bed. This was a fairly rare piece, reserved for the most luxurious homes, where it was often placed on a platform.

Outward-scrolling ends

The slight outward curve of the headboard and footboard contributes to the overall oval shape of the bed. This is an example of the excellent craftsmanship that went into this masterpiece.

Headboard with columns

The design of this extremely neoclassical headboard was derived directly from the Empire-style models. The only innovation is the type of wood used—a very light-colored wood that became one of the defining characteristics of the Restauration style.

▽ Lit en bateau *made of poplar, elm burl, ash burl, amaranthus, lemonwood from Santo Domingo and mahogany. The bed rests on a platform with two steps. This exceptional piece of furniture was made by François Baudry in 1827 for King Charles X. Musée des Arts décoratifs, Paris.*

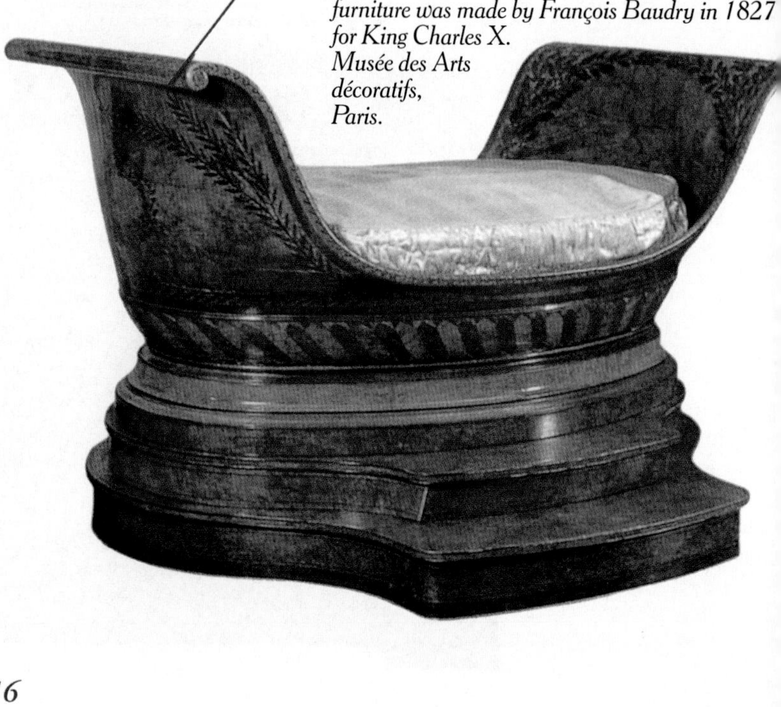

▷ *Dressing-table chair made of crystal, eglomized glass and gilt bronze. Crystal baluster legs in the front, a single square leg in the back. This remarkable piece of furniture comes from the dressing table ensemble purchased by the Duchesse de Berry from* L'Escalier de Cristal. *Musée du Louvre, Paris.*

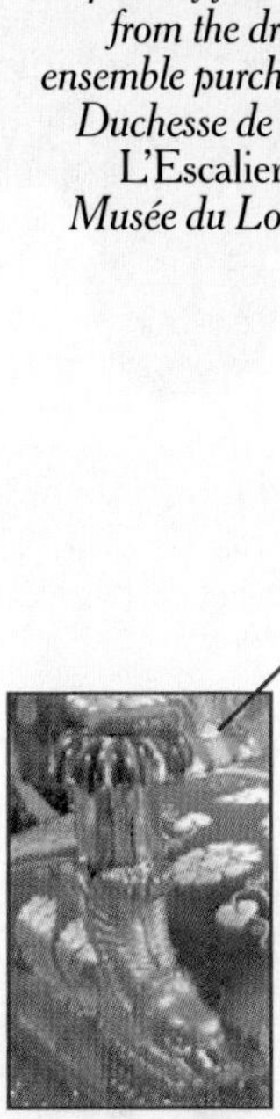

Dolphin-shaped arm stump

The dolphin motif, one of Louis XVI and Marie Antoinette's favorites, reappeared during the Restauration, where it was used widely on chests of drawers, desks and, above all, dressing tables and chairs. Finely carved, it is surmounted on this chair by a crystal panache representing a spray of water.

DRESSING-TABLE SETS

These pieces of furniture were placed in a corner of a master bedroom, generally near a window. The ensemble consisted of an armchair, a dressing table with a mirror (called the toilette) and a psyche. As these pieces became more visible elements of domestic furnishings, they also became increasingly extravagant. The Duchesse de Berry purchased a dressing-table set from **L'Escalier de Cristal.** ***It was as "splendid as a sparkling diamond," and was equipped with a music box which could play thirteen different songs in one hour.***

CHEST OF DRAWERS

The chest with three drawers, like the same piece during the Empire, had straight, console uprights. The keyholes of the three drawers were decorated foliated scrolls. The bronze ornamentation was limited to the drawer pulls and the handles. The upper drawer formed a tulip-shaped strip, and the case rested on low, thick legs.

The commode à vantaux *was a tier of drawers concealed behind two doors. It was sometimes a simple geometric shape, with few ornaments interfering with the austere design. The light-colored wood was subtly highlighted by one or two mahogany or bronze fillets on the doors and on the frieze. The doors opened to reveal three mahogany drawers. The solid chest rested on a plinth-type base.*

▷ *Chest of drawers. Walnut and walnut veneer, console uprights decorated with gilt bronze motifs of flowers and butterflies, tulip-shaped frieze, white marble top. Private collection, Avignon.*

Tulip-shaped frieze

The tulip-shaped frieze was a common feature on chests of drawers and secretaries. A drawer was often built into the frieze.

SMALL PIECES OF FURNITURE

Alongside chests of drawers, the fashion for small, multipurpose tables continued persisted. These included the travailleuse, *a small sewing table with a lid and a mirror; the* coiffeuse, *or dressing table, with a small, adjustable oval mirror framed by two swan's neck uprights; gaming tables, with rectangular top and four dished corners; and cylindrical, oval or pyramid-shaped* jardinières, *or plant-holders, supported by three or four high legs ending in lion's paw or scroll feet and richly decorated with inlaid motifs.*

◁ Jardinière, *or plant-holder that belonged to the Duchesse d'Angoulême. Mahogany and gilt bronze. Made by the École Royale de Arts et Métiers of Chalons, Musée du Louvre, Paris.*

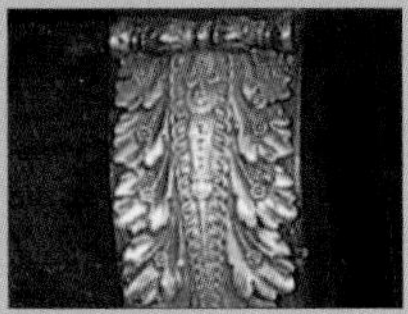

Wood and materials

Light-colored wood: spotted beech, varnished ash, elm, cherry, light-colored poplar, pearwood, plane tree, maple, bird's eye thuya, sycamore, lemonwood, orangewood, olivewood, boxwood root, acacia

Dark-colored wood: mahogany, palisander, amaranthus

Inlays of dark wood on light-wood backgrounds

Bronze sconces

Gray or white marble

Bright-colored Sèvres porcelain

Fabrics and upholstery

Silk, silk velvet, printed linen

Colors: white, the traditional color of the Bourbons; vivid colors such as coral, bright blue, orange, rose, lemon yellow and lime green

CHAIRS WITH PIERCED BACKS

Chair designs modified the Directoire and Empire lines somewhat by adding slight curves, making them look much more graceful and attractive.
The gondola chair, with a deeply curved back, was the most popular. Yet other chairs with straight backs were made, especially during Louis XVIII's reign, along with pierced splats decorated with neo-Gothic cathedral fretwork patterns and solid seat backs sculpted to look like drapery.
The overall shape of the chair followed the form of the chair back, and may have been square, rounded or deeply curved. The front of the apron was also straight.
The chair was always supported by saber legs in the back, and sometimes in the front as well. Other shapes for the front legs included tapered or baluster legs, console legs, cabriole legs, or legs with a slightly oblique shape. The crest rail and apron were often decorated with inlays of dark wood. The scroll-shaped armrests were characteristic features of Restauration-style chairs.

Pierced seat back

These were fairly rare, as most chairs were made with solid straight backs, a style inherited from the Empire. The pierced back or splat could be in the shape of a heart, lyre, vase, fan or simply a bar.

Scroll-shaped armrests

This was a permanent feature of chairs, whether they were designed for city or rural use. The shape of the scroll varied somewhat, and was more or less pronounced; it often ended with a swan or dolphin motif.

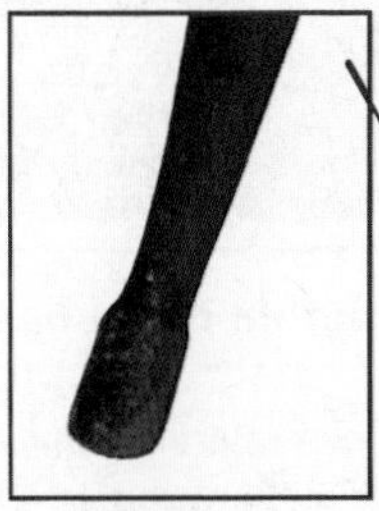

Hoof foot

This was a fairly unusual design, especially for a front leg. The inward-curving shape of the front leg, however, derived from the Greek-style *klismos*, was a frequently used design.

△ Armchair. Fruitwood. Pierced seat back. Saber legs ending with hoof feet in the front, spiral-curved armrests. Upholstered with chintz fabric made in the nineteenth-century fashion. Private collection, Avignon.

FRANCE

1830 1848

The Louis-Philippe Style

△ *Louis-Philippe's Grand Salon. Versailles. Grand Trianon.*

By Louis-Philippe's era, the bourgeois class had become influential enough to dictate its own taste in furniture. The results were simple but paradoxical. On the one hand, styles were geared toward increasing comfort and functionality, reflected in the furniture that was produced using industrialized processes. On the other, the bourgeoisie displayed a total rejection of modernity, turning instead toward imitation of antique styles. The neo-Gothic style of the 1830s was replaced by the neo-Renaissance and neo-Henri II styles around 1835, followed by Boulle copper and tortoiseshell marquetry, then a genre style that was an imitation of the Louis XV and Louis XVI styles in the 1840s. This practice, known as historicism, is based on an almost blind acceptance of copies. It triumphed during Napoleon III's reign and triggered a pan-European fashion for pastiche and eclectic movements. The Louis-Philippe style, also known as the Rococo Revival style, was strongly influenced by another fashion: Anglomania. Already in vogue during the Restauration, this fondness for all things English would be magnified by Louis-Philippe's nostalgic memories of the country in which he spent long years in exile. The only innovative elements that were introduced during this extremely conventional period were the creation of garden furniture for winter gardens and office furniture for the head of the household. These two specifically bourgeois concepts for interior design combined the Romantic fondness for nature and the needs of businessmen during this era of burgeoning industrialization.

The masters

***Claude-Aimé Chevanard (1798-1838): Ornamentalist, published a pattern book,* Recueil d'ornements.**

Alexandre-Louis Bellangé (1799-1863): Cabinetmaker.

Grohé Frères (1808-1885): German cabinetmakers who moved to Paris under Charles X.

Louis-Édouard Lemarchand (1795-1872): cabinetmaker specializing in copies of Boulle marquetry.

Michel-Victor Cruchet (1815-1877): Specialized in copies of Louis XV and Louis XVI chairs.

Georges-Alphonse Jacob-Desmalter (1799-1870): The last member of the Jacob family.

Wood and materials

Dark-colored woods: mahogany, palisander, yew, beech, walnut, walnut burl, ebony, ebonized pearwood and beech

◆◆◆

Compartments

Placed in the apron of the chest of drawers (often used for a fake drawer), this element appeared when the shelf of the small desk was lowered, revealing a series of small ebony storage compartments.

Medallions

The rich decor on the outside doors of this writing cabinet is mirrored by an equally sumptuous inside decor, consisting primarily of medallion motifs, a typical feature of the neo-Renaissance style. They decorate the central drawers.

Marble inlaid base

Marble inlays on tabletops and cabinets were a characteristic element of Renaissance furniture. During this period, rectangular plaques of pink and gray marble appeared, rather curiously, along the base.

WRITING CABINETS

△ *Writing cabinet. Palisander, ebony, palm tree, inlaid marble, leather.*
This is a perfect example of a Renaissance-style copy made for a rich bourgeois client.
This dual-purpose piece of furniture is displayed here as a desk.
Signed by Grohé Frères, 1839. Musée du Louvre, Paris.

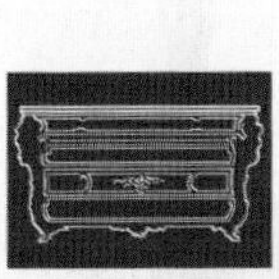

Chests of drawers and the fall-front desks that were generally made to match were designed according to the earlier Empire and Renaissance styles.
The difference between the latter and the bourgeois models was a total absence of marquetry and bronze. The sole ornamentation consisted of natural designs formed by the burl or grain of the various types of wood used (walnut, thuya). Keyholes were framed by extremely simple copper mounts.
Influenced by the English fashion for furniture that could be transformed to serve another function, a chest of drawers could become a dressing table by lifting up the gray marble top to reveal a basin.
Others could be transformed into a desk, with a tabletop fitted into the upper drawers, and drawers and compartments behind the doors, in a commode à vantaux, for example.
Writing cabinets and multi-purpose secretaries were made by some of the greatest cabinetmakers, who based their designs on Renaissance and seventeenth-century models. The results were even more surprising in that these particular pieces of furniture never existed during these earlier periods.

◆◆◆

Light-colored woods: thuya burl, elm burl, bird's eye maple, sycamore, lemon-wood, holly

Gray, black and white marble

Mother-of-pearl, pewter, bone, enamel, Sèvres porcelain, hard stone

Motifsand decorative elements

Rows of beads, bars, dolphins

Quatrefoil (four-lobed) motif

Carved palmettes, scrolls

Bracket feet with claws, frog leg's feet.

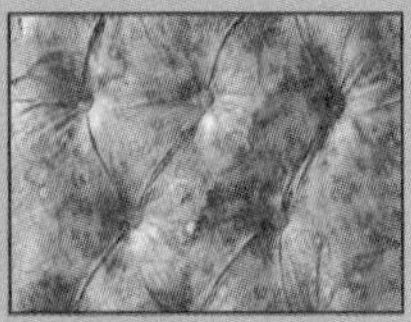

Fabrics and upholstery material

Tapestry with Oriental motifs

Strips of tapestry on velvet backgrounds

Quilted printed silks

Black horsehair, closely woven velvets, leathers

△ Guéridon. *Mahogany and gilt bronze. Musée des Arts décoratifs, Paris.*

THE *GUÉRIDON* AND THE *TRAVAILLEUSE*

Small tables and guéridons (pedestal tables) which were fashionable during the Restauration continued to be extremely popular.
Other tables, in addition to the travailleuse, or sewing table, included the vide-poches (known as a "tidy"), the reading stand and the sideboard, with two shelves of different sizes.
English-style tables became permanent fixtures in bourgeois interiors: the round library table with drawers in the apron became the family table, placed in the middle of the living room; the rectangular folding sofa-table on claw feet, was placed behind the sofa.
The fashion in bourgeois homes was for a profusion of small tables, hence the large number of round guéridons and tilt-top pedestal tables, which could be placed easily against a wall.
Other small tables and stools were used to display various objects and collectibles, which had become extremely important elements in interior design.

Cushion shelf

This shelf was used to hold sewing tools and work in progress. The shape of the cushion—neither oriental nor Chinese—the Gothic-style gallery and the uprights with bamboo patterns exemplify perfectly the period's unbridled fondness for exoticism.

◁ Travailleuse, *or work table, by Alphonse Giroux. Musée du Louvre, Paris.*

ARMCHAIRS

Chairs were the ultimate symbol of bourgeois comfort. Two new designs appeared: the Voltaire chair and the crapaud.

The crapaud chair was entirely covered with upholstery fabric, leaving no wooden frame visible whatsoever; it had a very high, wide back. Long fringed trim concealed the legs.

The Voltaire chair, probably the most famous of chairs made in the Louis-Philippe style, actually first appeared during the Restauration. It had a tall, scroll-topped back that curved inward just above the seat, console padded armrests, rear saber legs, front console legs or sometimes baluster legs; the various models always had castors.

The easy chair was an emblem of bourgeois comfort. It generally had a deeply curved back with curved uprights decorated with scrolls; bracket feet in the front and saber legs in the rear.

The gondola chair, which was still called a fauteuil de toilette, moved from the bedroom to the dining room, where it shared space with the straight armchair, which had a curved crest rail and solid seat back, with spiral armrests resting on a high, rectangular block connecting the apron to the legs.

Garden chairs were covered with a profusion of neo-Gothic and neo-Renaissance ornaments. They were made of cast iron and sometimes rattan or bamboo. These pieces were designed for winter gardens built into the wealthiest bourgeois homes.

Spirals

As opposed to the Renaissance-style spiral-turned elements, the neo-Renaissance spiral-turned elements of Louis-Philippe's era were not hand-carved, but were manufactured industrially on new machines that could produce large quantities of these elements.

△ *Neo-Renaissance armchair with spiral-turned uprights. High seat back upholstered with deep-buttoned silk. Padded armrests. Spiral-turned legs joined by an X-stretcher and mounted on copper rollers. Château de Versailles.*

▽ *Cathedral-style* jardinière *(plant-holder) with a decor of inlaid bone against a Rio rosewood background. Central metal compartment. The piece is supported by four Gothic-style legs, joined by an X-stretcher. Musée des Arts décoratifs, Paris.*

THE *JARDINIÈRE*

This small piece of furniture, which remained extremely popular throughout the entire second half of the nineteenth century, was a perfect vehicle for conveying the various characteristics of a style. Earlier styles were usually round or oval, while these ornamental tables tended to be made in small rectangular or square shapes, with a central metal compartment designed to hold potted plants or cut flowers.

France

1852 1870

The Second Empire Style

△ Napoleon III's office in the Tuileries. *Jean-Baptiste Fortuné de Fournier. Château de Compiègne.*

The proclamation of the Second Empire in 1852 ushered in an era of great prosperity for France and firmly established the supremacy of the bourgeois merchant class. A great revival in the arts and sciences followed, a movement encouraged by the emperor and empress. The major urban renewal project conducted by Baron Haussmann was undertaken with the aim of transforming Paris into a modern, well-proportioned city. Other major work included Charles Garnier's Opera, the development of the railway system, the opening of the first department stores and the first Universal Exhibitions (World's Fairs). All of this contributed to a cultural and social landscape that provided a backdrop for one of the most unusual styles ever seen. The Second Empire (or Napoleon III) style influenced virtually every sector, although some criticized it as the apogee of bad taste. There was an exuberance, extravagance, eccentricity and above all enthusiasm, joy and extremely high quality to the style—as perfect craftsmanship was the keyword guiding all production. The characteristic of this style was that it combined several other styles, borrowing from many different periods and countries. With so many accepted styles, furniture-manufacturers made fortunes. Elements were taken from the Renaissance, Louis XV and Louis XVI styles—the latter so important during this period that the Second Empire style is sometimes called the Louis XVI Revival style. Empress Eugénie was so enamored of Queen Marie-Antoinette that she promoted a Louis XVI Impératrice style. Added to these various styles were Japanese, Chinese and Islamic influences, a combination that sometimes produced rather surprising results: Indian ornamentation in caryatid shapes, imitation bamboo and cording in bronze, and Sèvres porcelain medallions framed by gilt bronze—not to mention the countless motifs of bright-colored sweet-briar and rose bouquets, pagodas, magots, trelliswork and birds. With such a vast ornamental vocabulary, Second Empire furniture will always be known as a pastiche style.

The masters

Alexandre-Georges Fourdinois (1799-1871): *Specialized in beautiful copies of marquetry.*

Henri Dasson (1825-1896): *Cabinetmaker and bronzesmith specializing in neo-Louis XV-style furniture.*

Guillaume Grohé (1808-1885): *Specialized in copies of all styles of furniture.*

Louis-Auguste-Alfred Beurdeley (1808-1882): *Copied eighteenth-century furniture for the imperial palaces.*

Charles-Joseph-Marie Jeanselme: *In 1847, took over the Jacob business and worked for the national palaces.*

Many companies: *L'Escalier de Cristal, Quetin, Duval Frères, Duvinage, Rousseau, Krieger, Mercier, Sormani: all specialists in copying every type of furniture and style, including Japanese pieces (some continued through the mid-twentieth century).*

OTHER FURNITURE

Large desks continued to be made in the style of the first Empire, but with a profusion of ornamentation.
The design for women's desks was derived from the Louis XV style, with curved shapes and a sophisticated mother-of-pearl, marquetry, porcelain and pewter decor.
Bookcases also became fashionable. Neo-Gothic or cathedral-style pieces were the most highly prized, but two-tiered bookcases made of black lacquered wood also appeared. The lower section was closed, while the upper section had two or three rounded glass doors. A multitude of elements contributed to the excess of ornamentation: painted decors, molding, bronze and mother-of-pearl inlays. Guéridons tables rested on caryatid or bamboo supports and had one or several shelves made of marble, malachite or Russian porphyry.

Arabesques on feet

With this style of furniture, every possible surface was decorated—especially the feet, where delicate arabesques and painted gilt foliated scrolls framed a central bouquet.

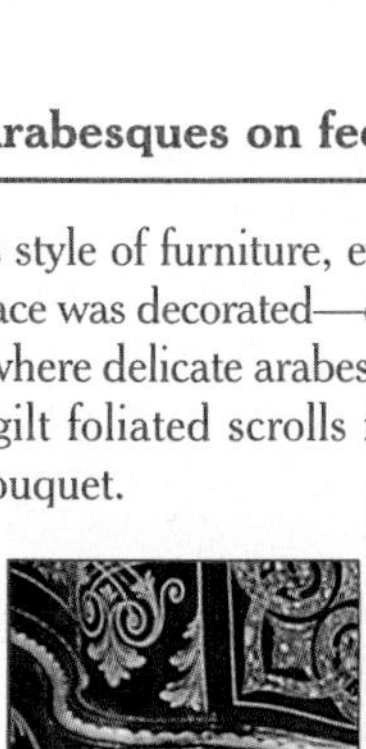

CHESTS AND CABINETS

The tall chest of drawers became an extremely common piece of furniture. This was a display piece designed to decorate an entrance of a living room. Both a chest and a low buffet, it sometimes had doors or drawers (four or five). The most common chests of this type were made in the Boulle style with inlays of tortoiseshell and copper, or in a style vaguely derived from the Louis XIV style, with a profusion of bronze and black lacquer and inlays of mother-of-pearl with a painted decor.

△ *Chest of drawers. Ebonized painted wood, inlays of mother-of-pearl with painted highlights, gilt bronze, motif of flowers and birds fluttering around a nest. Four drawers. 1855. Musée des Arts décoratifs, Paris.*

Pictorial pastiche

Furniture pieces became supports for brilliantly executed pictorial pastiches. Here, two lovebirds flutter around a nest holding two eggs, set in the midst of flowers painted in the manner of seventeenth-century Dutch still lifes.

▽ *Cabinet, black lacquered wood with mother-of-pearl inlay. Musée des Arts décoratifs, Paris.*

Mother-of-pearl inlays

Mother-of-pearl inlay was a characteristic feature of both the Second Empire and Victorian styles. Some inlays were brilliant examples of craftsmanship, as were the ornate arabesques framing the doors of the chest.

Wood and materials

Ebony, pitch pine, ebonized pearwood, rosewood, palisander, lacquered wood for small pieces of furniture

Electroplated gilt bronze used to create entire pieces of furniture, not just ornamental elements

Papier mâché, made from molded paper pulp, was used for mass production of chairs, pedestal tables and small pieces of furniture. They were often decorated with inlays of a type of mother-of-pearl known as "burgau" among antique dealers and furniture-makers.

Cuir bouilli, or molded leather, which resembled papier mâché

Cast iron, used as supports for furniture of state, pedestal tables and garden furniture

CHAIRS

Chairs played a predominant role in furnishing. They were, in a sense, the harbingers of a style. So many chairs in so many styles were made that it would be difficult to draw up a complete inventory. On the one hand were chairs made in a pastiche of Louis XV and Louis XVI styles; these were often so well imitated that an untrained eye could easily mistake them for authentic eighteenth-century pieces. On the other hand were all the whimsical pieces: chairs with designs imitating cording, bamboo and Chinese lacquer, papier mâché chairs with mother-of-pearl inlay, deep-buttoned armchairs with abundant trim, fumeuses, or smoking chairs that men could straddle to lean against the top, and, of course, the gondola chair in memory of the First Empire. The most famous were the giltwood or black wood charivari, with turned splats and a deep-cushioned seat—copies of these chairs are often rented for receptions today. The chauffeuse, designed for women who wanted to sit close to a fireplace, appeared under Louis-Philippe's reign. It came in all possible variations: imitation bamboo, giltwood or ebonized wood, papier mâché with mother-of-pearl inlays and black lacquer. Its chief feature was its very low seat and somewhat curved seat back, similar to the Voltaire chair.

◁ Chauffeuse. *Ebonized pearwood, seat decorated with stylized shells on the crest and seat rails. It stands on saber legs in the rear, curved legs to the front. Private collection, Avignon.*

▷ Gondola chair, *ca 1855. Papier mâché, ebonized wood, mother-of-pearl inlay and gilt paint. Musée des Arts décoratifs, Paris.*

▷ Wooden chair, *black lacquer and mother-of-pearl inlays. Musée des Arts décoratifs, Paris.*

▷ Chair of state. *Black lacquer, rectilinear seat back with a pediment on the crest rail. The chair stands on baluster-legs. Its function was purely decorative: it was designed to decorate an entry or formal living room. Private collection, Avignon.*

THE *CONFIDANTE*

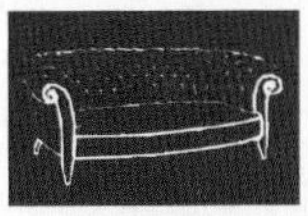

Known as confidantes and indiscrets, these love seats were the great innovation of the Second Empire. These pieces of furniture were designed to foster friendly conversation in a most comfortable setting. Cabinetmakers, furniture-makers and upholsterers used these pieces as supports to demonstrate the breadth of their skills. The confidantes and indiscrets were generally covered with deep-buttoned upholstery. The support, often on castors, was concealed under long fringe. The giltwood or ebonized armrests were the only visible woodwork. The confidante consisted of two reversed armchairs, joined by an upper S-shaped crest rail. The indiscret was formed of three armchairs, one of which was perpendicular to the other two; the crest rail was shaped like a three-bladed propellor.

◁ Confidante *with fitted cane seat. Musée des Arts décoratifs, Paris.*

POUFS

The pouf was the latest in fashion. It was a low, thickly padded stool that was highly versatile as an extra chair. It generally had a deep-buttoned upholstery with side skirts and trim that concealed the wooden frame. Some poufs were made as padded stools, usually deep-buttoned and supported by four short, carved wooden legs that were joined underneath the seat by an X-stretcher. The legs were designed to look like ropes, bamboo or even rockery. These backless seats were introduced into France sometime around 1830, after the development of coil-spring, deep-buttoned upholstery.

△ *Pouf with a cord motif support. Giltwood, Satin brocade, trim. Cord-like legs with X-stretcher in the form of a sailor's knot. Ca 1860. Musée des Arts décoratifs, Paris.*

◆◆◆

Chinese lacquer, japanning, black lacquered woods, porcelain plaques and medallions, inlays of copper pewter, bone, ivory, mother-of-pearl and tortoiseshell were all popular.

Fabrics and upholstery

Widespread use of upholstery padding, skirting and trim on chairs, sofas, settees and beds

Tapestry-makers play a decisive role in all Second Empire-style furniture

Quilted velvet with flower pattern (bright colors against a dark background)

Quilted bayadere velvet (wide multicolored stripes)

Brocaded satin, quilted silk

Bayadere trim

Chintz with floral prints

Bright colors: bright yellows, blues and red

SECRETARIES

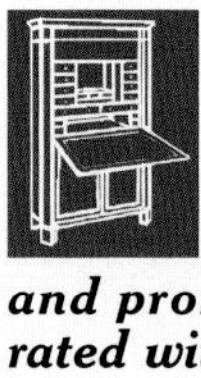

Secretaries were modeled after Louis XVI-style designs and profusely decorated with projecting molding and bronzes. Some had shelves, and some, though more unusual, displayed extraordinarily high levels of craftsmanship and imagination.

△ Secretary made by Tahan. Presented at Alphonse Giroux's stand at the 1855 Universal Exhibition in Paris. Made of carved linden wood, gilt bronze and porcelain plaques. Exuberant Rococo-inspired foliage decor. This is a very good example of the influence of the naturalist movement. The exceptional piece of furniture, midway between a woman's desk and a secretary, was immediately purchased by Empress Eugénie. Château de Compiègne.

TABLES

The mobility and small size of small tables and guéridons perfectly met the persistent and growing demand for comfort and efficiency. Their popularity (which began to grow during the reign of Louis XVI) continued unabated. These tables were usually manufactured in black lacquer or in wood painted with bouquets of flowers, modeled after the seventeenth-century Dutch style.
Nesting tables were designed in graduated sizes to fit one beneath the other when not in use. Usually four to a set, they were rectangular and decorated according to a common theme or with a variation of a theme on each table. The tilt-top table had a round or rectangular tabletop attached to a tripod by means of a tripod support. These tables were always ornately decorated with painted motifs and mother-of-pearl inlay.
The gaming table was either rectangular or square and was covered with felt. The tabletop folded in half. Made of ebonized wood or varnished curly-grained mahogany, it was often profusely ornamented. The travailleuse*, or work table, had a rectangular tabletop and opened to form a cabinet. It rested on four tall legs joined by a wide stretcher that formed a shelf. It was often made of papier mâché with mother-of-pearl inlay. Large dining room tables were of little interest, as they were usually copies of the Louis XVI, Regency or heavy Italian Renaissance tables (known as* cartibula*).*

△ Gaming table made in the manner of Boulle. Oak frame. Inlays of mother-of-pearl and brass. Musée Magnin, Dijon.

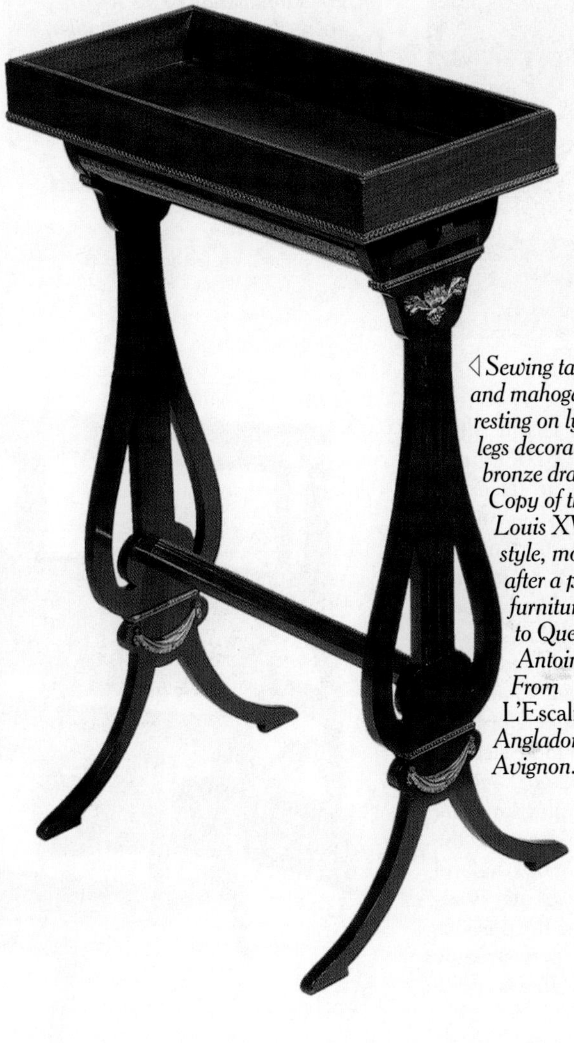

◁ Sewing table. Mahogany and mahogany veneer resting on lyre-shaped legs decorated with gilt bronze drapery mounts. Copy of the Louis XVI-Impératrice style, modeled after a piece of furniture that belonged to Queen Marie-Antoinette. From L'Escalier de Cristal. *Angladon Foundation, Avignon.*

UNITED KINGDOM

1800 — 1830

The Regency Style

△ English Interior. *Eugène Delacroix. Musée du Louvre.*

The first Regency style corresponds to the reign of George III, starting in 1800, and the regency of his son, the Prince of Wales, from 1811 to 1820. During this period, England appeared as the bastion of a certain "good taste," in opposition to what was seen as the excesses of the First Empire style—an attitude fueled by the fact that France and England were political enemies. Yet England borrowed and adapted much of the French ornamentation, notably the Egyptian motifs (symbols of the French conquests), which reappeared in a slightly different form on many Regency pieces of furniture. The first Regency style was strongly influenced by the drawings of the famous cabinetmaker Thomas Sheraton, published in his *Designs for Furniture* and *The Cabinet Maker and Upholsterer's Drawing Book*.

The characteristics of this furniture style had already been developed prior to the early nineteenth century: a Louis XVI inspiration reinterpreted with more slender, graceful lines, a fragile elegance combined with an impression of strength, austere ornamentation, exceptional marquetry work and a fondness for metamorphic furniture (pieces that could be transformed to serve another purpose). What is known as the second Regency style began when the regent was finally crowned king of England (becoming King George IV) in 1820. This style was characterized by greater ornamentation and exuberance; ornately carved motifs returned to the fore, and the previous graceful elegance was replaced by a sense of power. Furniture design was strongly influenced by the king's personal fondness for exoticism, imitation and chinoiseries.

The masters

Thomas Sheraton (1751-1806): Cabinetmaker and designer. His pattern books influenced furniture-makers throughout Europe and the United States.

Morgan & Sanders: They created elegant chairs and magnificent pieces known as metamorphic furniture.

Motifs and decorative elements

Favorite motifs during the Regency style: dolphins, rope and cable patterns, anchors, acanthus leaves, Greek palmettes and adaptations of the French neo-Egyptian motifs.

Under George IV: motifs of dragons, serpents, fantastic birds, magots, Chinese parasols, imitation bamboo, inlays of copper and tortoiseshell.

TABLES

As in all of Europe during this period, all kinds of tables were extremely popular, notably large dining-room tables. Made from the most beautiful cuts of mahogany, the tabletops rested on a single central column supported by a tripod base with claw feet or a concave plinth.
The sofa table, placed behind the sofas in a living room, was a variation of the Pembroke table with extra leaves. The drum table (known as the table de famille *in France) was a circular table with a series of drawers fitted into the apron. The breakfast table, with a rectangular tabletop, was supported by a central pillar resting on four concave feet with castors. Quartet tables were the great innovation of the Regency style: these were nesting tables, or several small tables that fit one beneath the other.*

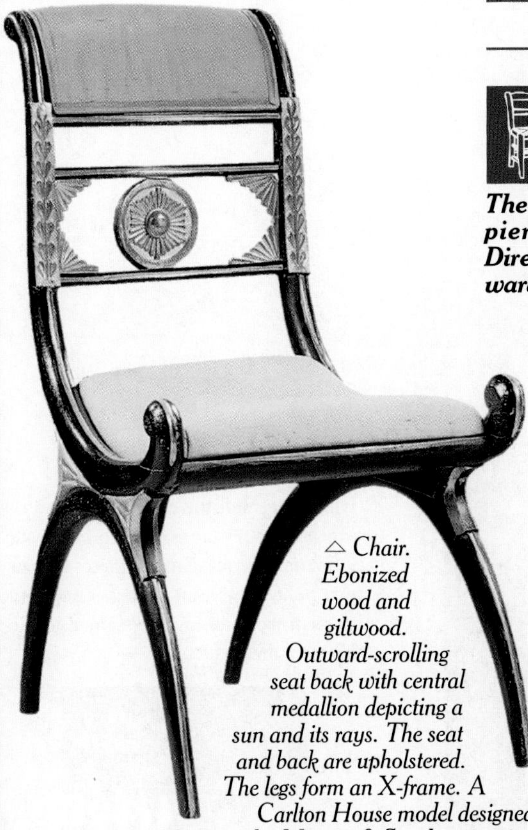

△ Chair. Ebonized wood and giltwood. Outward-scrolling seat back with central medallion depicting a sun and its rays. The seat and back are upholstered. The legs form an X-frame. A Carlton House model designed by Morgan & Sanders, inspired from the Greek klismos chair. 1815. Sotheby's, London.

CHAIRS

Chairs and armchairs made in the first Regency style had straight or curved legs, adapted from the Louis XV and Louis XVI styles.
The seat backs were solid with medallions or were pierced. Some designs were derived from the Directoire style, in which the seat back had an outward-scrolling curve.

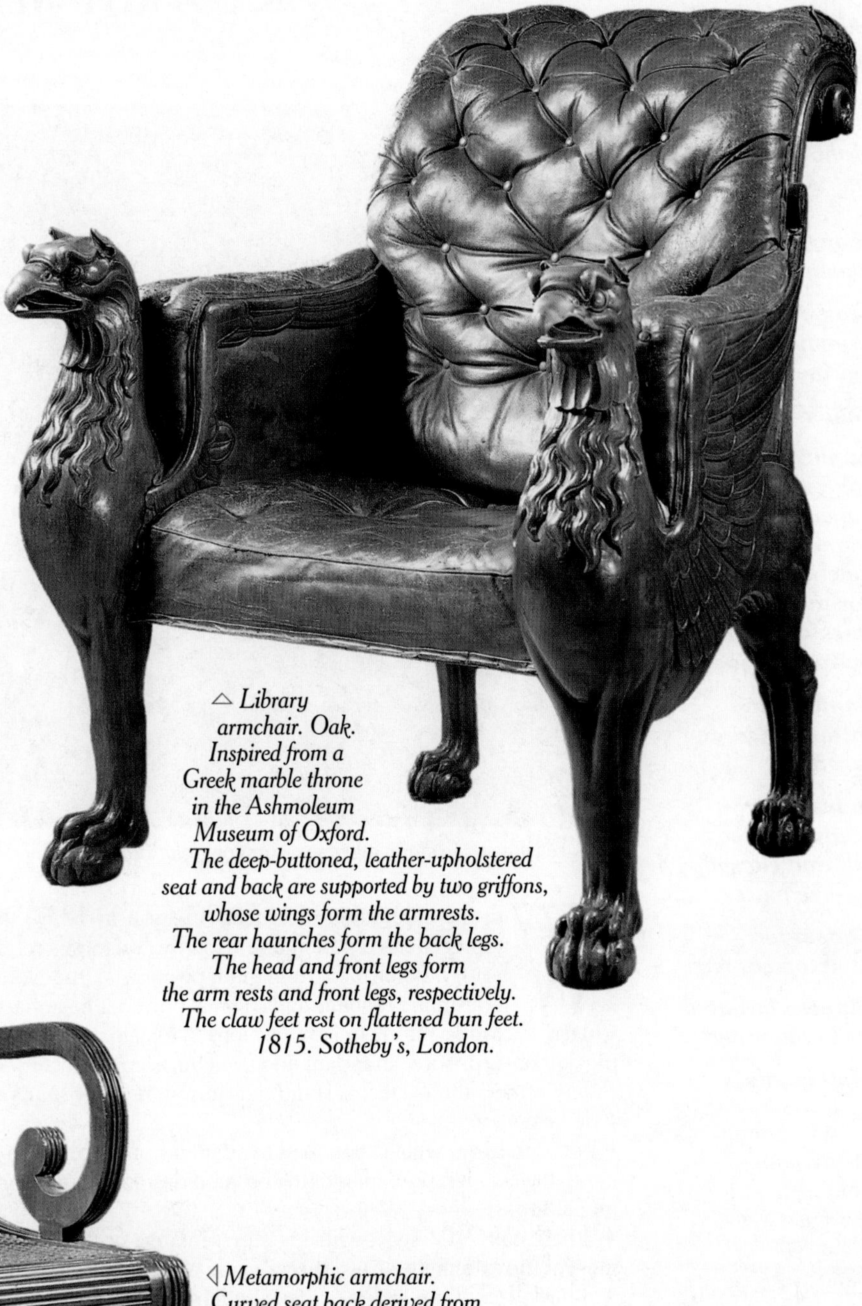

△ Library armchair. Oak. Inspired from a Greek marble throne in the Ashmoleum Museum of Oxford. The deep-buttoned, leather-upholstered seat and back are supported by two griffons, whose wings form the armrests. The rear haunches form the back legs. The head and front legs form the arm rests and front legs, respectively. The claw feet rest on flattened bun feet. 1815. Sotheby's, London.

◁ Metamorphic armchair. Curved seat back derived from an ancient Greek design, scroll armrests, saber legs. The seat is formed of a reeded seat rail concealing a mechanism that transforms the armchair into a stepladder. The seat back becomes the rear support of the ladder, the rear legs of the chair become the support for the middle steps, and the front legs separate into two sections. Made by B. Harmer from a design by Morgan & Sanders. 1815. Sotheby's, London.

United Kingdom

1837 – 1901

The Victorian Style

Wood and materials

Mahogany, walnut, walnut burl, beech, ebony, laurel, linden

Teak and camphor for marine furniture

Papier mâché

Application of colored pieces of paper on wood frame or papier maché, then covered with thick varnish to imitate lacquers

Bamboo and rattan for garden furniture

Industrially manufactured gilt and chased bronze pieces

Copper for tabletop corners

Chinese lacquers and japanning

Marble inlays

△ Benedicite: Grandmother's celebration. *John Henry Lorimer. Musée d'Orsay, Paris.*

With the coronation of Queen Victoria in 1837, the country entered an unprecedented period of prosperity. Victoria's reign, one of the longest in history, confirmed England's position as the world's greatest maritime, industrial, economic and colonial power. The impact on European styles of Queen Victoria's efforts to ease tensions between England and France was an explosion of surprising, abundant and sometimes contradictory elements.

A few principal movements stand out during the sixty-four years that the Victorian style held sway:

◆ Neoclassicism, which continued to adapt Thomas Sheraton's legacy, but by thickening the slender, pure lines of the brilliant designer and by adding increasing ornamentation.

◆ The Louis XIV style, which is representative of this style in name only, because most of the extremely curved pieces made were copies of the Rococo style.

◆ The Elizabethan style (or Elizabethan Revival), which never actually existed during Elizabeth I's reign; it was a combination of all the sixteen- and seventeenth-century English styles.

◆ The neo-Gothic styles, which combined metal, a material the furniture-makers had started to incorporate into their work, especially for garden furniture.

◆ The Late Victorian style, also called art furniture, which was very similar to the French Second Empire (Napoleon III style), sharing with it a taste for ebonized wood and gilt bronze mounts, and a fascination with Japan and its culture.

Maritime furniture was also made during this period and, although it was fairly marginal, it was a more austere style and a welcome change from the other styles. It was characterized by highly geometric shapes carved in beautiful wood (teak, mahogany or camphor wood). This was an eminently functional style of furniture, fitted with copper handles and with skillfully crafted copper mounts protecting the corners and edges.

Fringed trim

Trim concealed the castors and feet of armchairs that were entirely covered with upholstery. As small masterpieces in their own right, these trim elements required hours of work and were essential to the design of these chairs.

▷ *Easy chair. Covered with a Persian-carpet upholstery fabric known as turkeywork. Design by Liberty & Company. 1890. Sotheby's, London.*

CHAIRS

There were so many sofas and settees that a model existed for almost every specific purpose: for smoking, reading, sewing, writing, sleeping and so on. They were all deep-buttoned and extremely comfortable. The most famous sofa design appeared during the reign of William IV (1830-1837): this was the Chesterfield, with deep-buttoned upholstery and coil-springs.

Deep-buttoned leather

This was the apogee of Victorian comfort. Only the interior of the armrests and seat backs were deep-buttoned, never the seat itself.

△ Chesterfield armchair. Mahogany. Seat back and outward-scrolling armrests covered with deep-buttoned red-leather upholstery. The seat itself is not deep-buttoned. Saber legs in the rear and turned legs in the front, resting on four copper castors. 1835. Sotheby's, London.

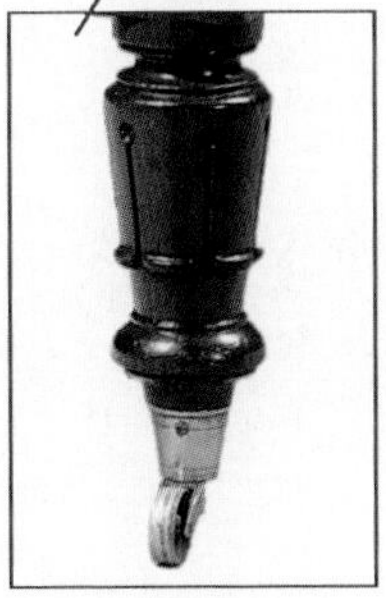

Castors

This major English innovation was invented in the eighteenth century and became an almost obligatory element in the nineteenth. Sometimes, however, the castors were fitted only to the front legs.

Fabric

Stretched leather, quilted leather for Chesterfield sofas and armchairs

Turkeywork: embroidered upholstery, imitative of Oriental carpets

Persian and Turkish carpets used to upholster armchairs and sofas

Quilted and/or printed velvets

Printed silk, damask, fabrics printed with Liberty & Company designs

Widespread use of tassels and fringe, notably on armchairs and sofas.

TABLES

All kinds of tables continued to be designed for the home. The most famous were the teapoy tables, small pedestal tables with three short legs, small bamboo stools, dumbwaiters (with two or more tiered shelves), japanned papier maché pedestal tables, gaming tables with a reversible, foldout checkerboard tabletop and nesting tables.

△ Dumbwaiter. Rosewood. The bottom shelf is supported by S-shaped legs, the second shelf, by turned columns. 1860. Sotheby's, London.

▷ Small pedestal table. Satinwood, rosewood and marble. Christie's, London.

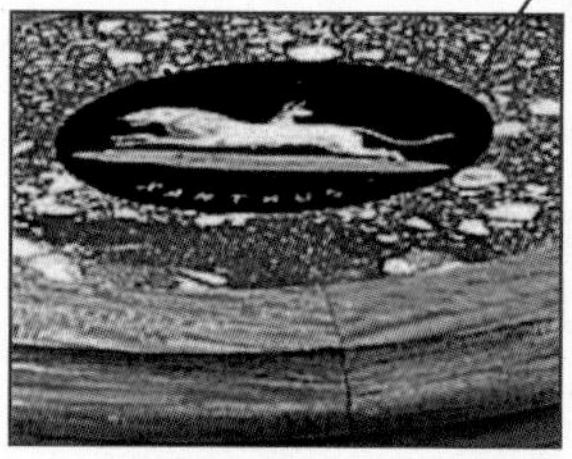

Central motif

This was a pastiche of pietre dure motifs taken from Italian Renaissance tables. In this case, it represents Xanthus, a river mentioned in *The Iliad*, framed by a circle of pink marble.

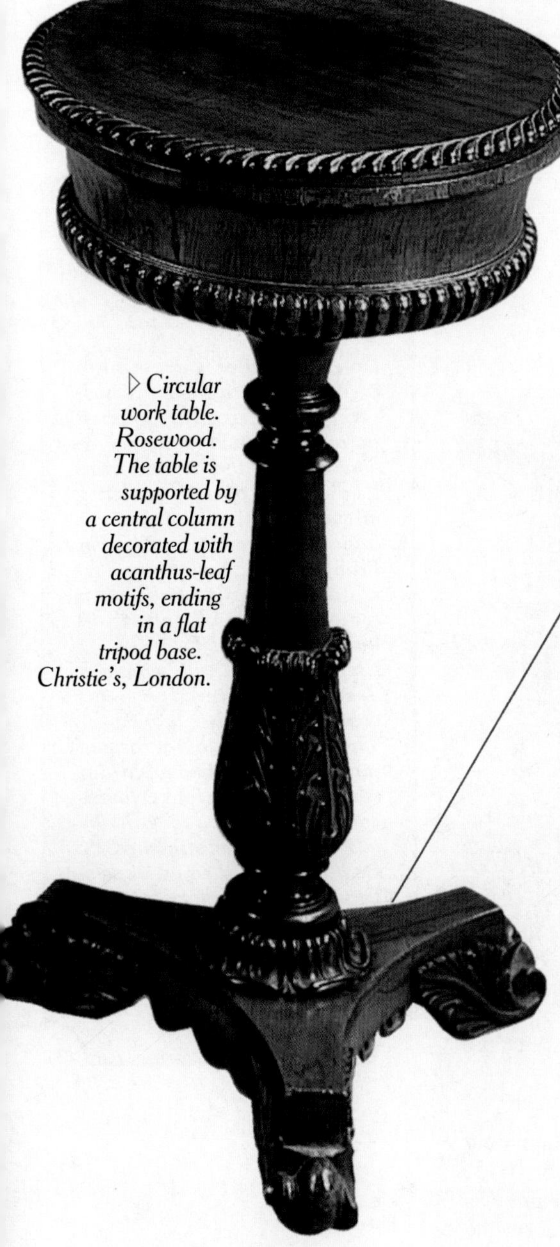

▷ *Circular work table. Rosewood. The table is supported by a central column decorated with acanthus-leaf motifs, ending in a flat tripod base. Christie's, London.*

Flat tripod base

This type of base, used generally to support a column, appeared throughout Europe during this period.

Finial

This ornament was a characteristic feature of the Renaissance style. On this piece, the finials are placed on the sides, while in the original style they were usually placed in the center of the stretcher.

△ *Elizabethan Revival rectangular work table. Rosewood. Interior compartment decorated with marquetry. The chest is supported by spiral-turned legs, joined by a spiral-turned stretcher with carved finials. Christie's, London.*

The masters

Josef Danhauser (1780-1829): Furniture-maker and principal proponent of the Biedermeier style. He inspired many other cabinetmakers, who adopted his simpler forms, restrained use of decoration and well-proportioned lines.

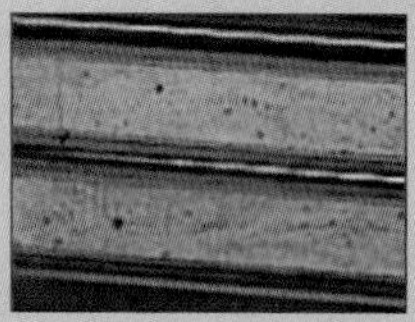

Wood and materials

Cherry

Maple

Pine

Karelian birch and, in general, all very light-colored woods

GERMANY

1815  1848

The Biedermeier Style

△ *Biedermeier Room. 1840. Regional Museum, Herrnhut.*

The Confederation of the Rhine, which Napoleon instituted after eliminating the Holy Roman Empire, was dissolved by the Vienna Congress of 1815. The German Confederation succeeded Napoleon's Confederation and was governed by the Emperor of Austria, who ruled as president. Hence, the German bourgeoisie in the early nineteenth century followed—quite willingly—the artistic and cultural influence of the Austrian capital, Vienna. The legendary conformity of the Austrian bourgeoisie found an enthusiastic following in Germany, symbolized by the emergence of a style developed, in part, by Josef Danhauser.

This style was not named for its creator, as it became known as the Biedermeier style, a name derived from the contraction of two names that symbolized the smug, narrow-minded bourgeois attitude of the reigning German conformity: Biedermann and Bummelmeier.

These two figures, who only actually existed via the incessant gibes of a popular satiric newspaper, were well-known throughout Germany for their aspirations to live with the families in "well-ordered," comfortable interiors provided, however, that they didn't cost too much. In retrospect, the Biedermeier style deserves more credit. It was largely derived from ancient Greek and Roman design principles, and therefore barely differed from most of the other styles of the era or the styles that preceded it. Its uniqueness resides in the extreme restraint with which Danhauser treated the ancient architectural elements, retaining, as it were, only the framework. Ornamentation and decorative motifs were banished, while the top priority was to use beautiful woods and simple forms. No bronze mounts or sculptures interfered with the curved or straight lines.

This is what created the elegance of this style, along with perfect proportions. Large-size pieces, such as armoires and bookcases, were often in the shape of simple Gothic curves with an extremely austere pediment, which was often supported by cylindrical columns, also devoid of any ornaments or fluting. Seat backs were often pierced with flat rod splats.

MAIN PIECES OF FURNITURE

Console tables were highly popular as "entre- deux," which referred to furniture placed between two windows.
The back of the méridiennes had an outward-scrolling curve. Sofas were the most important pieces of furniture in living rooms; they were surrounded by sofa tables on which various objects or oil lamps were placed.
Chairs were generally simple in design, upholstered in light-colored or bayadere fabric.
They were usually arranged around a large round table that was supported by four cylindrical columns joined together by a large plinth-like stretcher.
Bedrooms had their own specific pieces of furniture, consisting of an armoire, a dressing table, a bedside table and sometimes a chest of drawers.

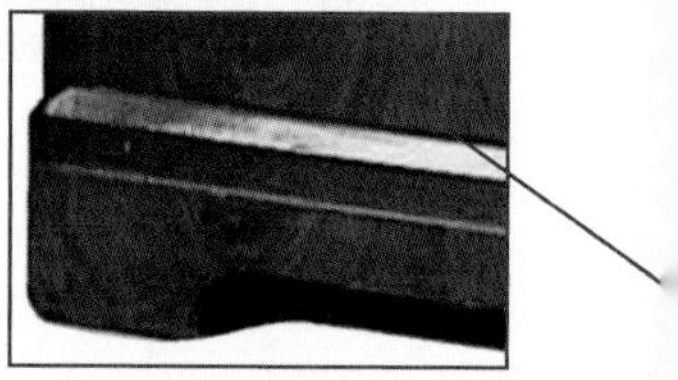

The base

The absolutely austere base combined curved lines on the side and geometric lines on the front.

SECRETARIES

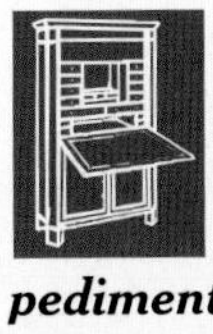

These pieces were always in a simple temple-like shape, i.e., surmounted with a Greek-style pediment. Secretaries were placed in living rooms. This element was inseparable from the sofa, armchairs and large tables found in all German bourgeois homes during this period.

Geometric pediment

This element was usually modeled after the pediment of a Greek temple. On this piece, the Greek form is itself surmounted by an extremely unusual, though splendid, rounded cornice.

Interior mirror

This element was similar to the seventeenth-century Italian cabinets or Empire-style console tables. It created a larger sense of depth by multiplying the motifs—the column was placed in the center to magnify this effect.

◁ Biedermeier-style secretary made of mahogany. A fall-front top opens to form a desk, revealing two rows of small drawers decorated with marquetry and mirrors and a central column. The lower section consists of three drawers resting on a base. Christie's, London.

Russia

1800  1825

The Neoclassical Style

△ *Alexander I's office. Alexander Palace, Pushkin.*

For many years, the lack of knowledge about the history of Russian history meant that it was often excluded from books about furniture. We now know just how splendid Russian furniture was. We also know that its entire history is somewhat ironic, because the stylistic principles for which it is criticized—copies, excess ornamentation and a somewhat pompous style—were exactly the same principles that swept through Europe in the second half of the nineteenth century. Between 1800 and 1820, Russia continued to adapt French furniture designs; the Directoire style was predominant at this time. It was known in Russia as the Jacob style and in France, as the Russian Jacob style. The only thing furniture had in common with the pieces made by the French cabinetmaker Jacob was the systematic use of mahogany. This style achieved an unprecedented success and would continue uninterrupted from 1800 to 1830. At the same time, a famous style known as the Russian Empire style appeared in 1800. This was the Russian adaptation of the ornamental motifs borrowed from ancient Egypt by way of the French Empire style. It remained in fashion until 1830 and produced a profusion of spectacular pieces of furniture. Furniture was made of natural woods (notably Karelian birch) and featured audacious forms and saber feet, along with a large number of highly detailed motifs, including standing sphinxes, busts of women wearing Nemes headdresses, Egyptian birds, eagles, sheaves of wheat framed by sickles, urns, dolphins encircling amphoras, swans with outspread wings, gigantic palmettes, intertwined hunting horns and arrows (singly, in clusters or crossed). The more audacious the motif (and the materials used), the more popular the piece of furniture. At the same time, in 1825, Russia became the first country in Europe to adopt the doctrines of an eclectic philosophy that espoused borrowing elements and characteristics of past styles. These included, among others, the use of giltwood, a Rococo adaptation of the Louis XV style with bucolic scenes of porcelain plaques, an Oriental reinterpretation of the neo-Gothic style for the furniture designed for the Alexandria Cottage in Petrodvorets, and the appearance of the two-headed eagle motif.

The masters

Heinrich Gambs (1765-1831): *German cabinetmaker who moved to Saint Petersburg in 1780.*

Andrei Voronikhin (1759-1814): *Architect who designed furniture made by Gambs.*

Carlo Rossi (1775-1849): *Architect who designed the Winter Palace and many pieces of furniture.*

Vassili Stasov (1769-1848): *Architect.*

Alexandre Pavlovitch Bryullov (1798-1877): *French furniture-maker who made the Pompeian furniture for the Winter Palace in 1837.*

Wood and materials

Mahogany, Karelian birch, black birch, maple

Giltwood and painted wood

Eglomized glass, colored glass

Bronze and porcelain for pedestal tables

Wing-shaped armrest

Armrests, made of wood carved in the workshop of Karl Scheibe, gilded in the workshop of F. Koelner and designed by Voronikhine, rested on a wood support patinated to look like bronze.

***Jardinière* support**

This is a unique feature in the history of furniture. The integration of a *jardinière* (plant-holder) in a furniture leg was a specific characteristic of the architect Voronikhin, who also designed an armchair whose armrests ended in a *jardinière* for the Pavlosk Palace.

JARDINIÈRES-DESKS

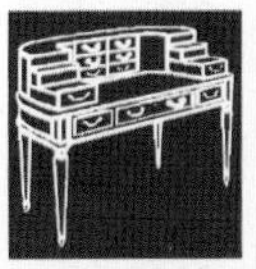

Desks were generally used as a pretext by cabinetmakers to display their skills. They were superbly luxurious and even whimsical, with an accumulation of patinated and gilt bronze elements, brass, precious woods, eglomized glass and porcelain. The most extraordinary examples were the famous* jardinières*-desks made between 1805 and 1815 by the cabinetmaker Heinrich Gambs, from drawings by the imperial architect Voronikhin for the Pavlosk Palace. These desks were decorated with gilt bronze trophies and urns; the unique feature of these desks were the dished corners that could hold plants and flowers.

◁ Jardinière-*desk made of mahogany and decorated with patinated bronze and gilt bronze vases and urns. Attributed to Heinrich Gambs after a design by Voronikhin. Paul I's apartment. Pavlosk Palace. Saint-Petersburg.*

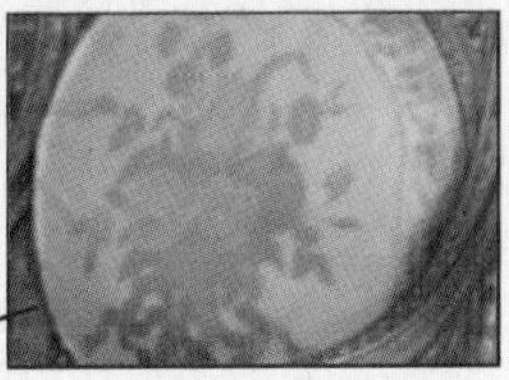

Italian-style seat backs

The rectangular seat back in the middle of which was fitted a padded and upholstered medallion was a common element in late eighteenth-century Russian furniture.

▷ *Italian-style armchair with flower-wreath motif and a medallion. Carved, painted and gilt wood. Maria Fyodorovna's apartment. Pavlosk Palace, Saint-Petersburg.*

ARMCHAIRS

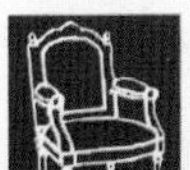

Armchairs followed the same pattern of extravagant and luxurious design that had overtaken all imperial furniture. Neoclassicism was expressed in a number of unbelievable richly ornamented chairs that adopted, and accentuated almost to the point of caricature, the characteristics of the Greek style: scrolls of acanthus leaves, saber legs and seat backs of various shapes (curved, lyre, outward-scrolling curves). For the Greek Room in the Pavlosk Palace, made of columns of green porphyry, the architect Voronikhin commissioned from the cabinetmaker Karl Schiebe a series of unusually exaggerated Greek armchairs.

EUROPE

1870 1900

The Eclectic Styles

△ The Fresco Room. *Elizabeth Frances Boyd. Musée d'Orsay, Paris.*

The first Universal Exhibition was held in London in 1851 at the Crystal Palace. A new idea gradually took hold and developed with the subsequent exhibitions held in 1867 (Paris), 1873 (Vienna) and 1876 (Philadelphia): eclecticism. Inspired by Victor Cousin's philosophical-spiritual movement, this movement appeared in Russia in 1825, in England in 1840 and in France during the Second Empire. The development of mass-production techniques for making furniture meant that "furniture houses" (the new masters in the field of furniture), such as that of Josef Danhauser, could offer a selection of designs extending over four or five centuries of successive styles.

The movement began in Russia in 1825 with Gothic copies that featured Oriental elements.

In England, various Revival styles flourished starting in the 1840s. The different styles included the naturalistic style and the Louis XVI Revival style, a sort of hybrid deep-buttoned Louis XV Rococo crossed with vaguely naturalistic themes. The Egyptian Revival style was nothing more than a disguised Empire style (in a resolutely anti-Napoleonic England, it was unacceptable to call it by its real name). The Elizabethan Revival was a mixture of neo-Jacobean and William and Mary styles, with a touch of Queen Anne for good measure! Finally, a much more interesting style, art furniture (1870-1890) appeared; this style was inspired by Japanese designs, but was fairly simple in form and prefigured the modern style. Between

◆◆◆

The masters

Édouard Lièvre (1829-1886): Designed many pieces of extravagant furniture, including a bronze bed of state.

Charles Hunsinger (1823-1893): Created cabinetry worthy of the great past masters.

Charles-Adolphe-Frédéric Wagner: Hunsinger's partner in the production of his masterpieces.

Charles-Guillaume Diehl: The most inventive cabinetmaker, who prefigured the modern style.

Eugène Grasset (1845-1917): Illustrator and ornamentalist with a passion for the Middle Ages and the Far East; he was a precursor of the Art Nouveau movement.

Ferdinand Barbedienne (1810-1892): Cabinetmaker specialized in the reproduction of ancient pieces of furniture, which had become highly fashionable.

Pagoda cornice

This superbly crafted cornice is not really Japanese; it could be Chinese, Thai, Burmese or even Indonesian. It mattered little, as long as it evoked the Far East and exoticism.

Painted panel

This is an oil painting by Édouard Detaille representing a Mongol or Tartar warrior, or perhaps a Samurai on horseback. The subject was meant to illustrate the armor-like appearance of the cabinet.

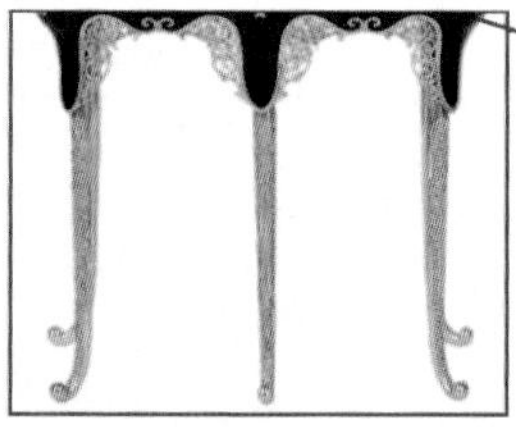

Tapered wand-like legs

This is the finishing touch to a piece of furniture already heavily ornamented with audacious details. Placing this structure on such slender legs almost defies the law of gravity.

JAPANESE CABINET

◁ *Japanese cabinet by Édouard Lièvre. 1877. Palisander, ebony, glass, engraved iron, bronze, oil painting on panel. The pagoda-shaped cornice was added as a supposed characteristic of Japanese art. Musée d'Orsay, Paris.*

Wood and materials

- *All types of wood*
- *Giltwood*
- *Painted wood*
- *Woods with industrially created patinas*
- *Silvered and gilt bronzes*
- *Chryselephantine sculptures*
- *Cloisonné*
- *Enamels*
- *Eglomized glass*
- *Iridescent glass*
- *Painted metal*
- *Lacquers*
- *Marquetry on ivory backgrounds*
- *Pietre dure marquetery*
- *Metal for folding furniture*
- *Rattan and willow for garden furniture*

△ The Student. *Francesco Oller y Cestero. Musée d'Orsay, Paris.*

◆◆◆

1890 and 1900, under the influence of such artists as Edward Burne-Jones or the writer John Ruskin, a heavy Celtic style, strongly influenced by the Middle Ages, persisted for several years.

In France, the use of varied furniture styles reached fever pitch. On the one hand was the type of furniture that had been exhibited at the Universal Exhibitions: it was overly historicized in concept, paid tribute to such diverse figures as Marie-Antoinette, Merovaeus and Joan of Arc, and favored extremely luxurious and abundant bronze ornamentation. These pieces were made by famous bronzesmiths and cabinetmakers, commissioned by furniture companies like L'Escalier de Cristal and the Fourdinois, Duvinage and Rousseau companies.

On the other hand was a composite-style of bourgeois furniture that literally overwhelmed interiors with fake Louis XV sofas, fake Charles X bedroom furniture, fake Louis XIV stools and, especially, fake Henri II dining room sets. These all appeared during the reign of Louis-Philippe and remained extremely popular and long-lasting, as the furniture continued to be made through the 1950s.

Finally, when Japan suddenly came to the attention of the West in 1868, the decorative paintings of the Edo period (1603-1867) and the brilliant works by master printmakers had an enormous impact. It was obviously a reinterpreted (and even distorted) Japanese style that appeared on French furniture. For the bourgeois of the period, Japan represented pagodas, bamboo and cloisonné. This latter technique, unknown in Japan, was invented and patented by the Duvinage company, which used it primarily in Japanese "vases" and extravagant lacquered and enameled pieces of furniture.

Germany used a pastiche flamboyant Gothic technique with exceptional skill. Later, in the same vein but with less successful results, after exhausting the possibilities of the more austere Biedermeier style, German designers plunged headlong into an outrageous neo-Rococo style. This was an exaggerated and almost unbearable pastiche of the eighteenth-century German Rococo style, which was already excessive itself.

In Austria, the Louis XV style was undergoing a revival, and it was adapted, even caricaturized, into an excessive Rococo style. Gilt elements and curves reached exaggerated proportions. A new movement began to coalesce which would "secede" from all these excesses: this was the Sezessionstil, or Secession style, Art Nouveau's precursor.

In the Netherlands, after years of an Empire style imposed by Napoleon's brother, King Louis, cabinetmakers started to create pastiche models of furniture from the Golden Age, especially large armoires with ornate marquetry.

In Italy, where the country was slowly recovering from the Napoleonic occupation, designers opted for a style that was close to the Louis-Philippe style, the Carlo Felice style, then, as in all the other countries of Europe, plunged into the Renaissance pastiche via a style called Dantesque.

Spain had the same difficulty in ridding itself of vestiges of the French Empire style. Eclecticism came to Spain via the Isabellino style, a pastiche of neo-Gothic and a Napoleon III Gothic troubadour style. Traditional furniture on the Spanish peninsula persisted beyond the various pastiches, thanks to its strong identity.

Eclectic-style furniture, whether defined as composite or historicist, remained popular throughout the world for seventy-five years (1825-1900), a feat that put an end once and for all to furniture styles named for sovereigns or political regimes.

JAPANESE CHAIR

▽ *An English chair inspired from a Japanese design. Black lacquer, fitted cane seat and seat back. 1895. Fondation Angladon, Avignon.*

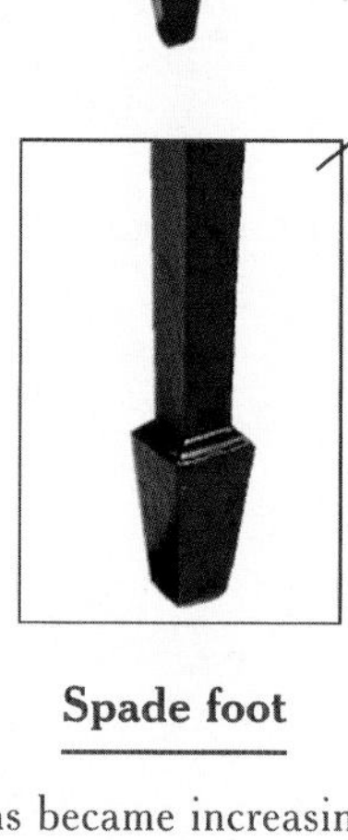

Spade foot

As forms became increasingly simplified, a surprisingly modern style appeared, in contrast to the usual stylistic excesses, exaggerations and hybrids of this period.

MEDAL CABINET

Cornice with coffin motif

Oddly enough, this piece of furniture features a cornice decorated with a coffin shape (that of Merovaeus). This morbidity goes well with the impression of overall heaviness created by this piece, which serves no useful purpose whatsoever.

Bull's head

This was supposed to be the most typical motif of the Gallic style, though no such motifs have ever been found. Magnificently sculpted by Emmanuel Fremiet, it depicts a yoked bull. At the bottom of the medal cabinet is a hoof, topped with a thistle, another "typical" Gallic ornament.

△ Medal cabinet by Charles-Guillaume Diehl. Displayed at the Universal Exhibitions of 1867 and 1873. This piece is typical of the eclectic style. Cabinetwork by Charles-Guillaume Diehl, sculptures by Fremiet. Oak and veneer of cedar, walnut and ebony, ivory inlay and silvered bronze. The central sculpture represents the triumph of Merovaeus, a Gallic chief who vanquished Attila in 451. "Gallic-style" ornamentation of harnessed oxen, harness ropes, salamanders and winged helmets. Musée d'Orsay, Paris.

UNITED STATES

1805 — 1840

The Directory-Sheraton Style

Wood and materials

Mahogany

Curly grained mahogany

Maple

Pine

Oak

Walnut

Fruit wood

Paint for rustic-style furniture

Dark green or black for chair frames

Indian red for large pieces of furniture

Stenciled motifs

Copper for sculpted mounts

△ The Portrait. *Dewey Bates. Christopher Wood Gallery, London.*

In the early nineteenth century, the United States combined the French Directoire and Empire styles, along with the English Regency style, to create a style known as the Directory-Sheraton, or American Regency style. This furniture style, which had some rather odd manifestations, remained popular through the mid-nineteenth century.

American furniture differed from European styles chiefly in the use of ornamental motifs. Shell motifs were not entirely abandoned, but were less important that sheaves of wheat, arrows, drapery, garlands and torches. The style adopted the saber foot from the French Directoire style, as well as the gondola shape for certain chairs and armchairs. Seat backs were often pierced and modeled after the slender lines of the Sheraton chairs. These were often adorned with such motifs as lyres, harps and hot-air balloons. Glossy varnish was applied to all types of wood, particularly mahogany; it was especially popular in the southern states.

The French influence reached the United States somewhat later than the English influence did. Although the Directory-Sheraton is exactly contemporaneous with the Regency style developed by Sheraton in England, it was nearly ten years behind the French Directoire style. The same phenomenon occurred with the influence of the Empire style, which reached the United States in the 1830s, while France was in the middle of the Restauration period. By the middle of the century, the most important influence was the English Victorian style, adapted in various forms in the United States: the southern states, for example, produced more sumptuous pieces than the northern states. By the end of the century, pastiche styles had invaded the United States, as everywhere else in the world, especially as the Americans demonstrated an extreme fondness, even passion, for these styles.

Rounded back

This type of Windsor chair prefigured the famous rocking chair.

MAIN PIECES OF FURNITURE

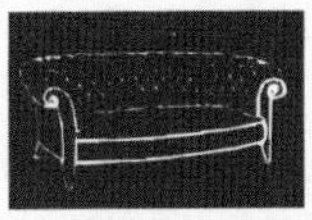

Many pieces of furniture were almost exactly like European models, although a few specifically American designs existed, such as the rocking chair.
The Hitchcock was a distinctive chair decorated with stencils, also known as a "fancy" chair.
The milk-safe was a type of food storage piece which is similar to a model made in regional styles in Europe.
The blanket chest was a fairly rustic chest of drawers which was used solely to store blankets.
The gate-leg table was exactly the same as the English design for which it was named.

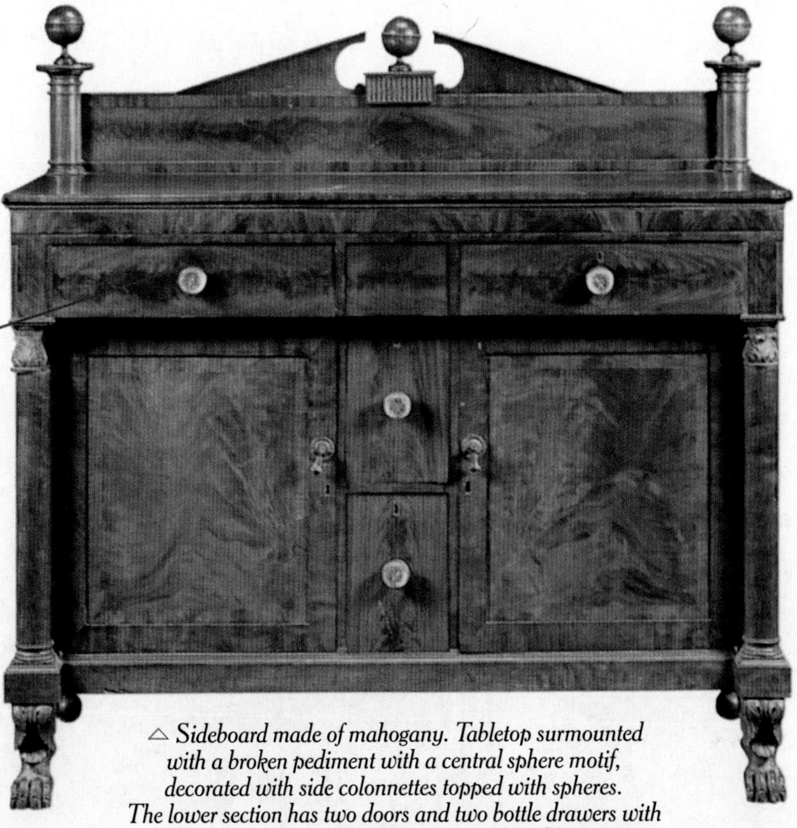

Crystal handles

Placed on drawers and bottle drawers, these handles display the great craftsmanship of this piece of furniture, which was actually a highly functional piece designed for a dining room or kitchen.

△ Sideboard made of mahogany. Tabletop surmounted with a broken pediment with a central sphere motif, decorated with side colonnettes topped with spheres. The lower section has two doors and two bottle drawers with beveled crystal handles. Column uprights. Claw feet. Signed by Michael Allison, New York. 1817. Christie's, London.

◁ Splendid Windsor settee made of bamboo and painted black. Back formed of 29 turned bamboo rods. Bamboo armrests supported by four thin rods and a bracket armstump made of bamboo rods of different thicknesses. The piece is supported by eight bamboo legs joined by an H-stretcher form of six bamboo rods. Made in Philadelphia in 1800. Christie's, London.

JAPAN

1850 1910

Discovery of a Style

△ *Detail of a triptych depicting an episode from the Chinese-Japanese War (1894-1895). Musée Guimet, Paris.*

Wood and materials

Indigenous woods

Oiled paper

Lacquers

Silk

The artistic history of Japan is not as old as China's, but it has certainly been as influential. The first contacts between these two countries took place sometime around AD 300. The artistic impact was enormous, and for several centuries, Japan merely copied the fashions (in clothes and in lifestyle) that came from China. Sometime around AD 400 , the country became unified and a Japanese state came into existence. By the end of the ninth century, Japanese art started to achieve a true national identity. When the Jesuit François Xavier discovered Japan in the sixteenth century, he found a culture in which almost every parameter had been defined nearly three hundred years earlier by the philosophical and religious influence of Zen Buddhism.

The Japanese culture did not really reach the West until 1868 and the advent of the Meiji government, which wanted to modernize the country and form contacts with the outside world. The decorative painting and master printmakers from the Edo era had an enormous impact on the West. This discovery had a decisive influence on late nineteenth-century and early twentieth-century Western painting, particularly among the French painters Monet, Manet, Degas and Vuillard, the Symbolists and the Nabis.

The respectful organization of empty space was the original concept governing Japanese art, homes and gardens. This was a Zen philosophical concept first developed in the twelfth century, which can be summed up as "simplicity equals perfection." This was diametrically opposed to the reigning styles in China and the West, where ornamentation and profusion were often the key principles determining the beauty of an object. Traditional Japanese furniture was reduced to the simplest possible expression and its designs were governed by extremely strict rules.

Aside from the religious and philosophical aspects, however, another important factor must be mentioned in terms of this furniture: the geographic situation of the island. Often hit by earthquakes, Japan learned early on to make lightweight structures of wood and paper that could withstand earthquakes. Japan was also influenced by the West: in the early twentieth century, a type of furniture design inspired from the French Louis XIV and Louis XV styles, as well as by English Georgian, Regency and fake Victorian styles, started to appear in "modern" Japanese interiors. This movement did not last very long and, soon after World War II, Japanese designers such as Noguchi invented structures modeled after classical Japanese models.

△ *Chair made of lacquered wood with giltwood fittings. Displayed with the Bodhisattva Fu, protector of revolving bookcases. Musée Guimet, Paris.*

▷ Detail of an eight-paneled screen representing actors interpreting Kit sune Ken. Musée Guimet, Paris.

THE MAIN PIECES OF FURNITURE

Seating furniture did not exist in Japan, because people sat on tatamis on the floor or sometimes on small silk cushions. There were no armoires or beds, either.
The bed was a type of mattress that was stored away each morning in a lacquered chest or behind a screen. The only pieces of furniture in the home were low, black-lacquered tables from the Edo period and cabinets reserved for shoguns' palaces. Writing tablets and screens were the two other main pieces of traditional furniture; they had sliding doors which were often entirely covered with a painted decoration.
The paint was applied over a background of gold leaf. The main themes were landscapes of the four seasons, animals, stilt-birds, pine trees, flowering trees (particularly cherries and plums), Mount Fuji, peonies, islands covered with vegetation and the sea.
The lack of furniture in the Zen Buddhist tradition meant that even the least important functional object in the home was showcased.
Combs, porcelain or lacquer dishes and stoneware or iron teapots, intensely beautiful and made with great simplicity, were considered to be major decorative elements.

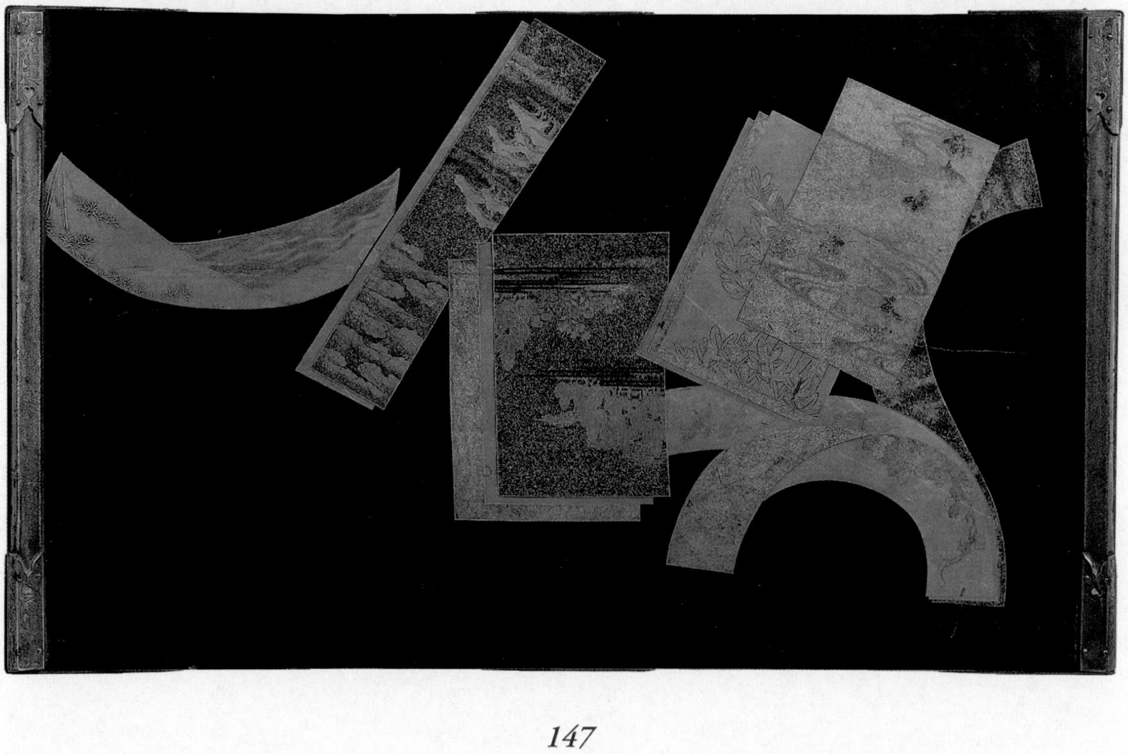

◁ Writing tablet made of black lacquer and gold leaf. Fondation Angladon, Avignon.

THE *20th* CENTURY

THIS CENTURY USHERED IN A NEW ERA OF INNOVATION AS THE MODERN STYLE SWEPT THROUGH EUROPE. ANY ELEMENT THAT RECALLED PAST STYLES WAS BANISHED, ESPECIALLY AT THE TURN OF THE CENTURY. ALTHOUGH WORLD WAR I PUT A BRUTAL STOP TO THE INVENTIVE SPIRIT OF THE MODERN STYLE, IT WAS ONLY A TEMPORARY HIATUS, AND A NEW BURST OF CREATIVE ACTIVITY OCCURRED AS SOON AS THE WAR WAS OVER.

In 1919, Walter Gropius founded the Bauhaus in Weimar, Germany. This was an experimental design school that acted as a catalyst for the Art Deco style and Functionalism. Developed just after the deprivations and tragedies of the war years (1914-1918), the Art Deco style burst onto the scene like a spectacular fireworks display.

It was the reigning style for more than twenty years, and in endlessly imaginative and elaborate ways, paralleled the development of the automobile, air travel and oceanliner voyages. Reserved to a wealthy and cultivated elite, Art Deco had its detractors, who criticized the fact that cabinetmakers were making outrageously priced pieces in an era still reeling from the shortages caused by the war years.

Functionalism proposed an entirely different approach, characterized by creative yet affordable furniture that relied on mass production techniques. Furniture had to be adapted to smaller apartments and to the budgets of the new middle class, a well-educated group of modest means.

By the 1960s, the Bauhaus principles had been fully assimilated, and creative individualism triumphed. The Design movement developed in Italy and Scandinavia and quickly spread to other countries.

In the 1970s, designers worked more closely with industrial processes so that their creations would become even more accessible to the general public.

Meanwhile, as these innovative movements developed, sales of antique furniture and copies of antiques soared. The success of antique dealers, second-hand shops and auction houses, linked to the acquisition of country homes, has continued unabated.

In the 1990s, as environment and waste management issues took on greater importance, a new international movement appeared that emphasized the recycling of discarded materials. This recycled furniture is extremely imaginative and has been exhibited in major galleries in Paris, London, Tokyo and New York.

◁ *Interior view of the orangery of Achim von Arnim's house. Wiepersdorf, Germany.*

The designers

***Michael Thonet (1796-1871):* German precursor of the Art Nouveau style, he started making mass-produced chairs beginning in 1850.**

***Hector Guimard (1867-1942):* French architect and pioneer of the Art Nouveau style that he discovered in Belgium and Great Britain. He is best known for the sinuous organic ornamentation on the entrances he designed for the Paris Métro stations.**

***Émile Gallé (1846-1904):* architect, ceramicist and cabinetmaker. A great Art Nouveau master and founder of the School of Nancy, he is more well-known for his colored glasswork and vases than for his furniture.**

***Louis Majorelle (1859-1926):* French decorator and cabinet-maker, also a master of the Art Nouveau style in France.**

◆◆◆

EUROPE

1890 1914

Art Nouveau and Modern Style

△ *Art Nouveau furniture. Horta House. Brussels.*

The movement that revolutionized art and fashion in the early years of the twentieth century appeared simultaneously in countries throughout Europe. Although the brilliant German furniture-maker and designer Michael Thonet deserves credit as a precursor to the new style, the Belgian architect Victor Horta is usually cited as the father of the Art Nouveau style. The villa he constructed in Brussels in 1893 was a clear announcement that a new style had begun.

In France, Nancy became the capital of Art Nouveau, and craftsmen, notably the glassmaker Émile Gallé, produced a wide range of objects that included furniture, glassware and stoneware.

The United Kingdom jumped onto the bandwagon in 1890 with a movement strongly influenced by the personality of Charles Rennie Mackintosh. Germany followed next, with the Jugendstil "new style." Though this style began in Northern Europe, it flourished in other regions as well. In Italy, it was known as the Stile Liberty or Stile Floreale, and it was the means by which designers, particularly Carlo Bugatti, moved away from the depersonalized styles and copies of the preceding century. The Arte Joven movement that first appeared in Barcelona also created a number of brilliant works, including buildings by the architects Antonio Gaudí and Montaner.

Designers broke totally with styles of the past, particularly with the classical influences of ancient Rome and Greece; they looked instead to the Ottoman and Islamic motifs (North Africa, Turkey) and to the Far East (Japan). They looked to nature and floral art for new motifs, including liana, tendrils, bent branches, algae, tubers, aquatic plants, women's arched backs, long wavy hair, Gothic tracery (one of Viollet le Duc's favorite motifs), the famous whiplash curve, insects and birds.

One of the guiding principles of this movement was to use a maximum of various art forms on the same piece of furniture, which meant that these pieces could only be made by multifaceted craftsmen and designers who were able to work as painters, cabinetmakers, glassmakers, bronzesmiths, ceramicists and even couturiers.

▷ *Armchair by Hector Guimard from the Coilliot home in Lille. Musée d'Orsay, Paris.*

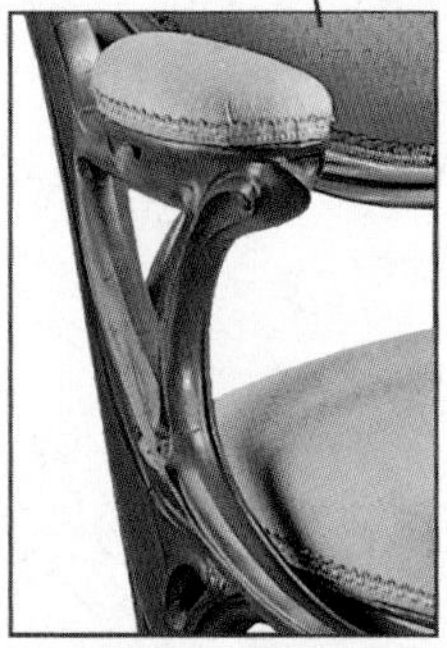

Organic inspiration

With the Modern style, it was the form that created the ornament. Seat backs, legs and seats made to look like branches or liana created the ornamentation, exactly like the entrances to the Paris metros, also designed by Hector Guimard.

THE BELGIAN SCHOOL

In the early twentieth century, Brussels was the undisputed capital of Art Nouveau, thanks to the unusual brilliance of the architect Victor Horta (1861-1947), who invented this movement that spread throughout all of Europe. The Belgian school also owes much of its success to another architect, Henry Van de Velde (1863-1957), who designed furniture devoid of any superfluous ornamentation, favoring instead the overall lines of the piece. Van de Velde's daring sense of design is still innovative today. He linked his modern aesthetic with a social content that he wanted Art Nouveau to promote, and was the first to envision furniture that would be both beautiful and affordable to all.

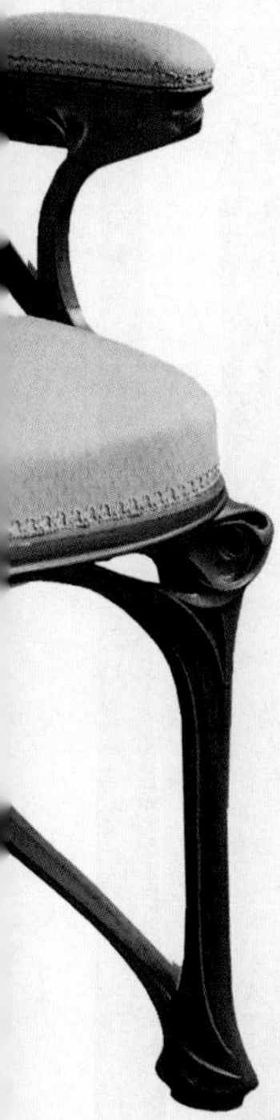

Superimposed drawers and compartments

The superimposition of two empty vertical compartments and two horizontal drawers on the side panels was a rather bold new approach to using volumes, in which a certain Japanese influence can be seen.

Stylized apron

This element supported a tabletop that was higher than the two compartments extending on either side. The lines are extremely simple and have no extra ornamentation.

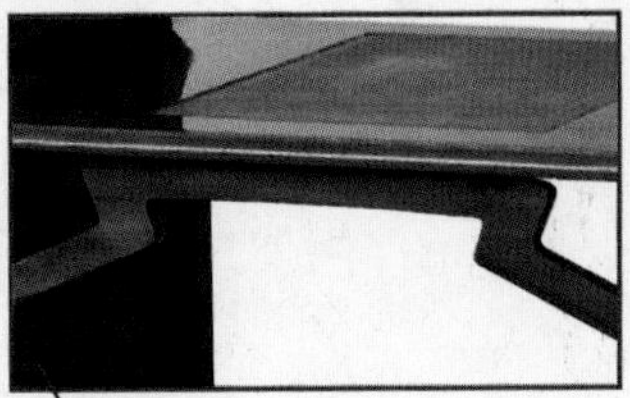

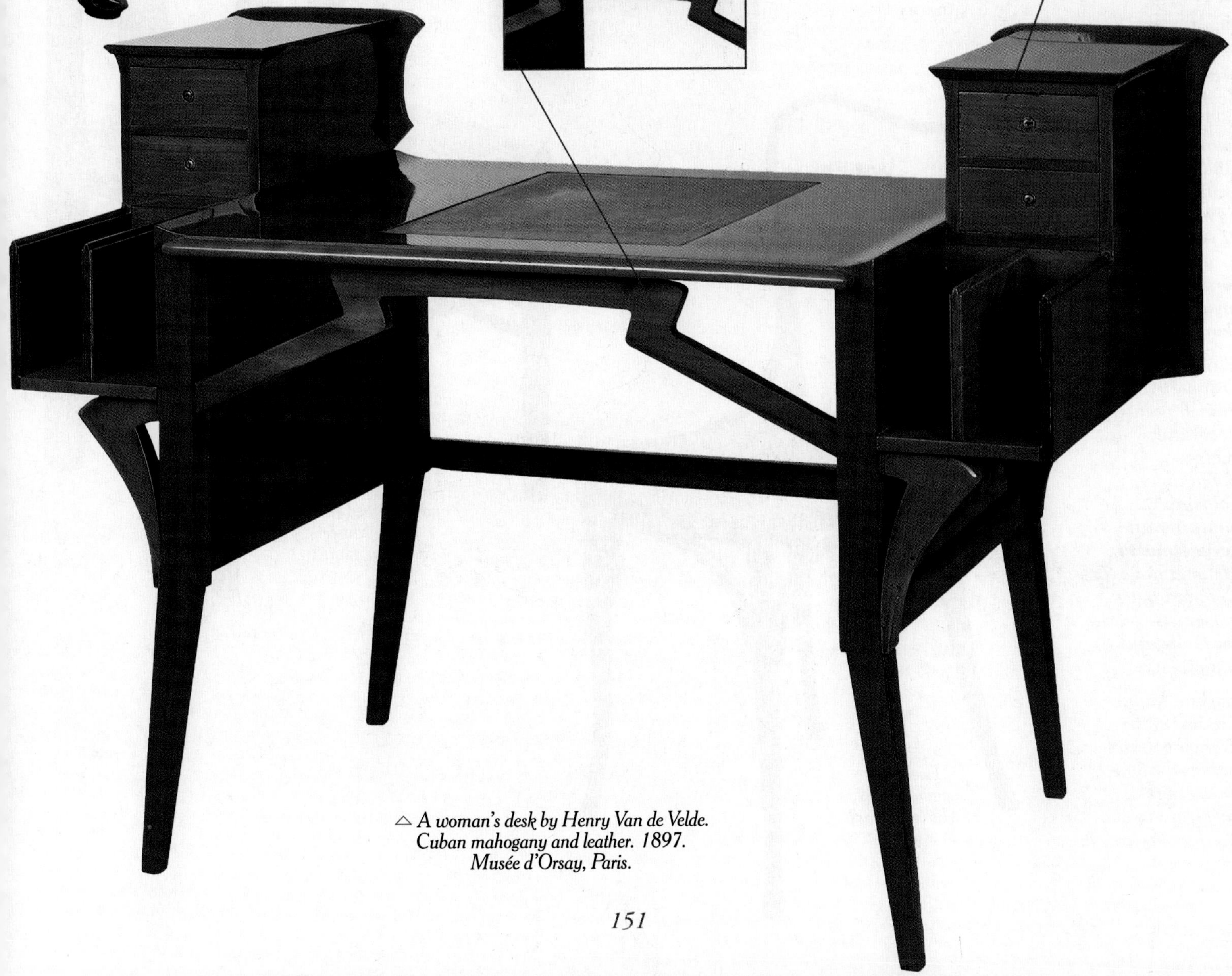

△ *A woman's desk by Henry Van de Velde. Cuban mahogany and leather. 1897. Musée d'Orsay, Paris.*

◆◆◆

In his Nancy workshop, Majorelle followed the same aesthetic principles and same ideals as Émile Gallé; his furniture was usually well-proportioned and elegant.

Charles Rennie Mackintosh (1868-1928): Scottish furniture designer, famous for his high-backed chairs and extremely geometric furniture.

Charles Robert Ashbee (1863-1942): Scottish designer. In 1888, he founded the Guild of Handicraft and in 1904, the School of Arts and Crafts; he created furniture with highly stylized floral motifs.

Victor Prouvé (1858-1943): French painter, decorator, sculptor, bookbinder, goldsmith, couturier and cabinetmaker. He is famous for the marquetry designs he made for Gallé and Majorelle.

Eugène Vallin (1856-1922): French cabinet-maker designed entire sets of furniture in the Modern style.

▷ *"Three-sheaf" chair by Émile Gallé. Walnut and goat-skin upholstery. Musée d'Orsay, Paris.*

△ *High-back chair by Charles Rennie Mackintosh. Tinted and varnished kheno. 1897. Musée d'Orsay, Paris.*

△ *Chair by Adolf Loos. Beech and caning. 1889. Musée d'Orsay, Paris.*

◁ *Chair by Frank Lloyd Wright. Oak and leather. 1908. Musée d'Orsay, Paris.*

CARLO BUGATTI

The furniture created by Carlo Bugatti (1865-1940) cannot be categorized to this day, although he was pursuing many of the same design issues as his contemporaries. He employed all kinds of unusual materials, drew his inspiration from Islamic and Japanese designs, and integrated copper plates, trim, pewter and ivory marquetry in the late nineteenth century. By the early twentieth century, however, his lines had become much simpler, although he continued the use of unusual materials. This innovative designer had two sons: Rembrandt, the famous animal sculptor, and Ettore, who designed the Bugatti automobiles.

△ *Chair by Carlo Bugatti. Mahogany, painted parchment. 1903-1904. Musée d'Orsay, Paris.*

△ *Armchair by Louis Majorelle. Walnut, various woods and fabric with floral motif. Musée d'Orsay, Paris.*

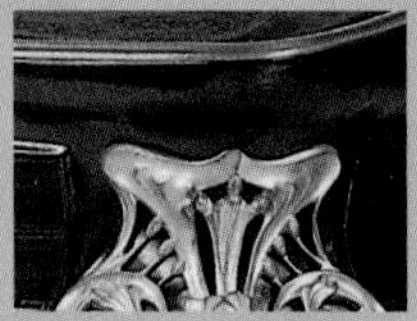

Wood and materials

For inexpensive industrial furniture: conifers, painted or used as veneer

For more expensive furniture: Brazilian mahogany, oak, walnut, pearwood

For marquetry: ebony, sycamore, walnut

Iron fashioned into spirals, ribbons, volutes, foliated scrolls and liana that followed the lines of the furniture

Enameled iron, fashioned in Modern-style shapes, particularly for utilitarian objects, bathtubs and furnaces

Inlays of ivory, mother-of-pearl, hammered and repoussé copper

Chased bronze

Glass and ceramics, used together on dressing tables

Stained-glass and tinted windows

Tapestries and fabrics with so-called Ottoman-style designs

THE FIRST ANTIQUE DEALERS

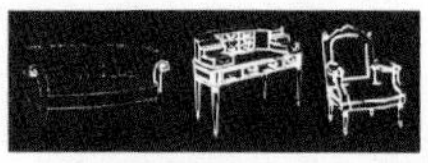

The business of dealing in antiques appeared just as nineteenth-century eclecticism was coming to an end and the Modern style was developing. It was between 1875 and 1890 that people became interested in the aesthetics and values represented by old furniture. Prior to this time, most people preferred to purchase a good, solid copy rather than acquire a ramshackle, albeit authentic, piece of furniture. Cabinetmakers made these copies according to old techniques and often incorporated fragments of authentic pieces of older furniture. Some cabinetmakers working in the Modern Style, such as Louis Majorelle or Eugène Gaillard, continued to use bronze mounts and marquetry, as in the eighteenth century, despite the new stylistic "rules."

Decorative sculpture

Unusual in the Modern style, this sculpture was a fairly common motif in work by Majorelle and Gaillard, who liked the tradition of bronze mounts. In this case, the bronze has been designed in one of the style's favorite motifs: an extremely slender, stylized orchid.

Concave edges

The inner edge was concave, while the outer edge mirrored this curve, in a harmonious geometric movement.

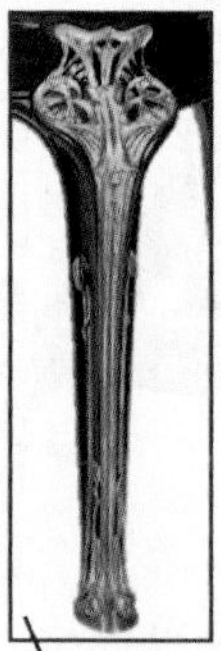

△ *Orchid desk by Majorelle. Mahogany, palisander, gilt bronze, leather. 1905-1909. Musée d'Orsay, Paris.*

Heart-shaped stretcher

The simple curves and movements that form a heart shape exemplify the stylistic lines of the Modern style.

△ Gaming table by Gallé. "Keep the hearts you have won." 1895. Musée d'Orsay, Paris.

Water lily bedside tables

Built directly into the headboard, the two bedside tables resemble two gigantic flat leaves of a water lily that look like they have grown on the upright of the bed, shaped to look like a tree trunk.

▽ Low bed with high headboard and low footboard, known as Padouk, with built-in bedside tables. By Eugène Vallin. 1900. Musée d'Orsay, Paris.

The designers

Émile Jacques Ruhlmann (1879-1933): One of the founders of the Art Deco style.

Pierre Chareau (1883-1950): He created simple, unornamented furniture, based on architectural lines. He introduced the use of chrome steel and nickel.

Eugène Printz (1889-1948): Cabinetmaker, he used palm tree and rosewood, brushed metal, aluminum and plate glass.

Robert Mallet-Stevens (1886-1945): Architect, he created extremely modern furniture.

Jean-Michel Franck (1895-1941): He created furniture from such fragile materials as shagreen and parchment.

Others: Charles Édouard Jeanneret, known as Le Corbusier (1887-1965), Jean Dunand, Paul Iribe, Jules Leleu, Louis Süe, André Mare, Marcel Coard, Clément Rousseau, Armand-Albert Rateau, Paul Follot.

EUROPE

1918  *1939*

Bauhaus and Art Deco

△ Interior. *Carl Grossberg. Private collection.*

In 1902, the Modern style was having some trouble gaining acceptance. At the same time, two young Austrian designers, Josef Hoffmann and Kolo Moser, submitted a totally new style of furniture to the Turin International Exhibition of Decorative Arts; their designs were a direct reaction against the "aesthetic mannerism" of the Modern style. This movement really took hold in 1919, when Walter Gropius founded the experimental Bauhaus school in Weimar, Germany, which aimed to break down the barriers between the structural and the decorative arts. This movement triumphed at the 1925 International Exhibition of Decorative and Industrial Arts, held in Paris (hence the alternative name for this movement, the "1925 style"). Luxurious furniture and more affordable mass-produced pieces were made according to the Bauhaus principles. Designers took over the role of ornamentalists, ordering furniture directly from cabinetmakers. The shapes were most often rectilinear, and cabinetmakers had specific instructions to avoid "any reference to the past." Ornamental motifs were eliminated, and metal and steel were used systematically to manufacture furniture. Steel tube frames were either chrome-plated or painted. In France, the Art Deco style found an enthusiastic outlet in the large department stores, particularly the Bon Marché, with the Pomone workshop. The Art Deco style was soon adopted as an official style: the French government opted for this style to decorate its ocean liners, including the *Normandie,* launched in April 1935. World War II seriously curbed the creative energy of this movement—which had already been censored in Germany under Hitler, where the state closed down the Bauhaus school in 1933. Many Art Deco designers moved to the United States, particularly to Chicago.

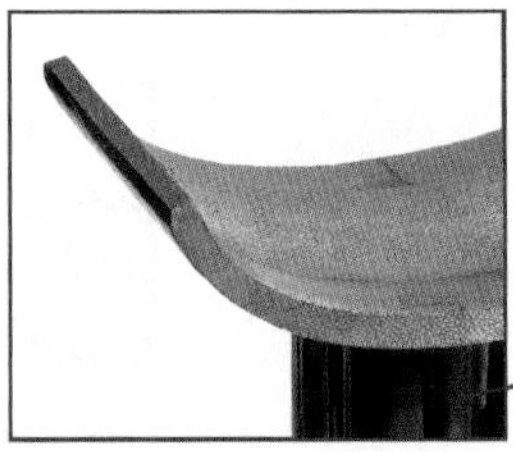

Shagreen covering

Art Deco designers loved to use shagreen. It was made from the skin of a dogfish that was colored pale green, pale blue or pale yellow. Fashionable in the eighteenth century, shagreen became popular again in the 1930s as a covering for all types of furniture, from chairs to chests of drawers.

Support inspired by African designs

The four wooden legs, carved and colored dark red, are joined in pairs by crosspieces forming Greek motifs. This design is particularly well suited to the African-inspired design, created by Pierre Legrain.

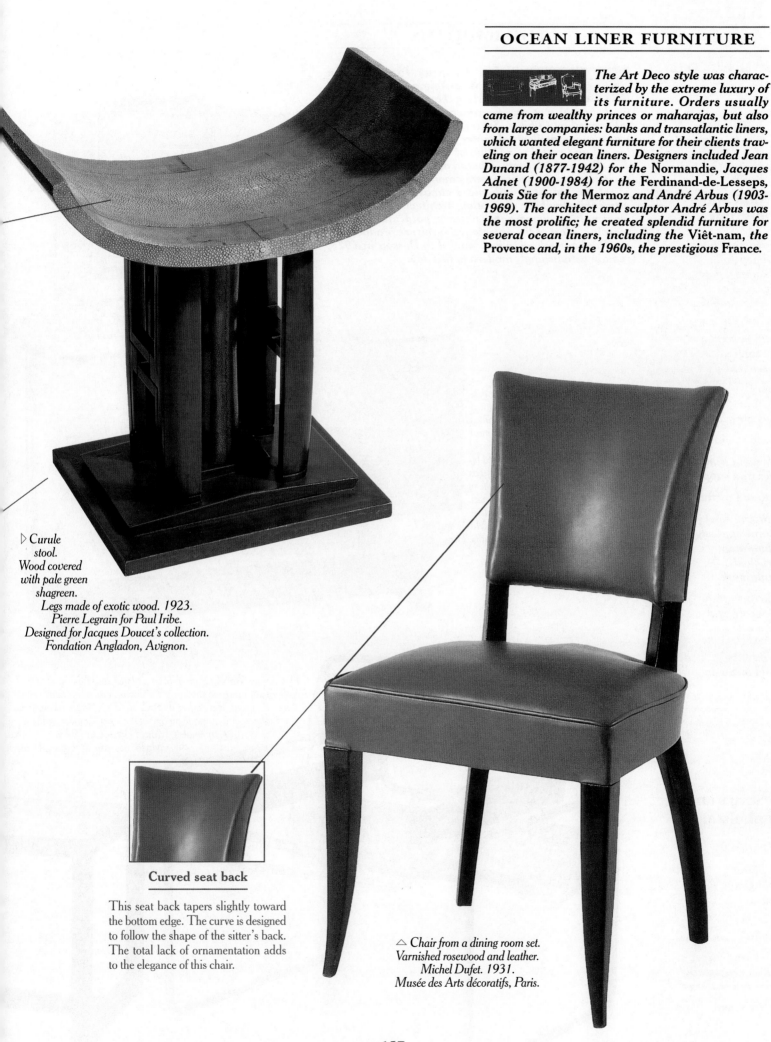

OCEAN LINER FURNITURE

The Art Deco style was characterized by the extreme luxury of its furniture. Orders usually came from wealthy princes or maharajas, but also from large companies: banks and transatlantic liners, which wanted elegant furniture for their clients traveling on their ocean liners. Designers included Jean Dunand (1877-1942) for the* Normandie*, Jacques Adnet (1900-1984) for the* Ferdinand-de-Lesseps*, Louis Süe for the* Mermoz *and André Arbus (1903-1969). The architect and sculptor André Arbus was the most prolific; he created splendid furniture for several ocean liners, including the* Viêt-nam*, the* Provence *and, in the 1960s, the prestigious* France*.

▷ *Curule stool. Wood covered with pale green shagreen. Legs made of exotic wood. 1923. Pierre Legrain for Paul Iribe. Designed for Jacques Doucet's collection. Fondation Angladon, Avignon.*

△ *Chair from a dining room set. Varnished rosewood and leather. Michel Dufet. 1931. Musée des Arts décoratifs, Paris.*

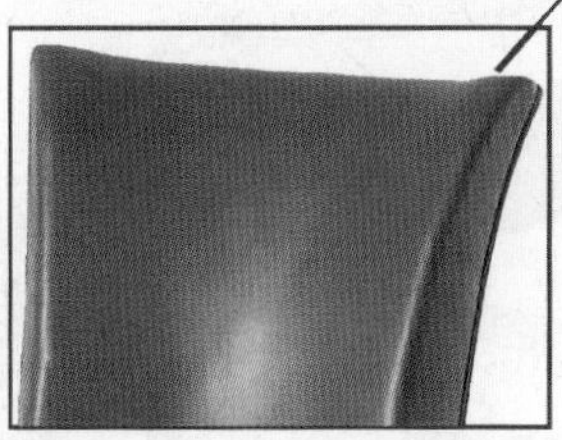

Curved seat back

This seat back tapers slightly toward the bottom edge. The curve is designed to follow the shape of the sitter's back. The total lack of ornamentation adds to the elegance of this chair.

Wood and materials

Macassar ebony, gaboon (or okoumé), palm tree, red or yellow Amboyna, mahogany

Lemonwood, sycamore, rosewood

Ivory

Gilt bronze

Copper and brass

Wrought iron for legs and supports

Painted metal

Chrome steel, stainless steel, aluminum, brushed aluminum

Mirrors, plate glass, crystal handles

White, beige and gold lacquers

Fabrics and upholstery

Leather

Colored shagreen, pony skin

Ocelot fur for sofas

Silk and velvet with geometeric printed patterns

Parchment

THE BAUHAUS

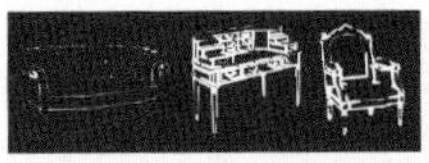

Walter Gropius founded the Bauhaus in Weimar, Germany, in 1919. More than just a school or a workshop, it was an experimental stylistic institute, influenced by Cubism, Surrealism and Primitivism. It was also an intellectual center researching the technological and social revolution of the 1920s and 1930s. The theory of relativity, Tibetan mysticism, yoga and a socialist vision of society were among the sources of inspiration. This style influenced almost all the applied arts: cabinetmaking, decoration, architecture, sculpture, glassmaking, typography, pottery, goldsmithery and weaving. Most of the objects and furniture produced by the Bauhaus school, which moved to Dessau in 1925, remain astonishingly modern to this day.

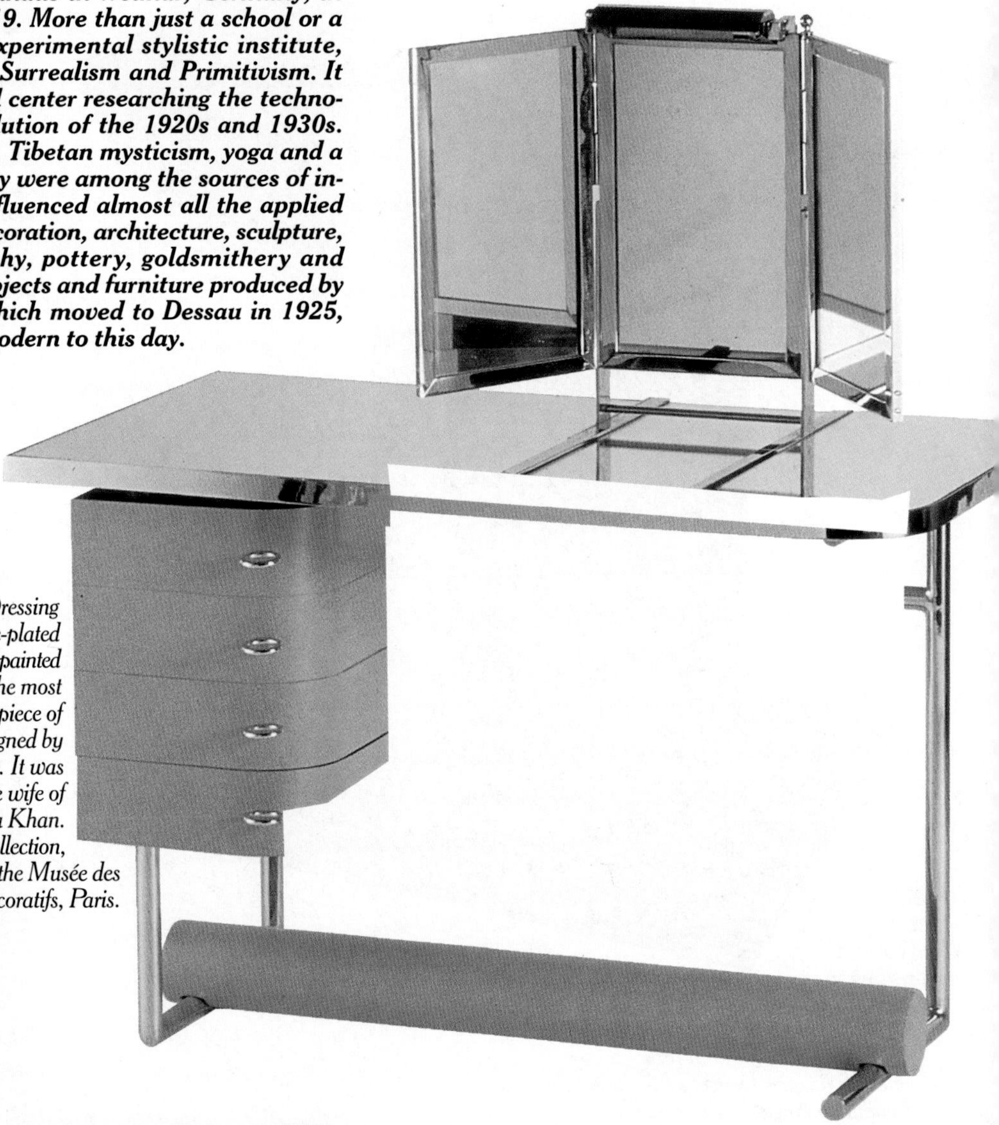

▷ Dressing table. Chrome-plated steel, mirror and painted metal. This is the most famous piece of furniture designed by René Herbst. It was created for the wife of Prince Aga Khan. 1930. Fnac Collection, on loan to the Musée des Arts décoratifs, Paris.

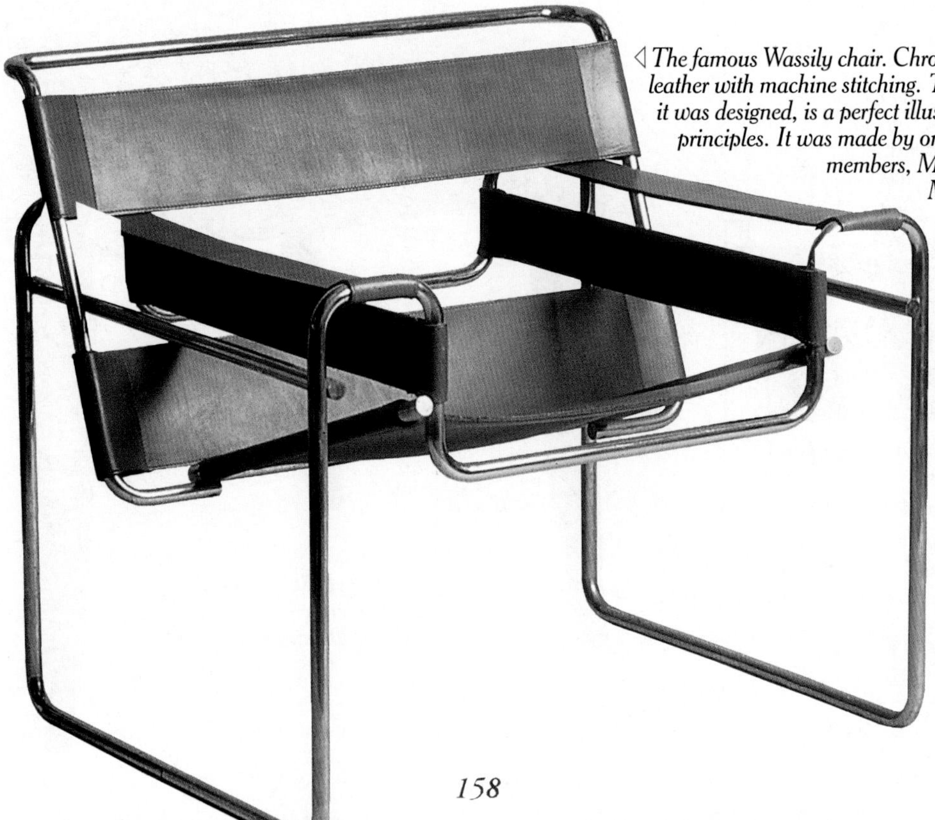

◁ The famous Wassily chair. Chrome-plated steel tubes and brown leather with machine stitching. This chair, copied endlessly since it was designed, is a perfect illustration of the Bauhaus aesthetic principles. It was made by one of the school's most eminent members, Marcel Breuer, in 1923. Musée des Arts décoratifs, Paris.

▷ *Three-tiered buffet, inspired by Cubism. Sycamore veneer and birch. 1923. By Sonia Delaunay. Musée des Arts décoratifs, Paris.*

▽ *Coffee table. Oak tinted black and white marble. The geometric shape is accentuated by the contrast between the black and white materials. Extremely modern for its time (ca 1910), this table prefigures the principles of the Bauhaus school. By Josef Hoffmann. Musée d'Orsay, Paris.*

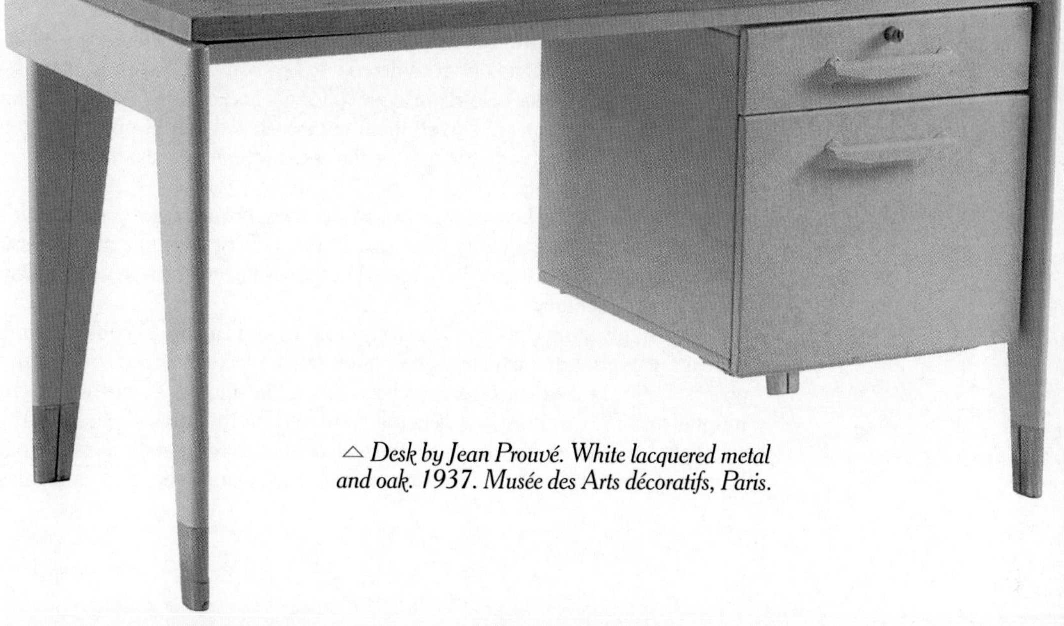

△ *Desk by Jean Prouvé. White lacquered metal and oak. 1937. Musée des Arts décoratifs, Paris.*

AFRICA

1920 1930

The Discovery of African Art

Wood

There were two categories of wood: hardwood used for furniture, and lighter, bombax-type wood used for masks. Some local woods were colored dark red with natural pigments or were colored black.

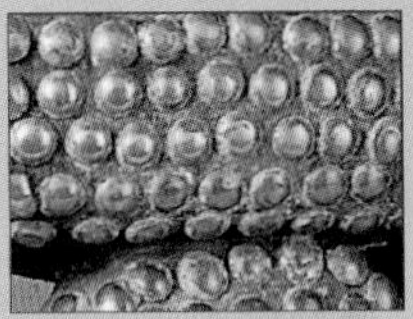

Ornaments

Copper or brass tacks, mirrors, fragments of mirrors, square pieces of metal, woven straw or dried grasses

Animal tusks and horns, contrary to popular belief, were never used in furniture

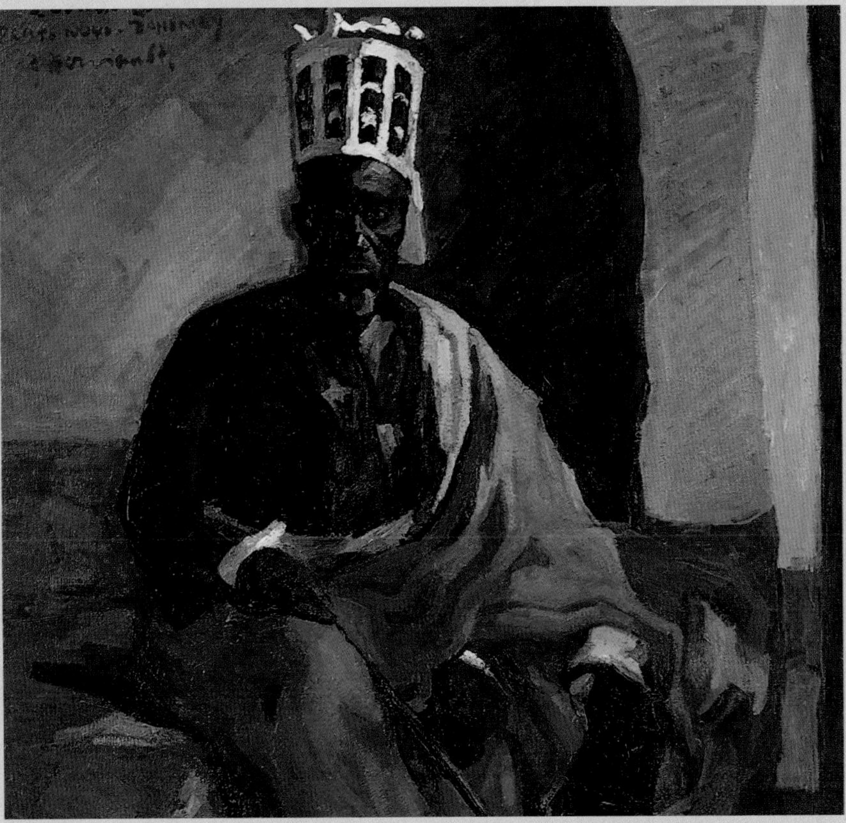

△ Zounon, King of the Night. Dahomey. *André Herviault. Musée national des Arts d'Afrique et d'Océanie, Paris.*

The performances of the famous Revue nègre, held in Paris after World War I, had a direct influence on contemporary music, painting, sculpture and fashion, but also, somewhat indirectly, on furniture design. The movement that appeared during the two world wars was based on a "black" aesthetic, a rather clumsy and colonialist attempt to model designs after African cultures, and in a wider sense, after so-called "primitive" cultures. This created an interest for African art, which gradually became an acceptable art form in the West.

Today, however, historians are aware that African art was already well known long before this period—but no one considered it to be "real" art. As early as the seventeenth century, curio collections belonging to art collectors and explorers contained magnificent masterpieces of African art. Artists themselves collected these works and often drew inspiration from them (with Picasso as the most often-cited example, along with the German Expressionists).

During the period between the two world wars, however, the general public became aware of this art in an entirely new way. In the 1930s, the influence of African art in Europe was similar to that of Chinese art in the seventeenth century and Japanese art in the nineteenth century.

African furniture consisted primarily of stools and chairs. The most common woods were indigenous, extremely strong species. Certain pieces included shimmering or bright objects made of various materials, such as nails, metal and bits of mirrors. Each piece was unique, and the furniture was generally reserved for the tribal chief, king, dignitary or sorcerer. The pieces were often sculpted with animal motifs (gazelles, insects, bats) or with human figures, especially in furniture made in East Africa (Kenya, Tanzania).

STOOLS AND CHAIRS

An invitation to sit down was a rare honor. In many African cultures, the person seated held the power. The chair, therefore, was reserved to an elite, to the wisemen and women, to the kings and to distinguished guests. No other piece of furniture exists in traditional African cultures: no bed, no table, no storage elements. The West discovered the marvelous African stools (particularly the thrones of the kings of Benin and Zaire) in articles and illustrations published by explorers.

Bat-head motif

Ornamental motifs were almost always inspired by the animal world, rarely the plant world, and were highly stylized. The decoration here consists of a series of bats' heads and large ears. The brass tacks indicate that this was a royal stool.

▷ *Royal stool from Cameroon (northwest province), with bat-head motifs and brass tacks. Musée national des Arts d'Afrique et d'Océanie, Paris.*

Spider-leg support

The furniture-maker imbued this ceremonial stool with an element of magic, making it even more inaccessible and disturbing. The seat is supported by an inverted set of frightening spider legs.

▷ *Dignitary's stool from Cameroon (western province, Bamiléké). The legs are made in the shape of a spider. Musée national des Arts d'Afrique et d'Océanie, Paris.*

◁ *Chair with a high seat back formed of a male figure with outstretched arms. Tanzania. Musée national des Arts d'Afrique et d'Océanie, Paris.*

EUROPE

1950 – 1960

Functionalism

The designers

Jean Prouvé (1901-1984): The leading figure of Functionalism, he promoted the idea of furniture for everyone.

Charlotte Perriand (1903-1999): A furniture designer, she worked with Le Corbusier, making innovative designs.

Louis Sognot (1892-1969): He specialized in rattan furniture.

Jean Royère (1902-1981): He traveled all over the Middle East, designed modern, luxurious environments.

Jacques Adnet (1900-1984): He created luxurious furniture sets.

Charles Eames (1907-1978) and Ray Eames (1912-1978): Leading post-war furniture designers.

Eileen Gray (1879-1976): She created lacquered metal furniture in an Art Deco style.

Emilio Terry (1890-1969): He created luxurious, caricatural furniture pieces.

△ *Furniture from the 1960s. Aulenti armchair and lamp. Elephant armchair by Rancillac. Musée des Arts décoratifs, Paris.*

All of Europe had to be reconstructed in the wake of World War II. Some artists, including Jean-Michel Franck and Pierre Chareau, had moved to the United States, which they viewed as a land of promise; many remained there. Others who had stopped working during the German occupation of Europe were able to get back to work. The world had changed, however, and the apartments being built were smaller than before. The guiding principles of modern design and expertise were hygiene, storage, efficiency, space-saving devices, affordable items and greater leisure time.

The four major movements that began just after the war are still relevant today:

◆ A style of furniture known in France as the Faubourg Saint-Antoine style (for the neighborhood in which it is made). These pieces were destined for a middle-class clientele and were poor copies of older styles, adapted to current fashion with little ornamental coherence.

◆ Luxury, high-priced and extremely high-quality pieces handmade by cabinetmakers. These were reserved to an intellectual, artistic and financial elite, as well as to national palaces of France. Jacques Adnet, André Arbus, Jean Royère and Emilio Terry were the great cabinetmakers of this period, creating exceptionally elegant and beautiful pieces.

◆ A movement aimed at providing the greatest possible selection of innovative furniture using new materials available for reasonable prices. Imaginative architects who wanted their designs to reach a broad public included Jean Prouvé, Charlotte Perriand, Louis Sognot (for rattan furniture), Charles and Ray Eames (for plywood or plastic and metal chairs) and the Danish designer Arne Jacobsen (wonderful armchairs).

◆ Finally, and unprecedented in furniture history: the popularity of antique furniture, available in specialty shops and at auction. This movement paralleled the increasing number of second homes owned by city dwellers and the desire to own "rustic" furniture—which is, in reality, the traditional furniture that has been produced for many years in the various French regions.

Free-form edges

Free-form edges on desks were meant to break the traditional symmetry between the two opposing sides, creating an innovative and elegant sense of harmony and balance.

▷ *Huidt and Molgarr-Nielsen chair. 1960. Musée des Arts décoratifs, Paris.*

FREE-FORM FURNITURE

Free-form furniture appeared in the late 1930s with designs by Charlotte Perriand in France, Carlo Mollino in Italy, Frederick Kiesler in the United States and Isamu Noguchi in Japan. Initially, they did not earn much recognition, but became very successful in the 1950s, when the designs were readapted by Jacques Adnet and Jean Royère (indeed, they were often classified as being in the "Royère" style). Characterized by rounded forms, circles, wavy lines and kidney shapes, free-form design was most often seen in luxury furniture. Ironically, it was far more unusual in more affordable furniture, for which this type of design was originally intended.

Brass and leather

The three drawers, like the rest of the desk, are entirely covered in hand-sewn saddle leather. Special care was taken with the places where the brass handles fit on to the leather, underscoring the luxuriousness of this exceptional desk.

▽ *Desk. This extraordinarily luxurious, yet functional piece has a wood and metal structure and is entirely covered with natural-colored sewn leather. The metal legs are also covered with sewn leather. The asymmetrical tabletop has one kidney-shaped end. Under this end is a magazine rack, made of three strips of leather, two swiveling shelves and a waste-paper basket. On the other end: a chest with three drawers, covered in sown leather. Brass handles. Jacques Adnet. Ca 1950. Fnac collection. On loan to the Musée des Arts décoratifs, Paris.*

Materials and upholstery

For high-priced furniture: marquetry using sycamore, carved walnut and lemonwood

Giltwood

Safety glass

Black marble

Celadon porcelain (greenware); brown lacquer set off with gold, blue lacquer, Beka lacquer

Chased and gilt bronze; patinated bronze

Aubusson tapestries

Wool fabrics

Saddle leather upholstery

For inexpensive, innovative furniture: rattan, woven rattan, beech, molded plywood, laminated teak, chrome-plated steel, lacquered sheet steel, perforated steel, aluminum, polyester reinforced with fiberglass, latex padding covered with fake leather of Skai, plastic wire

TRADE FAIRS AND BIENNIALS

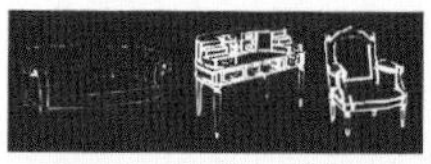

Fairs and biennials became the venues for showcasing the latest styles and new forms. With the creation of the Union des Artistes Modernes (UAM) in 1929 (the organization was dissolved in 1958) and their internationalist declaration, designers set forth their determination to break completely with the past and invent new concepts and new uses for furniture.
The Milan trade fairs, the Triennials and the Brussels Universal Exhibition in 1958 played a major role in the discovery of talented new designers.

△ Stackable chair, with a single piece seat and T-shaped back made of laminated teak. The legs are made of chrome-plated steel tubes. This famous chair was one of a series of stackable chairs designed from 1951 by the great Danish designer Arne Jacobsen. Musée des Arts décoratifs, Paris.

Polyester shell

Made from a single cast piece of polyester, this seat was incredibly strong. This was the first use of military research in the field of furniture: the chair was made by Zenith Plastics, a company that made parabolic antennas for American radars during World War II.

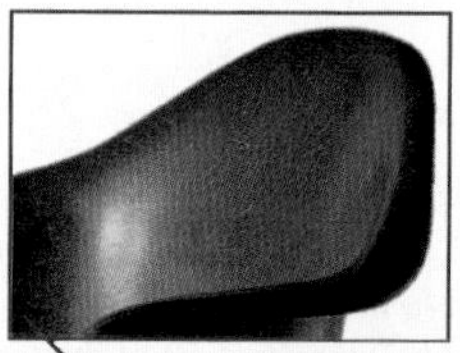

▷ Shell chair made of polyester reinforced with fiberglass. The legs are made of steel tubes, which cross in the center for support. Designed by Charles Eames (1907-1978). Made by Zenith Plastics Co, California. Manufactured by Hermann Miller, Furniture Company, USA. This was the first polyester shell chair exhibited in France. Musée des Arts décoratifs, Paris.

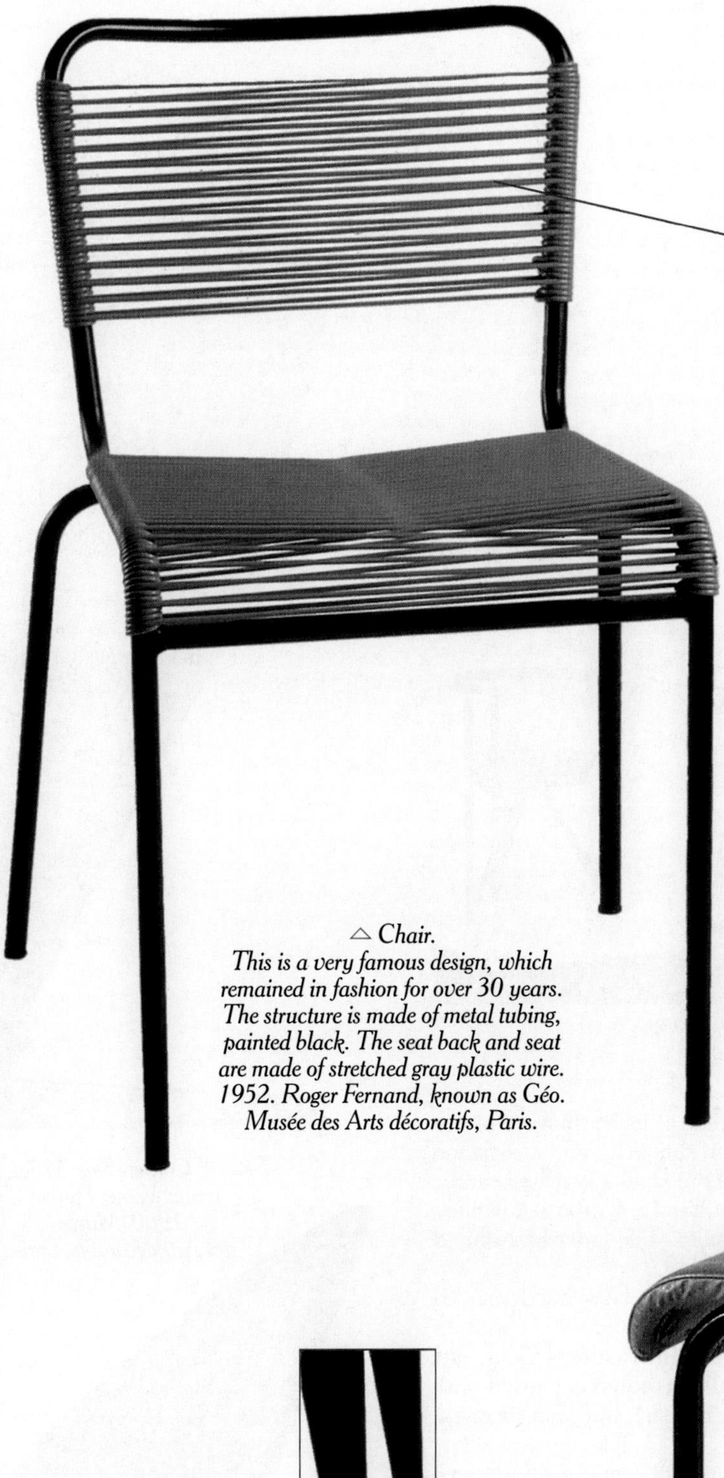

△ *Chair.*
This is a very famous design, which remained in fashion for over 30 years. The structure is made of metal tubing, painted black. The seat back and seat are made of stretched gray plastic wire. 1952. Roger Fernand, known as Géo. Musée des Arts décoratifs, Paris.

Woven plastic wire

This inexpensive and strong material made these chairs extremely popular.

Bent steel rear support

The rear legs are more structural in design than the front legs are. Jean Prouvé developed this form around 1935; this design was repeated in wood in 1942 and another all-steel version was created in 1947.

△ *Office chair, structure made of black-lacquered bent steel. The seat and back are covered with black Skaï. 1951 design. Created by Jean Prouvé. Distributed by Steph Simon. Musée des Arts décoratifs, Paris.*

The designers

Aalvar Alto (1898-1976): Finnish, he created extremely graphic furniture, made primarily of laminated wood.

Arne Jacobsen (1902-1971): Danish, his egg-, swan- and ant-shaped chairs took on the form of the human body.

Gio Ponti (1891-1979): Italian, he was famous for the absolutely pure lines of his chairs.

Carlo Mollino (1905-1975): Italian, he created furniture inspired by car designs.

Ettore Sottsass (born 1917): Italian, he invented the Memphis style in Milan in 1980.

Diego Giacometti (1902-1985): Italian, he created bronze and plaster furniture inspired by plants and animals, particularly for the Musée Picasso in Paris.

Olivier Mourgue (born 1939): French, he created the "Djinn" furniture line, with bright colors and sculptural lines.

EUROPE

1960  *1980*

Design

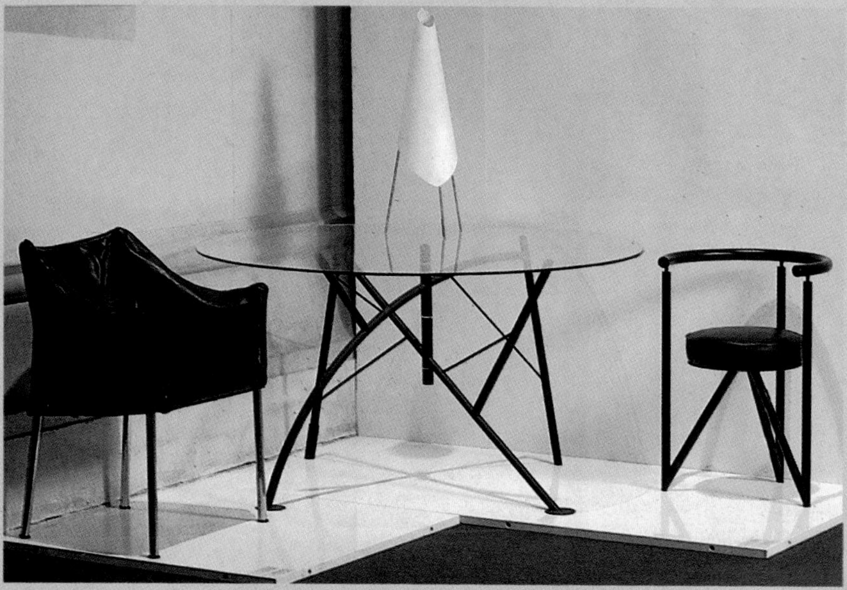

△ *Furniture by Philippe Starck from the 1980s. Musée des Arts décoratifs, Paris.*

The word "design" connotes a state of mind rather than a stylistic movement in a specific time. It is characterized by audacious forms, simplicity, and association of new or unexpected materials. The members of the Bauhaus school can be considered the predecessors of the design movement, as can Le Corbusier, Mallet-Stevens, André Arbus, Jacques Adnet and Aalvar Aalto. The latter had started designing extremely simple, stackable chairs as early as 1939.

Historically, design is defined as the movement of sleek, pure lines that developed long after World War II; the major designers were working in Scandinavia and Italy. A great deal of the furniture was distributed by the Knoll International Company, created in 1943 in New York by Hans Knoll. Knoll surrounded himself with famous architects (E. Saarinen, Mies van der Rohe, M. Breuer), who were researching new techniques.

In Scandinavia, the basic idea was to create furniture that combined traditional and new materials in forms that could be mass produced at the lowest possible cost.

In Italy, this movement offered designers an opportunity to finally leave behind the stylistic slump in which they had languished for many years. Minimalism, also known as essentialism, created (and continues to create to this day) marvelous pieces of furniture that were greatly inspired by industry, especially the automobile industry. Companies such as Alessi continued researching new forms that were then applied to small everyday objects.

The design movement came to France much later than elsewhere, in name at least. Its existence was officially recognized by the Ministries of Industry and Culture in 1979, with the creation of an association to promote innovation in furniture, the Valorisation de l'innovation dans l'ameublement (better known in France as VIA). It is responsible for encouraging the creation of "truly contemporary furniture."

Unofficially, however, the French had always been avid furniture buyers. In the early 1970s, alongside increasingly poor copies of antique furniture, there were a few attempts at creative, fairly inexpensive pieces, produced by the young designers who would later become famous. This was the case, for example, with the stackable plastic stools that the Prisunic chain stores ordered from the designer Andrée Putmann.

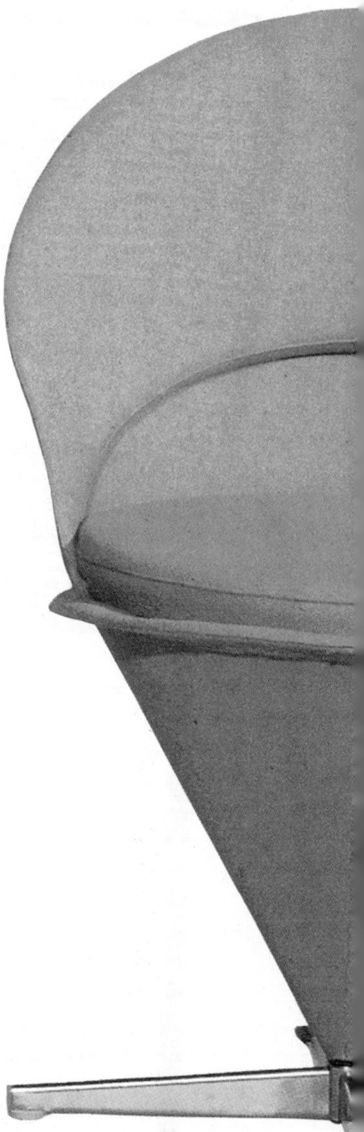

△ ▽ *Cornet chair. Metal, fabric. Verner Panton. 1960. Musée des Arts décoratifs, Paris.*

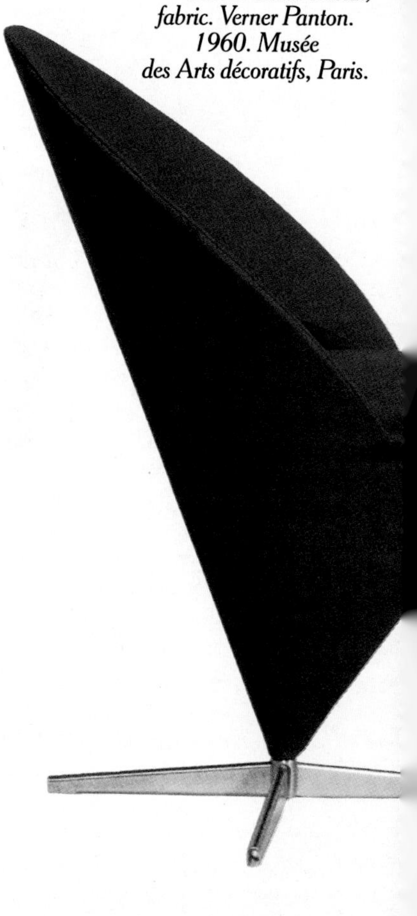

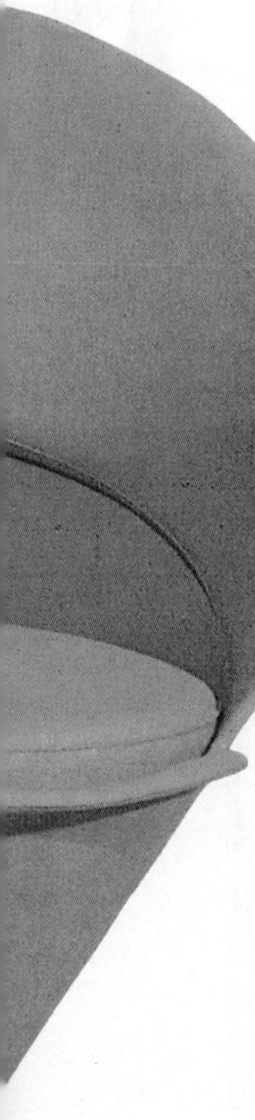

LARGE FURNITURE STORES

Toward the end of the 1960s, as mass-produced furniture became widespread, furniture started to be sold in large specialty furniture stores. Thousands of square feet were devoted to showrooms, where fully furnitured rooms displayed all types of different styles: dining rooms, living rooms, bedrooms and children's rooms.
With the exception of one British store and one Swedish store, which commissioned designers for their furniture, most of these other stores were not closely associated with designs produced by contemporary creators.

△ *AEO chair. Plastic, steel and fabric. Paolo Deganello for Archizoom. Musée des Arts décoratifs, Paris.*

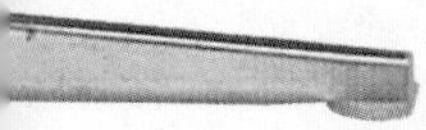

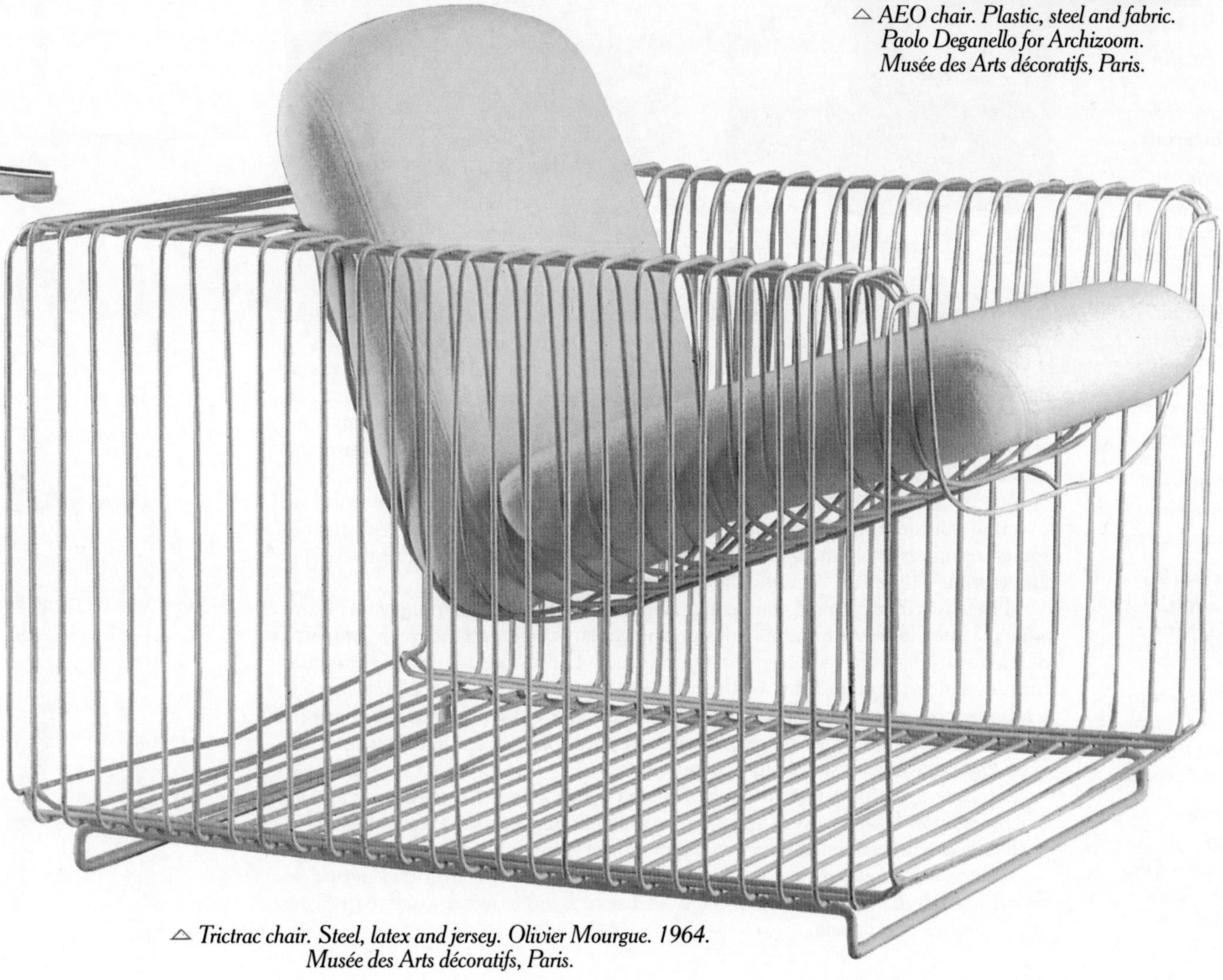

△ *Trictrac chair. Steel, latex and jersey. Olivier Mourgue. 1964. Musée des Arts décoratifs, Paris.*

U.S., EUROPE AND ASIA

1980 2000

Late 20th-Century Styles

The designers

Philippe Starck (born 1949): Extremely famous for his tables, chairs, libraries, restaurant decors and furniture for the Élysée Palace.

Jean-Michel Wilmotte (born 1948): Created furniture for the Élysée and the Grand Louvre.

Andrée Putmann (born 1925): Re-created designs by Mallet-Stevens, Le Corbusier and Eileen Gray.

Pierre Paulin (born 1927): Furniture from new materials.

Elizabeth Garouste (born 1949) and Matia Bonetti (born 1953): Imaginative furniture with rounded forms.

Olivier Gagnère (born 1952): Furniture made of metal structures and laminated wood.

Eric Schmitt (born 1959): Neo-Baroque chairs.

Yves Martenot: Imposing furniture inspired by the plant world.

Marco de Guetzel: furniture made from recycled materials.

△ *Furniture by Gaëtano Pesce. Musée des Arts décoratifs, Paris.*

Apart from the French association VIA (see p. 166), other elements played a major role in promoting contemporary designers and their furniture. The Yves Gastou gallery, for example, exhibited some of the most successful designs of the time. More official institutions, such as the Centre de création industrielle at the Georges Pompidou Center, were also influential: the exhibitions and retrospectives organized in the museum found an enthusiastic public, which, over the years, has become increasingly knowledgeable and demanding.

Many of these new forms would be adapted and sold throughout the world by two multinational home-furnishing companies: the Swedish firm Ikea and the Dutch company Habitat (the latter was founded by the English interior decorator and designer Terence Conran in the 1970s).

These two international giants offer an entire range of contemporary furniture, which is often far more tasteful in design and construction than the rustic copies of older furniture, which are also mass-produced. These companies also promote furniture incorporating some of the most sophisticated formal research in contemporary design, making it available to the general public at affordable prices. They also contribute to an entirely new design phenomenon: the importance of kitchen and bathroom designs and decoration.

Designers no longer create only furniture, but also refrigerators, washing machines, stoves, hoods over stoves, bathtubs, sinks and stereos. Design has made itself at home in the home, influencing almost every domestic object.

Ultimately, however, we do not yet have enough distance on this period to seriously analyze it. We should, perhaps, wait several more decades before drawing any definitive conclusions.

▷ *Bean chair. Wrought iron and velvet. Eric Schmitt. 1987. Musée des Arts décoratifs, Paris.*

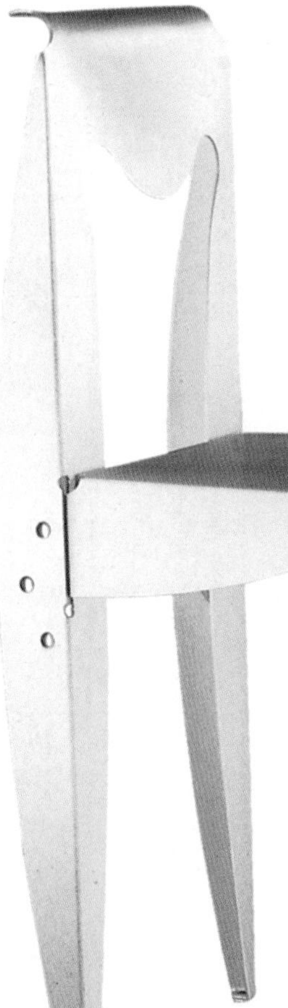

RECYCLED FURNITURE

The growing public awareness concerning environmental issues and a concern to protect limited natural resources inspired many contemporary furniture designers to experiment with new techniques. Rather than cutting down a tree to make a piece of furniture, young designers looked for alternatives to using wood. In the same vein, many designers in the United States, Asia and Europe took a good look at the mounting piles of discarded materials and initiated a movement to recycle much of society's waste products, giving them a new life. The materials used to make furniture range from cardboard to wire, sometimes resulting in some very odd shapes, which can still be seen today.

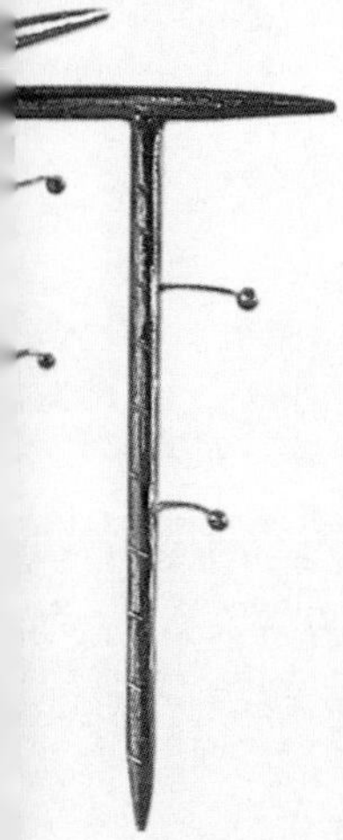

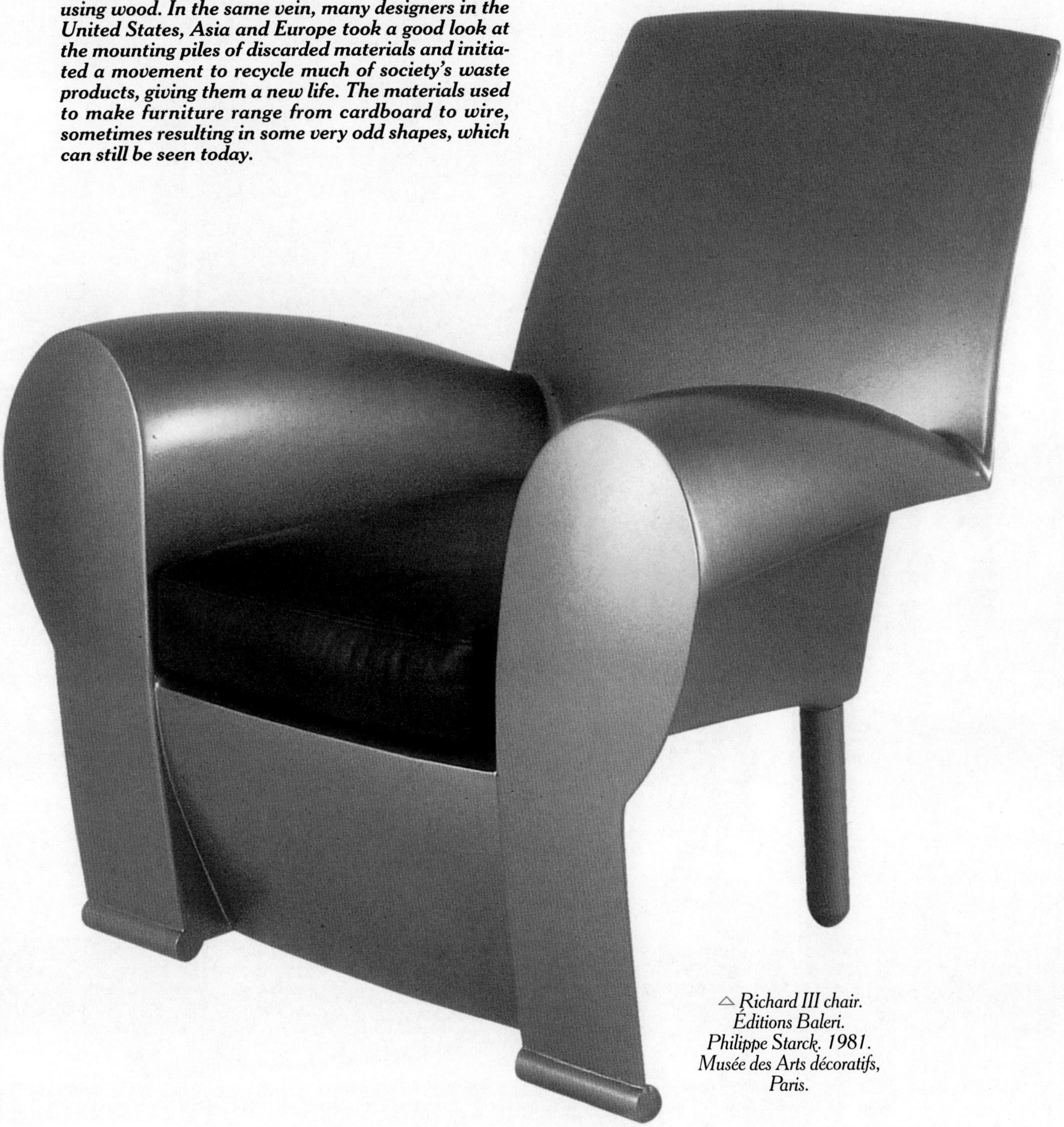

△ Richard III chair.
Éditions Baleri.
Philippe Starck. 1981.
Musée des Arts décoratifs, Paris.

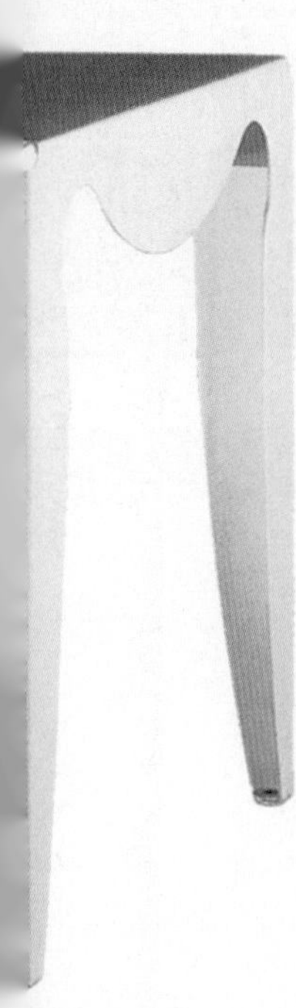

◁ Liberta chair. Aluminum.
Éditions Meritalia.
Afra and Tobia Scarpa. 1989.
Musée des Arts décoratifs, Paris.

FRENCH

REGIONAL STYLES

THE HISTORY OF REGIONAL FRENCH FURNITURE IS ALSO THE HISTORY OF RURAL, BOURGEOIS AND WORKING-CLASS SECTORS OF SOCIETIES. THERE ARE FEW EXAMPLES IN WHICH FURNITURE IS SO CLEARLY LINKED TO EVERYDAY LIFE AND REGIONAL ENVIRONMENTS.

The principal characteristics of regional furniture styles are their functionality, imaginative designs and steadfast transmission of traditional savoir-faire. Yet there are few remaining pieces of regional furniture older than the eighteenth century. Although certain Louis XIII pieces seem to prove the contrary, it is only because we underestimate just how great a difference there was between the city and the regions during the periods in question. Indeed, it took fifty years, and sometimes even a full century, before a style popular in Paris reached provincial cities. Once it did, it remained for many long years, with very few modifications. This explains why, in the early twentieth century, Louis XIII diamond-point armoires were still being made in southwest France, with the same tools that cabinetmakers used in the seventeenth century. Dating regional furniture is a difficult task, even for experts—and when, as occasionally happens, a date has been inscribed on a piece, it most often indicates a major family event, frequently a marriage.

Furniture was considered a sign of wealth only from the eighteenth century on. In the Middle Ages, furniture was limited to chests, used to store clothing, dishes and food; at night, the upper part was used as a bed. Later, more portable pieces of furniture appeared: stools, benches and bread kneading troughs, which were also used as tables. The armoire was developed in the eighteenth century, appearing first in the homes of provincial aristocrats and the bourgeoisie, for whom it represented the most important part of a bride's dowry. Later, the armoire became a common piece of furniture in more humble homes. Other types of furniture designed for specific uses gradually appeared, so that by the early nineteenth century, all the pieces of furniture we know today had been invented in one form or another.

The specific environment of each region was also decisive to furniture design. The most important factor was the type of wood used, which was always a local species found in the nearby forests. Ornamentation was highly inspired by the local flora and fauna. Finally, certain designs, such as box beds (unimaginable in hot regions), were clearly linked to climatic conditions.

Regional furniture—functional, unchanging and in harmony with nature—was rediscovered in the early 1970s, as people began to acquire vacation homes in the countryside. Today, these pieces can sell for astronomical prices at national and international auctions—a fitting turn of events for an art that had been underestimated for so long.

◁ *Normandy interior.*
Musée du Meuble normand,
Villedieu-les-Poêles.

The Alsatian

Style

△ *Alsatian dining area. Musée alsacien, Strasbourg.*

Alsatian furniture is rich and extremely diverse. The style changes fairly distinctly between Upper Alsace and Lower Alsace. The Upper Alsace style is characterized by an abundance—even an over-abundance—of ornate sculpted elements. The principal motifs include pilasters, spiral-turned columns, arches, acanthus leaves and pediments decorated with foliated scrolls—all clearly inspired by the Renaissance. In the midst of all these motifs, there sometimes appear masks or winged angels' heads, a specialty of the Jesuits in Molsheim. But the most characteristic feature of Alsatian furniture is the perfect mastery of marquetry, a skill developed early on (between 1650 and 1690); this technique was in its earliest stages in Paris during this time. The marquetry motifs were either geometric (checkerboards or stars) or clearly figurative (bouquets of flowers, birds and roses).

The furniture style in Lower Alsace consists exclusively of painted motifs on a characteristic blue background. These pieces incorporated a diverse range of geometric and plant motifs: six-pointed stars, fylfots (a swastika-like shape), rosettes, pretzels, tulips, carnations, mythological animals, lions, coats of arms, hearts and various arabesque shapes. This style of painting furniture was derived from the ancient Northern European tradition (in Sweden, Germany and Austria) of painting pine furniture to conceal the rough wood; these pieces were made from the sixteenth to the nineteenth centuries. The most beautiful examples date from the nineteenth century. The furniture painters mastered a wide palette of colors, and stenciled and freehand drawings displayed an exquisite level of refinement. These pieces are extremely rare and highly prized.

The masters

The Froydevaux-Kaeshammer dynasty produced the greatest cabinetmakers.

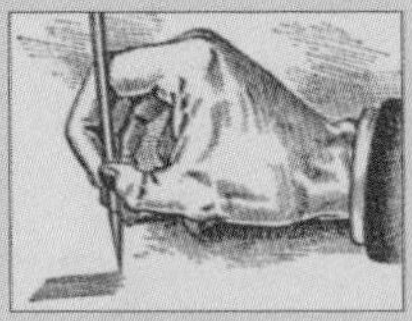

Inspiration

German Renaissance (17th century)

French Régence (18th century)

Rhine and Swiss furniture

Upper Alsace: ornately sculpted furniture

Lower Alsace: painted furniture

Wood

Walnut, oak, boxtree (marquetry), beech (for chairs), ebonized pearwood, cherry, plum

Pine and different conifer species, used for painted furniture, as well as for the interior sections of drawers and non-visible parts of furniture

CHESTS

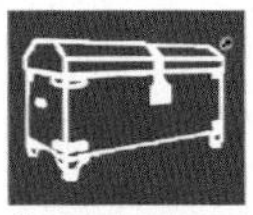

Chests are ancient furniture forms, the predecessor of all other furniture. The form was not forgotten by the Alsatians, who always used it to display their craftsmanship and savoir-faire.
The dowry chest, used to carry clothes and bedding, is one example; the date of the wedding and the bride's initials were always inscribed on the piece.
The most famous chest was the painted bourgeois-style chest, with a characteristic blue color. This was a flat-topped chest, with several panels on the facade decorated with stylized flowers. It stood on bun feet. The top was also divided into two panels. Other chests included a monumental, Renaissance-inspired piece, decorated with columns and ornate sculptures. Some were so large that they could be used as beds.
On the other end of the scale were small jewelry chests. The most elaborate of these were reproductions of small Renaissance cabinets.

▽ *Chest.*
Musée alsacien, Strasbourg.

△ Armoire-closet with two painted doors, 1812. Musée alsacien, Strasbourg.

THE ARMOIRE

Alsatian cabinetmakers illustrated their talents with exuberance on the many types of armoires. There were so many that it is hard to believe they could all come from the same region. The simplest and most famous is the two-doored pine armoire with a multicolored floral decor against a blue background. The most surprising were the rustic-style armoires, divided in half, with the vertical sections connected by wedges, and the so-called "slant" armoire, a narrow and extremely simple piece of furniture. Alsatian armoires, however, were generally ornately decorated. Some incorporated up to seven different types of wood to accentuate the difference between the light and dark colors. The façades were also decorated with many sculptures.

THE BUFFET

The two-tiered buffet was also a traditional dowry piece. The buffets were made all throughout Alsace starting in the second half of the eighteenth century. The size depended on the dimensions of the room it was designed for.
The olmer, like most two-tiered buffets, had an upper section used to store food, while the lower section was used for linen. Silverware drawers separated the two. But the unique feature of these buffets was a closet section extending the entire height of one side. A small niche, framed by a festooned molding, was sometimes added as a place to display small objects or carafes.
Many buffets were made of waxed walnut or oak. They were massive and rounded in shape, and stood atop large Renaissance-style bun feet. This impression of solidity was accentuated by the bonnet-scroll pediment and doors divided into compartments by hefty molding and sculptures.

△ Corner buffet with painted decor. Obermodern, 1813. Musée alsacien, Strasbourg.

▷ Chair with splayed legs. Musée alsacien, Strasbourg.

CHAIRS

The chair with splayed legs is the most typical example of Alsatian furniture. Its principal feature, as its name suggests, is the shape of the legs, an immediately recognizable and unprecedented form in the history of furniture.
The seat back was usually round, but was extremely irregular, with openwork designs and sculpted elements representing a multitude of different motifs dreamed up by the craftsman.
These were generally scroll shapes or designs inspired by local flora and fauna: hares, squirrels, wreaths of flowers, tulips, carnations, two-headed eagles, S-shaped intertwined hearts, entwined serpents, pretzels and so on.

The Auvergnat

Style

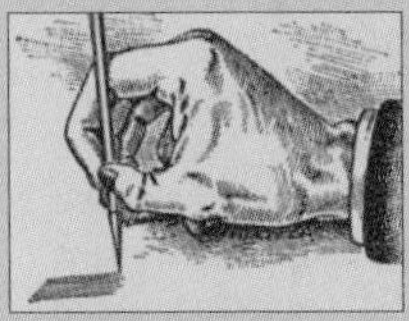

Stylistic inspiration

Louis XIII

Wood

Dark walnut, walnut in the Cantal region, fruit trees in the Velay region, cherry and beech for chairs

Different woods were often mixed together: pine bases, oak frames, ash drawers, walnut panels

△ *Interior of an Auvergnat home. Musée d'Art et d'Archéologie, Aurillac.*

This is functional furniture par excellence. The pieces are all massive and give an impression of solidity. The motifs seem to have existed forever. Many adopted the diamond and flattened diamond-point patterns of the Louis XIII style, while others were inspired from Gallic symbols: concentric circles, called bull's eyes, or disks symbolizing the sun and other planets. Other typical features include small and large balusters forming latticework or fretwork galleries, and straight moldings.

Locks and metal fittings are always extremely discreet; the small hinges are simple and keyholes are made of iron. Drawer pulls are often made in teardrop shapes, while locks are in cockscomb shapes.

The most common piece of furniture is the box bed, the Aurillac armoire with a protruding form, furniture from the lacemaking center of Velay, two-tiered buffets with flattened diamond-point patterns, chests, sideboards and benches. There are several different kinds of chests: grain chests, salt chests, bench-chests or ceremonial chests; the latter have rounded tops and panels decorated with geometric motifs.

Benches are generally made to double as chests, seating two people. This type of chest often contained salt and was placed near the fireplace to keep the salt dry; it is known as a *salis.* Some have a drop leaf and can be used as a dinner table or gaming table.

Three kinds of sideboards were used in the past: the sideboard-dishrack, modeled after a Brittany design; the sideboard-buffet, which had an upper section fitted with shelves; and a food storage sideboard.

△ Vaisselier-buffet, *or cupboard, with two doors, two drawers and four shelves. Musée d'Art et d'Archéologie, Aurillac.*

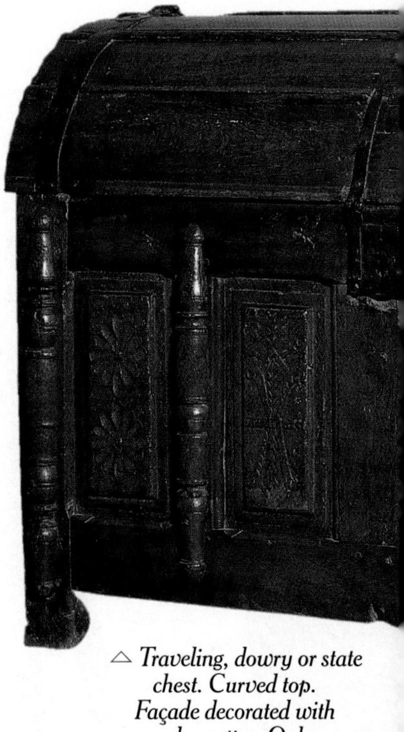

△ *Traveling, dowry or state chest. Curved top. Façade decorated with colonnettes. Oak. Musée d'Art et d'Archéologie, Aurillac.*

THE BUFFET OR SIDEBOARD

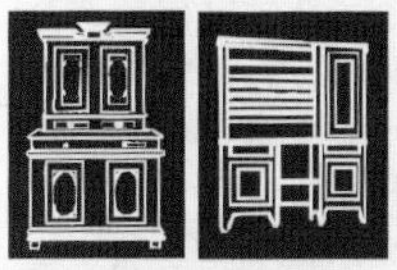

The two-tiered buffet is simple and massive in shape. It usually stood on bun feet, but could also be supported by simple stub feet. The door panels were carved with diamond patterns and were usually decorated in the center with a metal pendant in the shape of a teardrop or an iron rosette. The uprights of the buffet could also be decorated with colonnettes. The upper section of the buffet pictured here is narrower than the lower section, but another design, known as the buffet-bahut, also exists. In this piece, the upper section is flanked by a gallery of large balusters, somewhat like rougher versions of Provençal bread bins, to allow for air circulation.

▷ *Two-tiered buffet with four drawers. Pearwood, apple and oak. Musée d'Art et d'Archéologie, Aurillac.*

▷ *Bench-chest, or salis, for two people. Musée d'Art et d'Archéologie, Aurillac.*

The Bresse

Style

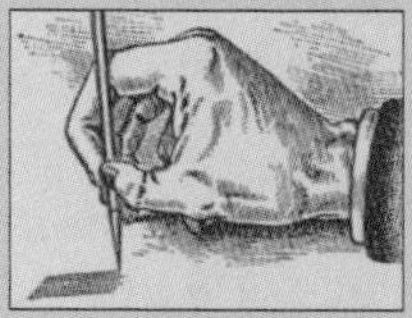

Stylistic inspiration

Régence

Louis XV

Wood

Walnut, oak and cherry for furniture frames

Elm burl and ash burl for doors and panels

△ *Farm in the Bresse region, near Bourg-en-Bresse.*

Bresse-style furniture, from a region northeast of Lyon, has been very popular since the late 1960s. Furniture pieces usually incorporate two woods of different colors; this association of light-colored and dark-colored wood gives it a sophisticated appearance.

Although inspired by the Louis XV style, most of the furniture was made in the early or mid-nineteenth century, with the exception of a few pieces that date from the late eighteenth century. Armoires, credences (or cupboards), buffets and sideboards with clock cases are the most representative examples of this style.

The decorative motifs were taken from local flora and fauna, as was the pattern throughout many regions; these included owls' heads, fighting birds, shells, aquatic plants (water lilies, flowers, gorse), vine stems, intertwined branches, leaves, acorns and flowerpots. Symbolic, geometric motifs were also used, such as a rosette in the middle of a circle motif (an extremely common design), as well as seemingly incongruous symbols such as the two-headed eagle of the Habsburg dynasty, a relic of the period when Bresse belonged to this family. Motifs were applied to panels and doors.

Cornices and pediments were often made in bonnet shapes. The lower crosspieces were always extremely ornamented and carved. The supports were often scroll feet, small hoof feet or bracket feet. Metal fittings, worked with exquisite skill, were small, wrought-iron brackets. The keyholes on armoires were placed high on the furniture piece and were elaborately shaped.

△ *Violin-shaped grandfather clock made of two different colors of wood. Walnut and ash burl. Dated 1825. Musée de Brou, Bourg-en-Bresse.*

THE *VAISSELIER* OR BUFFET

The Bresse-style vaisselier *(buffet) was an extremely elaborate piece of furniture made from the late eighteenth century to the early twentieth century. Many different designs exist, all made with two different colored woods (light and dark).*

The most spectacular example is the large vaisselier with three doors and three drawers. These elements were on the lower section, which was ornately sculpted and decorated, and framed by highly carved uprights. The lower crosspiece was decorated with garlands and was elaborately carved. The piece sat on either bracket feet or scroll feet.

The upper section was placed atop the lower section, but with a slight recess, forming a narrow tabletop. The section usually had several shelves (from three to six), with cross bars designed to hold plates placed on display.

Small, tabernacle-shaped armoires were placed on either side of the shelves. The main element of the buffet—the clock—was showcased in the center of the piece. Most often a rounded, violon-shape, the clock case was made of walnut or elm and was abundantly decorated with wreaths of flowers. Over the face of the clock was a small metal sculpture representing a rooster or a still life.

The top of the vaisselier had a baldachin with carved motifs. Most furniture from the Bresse region is dated and initialed.

△ *Two-tiered buffet. Walnut burl and ash burl. Musée de Brou, Bourg-en-Bresse.*

THE BUFFET WITH CLOCK

Like all Bresse-style furniture, the clock case was made using two different colors of wood. These clock cases were made in several shapes, but the most highly prized was the violin-shaped case, highly inspired by the Louis XV style, with a carved decor of shells and intertwined foliage.

The pediment was always curved. These rare pieces are generally dated on the inside and include the name of the owner.

The two-tiered buffet, also called a cabinet, was also highly inspired by the Louis XV style. It had an upper section with two doors and a curved pediment recessed from the lower section. The two sections were separated by a row of drawers.

△ *Sideboard with central clock case. Displayed without the clock face or mechanism. Two colors of wood, walnut and ash burl. Musée de Brou, Bourg-en-Bresse.*

The Burgundian Style

The masters

Hugues Sambin
Jean Demoulin
Claude Laborier

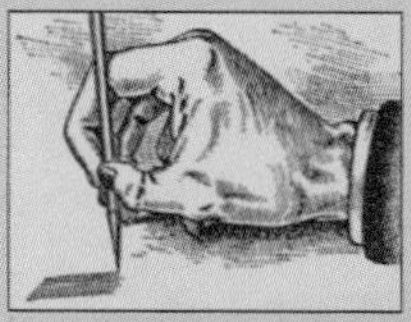

Stylistic inspiration

Renaissance
Louis XIII
Régence

Wood

Walnut, pearwood, cherry, elm burl or walnut burl, often used together for the panels of armoire doors

△ *Reconstruction of a Burgundian interior. Musée de la Vie bourguignonne Perrin de Puycousin, Dijon.*

With buffets and armoires, this style displayed the same overall characteristics as furniture designed during the Renaissance or Louis XIII's reign: many wide moldings and a profusion of carved elements.

Chests of drawers, however, followed the style initiated by Jean Demoulin, the unrivaled master of serpentine curves who worked for the Prince de Condé for many years. He specialized in japanning and highly curved, generous shapes that were meant to evoke the female body. The most typical chest of drawers comes from the region around Macon; these are extremely rounded and highly sculpted, with Louis XV legs and marble tabletops.

The metal fittings were elegantly worked with long, wrought-iron keyholes, a specialty of the Morvan region of France. The ends were often flame-shaped or were decorated with cockerel heads.

▷ Buffet-bahut *decorated with caryatid uprights, in the style of Hugues Sambin. Musée du Louvre, Paris.*

THE BUFFET AND THE *VAISSELIER*

Two types of two-tiered buffets existed: the gigantic buffet with eight doors and five drawers (with relatively little decoration, just wide molding, a projecting cornice and bun feet), and the true two-tiered* buffet-bahut. *This piece had a recessed upper section and was ornately decorated with Renaissance-style sculptures inspired by the school of Hughes Sambin, in other words, caryatids, wreaths, fruit, lions' heads, palm trees, masks and sinuous lines.

◁ Vaisselier *(buffet) from southern Burgundy. The plates, resting on cross bars, tilt forward. In versions from northern Burgundy, the plates tilt backward. The lower section has three doors. Musée de la vie bourguignonne Perrin de Puycousin, Dijon.*

The Lyonnais Style

The masters

Pierre Nogaret and his family
Canot
Levet
Lapierre
Philibert Delorme
Bernard Salomon
Pierre Woeriot

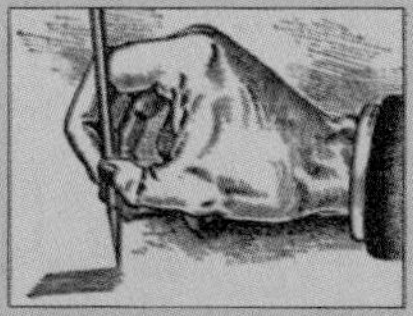

Stylistic inspiration

Renaissance
Louis XV

Wood and materials

Walnut
Oak
Cherry
Beech
Ash

△ *Lyon's "traboule" (covered pedestrian passageway) neighborhood, with a 17th-century tower staircase.*

In terms of furniture, the region of Lyon is characterized by a style that is far more urban and bourgeois than rural. During the Renaissance, Lyon was a cultured capital where a great deal of furniture was produced. It is therefore not surprising to find certain stylistic features of the period, primarily ornately sculpted elements, in this regional furniture.

Chests of drawers, chairs, armoires and buffets with central clock cases form the bulk of the furniture pieces produced in this region. The cabinetmaker Pierre Nogaret, who created extraordinary chairs, was an influential figure. Chests of drawers were made of walnut or fruit tree wood; they tended to be quite round in shape and had two or three drawers with copper handles, locks with quatrefoil motifs or high-relief shells as handles. Decorated with marquetry or grooves, the pieces were supported by tall cabriole legs with an elegantly carved lower crosspiece; some chests were supported by a Louis XV-style base. The designs and motifs were inspired by drawings and engravings published by Philibert Delorme, Bernard Salomon and Pierre Woeriot.

CHAIRS

The Nogaret chair is a walnut armchair inspired by the Louis XV style, but with wide, recessed and curved armrests. This extremely elegant chair was carved with flower and rococo motifs and upholstered with an Aubusson tapestry with a floral pattern. The designs for armchairs, chairs and sofas by Pierre Nogaret are particularly well-proportioned. All his furniture carry the estampille (the cabinetmaker's stamp) of Nogaret or of one of his students: Canot, Levet or Lapierre.

△ *Walnut chair with rounded seat back and cabriole legs. The crest rail is decorated with flowers. The seat is upholstered with yellow damask silk. Stamped by Nogaret in Lyon. Musée Vouland, Avignon.*

The Brittany Style

The masters

Allory family
Branthome
Berthelot
Boutin
Caucheu
Croizé family
David
Demeul
Julien Dondel
Peutrec
Piel
Jehan Tullon
Tulou family
Vassard

△ *Brittany interior. Musée des Amis de Guérande.*

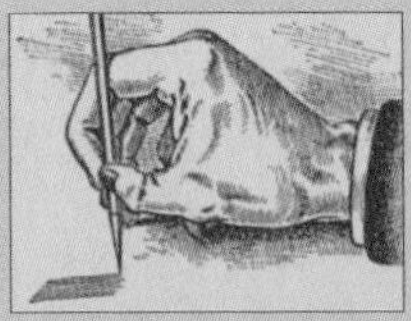

Stylistic inspiration

Louis XIII
Louis XIV
Louis XV

The Brittany style is one of the French regional styles that offers the greatest diversity in furniture, ranging from austere pieces painted with seafaring motifs to designs that are so that specific they do not exist anywhere else. The flax press or the *susbout* (a small armoire used to decant cider) are two examples. As in many other areas, the characteristics of the style differ within the region from Upper Brittany to Lower Brittany. In general, furniture design in the north was inspired by Louis XIV and Louis XV, while furniture in the south was a result of older and more varied influences (Louis XIII). In Vannes and Lorient the furniture incorporated marquetry; in Rennes, cherry was used; in Ouessant and Sein, furniture was painted blue; on Guérande, the armoires were red; in Cornouaille, the pieces were painted yellow with motifs from the Pont-l'Abbé region.

Yet all these pieces of furniture shared several features. The first was the round, concentric circle motif, inspired by Moorish designs (brought back by the many Breton sailors). This motif, which was used on every piece of furniture, was often combined with diamond-point or lozenge-shaped motifs. Brass or copper tacks were also used widely to accentuate sculptures. Spindles (slender turned columns) were placed on all box beds and buffets. It was not unusual to find Christian motifs (crosses, ostensories), Celtic motifs (spirals, knots) and Maltese crosses, taken from pattern books.

As in every other region, ornamentalists borrowed motifs from the local flora and fauna, which in this region were daisies, bunches of grapes, birds of prey and peacocks. Metal fittings were important in this furniture style and often were linked to sea voyages. In furniture from Saint Malo, for example, drawer handles shaped like crescent moons came from England or China. In Vannes, flame-shaped fittings were engraved with floral motifs. And in Quimper, they resembled sumptuous iron fretwork.

ARMOIRES

Armoires from Guérande were always painted bright red. This red was generally believed to be bull's blood and whitewash, until a scientific study suggested it could actually be red lead, used to protect the wood from the damp, salty air. This armoire had two doors and a straight cornice. Each door, divided vertically into three panels, was decorated with concentric circles, Maltese crosses or diamond-point motifs. Regardless of the patterns used, the middle panel always differed from the other two. The long, serpentine keyholes were made of brass. The armoire from the Guérande region is one example of the great diversity of Breton armoires, which include the armoire from Saint Malo, often made of mahogany, and the armoire from Rennes, with a characteristic crown-shaped cornice. Added to these are a multitude of small multi-purpose armoires, such as the flax press for storing flax and a spinning wheel, and the milk armoire, used as a larder.

△ Armoire from the Guérande region painted red. The two doors are decorated with concentric circle patterns and a diamond-point motif. Musée des Amis de Guérande.

△ Milk armoire from the Guérande region, painted red. This is a two-door larder resting on a chest with two shelves, used to store milk bottles. Musée des Amis de Guérande.

BOX BED

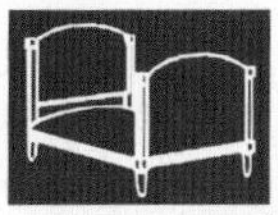

The box bed, known in the region as a gwele cloz, *is the most characteristic piece of furniture in Lower Brittany. It first appeared in the seventeenth century as a room within a room. Until the twentieth century, it was placed in the main room of the house, between the clock and the armoire. This specifically Breton placement of furniture, with the obligatory chest used as a step to reach the bed, is called the* trustel.

This arrangement could also be used for double box beds, in other words, superimposed beds (although only a few rare examples still survive). Although imposing in size, the Breton box bed was not very long, as people slept in a half-sitting position. The dimensions were invariable: 48 inches long, 72 inches wide and 100 inches high. Made of oak, cherry or chestnut, the box bed consisted of a front side with two uprights, joined by an upper crosspiece that forms a gallery topped by a cornice. The lower crosspiece was concealed behind the elaborately worked chest; a cradle could then be placed on this piece during the night. The bed opened either with one large or two small sliding doors. These were ornately carved and had a spy hole with an openwork design consisting of spindles. The more spindles a bed had, the wealthier the owner.

Geometric motifs were the most common, while stylized flowers, Celtic motifs, spindles and pilasters were used on the sides. In the Guérande region, the beds were painted red, like the rest of the furniture.

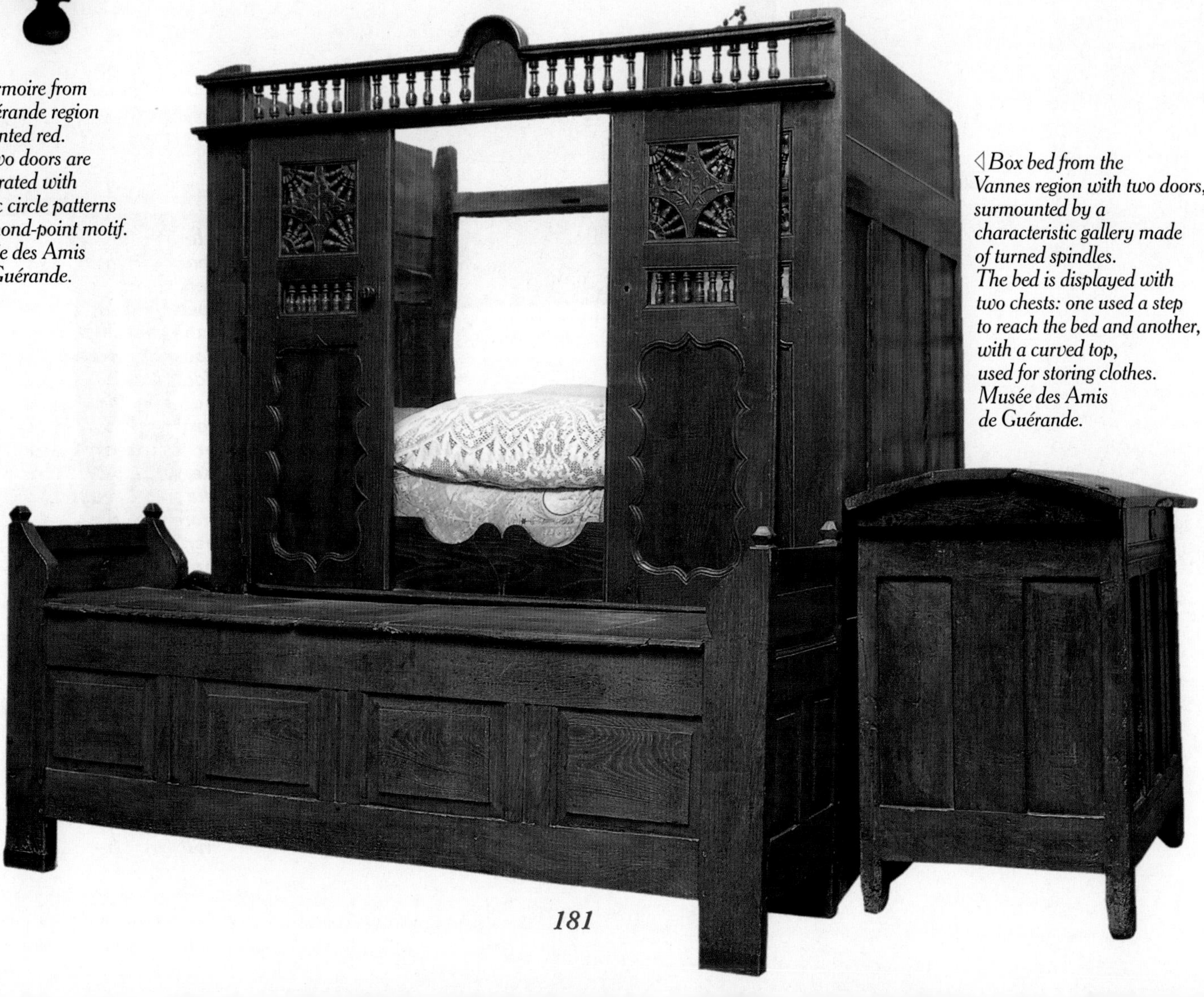

◁ Box bed from the Vannes region with two doors, surmounted by a characteristic gallery made of turned spindles. The bed is displayed with two chests: one used a step to reach the bed and another, with a curved top, used for storing clothes. Musée des Amis de Guérande.

Wood

Oak for panels, walnut for structures, boxwood and yew for balusters, cherry for sculptures, walnut, but also local wood known as **couëron** ***(a wood made rot-proof by soaking it in ponds), as well as driftwood.***

TABLES

Bin tables were not used to eat on. These bins or hutches were used as larders. The tabletop projects over the base on all four sides. The piece stands on short, rectilinear legs, joined by a wide H-stretcher. The top of the chest opened to give access to the food stored within. It was attached either by two sliding panels or by hinges placed on the side of the chest. The apron was very high—up to 16 inches—and was carved.

△ *Bin larder made of oak, with fall-front panel on the side. Musée des Amis de Guérande.*

△ *Dining room table from the Guérande region, painted red. Louis-XIII style, but made in the nineteenth century. Two drawers in the apron, turned legs, H-stretcher decorated with a central finial. Musée des Amis de Guérande.*

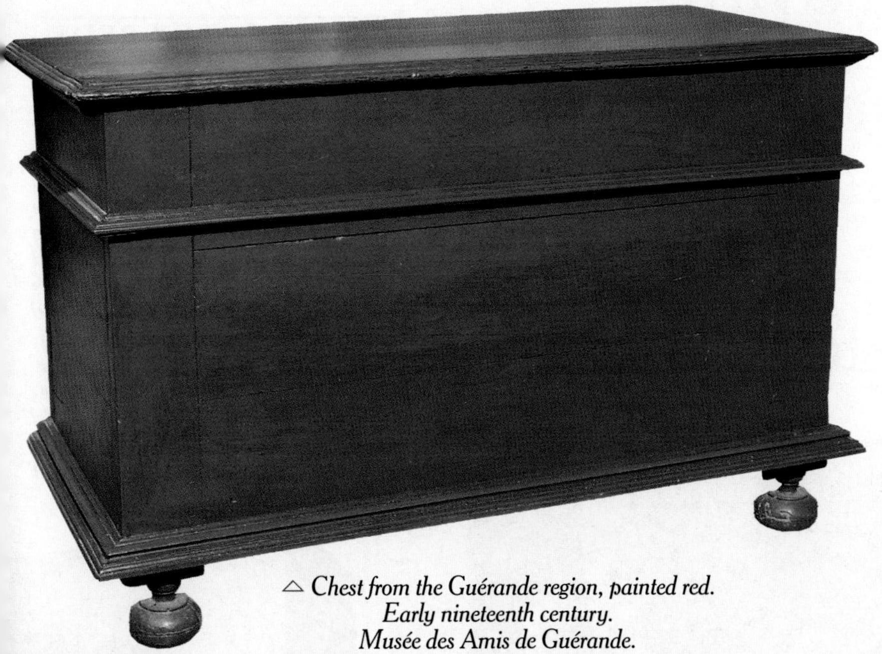

△ *Chest from the Guérande region, painted red. Early nineteenth century. Musée des Amis de Guérande.*

CHESTS

As in many French regions, the chest was important to a bride, and was especially so for marriages in wealthy families. As early as the fifteenth century, it was meant to hold the bride's dowry, and was therefore put on display so that all the guests could admire it and its contents.
The chests then became a kind of all-purpose piece of furniture, used as a table, larder, buffet, bench, step to reach a box bed, support for a cradle, a cupboard and even a bank. Two different types of chests exist in Brittany: the **grimoliou***, **a huge piece of furniture, six to ten feet long, with a curved top and a façade with panels carved with ornate geometric patterns; the other type, the*** **archiou***, **was smaller in size and had a flat cover so that it could be used as a table or a bench. In the Morbihan region, chests were decorated with inlaid woods, decors of hearts and stars and brass or copper tacks.***

◁ *Two-tiered buffet from the Guérande region, painted red. Musée des Amis de Guérande.*

BUFFET

The oldest buffets date from the mid-nineteenth century. They had two doors, topped by two drawers richly decorated with floral motifs, birds, and Celtic and religious (in Cornouaille) motifs. Brass and copper tacks were widely used as decorative elements, especially on more recent pieces.
The upper section, recessed slightly from the lower section, always had four shelves, whether it was the same width or narrower than the buffet below.
The latticework or bars holding the plates were decorated with alternating spindles and foliage. A clock was sometimes fitted into the center of the buffet. A flat cornice covered the top of the piece.

△ *Buffet from the Guérande region, with two doors and a case with four shelves. Musée des Amis de Guérande.*

The Savoyard

Style

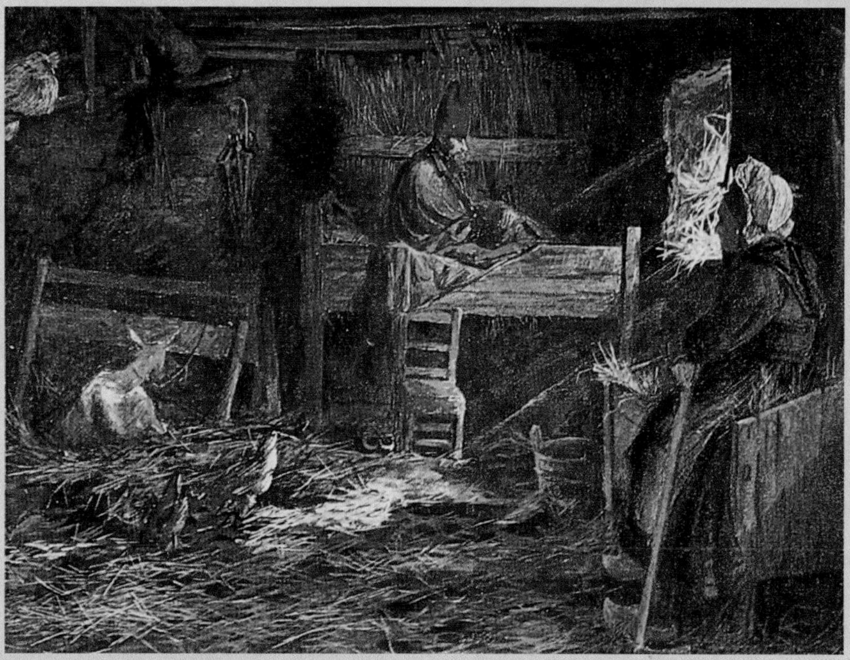

△ *Savoyard interior. Musée d'Art et d'Histoire, Chambéry.*

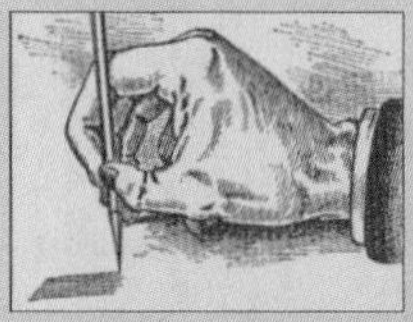

Stylistic inspiration

Renaissance

Hardware

Small wrought-iron hinges

This furniture, designed in a mountainous environment, is extremely rudimentary. Functional above all, the furniture pieces were almost always decorated with simple, hand-carved motifs, inspired by the usual religious or geometric ornamental patterns: revolving suns, rosettes, hearts, stars, diamond-point, Christian symbols and circles. The best-known hand-carved furniture comes from the Queyras region, where they were made as early as the fifteenth century. This furniture, made by farmers who were also wood-workers (of necessity), consists primarily of chests, two-tiered buffets, box beds, prayer stools and carved chairs, along with an imposing number of salt boxes and cheese-drying cabinets. This type of furniture is still made today, with the exact same designs.

Alongside this specifically mountain-style, austere furniture, generally made of pine and other conifers, there existed another style of furniture, that of the plains. This was fairly widespread in the towns located in the valleys, such as Chambéry and Annecy. These pieces were ordered by local dignitaries, who had reproduced—several decades after the fashion—the styles popular in Paris, with a special fondness for the Louis XV style. Furniture pieces made in this style include desks, dressing tables, chests of drawers, bookcases and bedside tables.

Clocks were often made of pine in mountain chalets, but were more sophisticated in the valleys; they were often built directly into the wall of the main room.

PARTIAL BOX BEDS

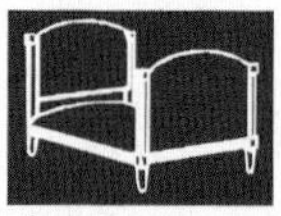

The partial box bed is another example of the austere Savoyard design. As its name indicates, the uprights form a sort of cage enclosure. These were carved with geometric motifs, as well as the initials of the owner and sometimes prayers or mottos. The front was closed off by curtains. The lower section sometimes had a drawer that could also be used as a crib. A bench was frequently placed in front of the bed.

CRADLES

The Savoy cradle was a crib placed on two curved pieces of wood forming rockers. It was shaped something like a trapezoidal trough with fairly high splayed uprights to protect the infant from the animals, which wandered freely about the room. The side panels had holes, meant for straps to suspend the

ARMOIRE

The armoire best characterizes the extreme simplicity of mountain furniture. It had two hand-carved panels fitted to a larch frame. There are no metal fittings; simple wooden pegs hold the doors closed, somewhat like certain Chinese armoires.

▷ *Shepherd's armoire made of pine. This is a characteristic example of the extremely austere design of mountain furniture. Musée d'Art et d'Histoire, Chambéry.*

◁ *Partial box bed resting on high feet; at night, sheep slept in the space underneath, thereby providing a certain amount of heat. Musée d'Art et d'Histoire, Chambéry.*

▽ *Cradle with side holes for straps to suspend it from the roof. Musée d'Art et d'Histoire, Chambéry.*

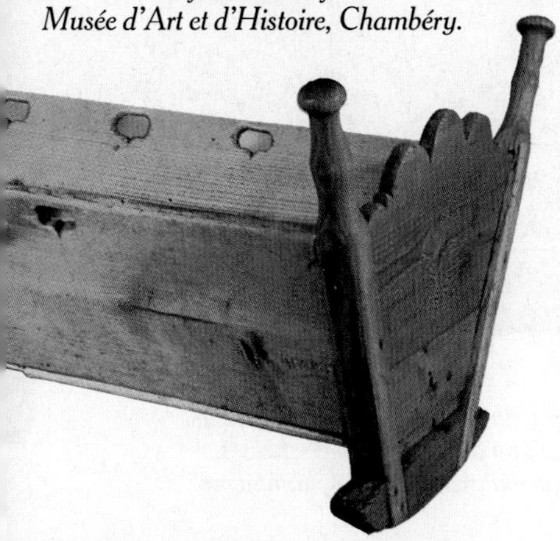

bed. Geometric motifs were carved on the rockers, on the cradle's headboard and on the base: they were intended to ward off evil spirits. It was not unusual to suspend the cradle from the roof, rather than place it alongside one of the beds.

CHESTS

Made of solid wood, generally of cembro pine, the chests from the Queyras region are somewhat different from other regions in that they have two interior compartments with locks. What really distinguishes them from others, however, is the ornate hand-carved decoration, a tradition that dates from the fifteenth century. Marked out with a compass or chisel, the various motifs—circles, seven-pointed rosettes, astral symbols and foliated scrolls—inspired from Renaissance styles were often carved while the wood was heated red hot. Tongue and groove joints, mortise and tenon joints, and dowels were used to assemble the structure. Chests were placed on the floor or stood on short, wide legs.

◁ *Chest made of larch from the Queyras region. The front is ornately decorated with carved rosettes and a gadroon pattern. Hinge plate and mounted lock. The uprights and crosspieces are connected by mortise and tenon joints. Made in 1739. Musée dauphinois, Grenoble.*

The Champenois

Style

Stylistic inspiration

Louis XIV

Louis XV

Louis-Philippe

Wood and materials

Oak, and sometimes walnut or cherry

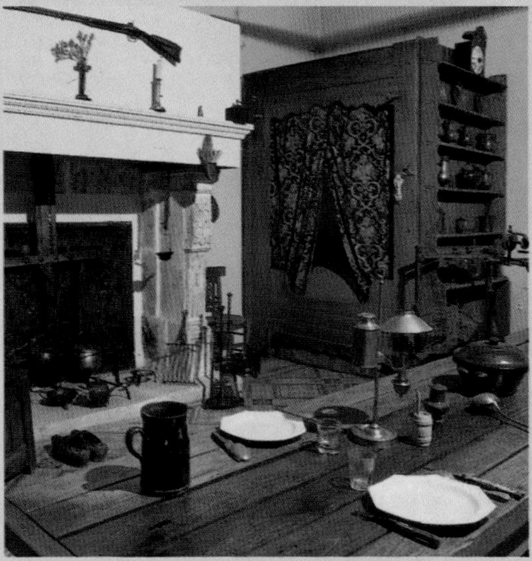

△ *Champenois interior. Musée municipal, Châlons-en-Champagne.*

Similar in many ways to the Parisian style, Champenois furniture nevertheless differs is a few elements: the scroll feet, projecting molding and heavy doors and cornices made of solid oak. The most characteristic examples of this style are the beds, painted gray, the small grape harvest tables and the buffets. Other pieces that stand out among the generally simple, though solid furniture, are the buffets that are called *ménagers* in this region, certain chairs and the clocks.

The hardware, made by a farrier, were Spartan in their simplicity.

The Champenois-style clock could stand over six feet high.

There were two types of clocks:

◆ One with a straight housing, resting on a square, undecorated base, with just a few moldings and heart or daisy motifs. The copper clock faces were extremely ornate.

◆ One with a more slender housing, which tapered toward the top and with a cornice carved with a shell motif and abundant decoration on the pediment, doors and base. This decoration incorporated a number of different motifs: birds and brightly colored painted floral decors, especially in the Aude region. The clock faces were made of faience,and a stone was used as a counterweight.

THE *MÉNAGER*

The three-door ménager was an oak buffet consisting of two sections of equal width. The most elegant was the double buffet, consisting of an upper section with profiled and carved uprights and a lower section resting on scroll feet. The lower section usually had two or three doors with a carved decor. Drawers were placed above these doors, along with a tabletop separating the two pieces. The upper section was slightly recessed and consisted of three shelves with a molding on each edge so that plates could be displayed on the shelves.

△ Ménager *with two doors and two drawers, surmounted by a case with three shelves. Musée municipal, Châlons-en-Champagne.*

The Île-de-France

Style

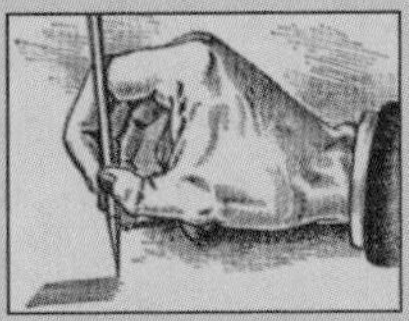

Stylistic inspiration

Gothic

School of Fontainebleau

Louis XIV

Louis XV

Louis XVI

△ *Farm in Île-de-France.*

Furniture made in the Île-de-France region was well-proportioned and well-designed. The proximity of Paris obviously influenced this style, which seems to summarize all the styles created in the capital, from the Gothic to the Louis XVI style. Some pieces of furniture, however, remained rustic, with features specific to the region. These included serpentine and curved pediments, deep molding, regularly spaced dovetail motifs and beautiful carvings of shells, foliated scrolls, rosettes, baskets, bouquets, masks and revolving suns, one of the preferred motifs in the region. The loveliest of these sculptures had extremely classical, inlaid patterns of ivory, mother-of-pearl, lapis-lazuli, colored marble or bronze. The legs were curved, when inspired by the Louis XV style, or rectilinear, a clear reference to the Louis XVI style.

The most highly prized pieces of furniture included the so-called *parisienne,* the Louis XV chest of drawers—that the Île de France region was one of the first to adopt—the Briard (or square) buffet and the hunting buffet with marble (a sumptuous piece of furniture). Metal fittings were extremely delicate, with openwork designs.

Wood

Wood from the Île-de-France forests: oak, beech, walnut, cherry fruit trees

Exotic marquetry woods and ebony

STORAGE FURNITURE

The Briard buffet, also known as a square buffet, was the simplest form of storage cabinet. Its design resembles closely the form of the large chest on legs made during the seventeenth century.

Most of these buffets had two doors with molding, in the Louis XV style, attached to fluted uprights in the Louis XVI style.

The so-called parisienne *was very narrow, but had two doors, which distinguishes it from the cupboards known as* bonnetières *or* homme-debouts, *which were common in this region. The Louis XIV-style panels were decorated with carvings or moldings. A shell motif sometimes decorated the top of the armoire.*

Chests of drawers were most often inspired by the Louis XV style, but included elements from the Louis XIV style. The piece had four rows of drawers, with copper handles decorated with a characteristic daisy motif. The legs were slightly curved.

△ *Square buffet, also known as a Briard buffet. Musée Briard, Jouarre.*

The Provençal

Style

The masters

Bernard Toro, a famous cabinetmaker and student of Pierre Puget, a sculptor from Marseille.

The Laffanour family, which has specialized in Provençal chairs since 1840.

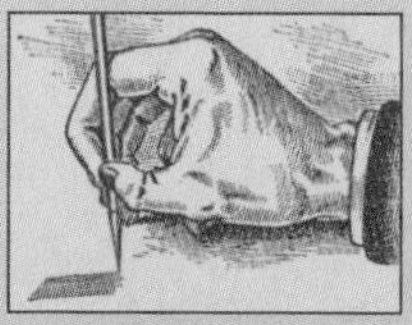

Stylistic inspiration

Upper Provence: ***Louis XIII***

Lower Provence: ***Louis XV*** ***Louis XVI***

△ A Provençal Kitchen. *Antoine Raspal. Musée Réattu, Arles.*

This is an exuberant style with curvilinear forms. The style of Upper Provence, however, is much more austere, massive and rigid than the style of Lower Provence. The latter can be divided into two major movements: the Arles style, with ornamental devices that include flowers and densely carved olive leaves; and the Fourques style, which is more sober, with spiral motifs and sunk carving.

The principal motifs include shells, roses, olives, olive branches, myrtle, almond trees, intertwined wreaths, pine cones, vines, wheat, flame ornaments and candlesticks; pediments were occasionally decorated with a pelican motif (as in Normandy). The piece generally stood atop scroll feet. Wood was often sculpted in openwork patterns, as were crosspieces.

Metal fittings were extremely important in this style and contributed to the exuberance of the furniture pieces. They resembled lacework of polished steel and were placed on the doors of armoires, buffets, drawers and even shelves. Keyholes were high, wide and scroll-shaped. Hinges were long and very thick, and made in olive or pine-cone shapes.

BREAD BIN

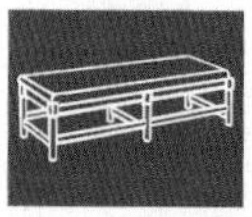

The panetière, or bread bin (paniero in Provençal), is a specifically local piece of furniture used to store the most important item of food: bread. Although it stands on legs, it was designed to be hung half-way up the kitchen wall, generally above the kneading trough.

The openwork structure, made of finely worked, thin spindles, allows for the circulation of air. A candlestick motif (a typical Provençal design) or flowers often decorated the middle of the crosspiece and the corners.

△ *Walnut bread bin. Muséon Arlaten, Arles.*

KNEADING TROUGH

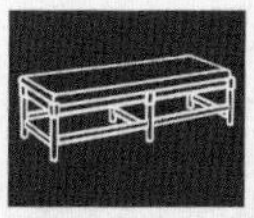

The kneading trough **(pétrin *or* mastres)** ***was generally inseparable from the*** **panetière** ***(bread bin) and the*** **tamisadou** ***(a sifting mill whose mechanical parts were concealed in a large decorated buffet). This piece of furniture has the oldest history of any other Provençal piece, as it dates from the thirteenth century. By the fifteenth century, it was the most important part of a bride's dowry, but it wasn't until the nineteenth century that the trough started to be sumptuously decorated with scenes from everyday life. It is designed in the shape of a trapezoidal chest standing on four turned legs, joined by an ornately carved crosspiece. The top is attached by hinges and was used to knead bread as well as to salt pork. The legs ended in scroll feet in Provençal and bracket feet in Nice, while the piece stood on a solid base in the Comtat Venaissin.***

▷ *Walnut kneading trough. Muséon Arlaten, Arles.*

Wood

Walnut, olive in marquetry, linden, pearwood, cherry, walnut, sorb tree, almond, orange, lemonwood and mulberry

THE ARMOIRE

The armoire or cupboard is generally an elaborately carved piece of furniture that was found both in the countryside and in the homes of the bourgeoisie. It was, as in Normandy, one of the main elements of a bride's dowry. Oddly enough, Norman and Provençal armoires share a number of characteristics. They both have a central section with molding and a highly ornate pediment decorated with the same floral, pelican, dove and acanthus-leaf motifs. Other designs included musical instruments and fruit. The armoire could be ten feet high in designs ranging from the exuberant Louis XV style in Lower Provence to an austere Louis XIII style in Upper Provence. The lower crosspiece was carved with openwork designs and the piece stood on scroll feet or bun feet. Each door was divided into two or three panels. The carved cornices were often bonnet-shaped. Even the hardware was finely worked. Made of walnut, almond tree, olive wood, rosewood or violetwood, the most highly prized armoires come from the Saint-Rémy-de-Provence, Beaucaire and Arles regions. These are decorated with olive and lemon motifs and are magnificently carved, often by Bernard Toro, from Toulon.

△ *Wedding armoire. Muséon Arlaten, Arles.*

△ *Waxed walnut salt box, with a drawer in the base. Muséon Arlaten, Arles.*

BOXES

Salt and flour boxes are small, abundantly decorated chests carved with the usual regional motifs (pine cones, olives, etc.), with the addition of motifs related to the specific nature of each chest. Certain salt boxes, for example, are decorated with motifs referring to fish and the sea, while flour boxes were adorned with seeds of wheat, sheaves or millstones. The salt box, or saliero, has a slightly slanting hinged top. The flour box, or farinïero, is opened by sliding up a vertical panel.

△ *Walnut flour box. Muséon Arlaten, Arles.*

△ *Chest with two drawers, inspired by the Louis XVI style. Walnut. Muséon Arlaten, Arles.*

CHEST OF DRAWERS

These chests were made in the Louis XV or Louis XVI style. The design originated in the eighteenth century for rich members of the bourgeoisie and the aristocracy. The chest has two or three drawers and is made of close-grained walnut. The top could be covered with marble, although this was more unusual. The legs were either high and curved, or short and straight, depending on the number of drawers it had. The front curved outward and was decorated with Rococo sculpture that was often quite extraordinary. The lower crosspieces were always elaborately worked. The metal fittings, which were extremely important decorative elements in these pieces, were generally made of burnished iron. An infinite number of variations on this form were made. In the Toulon, Marseille and Avignon regions, for example, the chests were lacquered—dark colors (red and green) in Marseille and Toulon, and pastel colors (olive green) near Avignon and Saint-Rémy-de-Provence. In the region around Arles, the sculptor Bernard Toro created extremely ornate work, especially for the façades of chests of drawers.

The Flemish

Style

△ *Flemish interior. Musée de l'hospice Comtesse, Lille.*

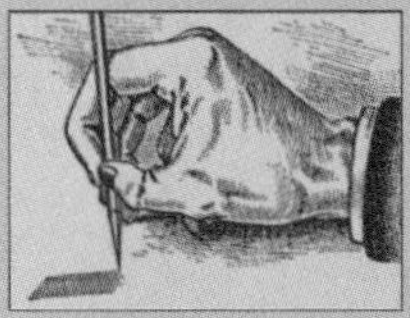

Stylistic inspiration

Renaissance

Louis XIV

Spanish

Dutch

Burgundian

Flanders belonged to Burgundy and then to Spain in the sixteenth century. The region retained many stylistic elements from these periods in both its architecture and furniture designs. Motifs such as opulent carvings of caryatids, lions' heads with iron rings in the mouths, atlases, flamboyant gadrooning, grotesque masks, crowns, projecting cornices and foliated scrolls were all taken from the Renaissance, as well as from the exuberant Spanish furniture made during the reigns of Charles V and Philip II. Nevertheless, Flemish furniture was functional above all, especially the storage pieces, which gradually became more decorative. There was also a large variety in the type of storage furniture, ranging from single-piece cupboards of all kinds (*ribbanks*), to two-tiered buffets, chests, credences, massive armoires (*kleerkas*) standing on bun feet, cabinets and more typical pieces such as the clothes cupboard.

The rest of the Flemish furniture—primarily chairs and tables—was also influenced by the Renaissance styles. These were elegant pieces of furniture, which contrasted sharply with the profusely ornamented storage pieces.

CHAIRS

Chairs fitted with rush seats are typically Flemish. They first appeared in the seventeenth century and have hardly changed since then. They are characterized by a seat back with four flat, undulating vertical rods. The two outside bars are spindle-shaped, while the two inner bars are somewhat flame-shaped. The crest rail, whether bonnet-shaped or carved, is often decorated with carvings of shells; it is always well-proportioned in relation to the rest of the chair. The seat is covered with rush. Another chair design was the cathedra, which was mid-way between the Gothic cathedrae and those inspired by the Renaissance.

△ *Chair with rush seat.*
Musée de l'hospice Comtesse, Lille.

△ *Cathedra chair, oak, late sixteenth century. Musée de l'hospice Comtesse, Lille.*

THE *RIBBANK*

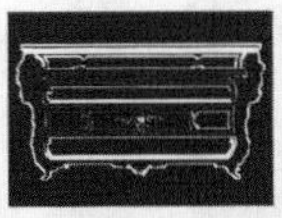

The ribbank is a massive, bulky piece of furniture with two doors, surmounted by an extremely ornate projecting cornice decorated with gadrooning. The two door panels are also ornately carved. The frame and crosspieces are decorated with carved caryatids, atlases and lions' heads. The piece often rests on large disk-shaped feet.

The ribbank is one of the many Flemish variations of storage furniture, which include two-tiered buffets, chests and buffets with two, three, four and even five doors.

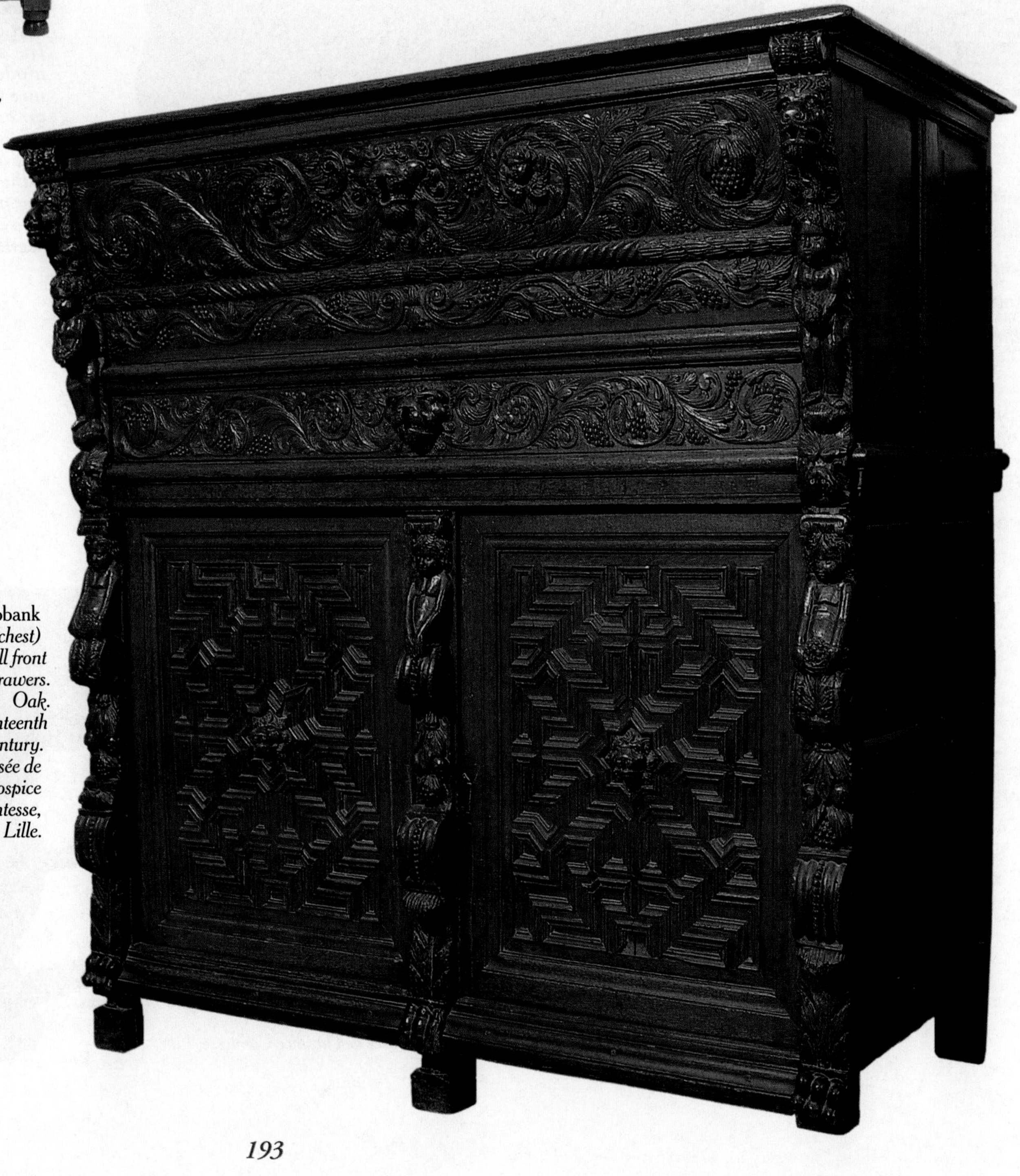

▷ Ribbank bahut *(chest) with fall front and drawers.* Oak. *Seventeenth century. Musée de l'hospice* Comtesse, *Lille.*

△ Bahut-crédence *from Brabant.*
Oak. Seventeenth century.
Musée de l'hospice Comtesse, Lille.

BAHUT-CRÉDENCE

The bahut-crédence is a two-tiered, ornately carved buffet, highly inspired by the Renaissance. Its unique feature is the upper section. It is much smaller than the lower section and forms a type of small chest placed on a ribbank-type lower section.
In some bahut-crédence models, the monumental cornice (it would be better to call it an entablature) on the upper section is supported by caryatids or atlases.
Other features of this surprising piece of furniture include two carved coffered panels per section and a drawer.

Wood

Dark oak
Cherry
Pearwood
Linden tree
Elm

RENAISSANCE TABLE

Flemish furniture clearly has none of the rustic aspects of other types of regional furniture styles. Tables perhaps best exemplify this.
While people in other regions in France were still eating off their laps, extremely sophisticated tables with baluster or carved legs were being made.
These four-legged tables, highly characteristic of the Renaissance, differ from the tables à l'italienne.

△ *Renaissance-style table with four baluster-turned legs.*
Oak.
Musée de l'hospice Comtesse, Lille.

The Franche-Comté

Style

The masters

Abraham-Nicolas Couleru

Marc-David Couleru

Pierre-Nicolas Couleru

and Georges-David Couleru

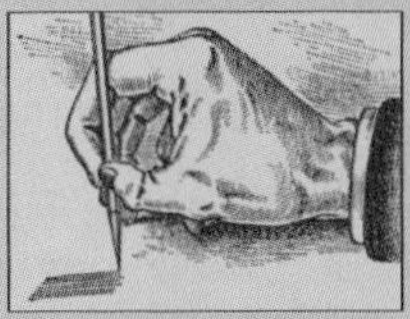

Stylistic inspiration

Louis XIV

Louis XV

Louis XVI

Burgundy

Lorraine

Champenois

Bresse

Hispano-Flemish

Wood

Walnut

Fruit trees

Oak

Pine

Beech

△ *A typical building in the countryside of the Franche-Comté region.*

This style of furniture is confusing in that armoires are called buffets and buffets may be called armoires. Franche-Comté furniture is characterized by well-proportioned designs, solidity and good craftsmanship. Designs have clear lines. The most striking aspect, however, is the family of cabinetmakers, the Coulerus, who influenced the furniture style.

The decorative motifs are purely geometric, and highlighted with floral motifs (leaves, clover). Furniture designs are accentuated by burning lines in the wood, creating trompe-l'œil grooved patterns. Spiral-turned columns are another decorative device. The façade of this type of furniture was often made of burl elm.

The most typical pieces of furniture are the clock, of course, as well as the Montbéliard armoire and the *vaisselier.*

The Montbéliard armoire, also known as a Protestant armoire, is a two-tiered buffet with four ornately carved doors, somewhat in the Moorish style. The unique features of these armoires were the two side handles, designed to make them easier to transport.

The *vaisselier* is an imposing piece of furniture, which can have up to six doors, five drawers and five shelves for dishes (which are always displayed tilted slightly backward).

CLOCKS

The Franche-Comté clock has such a familiar shape that it has become the model for almost all other grandfather clocks. The piece first appeared around 1830 and was adopted throughout all of France. The long case was made in the shape of a violin or a pyramid, or was merely straight. It had a vertical opening in the center to reveal the pendulum. There were many different designs. Some were extremely austere, made of painted and varnished pine; others had no decoration whatsoever; some were made of brightly painted pine; while still others displayed doors with carved moldings and motifs such as fleur-de-lys, crowns, eagles or cockerels. These differences in design are a function of the period during which they were made. All of the clocks were made in Morez, Morbier, Foncine or Besançon. The clock faces, fitted into round or straight cases, depending on the design, were made of enamel, faience or repoussée brass. The pendulums were made of bronze, embossed brass or brass painted with religious or romantic scenes.

▷ *A grandfather clock, known in the Comté region as a wedding clock, nineteenth century. Musée départemental d'arts et traditions populaires Albert-Demard, Champlitte.*

The Lorraine

Style

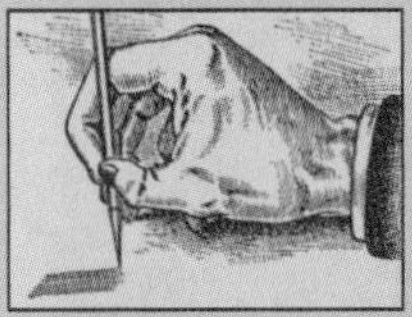

Stylistic inspiration

Louis XIII to Louis XVI, although predominantly Louis XV

Champenois

Wood

Oak, walnut, cherry, beech for chairs, pine and other conifers for chests

△ *Traditional Lorraine interior: canopy bed, Seille Valley. Musée historique lorrain, Nancy.*

This style is characterized by the rectilinear designs, with simple shapes, austere ornamentation and well-proportioned moldings. Two different types of furniture co-existed: pieces designed for the bourgeoisie, made of noble wood, and others made for the working class, produced from rougher wood or painted pine. The motifs were highly naturalistic (flowers, thistles) and could form an entire bucolic scene on a single piece of furniture. Marquetry, a specialty of the region, reproduced designs of small, finely pointed stars made from several different colors of wood. Other patterns included checkerboards, fillets and inlays, occasionally highlighted with pewter (particularly in the Dieuze region). The Gérardmer region is famous for the brightly colored chests painted in tones of red and green, or with wood-burned patterns. Furniture essentially consisted of four-poster beds with ornamentation of the visible side only, box beds with curtains (these often had a storage space underneath), trapezoidal- or semicircular-shaped kneading troughs, small pieces of furniture with inlaid decoration, corner cupboards, large wide armoires and clocks. Special mention must be made of the large buffets and *vasseliers*, which are specific to this region. The Lorraine also produced interesting tables, including a large table supporting by legs joined by turned H-stretchers and decorated with two finials on each side and a large central finial on the stretcher. This central finial resembled a fifth leg. Another amusing piece of furniture was the so-called lacework table, with a small tabletop supported by three splayed legs.

Latticework fittings were made of iron or brass and incorporated motifs of small vases. They were usually made in the forge of each village. Handles stretched along the entire length of a piece of furniture, often ending in daisy-shaped fittings.

CLOCKS

Starting in the eighteenth century, highly imaginative clocks were made for the bourgeoisie and the aristocracy. The designs are so diverse that it is hard to imagine they all belong to the same style. The opening on the case was made in a quatrefoil shape, typical of the region. The case was either straight (from Metz) or violin-shaped (from the Vosges). The cornice was bonnet-shaped or curved, while the piece stood on bun feet or scroll feet. The clock face was made of faience or repoussée copper or was stamped with popular motifs.

△ *Grandfather clock. Musée historique lorrain, Nancy.*

THE *VAISSELIER*

The Lorraine vaisselier (or credence) was a perfect case to display the plates and dishes made in the region's potteryworks, including some of the most famous in France: Lunéville, Niderviller and Saint-Clément.
Built with an oak or cherry frame, the Lorraine vaisseliers all shared one feature: The shelves (three or four) on the upper section did not have a gallery to support the plates. Instead, the shelves had a groove, in which the edge of the plate fitted.
The lower section has two doors surmounted by three central drawers with fittings made of copper or pewter. The door panels were decorated with a large quatrefoil motif. The piece stood on bracket feet.

△ *Buffet-dresser from Fraize. Musée historique lorrain, Nancy.*

CHESTS

The pine Gérardmer chest was often more than 6 feet long. It was extremely simple in design: flat sides, hinged top and visible strap hinges. The most popular decorations consisted of geometric, floral or religious motifs, which were burned into the wood with a heated chisel or iron. The chests sometimes were painted in vivid colors, primarily red and green, but also yellow, black or blue.

△ *Chest made of painted pine.*
Gérardmer region.
Musée historique lorrain, Nancy.

THE BUFFET

The large two-tiered crédence buffet was an imposing, multi-purpose piece of furniture. It generally consisted of four armoires, a shelf and a chest of drawers. Occasionally, the lower section also had a slant-top compartment, which opened to form a writing surface. The type of two-tiered buffet rarely had fewer than four doors, three drawers and three shelves fitted into an alcove surrounded by the armoires. The ensemble combined the Louis XVI style (structure) and the Louis XV structure (crosspiece and scroll feet) in an unusually harmonious way.

△ *Two-tiered buffet. Musée historique lorrain, Nancy.*

The Vendean, Poitou,

Aunis and Saintonge Styles

The masters

Vendée:
Charles Corbrejaud

Alexandre Jamouillé

Poitou:
Mourault

Étienne Barbaud

Jallet

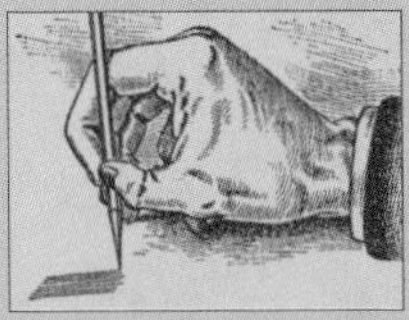

Stylistic inspiration

Vendean:
Louis XIII to Louis XVI

Netherlands

Poitevin:
Louis XIII to Louis XVI

Brittany

Saintonge and Aunis:
Louis XIV

Louis XVI

△ Bourrine *in the Monts region, in Vendée.*

Furniture in the Vendée region was remarkable graceful and refined. The light, austere forms, inspired by the Netherlands style, contribute a great deal to its style. The use of different species of wood to achieve contrasting colors created a polychromatic effect that was extremely elegant, especially as it imitated exotic woods. Motifs inspired by the Louis XIII through the Louis XV styles were combined with Brittany motifs of concentric circles and local motifs of flowers, crosses, hearts, fish and ducks.

Metal fittings were made of brass, steel or iron in the shapes of hearts, fleur-de-lys and cockerel heads.

The Poitou style does not differ significantly from the nearby regions, and indeed, it borrowed a great deal from Brittany and Bordeaux furniture styles. Motifs included Saint Andrew's crosses, daisies, garlands of figures, disks and diamond-point. Metal fittings extended along the entire height of panels and doors. The most representative piece of furniture was the *boîte à bonne Vierge,* which was a small chapel, like a display case, fitted into a buffet or an *homme-debout.*

Like the furniture in the nearby Vendée, the furniture made in the Aunis and Saintonge regions was extremely elegant and combined different types of wood (elm and ash) in elaborate marquetry patterns with very specific motifs: roses, stars, garlands of flowers, leaves and tureens. Often made by monks who were also fine craftsmen, this furniture frequently had religious connotations. The metal fittings were an important decor element and added a distinguished and refined touch. Fleur-de-lys, cockerel heads, clover and hearts were also commonly used motifs.

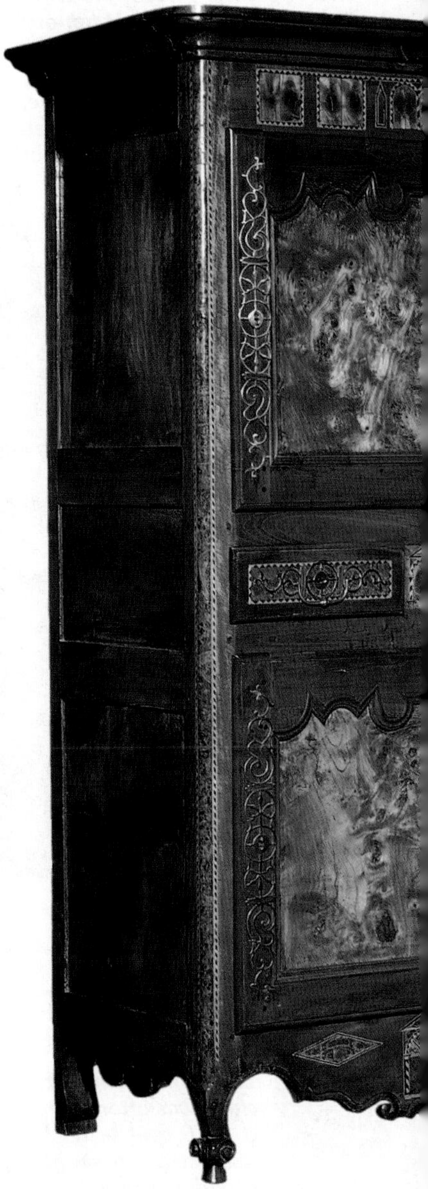

△ *Typical Saintonge cabinet. Cherry and elm burl for the door panels. Elaborate, long keyholes. Mid-nineteenth century. Musée vendéen, Fontenay-le-Comte.*

CABINETS

Cabinets from the Vendée region are unique in that they are not two-tiered pieces, as opposed to most cabinets, but stand as a single, tall piece.
The two doors, one above the other, are separated by a central drawer. This design makes these pieces look more like Louis XV armoires or secrétaires than cabinets. Like most of the furniture made in the region, they incorporate several different types of fruit trees and elm or ash burl. Moldings were sometimes accentuated by colored fillets.

▷ *Cabinet with painted moldings accentuating the forms. Maillezais region. Late nineteenth century. Musée vendéen, Fontenay-le-Comte.*

△ *Grandfather clock made of fruit wood and elm burl, resting on a base. Musée vendéen, Fontenay-le-Comte.*

CLOCKS

Clocks made in the Vendée region were usually austere. The top consisted of a medallion or open square section. A medallion placed on a straight case revealed the pendulum.
The piece stood on curved scroll legs, although occasionally on a base.
The combination of fruit tree wood and elm burl transformed even the most uninteresting clock into an extremely elegant and rich piece of furniture.

Wood

Vendée:
Fruit trees, cherry, walnut, young elm, oak, Nantes mahogany

Poitou:
Walnut, chestnut, cherry, ash burl

Aunis:
oak

Saintonge:
A combination of different trees and burls

Walnut and ash burl, cherry and elm burl

△ *Homme-debout. Musée vendéen, Fontenay-le-Comte.*

THE *HOMME-DEBOUT* AND THE ARMOIRE

The homme-debout *(literally, "upright man") is named for the fact that the piece was used during the French Revolution to hide royalists, who were forced to stand inside it. This is a narrow, one-door armoire with no central drawers, which differentiates it from the* bonnetière, *also with a single door.*
The door was often divided into rectangular panels decorated with a large rosette, placed in the center and surrounded by foliage or acanthus leaves. Some designs had marquetry of different types of woods and elaborately worked metal fitting.
Authentic examples of hommes-debout are extremely rare today. The maraîchine armoire is a typical piece of furniture from the Vendée. It has a single panel, decorated with asymmetrical molding on the crosspieces. Extremely austere in design, it rests on curved feet; the date it was made is engraved under the cornice.
Two other types of armoires exist: the armoire de moine, *a sacristy piece of furniture decorated with crosses and cherubs, and the armoire with two doors and three panels, decorated with Saint Andrew's crosses and standing on flattened bun feet.*

△ *Armoire from the southern Vendean woodlands. Late eighteenth century. Musée vendéen, Fontenay-le-Comte.*

The masters

Jean-François Hache

Christophe Hache (chests of drawers)

Pierre Achard (chairs)

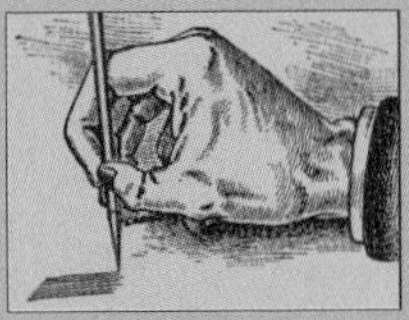

Stylistic inspiration

Louis XV

Louis XVI

Italy

Wood

Walnut and conifers

The Dauphiné

Style

△ *Interior of a Seyssins mill.*

The Dauphiné region created a highly distinct style of furniture, particularly in the cities. This was due to a dynasty of famous cabinetmakers, the Hache brothers, who became famous throughout France from the eighteenth century on for their large chests of drawers with elaborate marquetry patterns. They produced unusually sophisticated pieces for the bourgeoisie of Grenoble, accompanied by the refined chairs made by the furniture-maker Pierre Achard.

As for the mountain-style furniture, the Dauphiné region differs little from the Savoyard region. The regional pieces of furniture included armoires for storing clothes, tall larders, buffets decorated with a stone as in Lyon, *buffet-bahut* with four doors and *panetières* in the southern regions. Decorative motifs often included deep moldings, frequently accentuated by a thin line of black varnish.

Metal fittings were generally made of iron in an extremely simple design, except for those used on chests of drawers made by the Hache brothers. The contrast between the two styles is striking: they fashioned extremely sophisticated chased gilt bronze to create scrolls, intertwined foliage and Rococo-style shells, inspired by Italian styles.

CHESTS OF DRAWERS

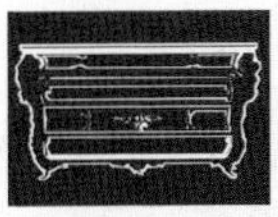

The chests of drawers made by the Hache brothers were designed in various styles: Régence, Louis XV or Louis XVI, with, in addition, a strong Italian influence and a distinct fondness for excessive decor.
The chest consisted of three large drawers with marquetry on the façade, sides and top. The essential decorative element was a marquetry pattern of flowers. The patterns followed the grain of the various woods, especially when roots and burls were used (in tinted or natural shades). These came from local trees, including the Alpine laburnum. The interior of the drawers was made of pine; the feet were square or scrolled and decorated with bronze fittings made in Paris, as were the chased bronze handles.
Another less sophisticated chest of drawers also existed. Called a* manette, *it was massive and extremely rounded in shape; it had magnificent carved wooden handles.

△ *Small chest of drawers, made of veneer marquetry with a cube design. In the center is a marquetry bouquet of flowers tied with a ribbon, framed by a chased gilt bronze cartouche. It has two drawers and rests on S-shaped feet. Brown breccia marble tabletop. A label in the upper drawer carries the inscription: "Hache à Grenoble, place Claveyson, 1775." Louis XV style. Jean-François Hache. Musée dauphinois, Grenoble.*

◁ *Louis XVI-style armchair. Tapered legs with stopped fluting. Fluted seat back and armrests. The entire chair is painted gray. The seat back and seat are upholstered with fabric depicting a bucolic scene. The uprights, seat rail and crest rail are joined by mortise-and-tenon joints. Pierre Achard. Musée dauphinois, Grenoble.*

The masters

Nicolas-François Banvilet

Louis Gabriel Jacquot (Vire)

Louis Quillard (Tinchebray)

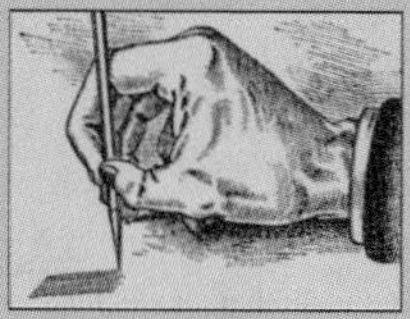

Stylistic inspiration

Rome

Gothic

Renaissance

Louis XV

Louis XVI

Île-de-France

The Normandy Style

△ *Normandy interior. Musée du Meuble normand, Villedieu-les-Poêles.*

The golden age of this style, characterized by harmonious proportions and highly diverse carved decors, was the seventeenth century. The predominant themes found on armoires—the chief principal piece of Normandy-style furniture—include bonnet-shaped cornices, curved doors and slightly inclined medallions. High-relief motifs included flowers and plants (acanthus leaves with the so-called pelican motif, roses, sheaves of wheat, bunches of grapes, baskets of flowers and marigolds) and animals (pairs of doves with outspread wings). Other geometric motifs used in the Normandy style include shells, medallions, beads, garlands, musical instruments and gardening tools, as well as a horn motif borrowed from the Rouen potteryworks.

The most beautiful metal fittings on Normandy furniture were made in Villedieu-les-Poêles; these were so famous that they were sent to regions all over France. The highly recognizable fittings included swan- or arabesque-shaped motifs. They decorated the entire width of the top of armoire doors.

WEDDING RITUAL

The wedding armoire was more than a piece of furniture; it was part of a true ritual. The ritual started at the birth of a young girl, and continued until she got married, at which time she received the armoire as a dowry, complete with all the necessary linen. Just after the birth of a daughter, the father would cut a dormant oak (in the winter) at the full moon. The wood had to be left to dry for at least six years. The day of the young girl's communion, the wood was split along the grain, then left to dry for several more years. Construction on the armoire began only once his daughter's hand was promised in marriage. A great deal of ceremony accompanied the move of the armoire from the family house to her new husband's home. When it arrived, the armoire was left open so that the entire village could admire the embroidered linen, part of the dowry. The wedding armoire was always between 7 ½ and 8 feet tall.

TABLES

The harvest table was an extremely austere long, rectangular oak table with a very thick tabletop. A sliding tray fitted under the table. The table stands on four or six square legs.

△ *Armoire from Cherbourg.*
Musée du Meuble normand, Villedieu-les-Poêles.

△ *Armoire from the Caux region.*
Musée du Meuble normand, Villedieu-les-Poêles.

△ *Harvest table.*
Musée du Meuble normand,
Villedieu-les-Poêles.

THE NORMANDY ARMOIRE

No piece of furniture illustrates a regional style better than the Normandy armoire. It is an almost mythical piece of furniture, recognizable from all others, regardless of the stylistic variations from one part of Normandy to another. Indeed, they are not all the same, depending on whether they come from Calvados, the Orne, the Eure, the Seine-Maritime or the Manche area. Significant differences occur in the shape of the cornice, the crosspieces, the medallions in the center of the panels, the feet and metal fittings.

The armoire from Caux is a spectacular piece, with a curved cornice and pelican bouquet motif. Others are distinguished by a drawer at the bottom or by a projecting cornice. All, however, have heavily decorated motifs in the center of the cornice, featuring carvings of doves with outspread wings and baskets of flowers. The central medallions on the doors may be unadorned or carved and surrounded by wide moldings.

A profusion of tracery, intertwined ribbons, baskets, fruit (except for apples), bunches of grapes and large daisies adorn the crosspieces of armoires from the Eure region. The piece stands on fairly high scroll feet.

◁ *Buffet made of apple. Musée du Meuble normand, Villedieu-les-Poêles.*

CLOCKS

Clocks, like chests, were also intimately linked to the wedding ritual, the difference being that the groom brought the clock to the couple's new home. A wide range of different designs existed. The most original and most famous is the demoiselle, with a violin-shaped case and beveled glass window just above the narrowest section. The most common clock was the straight-case grandfather clock with a top wider than the base. In the Dieppe region, the austerity of the case contrasted with the exuberant garlands of roses carved around the clock face. The Bayeux region produced a version that looked like an Egyptian sarcophagus with a circular top framed by carved flowers. The clock faces were made of brass with enameled Roman or Arabic numerals. Clock mechanisms came from Dieppe, Saint-Nicolas-d'Aliermont or even the Jura.

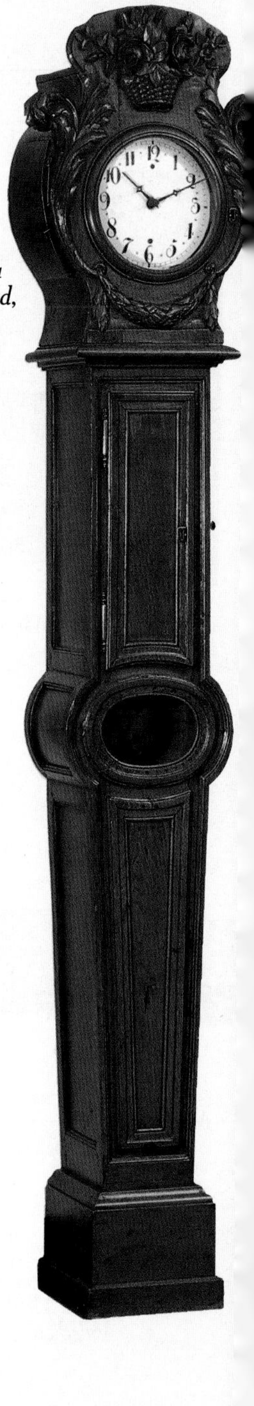

▷ *Grandfather clock from Bayeux. Musée du Meuble normand, Villedieu-les-Poêles.*

Wood

Stave oak for almost all furniture

Cherry

Walnut

Pine

Elm

THE *PALIER*

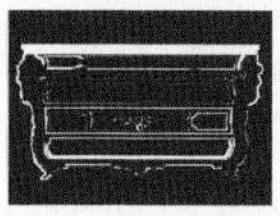

***The** palier **is a** vaisselier **that is somewhat smaller than a two-tiered buffet. It consists of a lower section with two square doors, decorated with carved foliage and supported by low, inwardly curving feet. The upper section was recessed and had several shelves with slender balusters designed to display pieces of faience produced in Rouen. In Upper Normandy, where it was associated with a small metal larder, it was known as an** ecuelle.*

The** faux-palier **consists of the lower section of a buffet, surmounted by a series of shelves used to store dishes. Notches were cut into the wood to suspend spoons.

▷ *Low sideboard from Vire. Musée du Meuble normand, Villedieu-les-Poêles.*

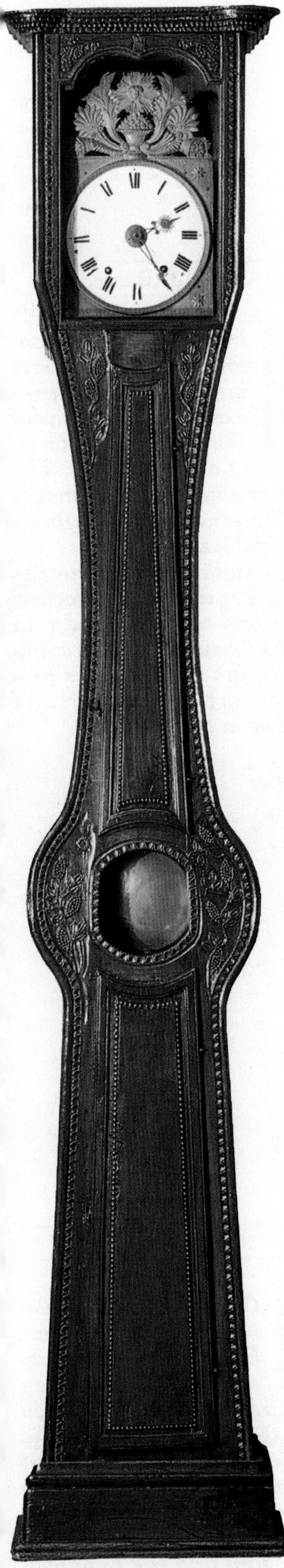

◁ *Box bed.*
Musée du Meuble normand, Villedieu-les-Poêles.

△ *Grandfather clock.*
Musée du Meuble normand, Villedieu-les-Poêles.

▷ *Two-tiered buffet from the Caux region.*
Musée du Meuble normand, Villedieu-les-Poêles.

BOX BED

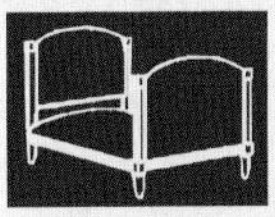

This type of bed was not completely closed off; at night the curtain was drawn to close off the bed section. This piece was tall and supported by fairly high legs. The lower crosspiece was sometimes decorated with a central motif. The upper section, generally narrow and with a curved outline, was frequently decorated with incised floral motifs.

BUFFET

The two-tiered buffet from the Caux region is characterized by a curved, elaborately carved cornice, generally in the shape of a basket handle or double cross. The structure was also carved, although it could be extremely sober in design, especially in two-tiered buffets with glass-front or wire mesh doors. Serpentine-shape molding decorated the doors of the lower section and the upper crosspieces. The feet were curved and covered with carvings of acanthus leaves. Some two-tiered pieces had removable bread boards. Other two-tiered pieces from Normandy are more exuberant in their decoration, with a broken cornice, religious subjects or figures sculpted in the round on the panels. In the Rouen region, they were used as display pieces, left open during meals to exhibit the dishes.

The Périgord and

Limousin Styles

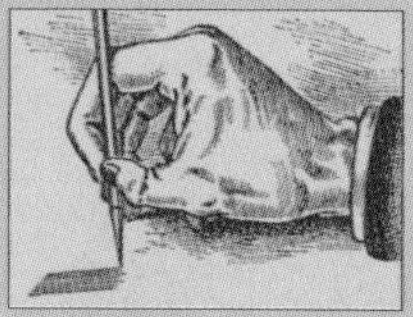

Stylistic inspiration

Louis XIII

Louis XV

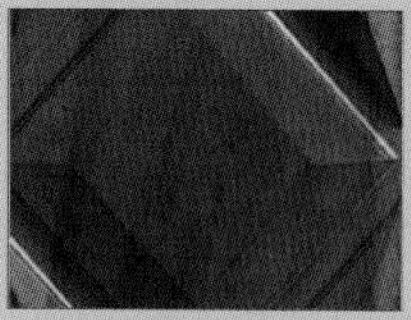

Wood

Light-colored walnut

Cherry

Pearwood

Chestnut

Beech

Elm

△ *Périgord interior. Musée des Arts et Traditions populaires du Périgord, Mussidan.*

Furniture from the Périgord region, often intended to display objects, was imposing, with thick moldings. The decorative devices were derived directly from the Louis XIII style and included Maltese crosses, Saint Andrew's crosses, diamond points, lozenges and triangles. Most of the furniture pieces (armoires, buffets, chests of drawers, scribans and *bonnetières)* rested on bun feet. Metal fittings, made of wrought iron, were generally discreet, with a fretwork motif. Hinges were wide.

Furniture from around Limoges was similar to that produced in the Périgord, yet it was somewhat heavier and more rustic. The armoire and buffet panels were decorated in a "chocolate bar" pattern, rather than diamond point. The most characteristic piece of furniture is the Aubazines armoire (twelfth century)— although few authentic examples of this piece still exist—and the cradle, suspended between two fixed supports.

ARMOIRES

In the Périgord region, armoires were always imposing structures—exact reproductions of the armoires produced during the Louis XIII style. The most common decorative motifs were diamond point, Maltese-crosses and lozenges.

The two main characteristics of the armoires were the projecting cornice and the flattened bun feet, which bear a striking resemblance to the feet of pieces produced during the William and Mary style in England.

CHAIRS

Chairs with turned elements (feet and seat backs) are particularly elegant. Shank-leg armchairs were often designed for chateaux. The bourgeoisie preferred these lovely walnut chairs (right) with openwork seat backs.

The same design appears in both the Périgord and the Limousin regions.

△ Armoire from the Périgord region with two doors, projecting cornice, two drawers and bun feet. Musée des Arts et Traditions populaires du Périgord, Mussidan.

THE BONNETIÈRE

The bonnetière is a typical piece of furniture from the Périgord region. It rested either on bun feet or on a simple wide base-board.
It was formed of two doors, one over the other, separated by a central drawer. The door panels were often decorated with diamond-point motifs. An imposing cornice surmounted the entire piece.

▷ Bonnetière with two doors and lozenge motifs. Cherry. Musée des Arts et Traditions populaires du Périgord, Mussidan.

◁ Farm chair from the Limousin region, with a short seat back. Musée des Arts et Traditions populaires du Périgord, Mussidan.

The Artois and

Picard Styles

The masters

Taupin

Demont

Pierre Dhéry

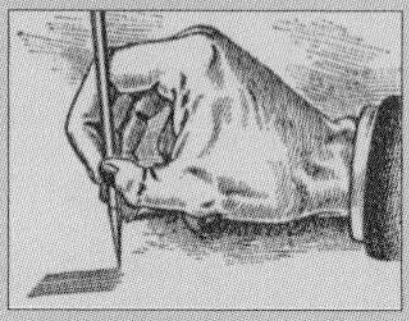

Stylistic inspiration

Renaissance

Louis XV

Louis XVI

Directoire

Île-de-France

Burgundy

Spain

Wood

Oak

Red cherry

Elm

Beech

Linden

Plum

Mahogany

△ *Old house in Beauvais, Oise.*

The differences between the styles of these two regions are so slight that they are generally discussed as a single region: the Artois-Picard. The Artois region was more highly influenced by Flanders, while the Picard looked toward the Île-de-France region. The furniture style is closely linked to the specific type of architecture. The ornamentation and decorative devices are almost the same: A stylized flower (or rose in Picard) adorned the end of a long sinuous branch, along with lozenges inspired by the Directoire, flowers, vases, hearts, Renaissance motifs, religious emblems and Louis XVI-style fluting. The linden tree was combined with oak to accentuate low-relief molding.

Metal fittings, made of wrought iron or brass, were extremely discreet in design.

BREAD TABLE

The Picard bread table is one of the many tables that are specific to the region, along with vigneron tables and changing tables. The bread table is a very famous piece. It was frequently used as a decorative piece of furniture, because it looks something like a pedestal table. It has a round tabletop, from $1\frac{1}{2}$ to 3 feet in diameter, and stands on a tripod base. Under the round top is a second triangular shelf meant to store bread (hence the name).

On most of these tables, one of the legs folded so that the table could be stored away.

In the seventeenth century, stew was placed on the tabletop and bread on the shelf underneath. Later, the bread table was used as an ironing board or as a sewing table.

THE SACRISTY BUFFET

The armoire à cheminée or sacristy buffet first appeared in the sixteenth century. Heavily inspired by the Renaissance style, it consists of two sections; the upper part is recessed and smaller overall than the lower section.

The lower section has two Renaissance-style doors, surmounted by two drawers.

The upper section has two doors surmounted by a frieze carved with a foliated scroll and flowers, and a broken or notched pediment with a religious motif.

The gap in the center of the broken pediment was topped by a dome housing a crucifix. The niche itself generally housed a statue of the Virgin Mary.

△ *Traite picarde (Picard milk chest) with two doors framed by two fluted uprights. Oak. Louis XV style for the doors, and Louis XVI style for the sides and the three small drawers fitted under the tabletop. Private collection. Ons-en-Bray.*

◁ *Sacristy buffet, inspired by the Renaissance with a decor of religious themes. The upper doors are carved with motifs representing the three theological virtues and the four cardinal virtues, framed by spiral columns decorated with branches of ivy. The lower panels are decorated with images of Charlemagne and of Saint Francis. Musée d'Art et d'Histoire. Hôtel de Berny. Amiens.*

THE *TRAITE PICARDE*

The traite picarde (Picard milk chest) was a very important piece of furniture. It is the perfect example of a piece of furniture designed for an architectural environment. The principal furniture element in a Picard home, this large storage piece (meant for linen and dishes) was custom-made to fit the room. It first appeared in the eighteenth century, when it was used to store the buckets after the cows had been milked. It was a low buffet with four, five, six or even eight panels; the piece could be up to 20 feet wide. Very shallow and low, it sometimes had drawers in the apron or was surmounted by a shelf for pots. Other designs included a clock case.

These milk chests were usually made in a Directoire-inspired style, but were occasionally inspired by the Louis XV style. A large number of different models exist, including the milk chest from Poix, a simple oak chest; the milk chest from Canaples, made of cherry with inlays of colored wood; the milk chest from Vignacourt, made of cherry with spectacular carving; and the right-angled milk chest, designed for the fireplace, which had a display case.

CHRONOLOGY

	DATES	STYLES	COUNTRY	CHARACTERISTICS
BC	2700-2190 BC	**OLD KINGDOM**	**EGYPT**	◆ Furniture with four rectilinear legs, connected by a stretcher.
	2300 BC	**DYNASTY VII**		◆ Lion's-paw feet for chairs.
	1580-1085 BC	**NEW KINGDOM**		◆ Skilled use of all different types of production techniques. Ivory inlays. All furniture is painted.
	900-400 BC	**BABYLONIAN EMPIRE**	**ASSYRIA**	◆ Technique of veneer is perfectly mastered. Chryselephantine sculptures. Painted furniture.
	500-100 BC	**ANCIENT GREECE**	**GREECE**	◆ Designs inspired from classical architecture. Curved seat backs. Painted furniture.
	206 BC on	**CHINESE LACQUER**	**CHINA**	◆ Functional furniture designed for traveling and copied identically from one generation to the next.
AD	From 300 BC to AD 330	**ROMAN EMPIRE**	**ITALY**	◆ Extremely luxurious and highly decorated furniture made with precious materials. Marquetry, veneer using precious metals, chased bronze. Painted furniture.
	330-500	**BYZANTINE**	**ITALY TURKEY**	◆ Imperial furniture sculpted from ivory.
	600-900 900-1100	**MEDIEVAL STYLE ROMANESQUE**	**FRANCE**	◆ Roughly made rudimentary furniture. Beautiful ironwork used in furniture joints. More marquetry and painted furniture.
1100-1500	1100-1250	**EARLY GOTHIC**	**FRANCE**	◆ Inspiration drawn from architecture, particularly from the new austere pointed arches in churches.
	1250-1390	**RAYONNANT GOTHIC**		◆ More highly ornamented shapes made from sculptured dark solid oak.
	1390-1500	**FLAMBOYANT GOTHIC**		◆ Excessive ornamentation. Most of the furniture, as well as the monuments and cathedrals, were painted.
16th cent.	1350-1600	**RENAISSANCE Florentine and Venetian**	**ITALY**	◆ Inspired from ancient Roman architecture. New techniques, marquetry is rediscovered.
	1490-1610	**FIRST AND SECOND RENAISSANCE François I and Henri II**	**FRANCE**	◆ Imitation of Italian renaissance in the François I (1515-1547) and Henri II (1547-1559) styles.
	1509-1603	**TUDOR**	**ENGLAND**	◆ Highly influenced by the Italian Renaissance (Venice).
	1508-1598	**PLATERESQUE**	**SPAIN**	◆ Italian, architectural and Mudejar influences.
	1500-1680	**AUGSBURG AND NUREMBERG**	**GERMANY**	◆ Architectural inspiration, intricate cabinetmaking and perfect mastery of marquetry.

DECORATIVE ELEMENTS	NEW FURNITURE	MATERIALS
	◆ Tables with four straight legs.	◆ Wood.
◆ Feet with five claws.	◆ Chairs, beds.	◆ Wood, woven straw.
◆ Stylized lotus flowers; gazelle and goat heads; lion, gazelle and bull legs.	◆ Tripod tables, storage elements, chests, small cabinets, beds.	◆ Painted wood, cord, ivory.
◆ Winged lions and horse heads; legs imitating animal hocks and lion's paws.	◆ Chairs, beds, tripod tables, superimposed storage chests.	◆ Ebony, rosewood, bronze, gold and ivory.
◆ Invention of the acanthus leaf design by Callimachus in the 4th century BC.	◆ Tables, *klismos* chairs with curved backs, beds, cupboards.	◆ Painted wood, ivory, strips of leather.
◆ Rectilinear furniture without ornamentation. Starting in the 14th century: motif of a lion's paw clutching a ball.	◆ Small, low tables, tables with two shelves, stools, small cabinets with drawers.	◆ Wood lacquered with 36 layers of red resin.
◆ Rosettes, laurel wreaths, lion's claws and heads, grimacing masks, X-stretcher.	◆ *Armorium* (cabinet for weapons), curule chairs and table, X-frame chairs, benches with straight back, klines.	◆ Painted wood with veneers of silver, bronze, ivory, ebony, marble.
◆ Motifs included foliated scrolls, flowers, animals and people carved into chairs.	◆ Coffres, *lectrins* (reading stands), richly carved chairs of state.	◆ Sculpted ivory, inlay wood.
◆ Ornamentation disappeared, with the exception of a few foliage motifs. Semicircular arch.	◆ Benches used as seats, tables and beds. X-frame chairs for palaces.	◆ Unpainted oak. Iron for hinges, straps.
◆ Geometric ornamentation derived from Romanesque art: tracery, checkerboards, chevrons.	◆ Chests, benches, armoires.	◆ Oak commonly used throughout the entire Gothic period. Wrought iron.
◆ Sculpted capitals. Motifs inspired from nature: stylized flowers, palmettes, rosettes, fleurons.	◆ Dressers, lectrins, lutrins.	◆ Painted wood.
◆ Turrets, diapering, pinnacles, Gothic arch, evangelical scenes, latticework sculpture.	◆ Chairs and settles.	
◆ In Florence: sculptures, foliated scrolls, angel heads, lions' heads. In Venice: Oriental motifs.	◆ Savonarola chairs, tables, *sedia dantesca*, *stipi*.	◆ Walnut, ivory, pewter, bronze, tortoiseshell, *pietre dure*.
◆ Abundant sculptures, including pilaster, caryatids, columns, acanthus leaves, feathers.	◆ Buffets, armchairs, *crédences*, *tables à l'italienne*, *caquetoires*.	◆ Oak and walnut.
◆ Motifs of the four Evangelists, chimerae, coils.	◆ Buffets cupboard, refectory table.	◆ Oak, inlaid boxwood.
◆ Polychrome paintings, bronzes, urns, grotesque ornaments.	◆ *Vargueño* desks.	◆ Walnut, ebony and ivory.
◆ Interplay between woods of different colors and materials including ivory, pewter, silver, mirros and tortoiseshell.	◆ Cabinets with two drawers on a carved support, press cupboards.	◆ Mixed materials.

	DATES	STYLES	COUNTRY	CHARACTERISTICS
17th cent.	1550-1690	**ORNAMENTALIST or GOLDEN AGE**	NETHERLANDS	◆ Rejection of the Italian Renaissance style. Ornamentalist Inspiration. Exceptional marquetry.
	1600-1690	**BAROQUE**	ITALY	◆ A quest for spectacular effects and excessive ornamentation. Straight lines are replaced by exuberant scrolls and curves.
	1603-1660	**JACOBEAN**	ENGLAND	◆ Influences: Palladium architecture.
	1605-1665	**PHILIP IV or CHURRIGUERESQUE**	SPAIN	◆ Derived from the exuberant scrollwork, columns, towers and decors by the architect Churriguera.
	1610-1661	**LOUIS XIII**	FRANCE	◆ Austerity and simple forms.
	1610-1680	**AURICULAR**	GERMANY	◆ Exuberance and a fondness of sculpture and decor.
	1660-1695	**WILLIAM AND MARY**	ENGLAND	◆ More sober furniture, with emphasis on burl, wood grain and veneers of contrasting woods.
	1661-1715	**LOUIS XIV**	FRANCE	◆ Geometric symmetry and rigor. Luxury, well-balanced style. Strongly influenced by cabinetmakers such as Boulle.
18th cent.	1700-1730	**RÉGENCE**	FRANCE	◆ Lines became more curved, furniture less symmetrical.
	1695-1714	**QUEEN ANNE**	GREAT BRITAIN	◆ Appearance of the curving cabriole leg.
	1700-1769	**PETIT BAROQUE**	ITALY	◆ Excessive carved elements, decor and trompe-l'œil.
	1700-1790	**DUTCH BAROQUE**	NETHERLANDS	◆ Bulging forms and curves on all types of furniture.
	1714-1760	**EARLY GEORGIAN**	GREAT BRITAIN	◆ Influences: China, Italian Renaissance, Louis XV.
	1715-1808	**ROCOCO AND NEOCLASSICAL**	SPAIN	◆ Exaggeration of the French Rococo and Italian Rococo styles.
	1723-1774	**LOUIS XV or ROCAILLE**	FRANCE	◆ Innovation, fantasy, asymmetry: more curves, counter-curves and serpentine shapes. Perfect craftsmanship. Cabinetmaker or furniture-maker's stamp is obligatory (1751).
	1725-1788	**ROCOCO**	GERMANY	◆ Exaggerated curves. Overabundance of ornaments.
	1730-1801	**NATIONALIST**	RUSSIA	◆ Development of an original and sumptuous Russian style.
	1750-1780	**CHIPPENDALE**	U.S.	◆ Symmetry. Combination of straight and curved lines.
	1755-1770	**TRANSITION**	FRANCE	◆ Rectilinear lines reappear, inspired from ancient furniture.
	1760-1800	**LATE GEORGIAN**	GREAT BRITAIN	◆ Innovation under the influence of three master cabinetmakers; comfort.
	1774-1792	**LOUIS XVI**	FRANCE	◆ Return to ancient Greek and Etruscan styles, neoclassicism: rectilinear lines, symmetry, geometry.
	1771-1792	**GUSTAVIAN**	SWEDEN	◆ Neoclassical furniture painted in pastel colors.
	1795-1804	**DIRECTOIRE**	FRANCE	◆ Inspired from ancient Egypt, Greece and Rome.
	1780-1810	**FEDERAL**	U.S.	◆ Adaptation of European neoclassicism.
	1769-1804	**NEOCLASSICAL**	ITALY	◆ Inspired from ancient Rome. Straight lines, symmetry.

DECORATIVE ELEMENTS	NEW FURNITURE	MATERIALS
◆ Foliated scrolls, lion heads, grotesque ornaments, caryatids, flowers, trompe-l'œil perspectives.	◆ Armoires, tables, cabinets decorated with marquetry, leather armchairs, cane-seat chairs.	◆ Walnut, palisander, ivory, ebony, tortoiseshell, bone.
◆ Architectural forms, cupids, lion heads, chimera, birds of prey, trompe-l'œil.	◆ *Stipi* (cabinets) on caryatid or atlante support.	◆ Ebony, ivory, mirrors, pewter, bronze, hard stone.
◆ Beads, vases, urns, balusters, St Andrew's cross.	◆ Gate-leg tables. Upholstered armchairs.	◆ Oak, bone, ivory.
◆ Polychrome motif set off with gold, Moorish motifs, column and tower motifs from Escurial Palace.	◆ *Contadores*, cabinets with borken pediments, *escritoria*, fall-front desks.	◆ Ebonized wood, mahogany, painted glass, ivory, bone.
◆ Diamond point, molding, bun feet.	◆ Upholstered chairs. Canopy beds.	◆ Oak, walnut.
◆ Sculptures resembling the interior of the ear, reliefs.	◆ Cabinets, press cupboards.	◆ Ebony, bone, mother-of-pearl, tortoiseshell.
◆ Baluster and bun feet. Foliated scrolls. Marquetry. Chinese lacquered panels.	◆ Chests of drawers, round pedestal tables, armchairs.	◆ Walnut burl, ash, violetwood.
◆ Motifs derived from ancient Rome, suns, armor, baluster legs. Silver furniture. (1689).	◆ Chests of drawers, confessional armchairs, consoles, sidetables, Mazarin desks, *lits à la duchesse.*	◆ Ebony, walnut, tortoiseshell, copper, silver, bronze.
◆ Motifs include espagnolettes, shells, palmettes.	◆ *Commodes-tombeau*, flat desks.	◆ Walnut, beech, amaranthus.
◆ First appearance of the claw-and-ball motif.	◆ Kneehole desks, sun tables, tallboys.	◆ Walnut, walnut burl.
◆ Trompe-l'œil, *scagliola* (imitation marble surface).	◆ *Studioli*, consoles, chests of drawers.	◆ Walnut, mother-of-pearl.
◆ Marquetry of contrasting wood and ivory.	◆ Secretaries with rounded forms.	◆ Walnut, burl, ivory.
◆ Bulging shapes, japanning.	◆ Bachelor' chests, dresssing tables.	◆ West Indian mahogany.
◆ Gilt surfaces, trompe-l'œil, colored backgrounds, mirrors.	◆ Chests of drawers, scribans.	◆ Walnut, ebony.
◆ Asymmetrical, cut-out motifs: shells, cartouches, diamond shapes, magots, monkeys; dolphins, marquetry, bronze, japanning, vernis Martin (a type of varnish).	◆ Chests with two or three drawers, slant-top desks, *bergères*, cabriole chairs, *duchesses brisées*, *bonheur-du-jour*, secretaries.	◆ Beech, oak, rosewood, violetwood, palisander, lacquer, mahogany.
◆ Cherubs, giant shells, drapery, quivers.	◆ Armoires, consoles, bookcases.	◆ Giltwood, painted wood.
◆ A mixture of all types of European ornaments and motifs.	◆ Tables, chairs, beds, desks.	◆ Blued steel from Tula.
◆ Broken pediments, urns, shells, umbrella motifs.	◆ Break-front commode and bookcase, wing chairs.	◆ Curly grained mahogany and mahogany.
◆ Greek-style decors, porcelain with decorative plaques.	◆ Same furniture as during the Louis XV style.	◆ Same as Louis XV style.
◆ Umbrella motifs, wreaths, bouquets, cameos.	◆ Bookcases, Pembroke tables, sofas.	◆ Mahogany, satinwood, maple.
◆ Fluted legs and reeding, ribbons, urns, trophies, beads, lyres, bouquets of flowers, rosettes, tracery, pine cones.	◆ Dining room tables, roll-top desks, all kinds of chairs, *coiffeuses.*	◆ Mahogany, exotic woods, painted wood, beech, oak.
◆ Sprays of flowers, flower buds, carved knots.	◆ *Klismos* chairs, desks with compartments.	◆ Painted pine, birch.
◆ Diamond shapes, sphinxes, quivers, palmettes, lions.	◆ Gondola chairs, daybeds, *somnos.*	◆ Walnut, beech, mahogany.
◆ Neoclassical motifs and ornaments.	◆ Consoles, desks, chairs, tables.	◆ Mahogany.
◆ Ribbing and fluting, winged lions.	◆ Settees, consoles, chests of drawers.	◆ Painted wood, mahogany.

DATES	STYLES	COUNTRY	CHARACTERISTICS
19th cent.			
1804-1815	**EMPIRE**	**FRANCE**	◆ Majestic, austere grandeur, developed as part of the Napoleonic propaganda. A passion for ancient Greece, Rome and Egypt, as well as for epic and monumental themes.
1800-1830	**REGENCY**	**GREAT BRITAIN**	◆ Graceful, slender, elegant forms, adapted from the Louis XVI style by T. Sheraton. Metamorphic furniture.
1800-1825	**NEOCLASSICAL**	**RUSSIA**	◆ Also often called the Russian Empire style.
1800-1840	**SHERATON**	**U.S.**	◆ Inspired from the English and French styles of the same name.
1810-1840	**EMPIRE**	**EUROPE**	◆ French Empire style imported to conquered countries.
1815-1830	**RESTAURATION**	**FRANCE**	◆ Rounded corners, return of emblems of the monarchy.
1815-1848	**BIEDERMEIER**	**GERMANY**	◆ Absence of motifs and ornamentation. Beautiful wood.
1821-1840	**CARLO FELICE**	**ITALY**	◆ Also called the Piedmontese style. Return of curved forms.
1830-1848	**LOUIS-PHILIPPE**	**FRANCE**	◆ Mass production. Bourgeois comfort.
1833-1868	**ISABELLINO**	**SPAIN**	◆ Romantic, neo-Gothic and neo-Baroque 17th cent style.
1837-1901	**VICTORIAN**	**GREAT BRITAIN**	◆ Pastiche of Gothic (Elizabethan) and Louis XV (called the Louis XIV) styles, with excessively ornamented neoclassicism.
1852-1870	**NAPOLEON III**	**FRANCE**	◆ Pastiche of styles from the preceding three centuries, either copied faithfully or mixed together to create eclectic, highly ornamented and original pieces of furniture.
1870-1900	**ECLECTIC**	**EUROPE**	◆ Mass production of copies of all types of older style of furniture. Discovery and adaptations of Japanese styles.
20th cent.			
1893-1914	**ART NOUVEAU**	**BELGIUM**	◆ Total break with styles from the past. Designers look for a new ornamental language inspired from architecture.
1885-1910	**SEZESSION STYLE**	**AUSTRIA**	◆ Naturalist inspiration; curves reign supreme.
1895-1914	**FLOREALE STYLE**	**ITALY**	◆ Far eastern inspiration. Designs by Carlo Bugatti.
1895-1914	**MODERN STYLE**	**FRANCE**	◆ Highly descriptive naturalism, by the School of Nancy. Designers become mutlidisciplinary.
1895-1914	**ARTE JOVEN**	**SPAIN**	◆ Break with the past, inspired by the architect Gaudí.
1918-1939	**BAUHAUS AND ART DECO**	**EUROPE**	◆ Spirit of innovation and creativity. Geometric structures, influence of African art and Cubism.
1920-1930	**AFRICAN ART**	**AFRICA**	◆ Unique and recent pieces, mainly for tribal chiefs.
1950-1960	**FUNCTIONALISM**	**ALL COUNTRIES**	◆ Internationalization of styles. Luxurious designer pieces co-exist alongside inexpensive, mass-produced furniture.
1960-1990	**DESIGN**	**ALL COUNTRIES**	◆ Styles are linked exclusively to the name of the individual designer. Designers replace the cabinetmakers of the past.
1980-2000	**FIN DE SIÈCLE**	**ALL COUNTRIES**	◆ Decoration becomes fashionable. Mass-produced design pieces.

DECORATIVE ELEMENTS	NEW FURNITURE	MATERIALS
◆ Straight lines. Symmetrical ornamentation. Motifs: bees, eagles, laurel wreaths, the letter "N" (for Napoleon), caryatids, sphinxes, swans.	◆ *Lits bateau*, sinks, dressing tables, *athéniennes*, bookcases, dining-room tables, cheval glasses, knee-hole writing desks.	◆ Mahogany (through 1808), walnut, lemonwood, elm burl, gilt bronze.
◆ Marquetry. Motifs: dolphins, ropes, anchors. Greek, Egyptian and Chinese (dragons, serpents) motifs.	◆ All metamorphic furniture. Dining-room tables, quartetto (nesting) tables, drum tables.	◆ Curly grained mahogany, satin-wood, spotted maple, shellac.
◆ Luxurious treatment of European ornaments.	◆ Court and state furniture, desks.	◆ Karelian birch, mahogany.
◆ Draperies, garlands, torches, seat backs made of rods.	◆ Hitchcock chairs, rocking chairs.	◆ Mahogany, ebonized wood.
◆ Same ornaments as the French Empire style.	◆ Same furniture as the French Empire style.	◆ Same as French Empire style.
◆ Swans' necks, fleur-de-lys, Gothic elements.	◆ Work tables, Voltaire armchair.	◆ Maple and all light woods.
◆ No motifs. Simple Gothic shapes and pediments.	◆ Chairs, *secrétaires*, bookcases, tables.	◆ All light woods.
◆ Inlaid patterns of dark wood on light-wood backgrounds.	◆ Armchairs, sofas, tables, bookcases.	◆ All light woods.
◆ Deep-buttoned upholstery and trim. Cyma recta corners.	◆ *Crapaud* armchair.	◆ Mahogany, maple, cherry.
◆ Gothic arches, curves and heavy ornamentation.	◆ All of the furniture listed above.	◆ Mahogany, dark woods.
◆ All motifs from the past, lacquers and inlaid copper, marble and mother-of-pearl. Deep-buttoned leather. Trim.	◆ Boat and garden furniture, leather-upholstered sofas, occasional tables.	◆ Ebonized wood, teak, papier maché, rattan, metal.
◆ Mother-of-pearl inlays on ebonized wood, bouquets of painted flowers, Boulle-style tortoiseshell inlays, neo-Rococo motifs, medallions and Sèvres porcelain.	◆ *Confidents, indiscrets, poufs, crapauds, guéridons,* (pedestal tables), nesting tables, work tables, tilt-top tables, dumbwaiters.	◆ Ebonized pearwood, ebony, pitch pine, bamboo, palisander, papier maché, mother-of-pearl.
◆ Fashion for bronze statues. Excessive use of bronze mounts. Lacquered panels and pagoda shapes inspired by Japanese design.	◆ All of the furnitures made in earlier styles. Purely decorative furniture.	◆ Woods used in the past, bronzes, lacquers, porcelain.
◆ Curvilinear shapes in slight relief, curves and whiplash curves. Stylized floral and foliage motifs.	◆ All the preceding furniture, plus dressing tables, armoires with glass panels, display cases, tables.	◆ Palisander, tinted walnut, cherry, lacquered wood.
◆ Industrial bentwood process.	◆ Chairs by Michael Thonet starting in 1860.	◆ Ebonized wood, tinted wood.
◆ Motifs of insects, birds and plants. Inlaid patterns.	◆ Desks, chairs, *secrétaires*.	◆ Copper, ivory, pewter, wood.
◆ Motifs of roots, algae, bent branches, liana, corkscrews, sinuous hair.	◆ Glass cases with bookshelves, dressing tables, complete dining-room and bedroom sets.	◆ Oak, mahogany, palisander, walnut, lemonwood, glassware.
◆ Anthropomorphic shapes and fantastic decors.	◆ Designed to be built into the architecture.	◆ All types of wood and mosaics.
◆ Style free of all ornamentation. Extreme care taken with the materials used (wood, copper).	◆ Bars, club chairs, oceanliner furniture design, low tables, sofas, armoires with mirrors.	◆ Macassar ebony, lacquered wood, palisander, shagreen.
◆ Sculptures of animal or human figures.	◆ Stools, chairs, thrones.	◆ All indigenous woods.
◆ Coexistence of entirely new forms invented by contemporary designers, alongside copies of old styles.	◆ All types of furniture.	◆ Tempered steel, polyester, plywood, sheet metal, rattan.
◆ Elimination of all superfluous ornamentation. A quest for simplicity, comfort and practicality.	◆ Storage furniture, closets, kitchen and bathroom furniture.	◆ Fiberboard, plastic, resin, steel, polished glass.
◆ Abandonment of any formal taboos.	◆ Office furniture. Furniture in kits.	◆ All materials.

A

Acanthus leaf: Ornamental motif reproducing the Mediterranean plant of the same name. Used for the first time in the 5th century BC by the Greek sculptor and goldsmith Callimachus, this motif reappeared in the Renaissance and was used regularly in all styles through the Empire style.

Apron: A horizontal element under the seat rail of a chair or tabletop. It is often carved or pierced.

Arabesque: A flowing, asymmetrical ornamental device representing foliage, scrolls or geometric patterns.

Arm stump: This is a vertical piece that supports the chair arm; it rises from the seat rail to the arm itself.

Armoire: French term for a wardrobe or cupboard.

B

Baldachin: A permanent ornamental canopy, as for a bed.

Baluster: Small turned or carved pillar or colonnette, often in a vase or pear shape. The design first appeared during the Renaissance.

Bergère: Primarily an 18th-century furniture form, in which the space between the armrests and the seat was closed.

Bucranium: Skull-shaped ornament used on a frieze.

Burgau: Bright, reddish-mauve mother-of pearl.

Burl: A dome-shaped growth on a tree; when sliced, it has a beautiful grain and is used for veneers. When large enough, it can be used for tabletops. Elm, walnut and yew have interesting burl wood.

C

Cabriole: Used in the 18th century to describe an upholstered chair or sofa whose back curved into the arms in a smooth line. Also used to designate a type of S-shaped leg.

Cartouche: Decorative device, inspired by ancient Roman ornamentation and used in the Renaissance, Baroque and Rococo styles.

Caryatids: A support sculpted in the form of a female figure; derived from ancient Greek architecture. The device reappeared in Renaissance styles, and later, in various neoclassical styles.

Chasing: This is a technique for decorating a metal surface. Chasing chisels (these have rounded edges rather than sharp ones) are used to emboss or engrave various figures or designs.

Chimera: A decorative motif consisting of a winged animal, usually with the head, body and front legs of a lion or goat, attached to a serpent's tail. Popular during the Renaissance.

Chryselephantine: This term describes objects made of or overlaid with gold and ivory.

Crest rail: The top rail of the back of a chair, mounted atop the stiles.

Crockets: A decorative device used in Byzantine and Gothic furniture. Carved flowers or foliage on an outer edge of a vertical element, such as a chair back.

Cross rail: The horizontal element of a chair back, below the crest rail.

Cyma recta: Molding or curve in which the upper part is concave and the lower part convex.

D

Denticulation: A decorative device consisting of a series of small tooth-like shapes, usually placed along the lower edge of a cornice. Derived from an ancient Greek motif and widely used in neoclassical styles.

Diapering: This is an ornamental pattern formed of small squares or diamond shapes, repeated in a checkerboard arrangement. This motif appeared in medieval furniture and architecture.

E

Ebeniste: The French term for cabinetmaker, as opposed to *ménuisier*, who was a joiner or furniture-maker. The French guild system maintained a strict division between the various crafts, and only a master craftsman could practice both disciplines.

Eglomisé: A decorative technique used in the 18th and 19th centuries; the reverse side of a glass panel was painted gold, white or blue and attached to or used as a door.

Entablature: An architectural term describing a horizontal element supported by columns of pilasters; some furniture designs adopted this form.

Espagnolette: A bronze decorative mount in the form of a female bust, popular during the Régence and Louis XV styles.

Estampille: The name or initials of the cabinetmaker or furniture-maker, applied to a piece of furniture using a heated iron. Starting in 1751, the Parlement of Paris decreed that cabinetmakers and furniture-makers had to apply this stamp by law. On chairs, this stamp is usually placed under the rear seat rail. On chests of drawers and

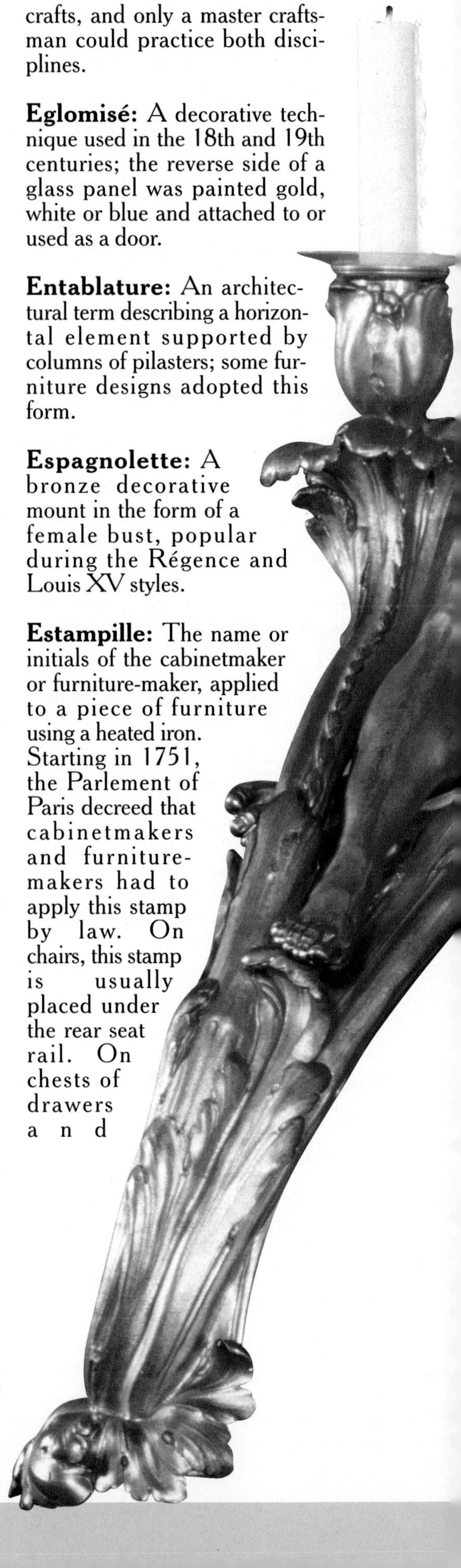

secrétaires, it is under the marble tabletop, and on tables, under the apron. A stamped piece of furniture is generally more valuable than an anonymous piece, but the master's signature does not necessarily mean that he actually made the work. The *estampille* remained obligatory until the end of the Ancien Régime. Although it became optional after the French Revolution, all the great French and foreign cabinetmakers continued to use it.

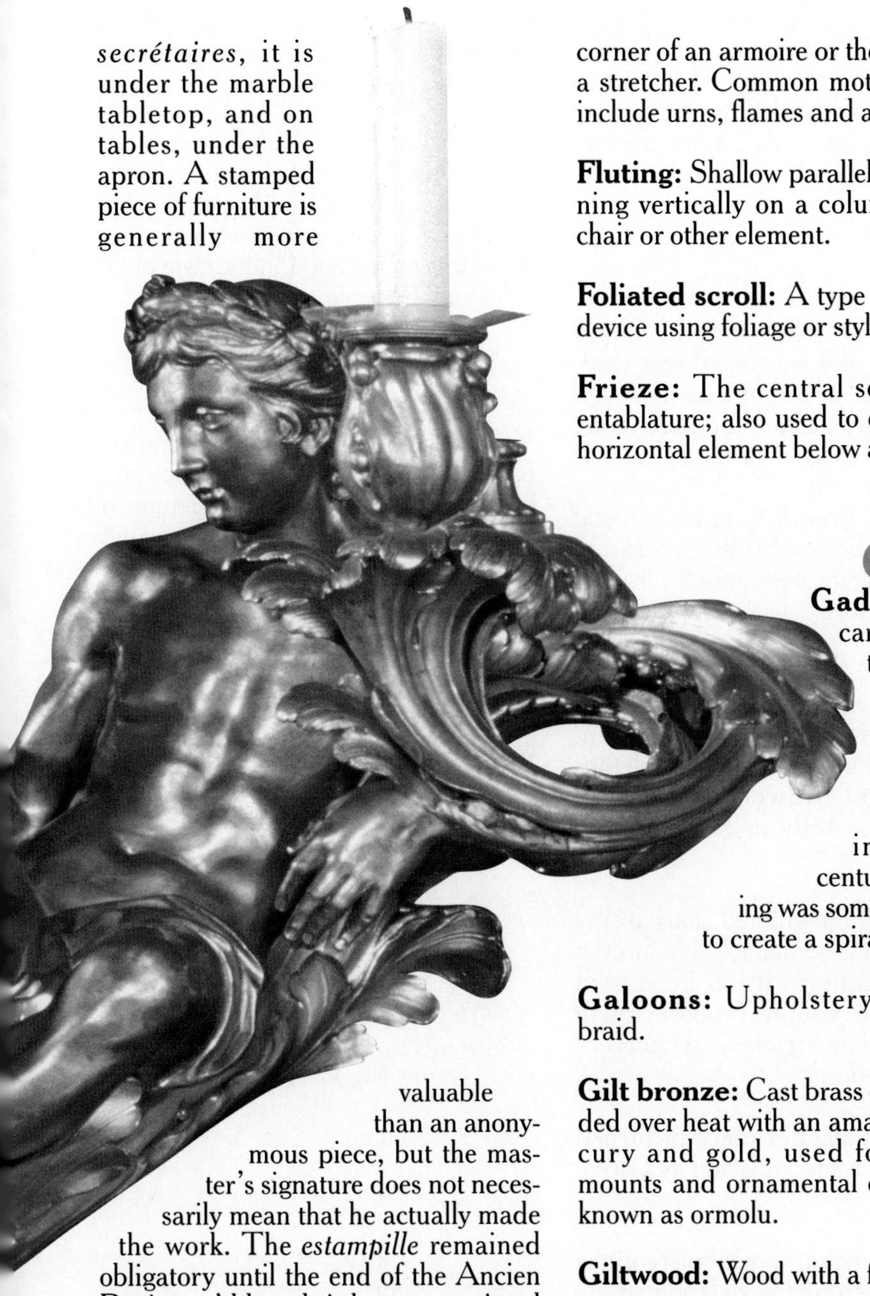

F

Fall front: The front section of a cabinet, drawer or desk that has a hinge at the bottom so that it can open by falling forward.

Fauteuil: French term for an upholstered armchair with open sides (as opposed to a bergère). This furniture form was developed in the 17th century.

Fillet: A narrow strip or band, often a piece of veneer, used to accentuate lines.

Finial: A turned or carved decorative device often used to terminate a structural element such as a bedpost, the corner of an armoire or the midpoint of a stretcher. Common motifs for finials include urns, flames and acorns.

Fluting: Shallow parallel grooves running vertically on a column, pilaster, chair or other element.

Foliated scroll: A type of decorative device using foliage or stylized leaves.

Frieze: The central section of an entablature; also used to designate the horizontal element below a tabletop.

G

Gadroon: This carved decorative motif consists of short vertical lengths of reeding. Widely used in the 18th century, the reeding was sometimes curved to create a spiral effect.

Galoons: Upholstery binding or braid.

Gilt bronze: Cast brass or bronze gilded over heat with an amalgam of mercury and gold, used for furniture mounts and ornamental objects. Also known as ormolu.

Giltwood: Wood with a finish of gold.

Guademecil: Spanish term for sheepskin leather with finely tooled, colored and gilded leather. It was widely used during the Spanish Renaissance.

I

Inlay: A decorative technique that creates a pattern of design by embedding pieces of one material into another, notably ivory, mother-of-pearl, tortoiseshell and bone on wood. The effect was often accentuated by using materials of different colors.

J

Japanning: This term refers to various methods of imitating oriental lacquers in Europe. It was widely used in the 17th and 18th centuries.

L

Lambrequin: A deeply scalloped piece of drapery, used as a valance; by extension, a fringe-like ornamental device carved on furniture, especially the apron of a chair, table or large piece of case furniture. These were very popular during the Louis XIV and Régence styles.

Linenfold: A decorative device that originated in 15th-century Flanders and spread throughout Europe. Often carved on panels and chests, it represents a piece of cloth arranged in vertical folds.

Listel: A narrow fillet.

Loper: This is a sliding arm that extended from a cabinet or desk to support the fall front of a desk.

M • N

Magot: A French term, originally signifying a grotesque monkey with no tail; in the 18th century, used to designate a grotesque oriental figure, primarily on porcelain.

Marquetry: A decorative veneer of wood (or other materials, including stone ivory and bone), consisting of small shapes inlaid to create a pattern or a scene. Marquetry developed in Germany, then spread to France in the early 17th century and to England in the mid-17th century.

Mascaron: A head, usually rather grotesque in style, viewed frontally.

Molding: Continuous strip of band of decoration with a shaped profile. Used to ornament edges or to create a linear decorative motif. Moldings come in many different shapes.

Mortise-and-tenon joint: A technique of joining two pieces of wood by a tenon (a projection, usually rectangular in shape) carved out of one end to exactly fit into the cavity, or mortise, or the other piece.

Mudéjar style: A Spanish decorative style developed by Moslems in Christian Spain. It incorporated complicated geometric inlaid patterns.

O

Ormolu: See gilt bronze.

Ornamentalist: A master draftsman, engraver, decorator or sometimes even an architect, who specialized in engravings of ornamental designs, called pattern books. Cabinetmakers and furniture-makers used these books as inspiration for their own designs. Ornamentalists played an essential role in determining styles from the 16th to the 19th centuries.

Ovolo molding: A convex molding, in an approximate quarter-round shape.

P

Palmette: A fan-shaped decorative device resembling a stylized palm leaf. It originated in ancient Egypt and became a common motif in the 18th century neoclassical styles.

Pediment: Arched or triangular ornamental element that surmounts case furniture such as armoires. It became extremely popular in the 18th century, particularly the type known as the broken (or scroll) pediment, which has a gap in the center, often used to display an object or a finial. Other types of pediments include the swan-neck pediment and the lattice (or fretted) pediment.

Pilaster: A shallow rectangular column or pillar set into or against a wall. Originally a structural element, it has been a widely used decorative piece in furniture since the Renaissance.

Psyche: The 19th-century French term (particularly during the Empire style) for a cheval glass, a portable full-length mirror mounted between two uprights.

Q ◆ R

Quadriga: In ancient Rome, a two-wheeled chariot drawn by four horses.

Quatrefoil: A decorative motif widely used in Gothic furniture consisting of a symmetrical four-lobed form, usually framed by a circle. It was revived during the neo-Gothic style in the 18th and 19th centuries.

Reeding: A decorative device consisting of parallel convex molding, the opposite of fluting.

Rep: A transversely corded fabric of wool, silk or cotton.

Rosette: A circular-shaped decorative device that was carved, inlaid or painted as a stylized flower with rose petals. It has been used since ancient Greece.

S

Saber leg: Derived from the Greek *klismos* chair, this leg curved rearward, resembling the sword of a cavalryman. It was popular in chairs and sofas in the late 18th and early 19th centuries.

Sabot: The French term for a metal (usually gilt bronze) fitting enclosing and protecting the bottom of the leg of a piece of furniture.

Scagliola: A material used since ancient Rome to imitate marble. It first appeared in furniture in the 16th century in Italy, and was used for tabletops and chests of drawers throughout Europe, expecially in 18th-century Florence.

Shagreen: Fine-grained shark or ray skin, ground flat so that the skin forms a granulated pattern. It has been used since the 17th century to cover small boxes, as well as stretched on panels as a furniture veneer.

Spindle: A slender piece of turned wood used in chair backs and as a decorative device.

Splat: The central vertical piece in the middle of a chair back. It is usually pierced or shaped to form a major decorative element. A chair may have a single splat or multiple splats.

Stile: The vertical member of a chair, including the rear leg and side support of the back, extending from the foot to the crest rail.

Stretcher: A horizontal bar used to join and strengthen the legs of chairs and tables. Specific stretchers are identified by name, such as the H-stretcher (the cross bar forms the letter "H"), the X-stretcher, etc.

T

Tester: Originally the term designating a headboard of a bed, but after the 17th century meant a canopy of wood over the bed.

Tracery: Ornamental work consisting of delicate, interlacing lines.

Trefoil: An ornamental device consisting of three lobes, radiating from a center. This was widely used in Gothic furniture and in tracery. It became popular again during the neo-Gothic style of the 18th and 19th centuries.

V

Valance: Horizontal strip of drapery hanging from the tester or canopy of a bed; it also refers to a short length of fabric hanging from a chair, concealing its legs.

Vermeil: A metal, such as silver or bronze, which has been gilded.

Volute: A spiral scroll used as a decorative motif for the ends of armrests, legs and other elements of a piece of furniture. It also designates the foliated spiral scroll used in Gothic architecture.

The page numbers in boldface refer to major developments; those in italics, to illustrations.

G

H

I

J • K

L

PHOTOGRAPH CREDITS

The front and back cover photographs are by Matthieu Prier, except for:

Musée des Arts décoratifs: Jaulmes L.-S. (D.R.) (cover: top, third from left)

AKG Paris: 90, 148-149, 150, 156; Cameraphoto, 93 (tl); J. Da Cunha, 98, 138, 139; S. Domingie /M. Rabatti, 15, 49, 93 (tr and b); H. Heine, 136

Christie's Images: 23, 43 (b), 44 (b), 45, 47 (b), 87 (b), 91, 95 (tl and b), 96 (b), 97, 101, 105, 134 (t and b), 135, 137, 145

Collection du Musée dauphinois: 185 (b), 201 (tr and b)

Collection du musée de Brou: H. Nègre, 177; M. Grefferat, 176 (r)

Collection Musée Albert-Demard, Champlitte: 195 (r)

D.R., 102 (r), 103 (b)

Dover: p. 4
Insets: 14, 18, 20, 22, 24, 28, 34, 40, 42, 44, 46, 48, 50, 52, 56, 62, 70, 72, 78, 84, 86, 88, 90, 92, 94, 96, 98, 100, 102, 104, 108, 114, 120, 124, 130, 132, 136, 138, 144, 146, 150, 156, 160, 162, 166, 168

Giraudon: 20, 25 (b), 46, 50, 92, 96 (l), 178 (t), 188; Lauros-Giraudon, 25 (t), 47 (t); Bridgeman-Giraudon, 86, 140, 144; Alinari-Giraudon, 94

Musée des Arts et Traditions populaires du Périgord, Mussidan: 206

Musée d'Art et d'Histoire, Amiens: 209 (b)

Musée d'Art et d'Histoire, Chambéry: 184 and 185

Musée de la Vie bourguignonne Perrin de Puycousin, Dijon: 178 (tl and b)

Musée alsacien, Strasbourg: 172 and 173

Musée historique lorrain, Nancy: G. Mangin, 196 (g), 197 (tl and bl); Mignot, 196 (r), 197 (r)

Musée des Arts décoratifs. ADAGP, 1998: L.-S. Jaulmes, 157 (b), 159 (bd), 163 (b), 165 (b); D.R.: L.-S. Jaulmes, 113 (b), 116 (b), 122 (t), 123 (b), 125, 126 (tr and bl), 127, 158, 159 (t), 162, 163 (t), 164, 166 (l), 167 (b), 168, 169; D.R.: S. Olivier, 166 (r), 167 (tr)

Muséon Arlaten, Arles: 190, 191 (b); B. Delgado, 189, 191 (tl); R. Wilson, 191 (tr)

Photo-contact, Beauvais: 209 (t)

Matthieu Prier: 12-13, 16, 17, 18, 21, 28, 30, 31, 32, 33, 35, 36, 39, 41, 51, 53 (tr), 58 (t), 60, 61, 62, 63, 64, 65, 66, 67, 68, 69 (t), 71 (b), 72, 73, 74, 75, 77, 95 (tr), 100 (bl), 106, 107, 118 (t), 119, 126 (tl and br), 129 (l), 142 (r), 147 (b), 157 (t), 170-171, 174, 175, 179 (r), 180, 181, 182, 183, 186, 187 (r), 192, 193, 194, 199, 200, 202, 203, 204, 205, 207

Réunion des Musées nationaux: 8 (tl), 8 (tr), 10, 11 (t), 11 (b), 14, 24, 26-27, 37, 38, 40, 53 (b), 57, 69 (b), 70, 78, 80 (tl), 83 (b), 84, 99, 104, 108, 111, 116, 123 (r), 140 (inset), 142 (l), 147 (t), 152(r), 153 (tl and r), 160 (l); Arnaudet, 48, 52 (tl), 52 (r), 58 (l), 79, 81, 82, 100 (r), 113 (t), 121, 122 (b), 124, 128, 132, 146 (t); M. Bellot, 80 (r), 118 (b), 130; J.-G. Berizzi, 42, 59, 102 (l); P. Bernard, 156 (r); G. Blot, 7, 19, 22, 34, 54, 55, 56, 76, 110 (t), 114, 154, 155; G. Blot /C. Jean, 44 (l); Chuzeville, 6-7, 8 (b), 29; M. Coppola, 115; Th. Girval, 71, 129 (r); Lagiewski, 109, 110 (b), 112; H. Lewandowski, 9, 143, 151, 158-159, 160 (r); Mathéus, 83 (t), 161; Mercator, 120; R.-G. Ojeda, 88, 150-151, 152 (tl), 153 (b); Ravaux, 53 (tl); J. Schormans, 141; G. Vivien, 117

Roger-Viollet – insets: 172, 176, 178, 184, 186, 188, 192, 195, 196, 198, 201, 202, 206, 208, 176 (l), 179 (l), 187 (l), 195 (l), 198, 201 (l), 208

Sotheby's Images: 43 (t), 85, 87 (t), 89, 103 (t), 131, 133